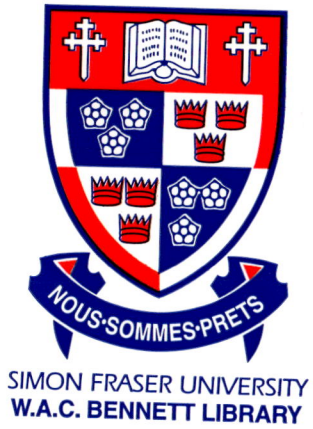

SIMON FRASER UNIVERSITY
W.A.C. BENNETT LIBRARY

LEIBNIZ AND THE ENGLISH-SPEAKING WORLD

The New Synthese Historical Library
Texts and Studies in the History of Philosophy

VOLUME 62

The titles published in this series are listed at the end of this volume.

LEIBNIZ AND THE ENGLISH-SPEAKING WORLD

Edited by

PAULINE PHEMISTER
University of Edinburgh, Scotland, UK

and

STUART BROWN
The Open University, Milton Keynes, UK

 Springer

A C.I.P. Catalogue record for this book is available from the Library of Congress.

ISBN 978-1-4020-5242-2 (HB)
ISBN 978-1-4020-5243-9 (e-book)

Published by Springer,
P.O. Box 17, 3300 AA Dordrecht, The Netherlands.

www.springer.com

Printed on acid-free paper

TABLE OF CONTENTS

CONTRIBUTORS

Philip Beeley lectures in History of Science at the University of Hamburg and is editor of Leibniz's philosophical writings and correspondence at the University of Münster.

Andreas Blank is Visiting Fellow at the Cohn Institute for the History of Philosophy of Science and Ideas at Tel Aviv University, Israel.

Martha Brandt Bolton is Professor of Philosophy at Rutgers University.

Gregory Brown is Professor of Philosophy at the University of Houston, Texas.

Stuart Brown is Emeritus Professor of Philosophy at the Open University.

Stephen H. Daniel is Professor of Philosophy at Texas A & M University.

Norma B. Goethe is Professor of Philosophy at the School of Philosophy, National University of Cordoba, Argentina.

Nicholas Jolley is Professor of Philosophy and Chair of the Philosophy Department at the University of California, Irvine.

Robert J. Mulvaney is Distinguished Emeritus Professor of Philosophy at the University of South California.

Ohad Nachtomy is Assistant Professor at Bar – Ilan University, Israel.

Pauline Phemister is Lecturer in Philosophy at the University of Edinburgh.

George MacDonald Ross is Senior Lecturer at the University of Leeds and Director of the Subject Centre for Philosophical and Religious Studies at the Higher Education Academy.

Justin E. H. Smith is Associate Professor of Philosophy at Concordia University, Canada.

Evelyn Vargas teaches in the Department of Philosophy, Universidad de La Plata, Argentina and is Adjunct Researcher for CONICET (*Consejo Nacional de Investigaciones Científicas y Tecnológicas*).

Catherine Wilson is Professor of Philosophy at the City University of New York and teaches in the Graduate Centre.

ABBREVIATIONS

A   *G. W. Leibniz: Sämtliche Schriften und Briefe*. Berlin: Akademie Verlag, 1923–. Referred to by series, volume and page number.

AA   *Kant's Gesammelte Schriften*. Göttingen: Akademie der Wissenschaften, 1902–. Referred to by volume and page number.

AF   *David Hume: Writings on Religion*. Ed. by A. Flew. La Salle, IL: Open Court 1992.

AG   *G. W. Leibniz: Philosophical Essays*. Ed. and trans. by R. Ariew and D. Garber. Indianapolis, IN: Hackett 1989.

AS   G. Dalgarno. *Ars Signorum, Vulgo Character Universalis et Lingua Philosophica*. London: J. Hayes 1661.

AT   *Oeuvres de Descartes*. Ed. by C. Adam and P. Tannery. Paris: J. Vrin 1964–74. Referred to by volume and page number.

BB   *Die Briefwechsel des Gottfried Wilhelm Leibniz in der Königlichen Öffentlichen Bibliothek zu Hannover*. Ed. by E. Bodemann. Hannover: Hahn 1895. Reprinted Hildesheim: Olms 1966.

BH   *Die Leibniz-Handschriften der Königlichen Öffentlichen Bibliothek zu Hannover*. Ed. by E. Bodemann. Hannover: Hahn 1895. Reprinted Hildesheim: Olms 1966.

C   *Opuscules et fragments inédits de Leibniz*. Ed. by L. Couturat. Paris: Alcan 1903. Reprinted Hildesheim: Olms 1961.

CL   C. S. Peirce. *Reasoning and the Logic of Things. The Cambridge Conferences of 1898*. Ed. by K. L. Ketner and H. Putnam. Cambridge MA: Harvard University Press 1992.

CN   *Charles Sanders Peirce. Contributions to "The Nation"*. Ed. by K. L. Ketner and J. E. Cook. 4 vols. Lubbock: Texas Tech University Press 1975–87.

CP   *Collected Papers of Charles Sanders Peirce*. Ed. by C. Hartshorne, P. Weiss (vols 1–6), and A. Burks (vols 7–8). Cambridge, MA: Harvard University Press 1931–58.

CSM   *The Philosophical Writings of Descartes*. Ed. and trans. by J. Cottingham, R. Stoothoff, and D. Murdoch. 2 vols. Cambridge, UK: Cambridge University Press 1984–85. Referred to by volume and page number.

CW   I. Newton. *The Principia: Mathematical Principles of Natural Philosophy*. Trans. by I. B. Cohen and A. Whitman. Los Angeles: University of California Press 1999.

D   G. W. Leibniz. *Opera Omnia*. Ed. by L. L. Dutens. 6 vols. Geneva 1768. Reprinted Hildesheim: Olms 1989. Referred to by volume and page number.

DB   *George Berkeley: Alciphron, or the Minute Philosopher: In focus*. Ed. by D. Berman. London and New York: Routledge 1993.

E   G. W. Leibniz. *Opera Philosophica*. Ed. by J. E. Erdmann. Berlin: Eichler 1840.

EP   *The Essential Peirce. Selected Philosophical Writings*. Ed. by N. Houser and C. J. W. Kloesel. 2 vols. Bloomington: Indiana University Press 1992–98. Referred to by volume and page number.

ERC   J. Wilkins. *An Essay Towards a Real Character: And a Philosophical Language*. London: S. Gellibrand 1668. Cited by part, chapter, section and page.

Essay   J. Locke. *An Essay Concerning Human Understanding*. Ed. by P. H. Nidditch. Oxford: Clarendon Press 1975. Referred to by book, chapter, and section.

F   *The Works of George Berkeley*. Ed. by A. C. Fraser. 4 vols. Oxford: Clarendon Press 1901. Cited by volume and page number.

FC   *Nouvelles lettres et opuscules inédits de Leibniz*. Ed. by A. Foucher de Careil. Paris: Durand 1857. Reprinted Hildesheim: Olms 1971.

FCO   *Oeuvres de Leibniz*. Ed. by A. Foucher de Careil. 7 vols. Paris: Firmin Didot Frères 1859–75. Referred to by volume and page number.

GG   J. Toland. *Letters to Serena* [1704]. Ed. by G. Gawlick. Stuttgart-Bad Cannstatt: Friedrich Frommann 1964.

GK   J. Locke. *Epistola de Tolerantia/ A Letter on Toleration.* Ed. by J. W. Gough and R. Klibansky. Oxford: Clarendon Press 1968.

GM   *Leibnizens Mathematische Schriften.* Ed. by C. I. Gerhardt. 7 vols. Berlin: A. Asher and Halle: H. W. Schmidt 1849–63. Reprinted Hildesheim: Olms 1965. Referred to by volume and page number.

GP   *Die Philosophischen Schriften von Gottfried Wilhelm Leibniz.* Ed. by C. I. Gerhardt. 7 vols. Berlin: Weidmann 1875–90. Reprinted Hildesheim: Olms 1965. Referred to by volume and page number.

Gr   *G. W. Leibniz: Textes inédits d'après les manuscrits de la Bibliothèque provinciale d'Hanovre.* Ed. by G. Grua. 2 vols. Paris: Presses Universitaires de France 1948. Referred to by volume and page number.

GW   *Briefwechsel zwischen Leibniz und Christian Wolff.* Ed. by C. I. Gerhardt. Halle: Schmidt 1860. Reprinted Hildesheim: Olms 1963.

HD   *The Works of Robert Boyle.* Ed. by M. Hunter and E. B. Davis. 14 vols. London: Pickering and Chatto 1999–2000. Referred to by volume and page number.

HF   G. W. Leibniz. *Theodicy: Essays on the Goodness of God, the Freedom of Man and the Origin of Evil.* Ed. by A Farrer. Trans. by E. M. Huggard. London: Routledge & Kegan Paul 1951. Re-published Peru, IL: Open Court 1985.

HGA   *The Leibniz-Clarke Correspondence.* Ed. and trans. by H. G. Alexander. Manchester, UK: Manchester University Press 1956.

HH   *The Correspondence of Henry Oldenburg.* Ed. by A. R. Hall and M. B. Hall. 13 vols. Madison: University of Wisconsin Press; London: Mansell; London and Philadelphia: Taylor and Francis, 1965–86. Referred to by volume and page number.

HTM   *The Leibniz-Arnauld Correspondence.* Ed. and trans. by H. T. Mason. Manchester, UK: Manchester University Press 1967.

K   *Die Werke von Leibniz*. Ed. by O. Klopp. 11 vols. Hannover: Klindworth 1864–84. Referred to by volume and page number.

KSC   *Correspondenz von Leibniz mit Sophie Charlotte*. Ed. by O. Klopp. 3 vols. Hannover: Klindworth 1873. Reprinted Hildesheim and New York: Olms 1970.

L   *G. W. Leibniz: Philosophical Papers and Letters*. Ed. and trans. by L. E. Loemker. 2nd ed. Dordrecht: Reidel 1969.

LBr   Niedersächsische Landesbibliothek, Hanover: Leibniz-Briefwechsel.

LH   Niedersächsische Landesbibliothek, Hanover: Leibniz-Handschriften.

LJ   *The Works of George Berkeley*. Ed. by A. A. Luce and T. E. Jessop. 9 vols. London: Thomas Nelson 1948–57. Referred to by volume and page number.

MA   *George Berkeley: Philosophical Works*. Ed. by M. Ayers. Rutland, VT: Charles E. Tuttle 1992.

MB   *G. W. Leibniz: Discourse on Metaphysics and Related Writings*. Ed. and trans. by R. N. D. Martin and S. Brown. Manchester, UK: Manchester University Press 1988.

MP   *Leibniz: Philosophical Writings*. Ed. and trans. by M. Morris and G. H. R. Parkinson. London: Dent 1973.

MT   *Berkeley's Principles and Dialogues: Background Source Materials*. Ed. by C. J. McCracken and I. C. New York: Cambridge University Press 2000.

OEP   *Margaret Cavendish: Observations on Experimental Philosophy*. Ed. by E. O'Neill. Cambridge, UK: Cambridge University Press 2003.

OH   *Otium Hanoveranum, sive Miscellanea ex ore et schedis illustris viri, piae memoriae, Godofr. Guilielmi Leibnitii* . Ed. by J. F. Feller. Leipzig: J. C. Martin 1718.

P   *G. W. Leibniz: De Summa Rerum: Metaphysical Papers 1675–76*. Ed. and trans. by G. H. R. Parkinson. New Haven and London: Yale University Press 1992.

PF M. Cavendish. *Poems and Fancies*. London: T. R. for J. Martin and J. Allestrye 1653. Reprinted Menston, Yorkhire: The Scolar Press 1972. 2nd impression, much altered and corrected. London: W. Wilson 1664.

PPO M. Cavendish. *The Philosophical and Physical Opinions*. London: J. Martin and J. Allestrye, 1655. 2nd ed. London: W. Wilson 1663.

RA [G.W. Leibniz]. *The Labyrinth of the Continuum: Writings on the Continuum Problem, 1672–1686*. Ed. and trans. by R. T. W. Arthur. New Haven and London: Yale University Press 2001.

RB *G. W. Leibniz: New Essays on Human Understanding*. Ed. and trans. by P. Remnant and J. Bennett. Cambridge, UK: Cambridge University Press 1996.

RC R. Cudworth. *The True Intellectual System of the Universe: Wherein all the Reason and Philosophy of Atheism is Confuted and its Impossibility Demonstrated*. London: Richard Royston 1678.

RCP *The Collected Papers of Bertrand Russell*. London and New York: Routledge 1983-.

SW *The Works of George Berkeley*. Ed. and trans. by G. Sampson and G. N. Wright. 2 vols. London: George Bell 1897. Referred to by volume and page number.

TSHT *The Correspondence of Isaac Newton*. Ed. by H. W. Turnbull, J. F. Scott, and L. Tilling. 7 vols. Cambridge, UK: Cambridge University Press 1959–77. Referred to by volume and page number.

UL *Correspondance de Bossuet*. Ed. by C. Urbain and E. Levesque. 15 vols, New edn. Paris: Hatchette 1909–1925. Reprinted Vaduz: Kraus 1965. Referred to by volume and page number.

W *Leibniz Selections*. Ed. by P. Wiener. New York: Charles Scribners 1951.

WF *Leibniz's "New System" and Associated Contemporary Texts*. Ed. and trans. R. S. Woolhouse and R. Francks. Oxford: Clarendon Press 1997.

WFPT   *G. W. Leibniz: Philosophical Texts*. Ed. and trans. by R. S. Woolhouse
       and R. Francks. Oxford: Oxford University Press 1998.

WML   *Thomae Hobbes Malmesburiensis Opera philosophica quae Latine
       scripsit omnia*. Ed. by W. Molesworth. 5 vols. London: J. Bohn
       1839–45. Reprinted as *Opera Philosophica Omnia*, with introduction by
       G. A. J. Rogers. Bristol: Thoemmes 1999. Referred to by volume and
       page number.

PREFACE

Most of the papers in this volume were originally presented as papers at a conference held in Liverpool in September 2003, also entitled "Leibniz and the English-speaking World." The conference was held under the auspices of the British Society for the History of Philosophy. It was also supported by the G.W. Leibniz Gesellschaft and the Leibniz Society of North America. The financial support of the BSHP, the Mind Association and the DAAD, as well as the hospitality of Liverpool University and the administrative assistance of Maureen Pilkington, is gratefully acknowledged.

The papers, which are previously unpublished, have subsequently been revised for this volume. Two of the chapters have been specially written for the volume. Chapter One, which is written by the editors, is intended to provide an introductory overview of the topic and to place the substantive papers within it. Chapter Seven, which is concerned with the connection between Leibniz's philosophy and that of the Cambridge Platonists, was commissioned to fill what appeared as a gap in the topics covered by the conference papers. Chapter Fifteen is based on a previously unpublished lecture that explores one aspect of the reception of Leibniz in America.

The Editors are grateful to the staff at Springer for their help in bringing this volume to publication.

P.P.
S.C.B.

STUART BROWN AND PAULINE PHEMISTER[1]

1. LEIBNIZ AND THE ENGLISH-SPEAKING WORLD

An introductory overview

Leibniz took an interest in a significant number of British thinkers of his day and corresponded with several of them. And there was attention to his philosophy in the English-speaking world in his own time and has been a good deal of attention since. Yet there has been no attempt to consider his philosophical connections with or reception in the English-speaking world in a systematic way. The literature has mostly focused on topics outside philosophy, such as Leibniz's visits to London in 1672 and 1676, his involvement in securing the Hanoverian succession and his controversy with the Newtonians over who could claim to have discovered the differential calculus. There has been discussion of certain appropriate topics in philosophy, especially of Leibniz's vainly hoped-for dialogue with Locke that resulted in his *New Essays*, the well-publicised controversy with Samuel Clarke, as well as the influence of certain British philosophers (notably Hobbes) on Leibniz's thought. But, in other respects, the Anglophone dimension of Leibniz studies is relatively neglected.

We hope with this volume to have begun to remedy this situation. Many avenues remain unexplored, however, as will be apparent even from this introductory chapter. Here we try both to provide an outline of the topic and to place within it the substantive papers that follow. We have divided these introductory remarks into three sections, beginning with the early period up to 1676, the year of Leibniz's second and last visit to London, on his way from Paris to take up the post in Hanover where he was to be based for the rest of his life. The second section covers the later period (1676–1716), when Leibniz was responding to British philosophy from the standpoint of his own mature thought as well as the early reception of his philosophy by British philosophers. The final section is concerned, as are the final three papers of the volume, with the later reception of Leibniz's philosophy in the English-speaking world.

1. LEIBNIZ'S EARLY CONNECTIONS WITH ENGLAND AND BRITISH PHILOSOPHY

Leibniz embraced Modern philosophy, with qualifications, in the 1660s. His lists of those he regarded as the pioneers of the new philosophy tended to repeat the same six names: Francis Bacon (1561–1612), Galileo Galilei (1564–1642), Thomas Hobbes (1588–1679), Pierre Gassendi (1596–1655), René Descartes (1596–1650)

1

P. Phemister and S. Brown (eds.), Leibniz and the English-Speaking World, 1–18.
© 2007 *Springer.*

and Kenelm Digby (1603–1685). So, for instance, he claims in his *Confessio Naturae contra Atheistas* (1669) that:

[…] we must agree with those contemporary philosophers who have revived Democritus and Epicurus and whom Robert Boyle aptly calls corpuscular philosophers, such as Galileo, Bacon, Gassendi, Descartes, Hobbes, and Digby, that in explaining corporeal phenomena, we must not unnecessarily resort to God or to any other incorporeal thing, form or quality […] but that so far as can be done, everything should be derived from the nature of body and its primary qualities – magnitude, figure and motion. (A VI ii, 489–90/ L 110)

It is noteworthy that this list includes three British philosophers and that mention is made of a fourth.

Leibniz's lists do vary, it should be said, and the inclusion of the now obscure Sir Kenelm Digby in some of them seems surprising. Digby was, however, the author of one of the first systematic expositions of the mechanical philosophy, published indeed in the same year as Descartes's *Principia philosophiae*. (1644). More work needs done on Leibniz's interest in Digby, and in his follower Thomas White.[2] But it seems clear that Leibniz was attracted to Digby's project partly because, unlike Descartes, he sought to reconcile the new philosophy with that of Aristotle. Leibniz also shared with Digby – in this case with Descartes also – the desire to demonstrate an incorporeal God and immortal souls on terms consistent with the new philosophy.

The early modern British philosopher who is most often mentioned in Leibniz's early writings is Hobbes. And some commentators have suggested that Hobbes was a major influence, not only on Leibniz's early philosophy but also on the later. This question of Hobbes's influence on Leibniz is considered in the first substantive paper in this collection, that by George MacDonald Ross.

Another of the founders of "Modern philosophy" whose influence on Leibniz is still a matter for discussion is Francis Bacon. On Leibniz's own account, in his 1675 letter to Foucher, Bacon was one of the first modern philosophers he read:

Bacon and Gassendi were the first to fall into my hands. Their familiar style was well-suited to a man who wanted to read everything. It is true that I had often glanced at Galileo and Descartes. But I have not long become a geometer and I was put off by their style of writing, which required a good deal of thought. (A VI ii, 247)

It is not certain what Leibniz specifically owed to Bacon. He certainly agreed with him about the collaborative nature of science and may have been influenced, at least indirectly, by his method.[3] It is more certain that Leibniz was initially attracted to Gassendi's atomism, as he confessed in a 1715 letter to Remond:

[…] his [sc. Gassendi's] thoughts satisfy me less now that they did when I first began to drop Scholastic views, when I was still a schoolboy. Since the doctrine of atoms gratifies the imagination, I committed myself to it. The void of Democritus and Epicurus, together with the incorruptible corpuscles of these two authors, seemed to me to remove all the difficulties. (GP III, 620/cf. L 657)

In this letter Leibniz argues that the philosophy of Gassendi could helpfully be used to introduce young people to natural science. But, as he implies, this is despite the fact that Bacon's atomism is not really true. Leibniz indeed made his critique of atomism a fundamental part of his later philosophy, rejecting atoms and the void for the identity of indiscernibles and the *plenum*. He was not alone in first being attracted to Epicureanism and then reacting against it. The same is true of Margaret Cavendish (1623–1673), Duchess of Newcastle, whose thought makes an interesting comparison with that of Leibniz, as Catherine Wilson brings out in Chapter 3.

Leibniz and the English Language

We have seen that the young Leibniz, on his own confession, wanted to read everything. And the same habit of voracious reading and curiosity about anything that was happening in the world of learning remained with him for the rest of his life. Given this motivation he would not have been deterred from reading books that struck him as interesting because they were in a language, such as English, which he hardly used. In 1671, for instance, he had read John Wilkins's *Essay towards a Real Character and a Philosophical Language*, and it is clear (see Chapter 4) that he understood it well enough. Again, in 1676, he was sent Boyle's *Some Physico-Theological Considerations about the Possibility of the Resurrection* (discussed in Chapter 6) and his notes show not only that he understood its drift but that he was able to make intelligent guesses as to the meaning of unfamiliar words.[4] By at least the 1670s, then, Leibniz had a competent reading knowledge of English, and it would have improved considerably in later years. In 1689 he made extensive notes on Cudworth's *True Intellectual System of the Universe*. In the 1690s he was already studying Locke's *Essay Concerning Human Understanding* in the original language, though he was glad when it appeared in French translation. He read and made notes on John Toland's *Christianity not Mysterious*, though when he and Toland met or corresponded they did so in French. He also read Berkeley's *Principles of Human Knowledge* and made notes (in Latin) at the back of his copy. These are works by authors whose relations with Leibniz are discussed in this volume. A complete list of the philosophical works in English he is known to have given some attention to would be a good deal longer.

English was already becoming an important language for philosophical exchanges even in the 1670s. But, in the middle of the seventeenth century, Latin was still *the* international language of academic communication. It was the language in which Leibniz made notes for his own use on philosophical matters. The editions of the works of English-speaking philosophers Leibniz would have preferred to use and to which he was more likely to have access would be in Latin. For example, he knew Digby's *Two Treatises* by one of the Latin editions, entitled *Demonstratio immortalitatis animae rationalis*, the title by which Leibniz refers to Digby's book when reporting his project of reconciling Aristotle with Modern philosophy.[5] He probably did not know the earlier English edition. George Dalgarno's *Ars signorum* (1661) only existed in Latin editions until very recently. Despite the trend towards the use of vernacular languages, which would eventually become all but universal, philosophers who wanted a more than national reputation took the trouble to have their works appear in Latin. The works of Henry More, for instance, were known to Leibniz through the edition of his *Opera Omnia* that was published in London in 1679.

Latin was still, in the mid-seventeenth century, a language in which scholars from different countries could write to one another and, if they met, converse. It was the language in which Leibniz corresponded with Henry Oldenburg, despite the fact they were both native German speakers. Latin was also the language in which Leibniz corresponded, in 1696, with the Oxford Professor of Geometry, John Wallis (1616–1703). However the necessary degree of linguistic competence would usually only be possessed by those who had attended a university and so it would usually be restricted to men and moreover to men who had been preparing for one of the established professions, such as the Church, law, or medicine. Women, aristocrats and many of the new men of science – to mention three overlapping categories of lay people who often took an interest in philosophical matters – would not usually have learnt Latin. Several of the figures of the Royal Society whom Leibniz met in London or with whom he might have liked to have a correspondence were not sufficiently versed in the language. The mathematician John Collins, for instance, was impressed by Leibniz but his Latin was poor and it was hard for them to communicate with one another when they met on Leibniz's second visit to London.[6] That might help to explain why there were no correspondences attempted between Leibniz and a number of the Royal Society figures, such as Robert Boyle, for whom he had a particular respect.

If competence in Latin could no longer be taken for granted in English scientists by the 1670s, its use had significantly declined by the early eighteenth century. When the then Secretary of the Royal Society, John Harris, wrote to Leibniz in 1710, he wrote in English and Leibniz replied in French: a solution to the problem of international communication he had already found with English correspondents, such as Lady Masham, who had not been trained in Latin. Leibniz's correspondence with the Scottish aristocrat Thomas Burnett of Kemnay, between 1695 and 1714, was entirely in French.

Leibniz, London and the Royal Society

Leibniz's first contact in London was Henry Oldenburg, who was one of the secretaries of the Royal Society from 1662 until his death in 1677. Oldenburg was a key figure, as Philip Beeley explains in Chapter 5, in facilitating Leibniz's introduction to members of the Royal Society and in promoting his eventual election to a fellowship.[7] Leibniz had dedicated part of his *Hypothesis physica nova* of 1671 to the Royal Society and it was reprinted by Oldenburg under its auspices.

Leibniz visited London twice, initially for a few weeks in January–February 1673 and later for a week in October 1676. The first visit was in the company of a nephew of his employer, the Elector of Mainz, and its ostensible purpose was diplomatic.

The English and French were at war with the Netherlands and the mission came with a proposal for a peace plan. Though the peace mission was fruitless Leibniz had an agenda of his own, as the visit to London provided him with an opportunity to attend meetings of the Royal Society and make the acquaintance of some of its most important members.

The Royal Society had been established in 1660 and given a Royal Charter in 1662. Its full title was "The Royal Society of London for Improving Natural Knowledge." Among its founder fellows who had connections with or were of interest to Leibniz were Robert Boyle, Robert Hooke, Sir Robert Moray, Henry Oldenburg, Dr John Pell, John Wallis and John Wilkins. Wilkins had died the previous year and Wallis was not in London. But, in addition to Oldenburg, Leibniz met Boyle, Hooke, Moray and Pell during this first visit. On his second visit, on his way from France to the Netherlands and bound for Hanover, he also made the acquaintance of John Collins, a Fellow since 1667 and by then librarian.

Some of those Leibniz spoke to were particularly interested in his mathematics. Pell, whose meeting with Leibniz at Boyle's house is briefly discussed in Chapter 6, was not impressed, suggesting that others had already done what Leibniz claimed to have originated. John Collins, on the other hand, seems to have got along well with Leibniz on his later visit, allowing him access to mathematical manuscripts in the Society's library.

Other members of the Royal Society were more interested in his calculating machine. He had brought a model with him and the first London visit afforded him the opportunity to demonstrate it to members of the Society. The machine was not yet working properly and Robert Hooke was very dismissive in his appraisal. Sir Robert Moray, on the other hand, was better disposed and he it was who put Leibniz forward for a fellowship of the Society. Leibniz was duly elected on 9 April 1673. When he returned to London in 1676 he brought with him a working model of his calculating machine, which he showed to Oldenburg, though he was not able to demonstrate it to other members of the Royal Society as meetings had not yet resumed after the summer recess.

Three of the papers in this volume explore the intellectual relations between Leibniz and founder members of the Royal Society. In Chapter 4, Andreas Blank considers his interest in a universal language, which was shared by, amongst others, John Wilkins.[8] In Chapter 5, Philip Beeley looks at Leibniz's relation to the theologian and mathematician, John Wallis. In Chapter 6 Stuart Brown reviews some aspects of Leibniz's reception of Robert Boyle, in particular his natural theology.

The history of Leibniz's relationship with the Royal Society does not end there. John Locke (elected 1668) and Isaac Newton (elected 1672) were already fellows when Leibniz visited, though he did not meet them. And Samuel Clarke, with whom he was to have had a correspondence that long defined his relationship to the English-speaking world, was eventually elected in 1735. The later part of this story is taken up in the next section.

2. LEIBNIZ'S LATER CONNECTIONS WITH ENGLAND
AND BRITISH PHILOSOPHY

Although Leibniz's second visit to London was his last, it did not mark the end of his connection with England or with British philosophers. On his return to Hanover, Leibniz served successively three Dukes of the House of Brunswick-Lüneburg: Johann Friedrich until 1679, his brother, Ernst August until 1698, and finally, Ernst's son, Georg Ludwig. Georg Ludwig became King George I of England in 1714 and for many years previously, Leibniz had been involved behind the scenes in negotiating the succession to the English throne. On philosophical matters in this later period there has been a deal of controversy about the possible influence on Leibniz of the Cambridge Platonists, especially Henry More (1614–1687) and Ralph Cudworth (1617–1688) and two philosophers allied to them: the younger Van Helmont, Francis Mercury (1618–1699) and Henry More's pupil, Anne Conway (1631–1679).[9]

Commentators have variously held each responsible for Leibniz's adoption of the term "monad" in the 1690s. In this context, Catherine Wilson (1989: 181) notes occurrences of the term in the writings of the Cambridge Platonists, pointing specifically to Henry More's *Enchiridion metaphysicum* (1671) and Ralph Cudworth's *True intellectual system of the universe* (1678). The former Wilson claims had reached Leibniz in 1679; the latter Leibniz read and annotated in 1689. She goes on to hypothesise that Leibniz's adoption of the term "almost certainly stems from the Cambridge group" (181), though not directly from the younger Van Helmont. Allison Coudert, on the other hand, argues for a far greater influence on Leibniz from the Aristotelian-inclined Francis Mercury Van Helmont than from the Platonists More and Cudworth (1995: 23–4), while Carolyn Merchant considers the possible influence of Anne Conway, suggesting that Leibniz may have appropriated the term "monad" from her work too (1979a).[10]

Whatever the source of Leibniz's terminology, it is undeniable that there is significant philosophical convergence between Van Helmont and Leibniz, ranging from the universal characteristic to the nature and relation of matter and spirit.[11] There is much still to be understood in this area, but we do know that Van Helmont was responsible for introducing Leibniz to Anne Conway's *Principles of the Most Ancient and Modern Philosophy*. Leibniz found her vitalist metaphysics of matter and spirit most compatible with his own (To Burnett, 24 August 1697: GP III, 217). Certainly, there is great similarity in their views, especially insofar as Leibniz advances an ontology of perceiving, embodied, living creatures, each grounded ultimately in primitive units comprising active and passive forces, but there are also significant differences, one of which being Conway's positing of Christ as mediator between God and finite creatures. Again, some progress has been made into uncovering the intellectual convergence between them,[12] but further research is needed to determine its extent and shed further light on the fundamental ontologies of each.

At the same time, Leibniz's connections with More and Cudworth are not to be dismissed. Leibniz was reading More at least by the late 1670s (Brown, S. 1990: 77 & 91n), but he probably did not read Cudworth until the late 1680s when he annotated a large part of the Cambridge Platonist's *True intellectual system*, having happened upon a copy during his visit to Rome.[13] More's vital principles and Cudworth's plastic natures resonate with Leibniz's re-introduction of substantial forms to counter overly materialistic and atheist tendencies of the modern philosophy. But the equivalence is not exact. Precisely where Leibniz situates himself in relation to Cudworth on the issue of plastic natures is the topic of Chapter 7.

Cudworth's daughter, Damaris Masham, also figures in the fuller account of Leibniz's connections with the English-speaking philosophers in the early 1700s. In the latter half of 1703 or early in 1704, she initiated a 2 years correspondence with Leibniz when she sent him a copy of her father's *True intellectual system*, though there is little overt discussion of Cudworth in the exchanges that follow. Nor does their correspondence touch on matters raised in Lady Masham's own published work. Her *Occasional Thoughts in Reference to a Vertuous or Christian Life*, promoting the role of reason in grounding moral and religious conduct, was published anonymously and anyway did not appear until 1705. Her *Discourse Concerning the Love of God* (1696), in which she argues against the Malebranchian John Norris, had also been published anonymously. But it seems that Leibniz only learnt of the work in 1706 when Pierre Coste made Leibniz a gift of his translation of it (GP III, 383). Even then, Leibniz was still unaware of its authorship, but may in any case have followed the common trend and attributed it to Locke. This is unfortunate for surely had he been aware of its true authorship, he would have engaged Lady Masham on matters moral and theological. As he indicates to Coste when thanking him for his gift, he had presented his own ideas on the love of God in his *Codex Juris Gentium Diplomaticus* of 1693 (GP III, 384). And the themes of love and justice would later play a prominent part in Leibniz's assessment of the third Earl of Shaftesbury's *Characteristicks of Men, Manners, Opinions, Times* (D V, 39–46/ GP III, 423–31)[14] and from which it is evident that Leibniz found in Shaftesbury's work much with which he could agree. Moral freedom also comes under scrutiny in Leibniz's critical examination of William King's *On the Origin of Evil* (1702) in an appendix to his *Theodicy* (1710).[15]

Rather than concentrating on her own works or on those of her father, Leibniz's letters to Damaris Masham focus on issues that pertain closely to the philosophy of John Locke, whom Leibniz knew to be part of the Masham household at that time. Leibniz himself was immersed in Locke's *Essay Concerning Human Understanding* during this period and he appears to have considered his correspondence with Lady Masham as an opportunity to draw Locke into direct debate or at least to elicit Locke's views on his own metaphysical position. He repeatedly encourages Lady Masham to discuss with Locke such issues as the materiality of the soul. Locke refuses to be drawn into direct confrontation, but Leibniz confided to Burnett his belief that Locke had nevertheless played a part in the correspondence (2 August 1704: GP III, 297–8). In 1707, he would admit to Coste that his regard for Locke's *Essay*, coupled with his correspondence with Lady Masham, had encouraged him

to work on his own *New Essays* and that he had done so in the hope that it would
lead to more direct contact with Locke himself (16 June 1707: GP III, 392).

Locke

Although for many years it had been Oldenburg who served as Leibniz's conduit for
news of developments in science and other fields in England, in the later period in
which Leibniz was focusing on Locke's philosophy, this role was played by Thomas
Burnett of Kemnay. Jolley describes Burnett as "Leibniz's principal correspondent
about the English intellectual scene during the whole period of his active interest
in Locke" (Jolley 1984: 36n).[16] In this role, Burnett

> undertook to keep Leibniz abreast of developments in many fields of enquiry: he did not fail to acquaint
> Leibniz with Locke's reputation as an economist and political theorist. But his correspondence reveals a
> marked bias towards theological issues, and this direction in his own interests caused him to give special
> prominence to the religious controversies in which Locke's works were engaged. (Jolley 1984: 52)

Burnett drew Leibniz's attention to the increased demand for Socinian treatises in
England (Jolley 1984: 43). Leibniz had read Locke's *Reasonableness of Christianity*,
which brought charges of Socinianism against Locke and Burnett introduced him
to the Bishop of Worcester, Edward Stillingfleet's response, the *Vindication of the
Doctrine of the Trinity*, describing it as "a polemic directed against the deists and
socinians" (Jolley 1984: 51). Burnett told Leibniz of the publication of Locke's
anonymous *Second Vindication of the Reasonableness of Christianity* (Jolley 1984:
48) and kept him informed about the ensuing and increasingly heated theological
exchange between Locke and Stillingfleet (Jolley 1984: 51). The contrasting views
of Leibniz and Locke on the issue of religious toleration, seen in the context of
Leibniz's *New Essays on Human Understanding*, are discussed by Nicholas Jolley
in Chapter 9.
    It was to Burnett in March 1696 that Leibniz sent his preliminary thoughts on
Locke's *Essay Concerning Human Understanding*, which had been published in
1690. Following Leibniz's instructions, Burnett passed these to Locke. Leibniz
continued to correspond with Burnett but never managed to persuade Locke to enter
into direct correspondence. Locke's unenthusiastic opinion of Leibniz is known to
us through some rather disparaging comments on Leibniz's thoughts on his *Essay*
which Locke included in a letter to his friend, William Molyneux, in 1697. He
also declares himself unimpressed by Leibniz's paper *Meditations on Knowledge,
Truth, and Ideas*. This is surprising since there Leibniz sets out distinctions among
clear and distinct ideas that are not unlike those Locke makes in his *Essay*. Leibniz
persisted, sending further papers to Burnett to be passed onto Locke. None elicited
the desired reply from Locke himself. Leibniz persisted in his engagement with
Locke's *Essay*, however. When, in 1700, Coste, at that time tutor to Lady Masham's
son, published his French translation of Locke's *Essay*, Leibniz claims that it was
his re-reading of the *Essay* on the appearance of the French version that spurred
him to begin work on an extended response, begun in 1703 and which eventually
became his *New Essays on Human Understanding*.

Written as a dialogue, Locke's views, presented by Philalethes, are given mainly as quotations taken from Coste's translation. Leibniz's responses are presented by Theophilus. The fictional interchange between the two men ranges over topics as diverse as innatism, the nature of substance and matter, including the thorny question whether matter might think, freedom and personal identity. Leibniz's choice of dialogue form for the *New Essays* as a means of resolving philosophical disputes with Locke is discussed in depth by Bolton in Chapter 8. Without doubt, Leibniz hoped that the *New Essays* would serve to elicit further responses from Locke, but Locke was not to be drawn. The English philosopher's health was failing. Locke died in the autumn of 1704, at which point Leibniz abandoned plans to have the work published. All the same, references to later events within the text itself lead Remnant and Bennett to conclude that Leibniz continued revising the work at least a little after Locke's death (RB xii). The *New Essays* were published posthumously in 1765.

Newton and Clarke

Just as Locke hovers in the background of Leibniz's correspondences with Burnett and Masham, Leibniz's correspondence with Clarke takes place under the shadow of Newton. Clarke was not only a follower of Newton; he was also Newton's priest and the two men no doubt had frequent contact with one another. Certainly, we may assume that Newton would not have objected too strongly to any of the views Clarke propounds to Leibniz and he may even have suggested many of them himself. But, as Vailati has argued, the Clarke of the Leibniz correspondence is an independent thinker whose views may coincide with Newton's but are nonetheless his own (Vailati 1997: 4–5/ cf. Ariew 2000: x–xi). In the exchange with Leibniz, Clarke is not, or is not only, Newton's mouthpiece. In this respect the correspondence with Clarke is unlike that Leibniz enjoyed with Burnett and to some extent also that with Masham. Between Leibniz and Clarke transpires a properly intellectual debate in which each correspondent responds to the views of the other on a range of metaphysical and scientific issues from his own reasoned position. And because Leibniz in this correspondence in particular calls upon various principles, such as those of Sufficient Reason, Contradiction and the Identity of Indiscernibles, Leibniz's letters serve to give us valuable insight into the parts played by the principles in the justification of his philosophical system.

The correspondence begins with a letter from Leibniz to Princess Caroline in 1715.[17] As the daughter-in-law of Leibniz's employer, George Ludwig, Caroline had relocated to England with the rest of the Hanoverian court apart from Leibniz when Georg Ludwig ascended the throne of England as King George I on the death of Queen Anne in 1714. As the wife of the new Prince of Wales, Georg August, Caroline would later become Queen when her husband ascended the throne as King George II. In his letter to the Princess of Wales, Leibniz, having been kept well informed of ongoing theological debates in England by Burnett, remarks that natural religion was in decline in England and specifies Locke and Newton as major participators in the decline. Caroline passed the letter to Samuel Clarke and a short correspondence from 1715 to 1716 between Leibniz and Clarke followed. The correspondence consists of five letters on each side if we count Leibniz's initial letter to Princess Caroline as the first letter in the correspondence. Clarke has the final word since Leibniz died before he could reply to Clarke's fifth letter. Clarke published the correspondence in both English and French in 1717.

Locke had undermined established religion by entertaining the possibility that the soul might be material and although he himself had since died, his followers did not renounce the suggestion. Newton posed a threat because he even went so far as to entertain the possibility that God is a material thing. Leibniz derives this conclusion from Newton's claim that space is "an organ which God makes use of to perceive things by" (Ariew 2000: 4). Clarke denies the charge on Newton's behalf, drawing a distinction between space as God's *sensorium* and space as a medium used as God's instrument of perception. In his first letter, Leibniz had also accused Newton of regarding God as having made an inferior universe which requires God's intervention from time to time to correct or mend it. Instead, Leibniz proposed his own doctrine of pre-established harmony, according to which God creates a fully harmonious universe that, once created, runs according to a perfect plan and not requiring recourse to God's intervention. Clarke responds, claiming that God does not need to mend His creation, but continually preserves, governs and inspects it. These themes form the basis of subsequent letters that take the reader further into discussion of the absolute or relative nature of space and time, the pre-established harmony, the possibility of the vacuum and atoms, and the concept of gravity or "action at a distance", to which Leibniz had already raised objections in his *Theodicy* in 1710 (*Preliminary dissertation on the conformity of faith with reason*, §19: HF 85–6) and which he here rejects on the ground that it would involve a perpetual miracle. Clarke objects that Leibniz's pre-established harmony is subject to this charge more so than is Newton's theory of gravity. This charge is the central concern of Gregory Brown's contribution to the present volume (Chapter 10).

Long before the *Correspondence with Clarke*, Leibniz's name had been linked with Newton's due to the dispute between the two men as to which of them had first discovered the calculus.[18] The dispute links their names to this day. As noted in the first section, Leibniz's relations with the Royal Society had been good in his early life, but they were stretched to the point of no return by the increasingly acrimonious priority dispute. Leibniz had published his results in the *Acta Eruditorum* in October 1684, in a paper entitled *A New Method for Maxima and Minima*. It is believed that Nicolas Fatio de Duillier was the first to raise the accusation of plagiarism against Leibniz (Ariew 2000: viii), but the charge became more pressing on the publication, in 1710, of the *Philosophical Transactions* of the Royal Society for 1708, in which John Keill claimed that Leibniz had merely invented a new symbolism for what was effectively the Newtonian calculus (Aiton 1985: 292). Leibniz asked the Royal Society to defend him and a committee was instructed to investigate (Aiton 1985: 338). Its report, published in 1713 as the *Commercium epistolicum*, upheld Keill's charge, but it is now known that it was written in large part by Newton himself (Ariew 2000: ix). That same year, Leibniz published an anonymous defence, the

Charta volans or flying sheet, in the *Journal littéraire*, to which Keill responded in 1714 (Aiton 1985: 338–9). In the end, Abbé Conti assembled an independent group made up of foreign ambassadors to investigate the case. They advised that Newton write personally to Leibniz, which, with the King's approval, he did (Aiton 1985: 339–40). Leibniz replied via Conti in April 1716 (Aiton 1985: 339–40), but the matter was still unresolved when Leibniz died later that year.

As it progressed, the dispute between Leibniz and Newton came to be regarded not merely as a dispute between its two protagonists themselves, but also as in terms of national rivalry between Germany and England.[19] This aspect is probably the real reason why the king steadfastly refused to grant Leibniz leave to join the rest of the Hanoverian Court in London, despite the efforts of Princess Caroline to persuade the king otherwise. George I's official stance was that permission was denied because Leibniz had not yet completed the history of the House of Brunswick-Lüneberg commissioned by his father, Ernst August. It is known that Leibniz desired that George I to appoint him as official court historian in England, a position the king was prevented from bestowing under the terms of the Act of Settlement (Brown, G. 2004: 287), but the commonly-held assumption that Leibniz also wanted to join the court in London has been called into question by Gregory Brown,[20] who suggests that concern for the position and reputation of Princess Caroline was one reason for his reticence (Brown, G. 2004: 264–8).

Later Reception

The question of Leibniz's reception among English-speaking philosophers towards the end of his life and in the immediate aftermath of his death brings to the fore the two major figures of Berkeley and Hume. Berkeley himself refers to Leibniz in *De Motu*, in connection with Leibniz's views on metaphysical and physical forces (MA 212, 214), and in *Alciphron* in regard to physical forces (DB 127). We know from the marginalia of his own copy that Leibniz read the Irishman's *Principles of Human Knowledge*, but we have no evidence that he sought to engage directly with Berkeley on philosophical matters in the way that he had with Locke. We can only speculate about the reasons for Leibniz's reticence, but as Stephen Daniel points out in Chapter 11, their understanding of each other's thought was restricted by limited acquaintance with each other's writings. Daniel argues that misunderstanding of each other's philosophies obscured the common ground between them. In fact, he suggests, their philosophies are much closer to one another than either suspected, not only in their views on abstract ideas, primary and secondary qualities and the anti-Newtonian relational character of space and time, but also on the question of the reality of bodies and their common belief that bodies exist only if they are sensed.

Hume did not always understand Leibniz well either. For instance, in the tenth dialogue of his *Dialogues Concerning Natural Religion*, Hume attributes to Leibniz the denial of the very existence of pain and suffering when in fact Leibniz explicitly acknowledges such evils as essential to the perfection of the best possible world (AF 256). This aside, there are aspects of Hume's philosophy that are arguably of

Leibnizian origin. In Leibniz's theory of monadic substances whose qualities are perceptions and appetitions may be found a precursor of Hume's bundle theory of the mind. Certainly, their views on personal identity are remarkably close, despite Hume's rejection of Leibniz's metaphysics of substance. Hume's distinction between truths of fact and truths of reason parallels Leibniz's distinction between contingent truths whose truth rests upon the Principle of Sufficient Reason and absolutely necessary truths whose truth can be known by means of the Principle of Contradiction. Moreover, Hume's account of causes and effects as distinct existences appears to echo Leibniz's doctrine of pre-established harmony.[21] On the other hand, however, Michael Haynes (1988) believes that Hume's denial of necessary causal connections can only be made compatible with his Newtonian inclinations in respect of the mind if they are understood as a criticism of Leibniz's insistence that there can be no action at a distance.

In theory, both Berkeley and Hume had access to a limited range of Leibniz's writings; in practice their access would have been even more restricted. Bearing in mind that Clarke had published his correspondence with Leibniz as early as 1717, Catherine Wilson's account of the situation prior to 1768 may be taken as definitive:

> Until 1765 when Raspe published his two-volume collection, which included the *New Essays*,[22] and Dutens his six-volume collection in 1768, understanding Leibniz was based on (in addition to the *Theodicy* and Pierre Bayle's entry on the theory of pre-established harmony in his *Historical and Critical Dictionary*), Pierre des Maizeaux's *Recueil des pièces diverses*[23] of 1720 (which included the Leibniz-Clarke correspondence), Leibniz's late letters to Remond, some reflections of Locke's *Essay*, short papers on "enthusiasm," Shaftesbury, and Bayle – as well as a treatise on fatalism which was not by Leibniz. Besides, the *Monadology*, the *New System* and the *Principles of Nature and Grace* went through several editions, and the *Protogaea* was finally published in 1749. [Scheidt, ed.].[24] (1995: 443)

The philosophers discussed in the next and final section were in a far more enviable position. In the nineteenth century, to the collections of Raspe and Dutens (D) were added the editions of Erdmann (E) in 1840 and of Gerhardt's editions of 1849–1863 (GM) and 1875–1890 (GP), while the twentieth century witnessed the publication of editions by Couturat in 1903 (C), Grua in 1948 (Gr) and of course the ongoing publication of Leibniz's corpus in the project of the Deutsche Akademie der Wissenschaften (A).

3. THE RECEPTION OF LEIBNIZ'S PHILOSOPHY IN BRITAIN AND AMERICA IN THE NINETEENTH CENTURY AND BEYOND

There has been little systematic attempt to examine the reception of Leibniz's philosophy in the English-speaking world or indeed in any part of it.[25] In this respect Leibniz has been less well favoured than, for instance, Spinoza.[26] Like Spinoza, however, Leibniz appears to have been largely unread and either ignored or lightly dismissed by English-language writers during the late eighteenth and early nineteenth centuries.[27] Indeed the historian W.R. Sorley claimed of this period of British philosophy that

[...] until the influence of Kant and Hegel made itself felt in the nineteenth century, English [sc. British] philosophy pursued an independent course. Spinoza was little known and avoided [...] Leibniz was equally neglected. (Sorley 1920: 299)

This claim may well be true, at least of the broad picture. Part of the explanation is that eighteenth century British thinkers had little time for metaphysical hypotheses. Moreover there was little interest in the history of philosophy during this period, at least in what was included for publication.[28] What approximated to histories of philosophy tended to be Enlightenment stories of progress. Leibniz could certainly expect to receive a mention in such stories, though it was not because his metaphysics was thought to be worth considering. For instance, the distinguished Scottish philosopher, Dugald Stewart, in his *Dissertation on the Progress of Metaphysical, Ethical and Political Philosophy* (1815), saw little need to argue for his claim that, in the estimation of the learned world, Leibniz's monads and his pre-established harmony ranked with the vortices of Descartes and the plastic nature of Cudworth.[29]

Sorley gives the credit for the revival of interest in German philosophy to the erudite Sir William Hamilton. Hamilton had studied at Glasgow but won a scholarship for Scottish students at Oxford (between 1807 and 1811) where he made private studies in the history of philosophy and in German philosophy before returning to Edinburgh, where he was to become Professor of Logic and Metaphysics. He was especially taken by Kant but recognised Leibniz as an important predecessor who had indeed been the first to recognise some important truths. Hamilton seems to have been the first writer in the English-speaking world to pay attention to the *Nouveaux Essais*, though it had been published by Raspe as far back as 1765. Hamilton claimed that though it was

of all others the most important psychological work of Leibnitz, [the *Nouveaux Essais*] was wholly unknown, not only to the other philosophers of this country, but even to Mr Stewart, prior to the last years of his life. (Hamilton 1859–1860: II, 359)

Leibniz was the first philosopher, according to Hamilton, to recognise the quality of necessity or the impossibility that it should be otherwise as what distinguished a priori cognitions from empirical ones, though it was not until Kant had shown its importance that "the attention of the learned world was called to the scattered notices of it in the writings of Leibnitz" (Hamilton 1859–1860: II, 359).

Interestingly, Hamilton had no more time for Leibniz's metaphysics than had Stewart before him. Having included Leibniz's hypothesis of pre-established harmony as amongst the options for explaining the relation of the soul and the body, Hamilton went on to say: "It is needless to attempt a refutation of this hypothesis, which its author himself probably regarded more as a specimen of ingenuity than as a serious doctrine."[30]

Ironically, however, Hamilton appears to have been a key figure in the stimulating an interest in Leibniz's metaphysics. He presented one of his favourite

Alexander Campbell Fraser, with what the latter referred to as "a beautiful edition of the philosophical works of Leibniz"[31] and this gift bore fruit in 1846, in what seems to have been the first proper article on Leibniz and his philosophy to appear in the English language.[32]

Fraser, who is best known for his editions of Berkeley, had offered the editor of the *North British Review* a choice between an article on Leibniz or one on Berkeley. And it is likely that he had already formed the opinion, expressed in his article, that Leibniz and Berkeley, whilst representing "opposed schools of philosophy", were both thinkers "whose speculations conducted them to immaterialism" (Fraser 1856: 47). The editor chose Leibniz with the brief that the article deal with the man and not primarily with abstractions. Fraser obliged, following the then recent biography by Guhrauer in his biographical outline. But he also sought to present some kind of apology for Leibniz's metaphysical speculations:

Besides their intrinsic value, they are connected with an important epoch in the history of modern speculation. This philosopher looms vast even in the distance, at the entrance of the labyrinth of recent German philosophy. (Fraser 1856: 4)

Leibniz's discussions, he went on to claim, "have given birth to the philosophical systems of Kant, Fichte, Schelling and Hegel" (Fraser 1856: 14).

Fraser was Professor of Logic and Metaphysics at Edinburgh for 35 years and many of his students themselves became professors of philosophy not only in Britain but throughout the English-speaking world. One of his former students was Robert Latta, whose edition of Leibniz's *Monadology and Other Philosophical Writings* (1898) was to become a standard one for much of the twentieth century. Latta was one of the first Britons to write a doctoral thesis on Leibniz and the exegetical part of the introduction to his edition was derived from this thesis. Of particular interest in the present context is his "Historical and Critical Estimate of Leibniz's Philosophy", which not only sought to place Leibniz in relation to Wolff, Kant, Fichte and Hegel but gave special attention to two philosophers who were very influential in the late nineteenth century but who have subsequently fallen into neglect: Herbart and Lotze.

Latta began the preface to his edition with these remarks:

In this country Leibniz has received less attention than any other of the great philosophers. Mr Merz[33] has given, in a small volume, a general outline of Leibniz's thought and work, Professor Sorley has written for the *Encyclopaedia Britannica* a remarkably clear, but brief, account of his philosophy, and there are American translations of the *Nouveaux Essais* and of some of his philosophical papers. That is very nearly the whole of English writing about him. (Latta, ed. 1898: v)

Latta seems to have been aware of the translations of various Leibniz pieces that were published in the *Journal of Speculative Philosophy* in the 1880s.[34] He seems also to have known of Langley's translation of the *Nouveaux Essais* of 1896.[35] It is unclear whether he knew of the collection of Leibniz papers (Duncan, ed. 1890) translated by G. M. Duncan of Yale. And he seems not to have been aware of Dewey's then recent book (Dewey 1888) on the *New Essays*.

By 1898 indeed the interest in Leibniz's philosophy had grown very considerably. For instance, two of the leading philosophers then at Trinity College, Cambridge were significantly influenced by Leibniz: James Ward, who had studied with Lotze in Gottingen, and John Ellis McTaggart, whose system had affinities with Leibniz's monadology. Bertrand Russell had been taught by them in the mid-1890s and was by 1898 a Fellow of Trinity himself. Indeed, it was in the academic year 1898–1899, as Norma Goethe explains in Chapter 13, that Russell stood in for McTaggart by giving a course of lectures on Leibniz. This course of lectures gave rise to Russell's most enduring contribution to philosophical scholarship, *A Critical Exposition of the Philosophy of Leibniz* (1900). Norma Goethe is concerned in her contribution to show how Russell made Leibniz into a "fellow spirit."

Russell's way of approaching Leibniz made his philosophy of interest to many who were not attracted by his metaphysical conclusions. His *Critical Exposition* remained a starting point for students in the analytical tradition for much of the twentieth century even though they often disagreed with his interpretations. Leibniz was also, in many ways – one of which is explored by Ohad Nachtomy, in Chapter 14 – an important influence on the development of Russell's own philosophy.

Though Russell had available to him the translations of Latta, Duncan and Langley, only Latta's translations satisfied him, the others usually requiring correction, in his opinion. Russell worked mostly from the original language editions by Gerhardt of the philosophical and mathematical writings. Though he admitted that he "had learnt more [from] [...] Erdmann's excellent account in his larger history (1842) [...] than from any other commentary" (Russell 1900: xiii), he largely wrote his *Critical Exposition* without reference to the secondary literature. A single critical reference to Latta's account marks the extent of his attention to the literature in English.

The Reception of Leibniz's Philosophy in America

There was a considerable influence of British philosophy on American in the late eighteenth century, especially of the philosophy of Locke. By the 1820s, however, according to a contemporary account, the works of Locke, formerly the textbooks in American colleges, had given way "to the Scotch writers; and Stewart, Campbell and Brown are now almost universally read as the standard authors on the subjects of which they treat." (Marsh 1913: 136). The author of this account, James Marsh, for many years Professor of Moral and Intellectual Philosophy at the University of Vermont, much regretted this situation. Marsh himself was a student of Kant and of German philosophy and a keen disseminator of Coleridge's philosophy. The "Burlington Philosophy" which Marsh established at Vermont was an important influence for John Dewey and his anti-empiricist book (Dewey 1888) on the *New Essays*.

Charles Saunders Peirce was another of those philosophers who found their way to Leibniz via Kant. Evelyn Vargas, in Chapter 12, begins by noting that Peirce's views on Kant have been studied extensively, there has been little attention to what he thought about Leibniz. This, as she points out, is surprising, given that Peirce regarded Leibniz's reasoning as far more accurate than "that of Kant or almost any other metaphysician that can be named." The contribution of Vargas relates to what Peirce perceived as a blind spot on Leibniz's retina which allowed him to accept some serious inconsistencies and absurdities.

In America, as in Britain, there was a contrast between those who valued Leibniz's logic (like Hamilton, Peirce and Russell) and those who were taken by his metaphysics, especially his monadology. Amongst the latter there were those, in the nineteenth century and twentieth century, who were inclined to what became known as "personal idealism" (Mulvaney 2001). Included in this group also are those known as the "St Louis Hegelians" who founded *The Journal of Speculative Philosophy* and kept it running from 1867 till 1893. This group, who included Thomas Davidson (1840–1900), sponsored the publication of some of the earliest translations into English of Leibniz's metaphysical writings.[36]

This division remained of importance in the twentieth century, with figures like H. Wildon Carr[37] (in Britain) and Leroy Loemker (in America) taking to the metaphysics and philosophers in the analytic tradition taking to the logic. That part of the Leibniz story, however, largely remains to be told. Robert J. Mulvaney's chapter in this volume does, however, link Loemker's interest in Leibniz with the tradition of American personalism.

NOTES

[1]   Sections 1 and 3 were written by Stuart Brown and Section 2 by Pauline Phemister.

[2]   There is a brief discussion of Digby in Mercer 2001.

[3]   Through the intervention of Boyle, whose relations with and influence on Leibniz are discussed in Chapter 6.

[4]   In his notes Leibniz guessed rightly that "poppy" meant "papaver", though he was not certain. See A VI iii, 238.

[5]   In a letter to Jakob Thomasius, A VI i, 168. See W 54.

[6]   See also Beeley 2004.

[7]   See Aiton 1985: 66. Aiton's opinion, with which I agree, is that "Leibniz could read English but probably could not speak it very well."

[8]   George Dalgarno was not a member of the Royal Society, perhaps because he was a school teacher in Guernsey by the time it was constituted. Nonetheless his work was known to a number of its members in addition to Wilkins. The first version of his book was vetted by Boyle and Pell.

[9]   On Leibniz and More, Conway and Van Helmont, see Brown, S. 1990 and 1997.

[10]   But in dissent, see Brown, S. 1990: 83–4.

[11]   Coudert 1995: 141–54.See also Brown, S. 1990.

[12]   Merchant 1979.

[13]   André Robinet traces these and later annotations from 1704 in Robinet 1997.

[14]   Leibniz appended his remarks to a letter to Coste dated 30 May 1712 (GP III, 421–3).

[15]   The only research relating Leibniz and King of which we are aware is that of Sean Greenberg, "Leibniz, King, and the *Theodicy*" (unpublished). Greenberg notes there that Leibniz held King's work in high regard.

[16]   What follows is based in large part on Jolley's account, which is recommended.

[17]   The importance of the relation between Princess Caroline and Leibniz to our understanding of the political, theological, and philosophical dimensions of the exchanges between Leibniz and Clarke are discussed in Meli 1999 and in Brown, G. 2004.

[18] For a excellent detailed analysis of the physical and mathematical issues involved in the dispute, see Meli 1993.

[19] Leibniz had worked long and hard to secure the Protestant Hanoverian succession to the English throne. He had suggested the possibility of a Hanoverian succession to the Duchess of Celle, encouraging her to mention it to King William III (Aiton 1985: 228). His intervention led eventually to the Act of Settlement in 1701, establishing the succession in favour of Hanover. Leibniz continued to promote the Hanoverian succession at every opportunity, even issuing an anonymous pamphlet detailing the mutual benefits of English and German co-operation (Aiton 1985: 229). The king's decision effectively deprived Leibniz the fruit of his efforts.

[20] G. Brown (2004: 264–8).

[21] Vadim Vasilyev (1993) discusses Hume's debt to Leibniz doctrine of pre-established harmony.

[22] "Raspe, *Oeuvres philosophiques latines et françoises de feu M. Leibnitz*, 7 vols." (Wilson, C. 1995: 470n).

[23] "des Maizeaux, *Receuil des pièces diverses sur la philosophie, la religion naturelle, l'histoire, les mathematiques, etc.*" (Wilson, C. 1995: 470n).

[24] Wilson adds: "Other early collections included: Feller, *Otium hanoveranum sive Miscellanea, ex ore et schedis illustris viri*; C. Kortholt, G. G. Leibniz, *Epistolae ad diversos, theologici, iuridici, medici, philosophici, matematici, et philologici argumenti*" (Wilson, C. 1995: 470n).

[25] The only person, so far as I know, who has done any sustained work in this area is Robert J. Mulvaney, who has had a particular interest in the American reception of Leibniz. See Mulvaney 1996 and 2001.

[26] There is nothing to compare, for instance, with Wayne I Boucher's six-volume collection of reception source material, *Spinoza: Eighteenth and Nineteenth Century Discussions* (Bristol: Thoemmes Press, 1999).

[27] Catherine Wilson, in her essay on "The Reception of Leibniz in the Eighteenth Century", justifies focusing on Germany since "it is only in Germany that there is anything like a continuous story to tell. In England, Leibniz became, after his death, little more than a name and a symbol – a threat to the honor of Newton and to the national honor as well." (Wilson, C. 1995: 443–4)

[28] Remnant and Bennett claim: "Until the 1970s the English-language literature on Leibniz tended to neglect the *New Essays* ..." (RB xxxv) That may be true of the literature of the twentieth century. But, for some nineteenth century philosophers, including Hamilton and Dewey, it was Leibniz's main work. And for those exercised about Locke's philosophy, which still loomed large in the English-speaking world in the nineteenth century, its prominence is understandable.

[29] See Stewart 1829: VI, 265.

[30] Hamilton 1859–1860: II, 304. Leibniz received some defence from his treatment at the hands of Hamilton from an unlikely quarter. John Stuart Mill, in his *Examination of Sir William Hamilton's Philosophy* (1865), complained about the way in which Hamilton failed to really understand the historical philosophers to whom he referred, considering their doctrines in isolation from the philosophies of which they were a part. No philosopher, according to Mill, sought to connect his various doctrines so carefully into a single system as did Leibniz. And so Hamilton's treatment of Leibniz, according to Mill, shows him in the worst light as an historian of philosophy: "Other examples may be given, though none greater than this, of Sir W. Hamilton's inability to enter into the very mind of another thinker." (Mill 1865: 502) Even Mill, however, did not regard Leibniz's philosophy as a serious option. His point is that Leibniz was driven to his metaphysical conclusions by a "logical necessity". To understand him, according to Mill, we need to see his monads, his pre-established harmony, his necessitarianism and his optimism as all part of the same system. Mill compares Leibniz's conclusions with Descartes's conclusion that animals are automata, remarking that Descartes was driven to his conclusion "far more absurdly". The implication is, even if not as absurd as Descartes's conclusion that animals were automata, Leibniz's conclusions were nonetheless entirely implausible.

[31] Fraser 1904: 58. It seems likely that the edition in question was that of Erdmann, which is entitled *"Opera philosophica"*, and to which Fraser refers in some detail in his article. There is a slight discrepancy between the date of the gift, as Fraser recalls it (sometime at the end of the winter of 1838–1839), and

the publication of Erdmann's edition (1839–1840). But Hamilton was a figure of international eminence by then and so may have received an advance copy.

[32]   The article was published in the *North British Review* in 1846 and included in Fraser 1856: 1–56.

[33]   Merz 1884 is the first book on Leibniz in English. Merz was English-born and he later lived in England. But his parents were German and he studied at various German universities, including Gottingen, where he knew and was influenced by Lotze. See the entry on him in the Thoemmes *Dictionary of Nineteenth-Century British Philosophers* (Mander and Sell, eds. 2002: 782–6). Merz does not refer to any English writing on Leibniz and his chapter on "The Fate of Leibniz's Philosophy" is largely concerned with Leibniz's philosophical descendents in Germany insofar as it is concerned with named individuals.

[34]   *The Journal of Speculative Philosophy*, published between 1867 and 1893, contained a number of Leibniz translations, such as: Monadology (vol. 1), the nature of the soul (vol. 2), "Platonic enthusiasm" (vol. 3), "On the doctrine of a universal spirit" (vol. 5) as well as translations of other German philosophers such as Kant, Hegel, Fichte and Lotze.

[35]   See Langley, ed. 1896.

[36]   For a fuller account see J. A. Good's introduction to the republication of all 22 volumes of *The Journal of Speculative Philosophy, 1867–1893* (Good ed. 2002).

[37]   As well as his commentary on the *Monadology* (Carr ed. 1930) Carr elaborated a Leibnizian metaphysics of his own in two monographs: Carr 1922 and 1930.

2. LEIBNIZ'S DEBT TO HOBBES

I. INTRODUCTION

My title might suggest that I am going to argue for a strong Hobbesian influence on Leibniz's philosophy. However, it is notoriously difficult to establish direct influences in the history of philosophy, and especially so in Leibniz's case. He was a voracious reader, and even while developing the earliest versions of his system when he was still a student, he had at his finger-tips an impressive range of authors – ancient, medieval, and contemporary. In most cases, one and the same doctrine or concept can be found, with greater or lesser variation, in a number of books Leibniz will have been familiar with. It is therefore unclear which he will have been indebted to in particular – and the more widely spread an idea, the more likely he is to have come under its influence. For example, one of Leibniz's aims was to reconcile Aristotelianism with the new mechanistic philosophy; but it makes little sense to ask which modern philosopher in particular converted him to the mechanistic worldview. On repeated occasions, Leibniz himself merely provides a list, such as "Galileo, Bacon, Gassendi, Descartes, Hobbes, and Digby,"[1] without giving priority to any one author.

Leibniz was certainly eclectic, and he quite consciously set out to produce a system which would incorporate what he believed to be true in different, conflicting philosophical systems, while rejecting what was false. In his own words, his system would be a "harmony of the philosophers."[2] As he wrote in his *Clarification of Mr Bayle's Difficulties* of 1698:

Consideration of this system [of mine] makes it evident that when one comes down to the basics, one finds that most philosophical schools have more of the truth than one would have believed.... [They] come together as at a centre of perspective, from which an object (confused if looked at from any other position) displays its regularity and the appropriateness of its parts. The commonest failing is the sectarian spirit in which people diminish themselves by rejecting others. (GP IV, 523–4)

Or as he put it more succinctly in a letter to Nicolas Remond of 1714: "Most philosophical schools are largely right in what they assert, but not so much in what they deny" (GP III, 607).

Although it is a fruitless project to champion one individual philosopher as *the* most important influence on Leibniz, it is nevertheless worthwhile to explore similarities wherever they may be found, in order to fill out the details of Leibniz's eclecticism. And sometimes there may be concrete evidence of a unique influence on a particular doctrine. So, while I do happen to believe that Hobbes has been relatively neglected as a source for Leibniz's ideas, I should not be taken as *championing* Hobbes, in the way that Catherine Wilson[3] does, or that Christia Mercer champions Aristotle (Mercer 2001), Konrad Moll champions Gasssendi

19

(Moll 1968–1996), or Ludwig Stein champions Spinoza (Stein 1890) as the main source for his early philosophy.

In this paper, I shall concentrate on Hobbes's and Leibniz's *metaphysics*. This may seem a surprising limitation, because Hobbes is now generally thought of as a political philosopher. However, in his own lifetime, Hobbes was known (on the Continent, at least) as first and foremost one of the leaders of the modern movement in theoretical philosophy and science, and it is here where his influence on Leibniz is strongest.

Nevertheless, it is arguable that, even in his political philosophy, Leibniz was significantly influenced by Hobbes. Patrick Riley[4] and others may have been misled by Leibniz's repeated rejections of Hobbes's political system as a whole into neglecting the extent to which Leibniz was stimulated by an admiration of certain aspects of Hobbes's approach, while being repelled by its apparently[5] atheistic conclusions.[6] Ursula Goldenbaum[7] has unearthed evidence that Leibniz was perceived by those who knew him best (in particular Christian von Boineburg) as a Hobbesian and Spinozist, rather than being the traditionalist Aristotelian that Christia Mercer would have us believe. Goldenbaum argues convincingly that Leibniz accepted the Hobbesian position that humans act only for their own advantage, and that Leibniz's problem was to reconcile individual self interest with the common good. He found the solution in the non-Hobbesian concept of love: "We love a thing whose happiness is pleasing to us."[8] In other words, an individual who is motivated by Christian love will act altruistically, because altruism is a source of pleasure.

2. LEIBNIZ'S KNOWLEDGE OF HOBBES

Leibniz was sufficiently impressed by Hobbes's philosophy to try to enter into correspondence with him. Two letters survive: one written on 13/23 July 1670 (A II i, 56–9) and the other around 1674 (A II i, 244–5). It is certain that Leibniz received no reply to the first,[9] and it is almost equally certain that the same is true of the second. Near the beginning of the first, he makes the following significant claim: "I believe I have read most of your works, whether separately or in the collected edition" (A II i, 56).

The collected edition which Leibniz refers to was published in Amsterdam in 1668.[10] Hobbes's motive was to boost his posthumous reputation as a major philosopher on the Continent (he was already in his 80s), as a counterbalance to his uneasy mix of neglect and notoriety at home. Although Leibniz had access to this edition soon after it was published, he had already read some of Hobbes's works in separate editions. Either way, his claim is fully vindicated by the range of works he refers to explicitly in his early writings: *De corpore, De homine, De cive, Leviathan, De principiis et ratiocinatione geometrarum, Examinatio et emendatio mathematicae hodiernae,* and *Problemata physica.*[11] There can be no doubt that Leibniz had studied Hobbes with great care by the end of the 1660s.

As I said earlier, many of the philosophical tenets Leibniz shared with Hobbes were held in common by others. Examples are: that space is a plenum, that there are no indivisible material atoms, that individual natural phenomena are to be explained in terms of the laws of mechanics and not in terms of final causes, and so on. Such ideas were generally in the air, even if not all the moderns espoused all of them. However, other, more specific ideas were Hobbes's own. I shall cover three clusters of such ideas relatively briefly, and then discuss a fourth one in greater detail, since it has been generally overlooked.

3. IDEAS LEIBNIZ DERIVED FROM HOBBES

Logic as Computation

In 1887, the Hobbes scholar, Ferdinand Tönnies, claimed (Tönnies 1887) that the basic idea of Leibniz's combinatory art, as well as his plan for a universal character-istic, could be traced back to Hobbes. In 1901, the Leibniz scholar, Louis Couturat, published a detailed rejection of this claim.[12] In fact both writers ranged more widely than this, with Tönnies looking for similarities between the two philosophers, and passages where Leibniz praises Hobbes; and Couturat looking for dissimilarities, and passages where Leibniz criticises him. However, both might be right in what they assert, and wrong in what they deny.

The crucial passage in Hobbes is *De corpore* 1.2:

> By 'reasoning' I mean computation. But to compute is *to unite a number of things added together into a single total, or to know the remainder when one thing is taken away from another*. So reasoning is the same as *adding* and *subtracting*. I do not mind if you add *multiplying* and *dividing*, since *multiplication* is the same as the *addition* of equals, and *division* is the same as the *subtraction* of equals as many times as is possible. Consequently, all reasoning is reduced to two operations of the mind, namely *addition* and *subtraction*.

And again in 1.3:

> Consequently, it would be wrong to confine computation (i.e. reasoning) to numbers, as if humans were distinguished from other animate beings only by their ability to count (as Pythagoras is said to have believed). This is because it is also possible to add a magnitude to a magnitude, or to subtract a magnitude from a magnitude, and similarly with bodies, motions, degrees of quality, actions, concepts, proportions, sentences, and names – which cover all branches of philosophy.

Hobbes's original and radical idea was that, instead of there being distinct kinds of reasoning (syllogistic, arithmetical, geometrical, etc.), all human reasoning was reducible to the single mental operation of adding or subtracting names, or propo-sitions consisting of names. Ultimately, logic was to be regarded as a species of arithmetic.

Leibniz approved of this. Referring to the first of the above passages, he wrote:

> Thomas Hobbes, that most profound investigator of the principles of all things, rightly laid down that every operation of the human mind is *computation*, and by this is to be understood either *adding* a sum or *subtracting* a difference.[13]

What Tönnies rightly saw was that Leibniz was indebted to Hobbes for the central idea that all reasoning was computation (or "calculation" in Leibniz's preferred terminology), and hence a kind of arithmetic or algebra. Without this idea, Leibniz would never have developed his combinatory art, nor his universal characteristic, which he envisaged as an arithmetically notated system of all possible concepts. His vision was that, since all reasoning was in principle computable, the day would come when inconclusive argumentation would be a thing of the past. As he wrote in an undated note:

> But to return to the expression of thoughts by means of characters, I thus think that controversies can never be resolved, nor *sectarian disputes* be silenced, unless we renounce complicated chains of reasoning in favour of simple *calculations*, and vague terms of uncertain meaning in favour of determinate *characters*.
>
> In other words, it must be brought about that every fallacy becomes nothing other than a *calculating error*, and every *sophism* expressed in this new type of notation becomes in fact nothing other than a *grammatical* or *linguistic error*, easily proved to be such by the very laws of this philosophical grammar. Once this has been achieved, when controversies arise, there will be no more need for a disputation between two philosophers than there would be between two accountants. It would be enough for them to pick up their pens and sit at their abacuses, and say to each other (perhaps having summoned a mutual friend): "Let us calculate." (GP VII, 200)

This echoes Hobbes's ambition to replace the disputes of "dogmatic" philosophy with the consensus characteristic of "mathematical" philosophy, by applying the methods of the latter to the natural and human sciences.[14]

If Tönnies had been more attuned to the latest developments in logic, he could have gone further, and pointed out that Leibniz nearly succeeded in developing a complete Boolean algebra – the final fulfilment of Hobbes's dream of logic as a species of arithmetic.

What Couturat did was to show that none of the details of Leibniz's logic are to be found in Hobbes, and indeed that Hobbes lacked the logical and mathematical ability to make any formal advances. However, this does not detract from Tönnies's insight that Leibniz was inspired by Hobbes's unique vision, even if Hobbes himself was unable to develop it. Couturat was wrong to dismiss Hobbes's influence on Leibniz simply on the grounds that Hobbes had failed to do what Leibniz subsequently achieved by standing on his shoulders.

The Definition of Truth

One of the most distinctive features of Leibniz's philosophy is his claim that in every true proposition, the concept of the predicate is contained in the concept of the subject.[15] When I say "distinctive", I do not mean that he was the first to define truth in this way, since the same definition is to be found in scholastic philosophy, at least as a definition of universal truth.[16] Leibniz's originality lay in extending it to all truth, thus giving rise to his principle that all truth is analytic, and its corollary that every individual has a complete concept.

Leibniz may have been encouraged by finding something very similar in Hobbes's writings. In *De corpore* 3.7 ("True and False"), Hobbes writes:

A *true* proposition is one in which the *predicate* contains the *subject*, or in which the *predicate* is the name of everything of which the *subject* is the name. For example, "A human is an animal" is a true proposition because whatever is called "human" is also called "animal". And "Some human is sick" is true, since "sick" is the name of some human. A proposition is called *false* if it is not true, or if its *predicate* does not include its *subject*; for example "A human is a stone."

There is, however an important difference, namely that, whereas Leibniz's definition is *intensional*, Hobbes's definition is *extensional*. That is to say, for Leibniz the predicate "animal" is contained in the concept of "human", because being an animal is part of the concept of being a human (a human is a rational animal). For Hobbes, by contrast, the concept of "human" is contained in the predicate "animal", because humans are a sub-set of animals. In a sense the definitions are equivalent, since any proposition expressing the predicate as contained in the subject intensionally can be replaced by one expressing the subject as contained in the predicate extensionally.

One reason why Hobbes preferred the extensional approach was because it fitted the traditional "tree of Porphyry", according to which the lowest species, such as humans, come under or are contained within a hierarchy of genera, with the highest genus of substance (or in Hobbes's system, body) at the top. He reproduces the "table of predicaments of bodies" in *De corpore* 2.15, and in 2.16 he comments:

Secondly, it should be observed that, in the case of *positive* names, the lower is always contained in the higher; whereas in the case of negative names, the higher is contained in the lower. For example, "animal" is the name of every human, and therefore includes the name "human" in itself; but since "non-human" is the name of everything which is not an animal, the name "non-animal" which is placed above it is contained by the lower name "non-human."

In other words, there are more animals than humans, since there are some animals which are not humans; and there are more non-humans than non-animals, since some non-humans are animals.

However, a more important reason for Hobbes to prefer the extensional approach was the metaphysical one that it was consistent with his nominalism. In Hobbes's ontology there was no room for anything other than individual bodies. Although names could have universal import as human artefacts (sounds in the air, or marks on paper), there were no concepts with an existence independent of human beings. So there was no problem (on this account, at least) over saying that humans are a sub-set of the bodies to which humans apply the name "animal." Although an intensional approach is equivalent in practice, it is ontologically very different, in that it implies the existence of real essences or independently existing concepts which can be said to be contained within one another.

It is true that Leibniz had a brief flirtation with nominalism,[17] and one which left a lasting mark in the form of his lifelong and fruitful concern with the importance of notation in areas such as the universal characteristic, logic, and the calculus. However, even at his most nominalist he regarded Hobbes's version of nominalism as unacceptably extreme, and he always retained a belief in the objective existence of concepts, which made an intensional approach to the issue of concept inclusion more natural.

There is a further question as to whether Hobbes anticipated Leibniz in making his definition of truth apply to all truths, or only to universal truths. Although the passage from *De corpore* 3.7 quoted above seems to apply to all truths, it is a general feature of Hobbes's writings that he is thinking mainly of "scientific", or necessary and universal knowledge, and not of "historical", or merely empirical knowledge. Thus in *De corpore* 3.10 ("Necessary and Contingent Propositions"), he writes:

Again, in every necessary proposition, the *predicate* is either equivalent to the subject (as in "A human is a rational animal"), or part of an equivalent name (as in "A human is an animal").... But this is not the case with contingent propositions. Even if it were true that "Every human is a liar," the word "liar" is not part of the compound name to which the name "human" is equivalent. So the proposition will not be called *necessary*, but *contingent*, even if it is contingently the case that it is always true.

So, although Leibniz may well have been influenced by Hobbes's definition of truth, he developed it far further than Hobbes could have envisaged.

A corollary of Hobbes's definition, reinforced by his nominalism, is a stress on the importance of verbal definitions as the foundation of all logical reasoning. One of the characteristics of Hobbes's writing is that he prefaces his arguments with long lists of definitions of key terms – a particularly good example being Chapter VI of *Leviathan*. Leibniz adopted a similar approach in many of his early writings, such as the *Theoria motus abstracti*, and his private notes include long lists of definitions of terms relating to particular topics.[18] These were a preliminary to Leibniz's ultimate goal of constructing a universal characteristic, in which concepts would be notated arithmetically, in such a way that their logical relations would be patent. This would make it possible to calculate mechanically whether any given proposition was true or false. Yet again, Leibniz's ambitions far outstripped those of Hobbes; but the central idea that the definition of names lies at the root of all reasoning is something Leibniz owed to Hobbes, who was unique among early modern philosophers for his stress on language.

The Concept of Conatus

One of the key concepts in Hobbes's system is that of *conatus* or "endeavour." Its primary occurrence is in his physics, where it serves to make up one of the many deficiencies of Cartesian physics. Descartes had tried to explain everything in terms of the two fundamental concepts of extension and motion; but it soon became evident that more concepts were needed to account for the phenomena – in particular, the concepts of mass and of force. Hobbes implicitly recognised the conceptual difference between a massy object and an equal volume of empty space by making size and shape accidents of body, as something existing in its own right, independently of its extensional properties. Even though he agreed with Descartes that there was no empty space, this was a contingent fact, rather than a necessary truth following from Descartes's thesis that the *essence* of matter was extension, and hence that there could be no extension without matter.

Force was more problematic, because, unlike matter and motion, it was not directly observable, and therefore uncomfortably close to the occult virtues which the moderns were so concerned to eliminate from the description of nature. Hobbes got round this problem by postulating *conatus* as a limiting case of motion, which *is* observable. In *De corpore* 15.2, he writes:

I shall define *conatus* as *a motion through a space and time which is less than is given, i.e. is determined, whether by being displayed, or by being assigned a number*; in other words, *it is a motion through a point*. In order to explain this definition, I must remind you that by 'point' I do not mean that which has no quantity, or which cannot conceivably be divided, since there is no such thing in the real world. Rather, it is that the quantity of which is entirely disregarded, in other words, that of which neither the quantity nor any part of it enters into the calculation for the purposes of demonstration. So a point should not be taken as indivisible, but as undivided.[19]

Just as a real point is an infinitesimal – greater than a mathematical point, but smaller than any given quantity – so a conatus is an infinitesimal motion. *Conceptually* it is still a motion, but its primary function is not to be the smallest component of a macroscopic motion, but to be the force[20] which initiates a motion. Thus, in the same chapter he says:

I define *resistance, when two moving bodies come into contact*, as *a conatus contrary to a conatus, whether wholly, or in a particular part.*

And:

to define what it is to *push: We say that one of two moving bodies pushes the other, when its conatus brings it about that the whole or part of the other leaves its place.*

As a force, a *conatus* is importantly different from an ordinary motion in that any given body can have only one motion at a time, but it will be subject to a variety of conatuses,[21] of which its actual motion is the resultant. Indeed, Hobbes held that every conatus is propagated to infinity through the plenum,[22] from which it follows that every body is subject to an infinity of forces. A corollary is that no body is absolutely at rest. Quite apart from the lack of a fixed point of reference in an infinite universe, even bodies which are apparently at rest relative to their neighbours are internally vibrating because of the conatuses acting on them. Rest is a state in which the forces are in equilibrium, and a body will spring into motion as soon as the balance is disturbed.

Leibniz draws heavily on Hobbes's concept of *conatus*, both in his letter to Hobbes of 1670, and in his *Theoria motus abstracti* of 1671. Although Leibniz diverges from Hobbes on points of detail, his broad position is that the smallest components of the material world are infinitesimals; that they are endowed with conatuses which are infinitesimal motions; that conatuses are propagated to infinity in the plenum; that a given body is subject to a multiplicy of conatasus at one and the same time; and that nothing is absolutely at rest.[23]

While this is by no means yet Leibniz's mature system, the seeds of it are clearly present, and it is equally clear that he stood on the shoulders of Hobbes for many aspects of it. Hobbes had gone as far as he could, and he was not mathematician enough to develop his concept of *conatus* into the calculus, as Leibniz did a few years later. Nor could Hobbes resolve the ambiguity of *conatus* being at the same time nothing other than a motion, and yet also the cause of motion. Leibniz resolved the problem by spiritualising Hobbes's infinitesimal atoms into non-spatial monads characterised by active and passive powers, and relegating motion itself to the realm of phenomena perceived by monads. Nevertheless, there is still a striking similarity between Hobbes's material universe, consisting of a dynamically interconnected plenum of infinitesimal particles, each pulsating with motion, and Leibniz's mature vision of a spiritual universe, consisting of unities striving for perfection, and accommodating themselves to each other through the universal harmony.

However, *conatus* as force is only one half of the story. Hobbes also used the concept of *conatus* to solve the mind/body problem. In the pre-modern period, the predominantly Aristotelian worldview fudged the issue by postulating mind and body as different aspects or components of one and the same individual substance (form and matter). Both Hobbes and Descartes independently sharpened the issue in their own distinctive ways: Hobbes with his uncompromising materialism, which excluded mind as a distinct ontological category; and Descartes with his uncompromising dualism, which made any interaction between mind and matter problematic.[24] Although Hobbes's first published philosophical work was his objections to Descartes's *Meditations*, it is unlikely that his own account of the relation between mind and body was a reaction to Descartes, because he regarded Descartes's concept of immaterial substance as totally absurd.[25] Nevertheless, Hobbes did have to explain how our everyday experience of consciously controlling the behaviour of our bodies is compatible with a materialist ontology.

In *Leviathan* 6, Hobbes takes it for granted that, since human beings are material objects, all their activities are motions. He distinguishes between purely physical or "vital" motions such as the circulation of the blood or breathing, and "animal" or "voluntary" motions, in which the imagination stimulates a new motion which would not otherwise have occurred. As with the inanimate realm, where a *conatus* is an infinitesimal motion giving rise to a macroscopic motion, in the animate realm, a volition is likewise an infinitesimal motion giving rise to a macroscopic motion: "These small beginnings of Motion, within the body of Man, before they appear in walking, speaking, striking, and other visible actions, are commonly called ENDEAVOUR."

So there is an exact parallel between *conatus* or endeavour in the inanimate and the animate realms. Just as there is no need to appeal to occult forces to account for motion in the inanimate realm, there is no need to appeal to similar forces in the animate realm. Volitions are nothing other than small beginnings of motion, and they do not imply a separate, immaterial substance which stimulates the body into action.

Leibniz was fully aware of the significance of Hobbes's concept of *conatus* for overcoming the Cartesian problem of how mind can influence matter (and *vice versa*) if they are totally different categories of entity. His solution was to avoid Cartesian dualism in the first place, by locating minds at unextended points, and equating *conatus* with volition. Thus in the *Theoria motus abstracti*, he says that this concept of *conatus* "opens the door to arriving at the true distinction between body and mind, which no-one has hitherto discovered" (GP IV, 230).

He explains this further in an undated letter to Arnauld. After summarising the *Theoria motus abstracti*, he writes:

> Further, from these propositions I reaped a huge harvest, not only in demonstrating the laws of motion, but in the philosophy of mind. For having demonstrated that the true location of our mind is a sort of point or centre, from this I deduced some surprising consequences about the indissolubility of mind, about the impossibility of refraining from thinking, about the impossibility of forgetting, and about the true and hitherto unknown difference between motion and thought – that thought consists in *conatus*, just as body consists in motion. (GP I, 72–3)

So we have Leibniz's own word for it that many of his key metaphysical doctrines originated in the concept of *conatus*, which he owed to Hobbes.

All Bodies Perceive

For the rest of this paper, I shall focus on a related point of similarity between Hobbes and Leibniz which has not received much attention,[26] namely their both holding that all bodies perceive, and that the difference between inanimate bodies and animals is that the latter *remember* their perceptions.

Hobbes's account of sensation is briefly as follows. Changes take place only when one body moves against a body adjacent to it. So a change in the sensory state of a sentient being can take place only if a body sets up a motion in a sense organ. In the case of touch, the motion is direct. In the case of vision, the brightness of a luminous body consists in a pulsating motion, which causes a vibration in the ether; and the part of the ether adjacent to the eye causes a motion in the eye. Again, sound consists in a vibration, which causes the air to vibrate, and the part of the air closest to the ear sets up a motion in the ear – and similarly with the other senses. But as yet there is no sensation. Once a motion is set up in the sense organ, it propagates a similar motion along the nerves, through the brain, and down to the heart. In the heart, it meets with an equal and opposite reaction, which travels back along the same route until it arrives back at the sense organ. Then and only then a "phantasm" is generated by the opposition between the two motions. This phantasm is the sensory image of which we are directly aware, and it appears to be external to us because of the outward motion from the heart and brain.[27]

There are, of course, many problems with this account. But what concerns me here is the difference between three kinds of being: human beings, sentient beings or animals, and non-sentient beings or inanimate matter.

Hobbes is quite explicit that sensation is the same in animals as in humans.[28] In this he differs from Descartes, for whom animals are automata, with no awareness of their sensations. Indeed, it is a corollary of Hobbes's materialism that he makes much less of a divide between humans and other animals, since he does not explain consciousness as the function of an immaterial soul (in fact he does not discuss consciousness as such at all). For Hobbes, what distinguishes humans is their possession of *reason*, and reason consists in nothing more than the ability to *name* things so as to construct a language, and to perform computations involving names. So if a human and an animal observe the same scene, the only difference is that the human can add a linguistic running commentary. As Hobbes says in the sixth objection to Descartes's *Meditations* (and bear in mind that he uses the word "thought" both for perceptions and for rational conceptions):

> but thought can be similar in humans and in animals. For when we assert that a person is running, we do not have a thought which is any different from that had by a dog watching its owner running. So the only thing that assertion or negation adds to simple thoughts is perhaps the thought that the names which the assertion consists of are the names of the same thing in the mind of the person doing the asserting. This is not to involve in a thought anything more than its resemblance to its object, but to involve that resemblance twice over. (AT VII, 182)

If we now turn to the difference between animals and inanimate matter, Hobbes has a problem. His account of sensation in sentient beings is purely mechanical, as it has to be if he is to avoid appealing to animal souls. But the crux of his explanation is that phantasms occur spontaneously at the meeting point between two equal and opposite motions. Or, one might say, a phantasm *is nothing other than* this meeting of motions, since no new matter can come into being, and there can be no such thing as an immaterial sensory image. If so, there is no justification for restricting phantasms to sense organs. Why should not a billiard ball be said to "sense" the impact of the white, and therefore to have a phantasm of it? All Hobbes's account of sensation does is to describe the route taken by a pressure wave so that there is an equal and opposite reaction at the surface of the sense organ; it does not explain why only sense organs should have phantasms.

Hobbes considers this question in *De corpore* 25, Article 5, headed "Not all bodies are endowed with sensation". He says:

> Even though, as I have said, all sensation occurs by reaction, it is not necessarily the case that whatever reacts has a sensation. I know there have been philosophers, and learned ones at that, who have held that all bodies are endowed with sensation; nor do I see how they could be refuted, if the nature of sensation consisted in reaction alone. But even if bodies other than sentient ones had some sort of phantasm whenever they reacted, it would cease as soon as the object went away. Unless they had organs capable of retaining an impressed motion even after the object had gone away, as animals have, their sensation would be unaccompanied by any memory that they had sensed — and this has nothing to do with the sort of sensation we are talking about here.

He doesn't *quite* say that all reactions result in a phantasm, but he comes very close to it. What he does say is that having a phantasm is not sufficient for sensation, because sensation requires memory. In other words, bodies are consciously aware of what impinges on them, or have sensations, only if they have a memory in which they can retain the phantasm beyond the instant in which it occurs. This is identical to Descartes's explanation of how we can sleep, given that the soul must always think, since thought is the essence of the soul. When we are awake, we remember our previous thoughts; but when we are asleep, we forget our thoughts from one instant to the next. Both Descartes and Hobbes hold that memory is integral to consciousness, whether or not consciousness requires a separate immaterial substance.

But Hobbes goes further in explaining why memory is necessary. In the same Article he continues:

> By 'sensation', we customarily mean a sort of judgment, based on phantasms, about the things which are the objects of sensation. More specifically, we compare and distinguish phantasms; and this is possible only if the motion in the organ which gave rise to a phantasm continues for some time, and the phantasm itself is brought back during that time. So the sort of sensation I am talking about (which is what is meant by 'sensation' in ordinary language) is necessarily accompanied by a memory, which enables us to compare earlier sensations with later ones, and to distinguish one from another.

Here, Hobbes seems to have forgotten that he is talking about animals as well as humans, since he says that sensation is a form of *judgment*, and he talks of "us". Nevertheless, animals do have memories, and inanimate objects do not. Moreover, Hobbes's point that sensation is *necessarily* accompanied by memory is a good one, since sense organs would be without a function unless they enabled animals to make comparisons and discriminations.

Hobbes then draws a further conclusion, which is that we must have a successive *variety* of phantasms in order to be said to sense anything, otherwise we have nothing to compare our present phantasm with. He gives the example of someone confronted with an unchanging perceptual state:

> I might say that you were absorbed in the thing, and perhaps that you were looking at it; but that you were oblivious. I would not say that you *saw* it. So it comes to the same thing whether you sense one thing all the time, or do not sense anything at all.

On the same grounds, in the *Ten Dialogues* (WME VII, 83), he says that a new-born baby does not sense when it first opens its eyes, but only after it has had enough phantasms to be able to distinguish one from another.

In short, there are three levels of awareness, and everything in the universe is aware at one or other of these levels. At the lowest level, inanimate objects have phantasms when they interact, but they do not have sensation. Animals do have sensation, because they can remember previous phantasms, and compare and distinguish them. Humans have the additional capacity to reflect on their sensations using language.

Coming back to Leibniz, he too, at least in his mature philosophy, holds that everything in the universe is a perceiver. Monads that are not souls of animals perceive unconsciously (they only have *petites perceptions*);[29] animals perceive consciously; and humans have the additional capacity for *apperception*, which includes reason, self-awareness, and a moral sense.

Of course, there are still many differences between the two philosophers. The biggest difference is that for Leibniz all substances are *essentially* perceivers and are not extended, whereas for Hobbes all substances are essentially extended, and are perceivers only in so far as they interact with other substances (though they are in fact doing this all the time). Nevertheless, it is remarkable that a materialist such as Hobbes could talk of inanimate matter as perceiving at all.

As I hinted above, the reason for this is that Hobbes is a monist. As a materialist monist, he is committed to denying any absolute difference in kind between inanimate bodies, animal bodies, and human bodies. Even God is a body, or body in general.[30] Their basic ingredients are the same, and they operate in accordance with the same mechanical laws. Consequently, both the animal function of sensation and the human function of rational thought must be reducible to elements which are found throughout the material world. For Hobbes the common element is the mutual action and reaction of colliding bodies; and if this is describable in terms of phantasms in the case of sense perception, then it ought to be describable in these same terms in the case of non-sentient bodies. That is why the difference between the animate and the inanimate must be attributed to something else, namely memory. Of course, memory in turn must be reducible to mechanical interactions of bodies; but it is reasonable to suppose that only *some* bodies are sufficiently complex to be able to store copies of phantasms (namely animal bodies), whereas the majority are not.

But Leibniz is also a monist, albeit a spiritualist one. Consequently, he too must reduce all the phenomena of nature to items of the same kind. He starts from the other end, by making something analogous to human and animal perception the essential property of substances, and he explains phenomena such as the extension and mass of bodies in terms of these perceptions. So, paradoxically, although the two philosophies seem diametrically opposed, they have it in common that if *anything* perceives, then in some sense *everything* must perceive.

I am not going to argue that Leibniz got the idea that inanimate objects perceive from Hobbes. Hobbes himself is quite cautious about it, and in the passage from *De corpore* 25.5 quoted above, he remarks that other philosophers have held that "all bodies are endowed with sensation". He doesn't say which philosophers in particular he has in mind, but vitalism was widespread in the seventeenth century. Indeed, one way of looking at Leibniz's philosophy is to see him as bringing about a reconciliation between vitalism on the one hand, and mechanism on the other.

However, although Leibniz cannot be said to have got his vitalism from Hobbes, he *does* seem to have been influenced by Hobbes's theory that the difference between inanimate bodies and animals is that the latter have *memory*. In his *Theoria motus abstracti*, the work which owes more to Hobbes than any other, he writes as follows:

No conatus which does not result in motion lasts more than an instant, except in minds. For what happens at an instant is a conatus, whereas what happens over time is the motion of a body. This opens the door to arriving at the true distinction between body and mind, which no-one has hitherto discovered. For every body is a momentary mind, or a mind that lacks *memory*, because it does not retain its own conatus together with the contrary conatus of another body beyond an instant. But two things are required for there to be *sensation*, namely action and reaction, or in other words comparison, and hence *harmony* — and also *pleasure* or pain, without which there is no sensation. So a body lacks memory; it lacks any sensation of its actions and passions; and it lacks thought.[31]

The concept of a non-sentient body as a "momentary mind" lacking memory is absolutely crucial for his later conception of primitive monads as unconscious perceivers belonging to the same ontological category as conscious perceivers. This is clearly a debt he owes to Hobbes.

In his later writings, Leibniz lays more stress on the idea of distinctness, and he sometimes implies that the difference between the perceptions of bare monads at one extreme, and humans at the other, is one of degree, namely the extent to which they are obscure and confused or clear and distinct. Indeed the main function of sense organs is to focus the infinitely confused mass of forces acting on us into a distinct representation of reality. However, he never abandoned the idea that memory is also essential for distinguishing between bare monads and animals. For example, in *Monadology* §19 he says:

If we are willing to give the name 'soul' to everything which has perceptions and appetites..., then all created simple substances (monads) could be called 'souls'. But since sensation is something more than simple perception, I am prepared to accept that the general name 'monad' or 'entelechy' is sufficient for simple substances which only have simple perceptions, and that we should reserve the name 'soul' for those which have more distinct perceptions accompanied by memory. (GP VI, 610)

And a little later, in §25, he makes it clear that he is talking about all animals, and not just human beings:

We also see that Nature has given heightened perceptions to animals, through the care it has taken to supply them with sense organs...(GP VI, 611)

He then goes on to say how memory enables animals to reason in an empirical way through the association of ideas. What distinguishes humans from animals is not a superior consciousness of what we experience, but the ability to know necessary and eternal truths over and above what is given in experience (§29: GP VI, 611) – another point in common with Hobbes.

4. CONCLUSION

To sum up, Leibniz's relationship with Hobbes is an excellent example of his willingness to incorporate into his own philosophical system any good features he found in other philosophers, however much he might disagree with them in other respects. He completely rejected Hobbes's materialism, alleged atheism, and most of his political philosophy. There is no way Leibniz could be described as a Hobbesian, even in the early 1670s when he was most immersed in Hobbes's writings. Yet, despite their differences, he found much to admire in Hobbes – not least his approach to logic and truth, his concept of conatus, and the way he distinguished between the perceptions of inanimate bodies, animals, and humans.

NOTES

[1] For example, *Confessio naturae contra atheistas* (A VI i, 489–90).

[2] For example, he uses the expression in a letter to Peter Moller/Müller of 2 January 1699 (BH 189). It so happens that, in this particular passage, the "philosophers" he is referring to are alchemists; but it is a frequent theme in Leibniz's writings that he is seeking to harmonise different philosophical schools.

[3] See Wilson, C. 1997. See also Bernstein 1980.

[4] See Riley 1996: esp. 91–8.

[5]   I say "apparently", because Hobbes's political writings, especially *Leviathan* and its Latin appendices, are permeated by far more fundamentalist Christianity than anything written by Leibniz.

[6]   For example, in his *Specimen quaestionum philosophicarum* of 1664 (A VI i, 84), he says that "the otherwise very acute man, Thomas Hobbes ... almost abandoned religion" in holding that "our soul is corporeal and by its nature mortal."

[7]   Ursula Goldenbaum, "Hobbes and Spinoza as the Heroes of the Young Leibniz. Leibniz as Belonging to the Modern", paper delivered at a conference on *The Young Leibniz*, at Rice University, Texas, Easter 2003.

[8]   *Elementa iuris naturalis*, A VI i, 457.

[9]   According to Philip Beeley, in a verbal communication, the letter was not forwarded to Hobbes, because of his dispute with the Royal Society.

[10]   *Thomae Hobbes Malmesburiensis opera philosophica, quae Latine scripsit, omnia* (Amsterdam, Ioannes Blaeu, 1668). This includes the Latin version of the *Leviathan*, the appendices to which are the main sources for Hobbes's materialist theology.

[11]   A VI ii, *Schriftenverzeichnis zu* VI i *und* VI i, 684.

[12]   Couturat 1901, Appendix 2, "Leibniz et Hobbes, leur logique, leur nominalisme", 457–72.

[13]   *Dissertatio de arte combinatoria*, GP IV, 64.

[14]   Cf. the Epistle Dedicatory to the *Elements of Law*, and (less succinctly) the Epistle Dedicatory to *De corpore*.

[15]   For example, in a letter to Arnauld of June/July 1686, GP II, 52: "semper enim notio praedicati inest subjecto in propositione vera." On other occasions he omits any reference to notions or concepts – for example, the *Specimen inventorum de admirandis naturae Generalis arcanis*, GP VII, 309, begins: "In omni veritate universali affirmativa praedicatum inest subjecto [...]."

[16]   Cf. Brown, S. 1984: 74, 82.

[17]   See in particular the *Preface to Nizolio*, GP IV, 127–62.

[18]   For example, Gr II, 512–45.

[19]   Hobbes's contemporary translator glosses "id est, *per punctum*" as "that is, motion made through the length of a point, and in an instant or point in time." J. W. N. Watkins treats the translation as if it were Hobbes's own words. (Watkins 1973: 87–8).

[20]   Hobbes does not himself call conatus a force. Instead, he uses the word *vis* or "force" in the idiosyncratic sense of "*impetus multiplied either by itself, or by the magnitude of the moving body, by virtue of which a moving body exerts more or less action on a body resisting it.*" (*De corpore* 15.2).

[21]   I know that the plural of *conatus* in Latin is *conatus*; but if it is used as an English word, the plural needs to be the inelegant "conatuses" in order to avoid ambiguity. I wish we could agree to use the word "conation" instead, since it does have a plural.

[22]   *De corpore* 15.7.

[23]   *Theoria motus abstracti*, GP IV, 221–40, esp. 228–30. I have merely sketched the points of similarity. Much more detailed comparisons of Hobbes and Leibniz on *conatus* are to be found in Watkins 1973 and Bernstein 1980.

[24]   I say "uncompromising" in accordance with the popular view of Descartes; but there are places where he seems to proposes a trialistic ontology, with the union of mind and body as a third kind of substance. See *The Principles of Philosophy* I.48 (AT VIII-1, 23), and the letters to Princess Elizabeth of 21st May and 28th June 1643 (AT III, 664ff. and 680ff.). However, postulating the human being as a distinct substance *sui generis* does nothing to make mind/body interaction more intelligible.

[25]   *Leviathan* 34: "And according to this acceptation of the word, *Substance* and *Body*, signifie the same thing; and therefore *Substance incorporeall* are words, which when they are joined together, destroy one another, as if a man should say, an *Incorporeall Body*."

[26]   Exceptions are Čapek 1973 and Wilson, C. 1997: esp. 343.

[27]   Hobbes's main account of perception is in *De corpore* 25.2.

[28]   Chapter 25 is entitled "Animal sensation and motion", and he refers to "sentient beings" in general, not just to humans.

[29] Catherine Wilson suggests that Leibniz may have derived the concept of a *petite perception* from Hobbes. (Wilson, C. 1997: 346) Although Hobbes doesn't use the term, in *De corpore* 29.2 he gives the example of our being able to hear the roar of the sea without consciously hearing individual waves – precisely the same example as Leibniz later gives in the *Nouveaux Essais* (A VI vi, 54).

[30] In the Appendix to the Latin version of *Leviathan*, Chapter 3 (WML III, 561), Hobbes states boldly that *Deus est corpus*; but it is ambiguous whether this should be read as "God is body" (in general), or "God is *a* body". I prefer the former reading.

[31] GP IV, 230. Cf. the letter to Arnauld, GP I, 73.

3. TWO OPPONENTS OF MATERIAL ATOMISM

Cavendish and Leibniz

Margaret Cavendish (1623–1673) and G.W. Leibniz (1642–1716) are natural subjects for comparison. Both philosophers embraced Epicurean atomism in their youths and later rejected it. They both became pananimists who took perception as a primitive term in their systems. Both wrote philosophical works that their critics considered fanciful, though this criticism applied rather widely at the end of the seventeenth century. Cavendish lived for a time in Paris, where she met a number of natural philosophers; Leibniz visited England and followed English natural and experimental philosophy with interest. Cavendish was specially interested in Descartes; Leibniz refers to the texts of Henry More, Anne Conway, Ralph Cudworth, Robert Boyle, and Robert Hooke, as well as Hobbes, Locke, and Newton. Though there is no evidence that Leibniz read Cavendish, comparison of their texts reveals the very close relations between English and Continental philosophy existing at the time and their engagement with a common set of issues.[1] The confluence of their objections to Epicurean atomism demonstrates the improbability – as if more demonstrations were needed – that Leibniz's theory of monads and pre-established harmony was an unanticipated extension of a theory of concepts, rather than a considered alternative to a powerful but at the same time morally and theologically troubling system of natural philosophy.

A further reason for comparing the two is that their often parallel assertions reflect markedly different underlying philosophical views and generated dissimilar fates. Although their diagnosis of the weaknesses of neo-Epicureanism coincides, Leibniz is deemed a critic and developer of the Cartesian tradition, while Cavendish has no such place in the historiography of philosophy. This difference cannot be explained by the quantity published by either philosopher, for Leibniz, though prolific, published relatively little philosophy before the *Theodicy* and was known to readers chiefly though his articles and critiques in the *Acta Eruditorum*. Cavendish's *Poems and Fancies* by contrast caused a sensation on its publication in 1653. Yet her 23 volumes of poems, orations, letters, plays, observations, biography and treatises on natural philosophy were little credited until recently. Henry More told Anne Conway that Cavendish was safe from "anyone giving her the trouble of a reply," and although More did in fact engage with her without citing her, he spoke for most of his contemporaries, except Joseph Glanvill, who wrote to her, Walter Charleton, who showed considerable moral courage in praising and defending her to the Royal Society, and (in a small way) Christiaan Huygens.[2]

Cavendish's lack of reputation is in some respects easy to explain. The education of women was acknowledged to be worse in the seventeenth century than it had

P. Phemister and S. Brown (eds.), Leibniz and the English-Speaking World, 35–50.
© 2007 *Springer.*

been in the sixteenth, and most aristocratic women could barely write or spell. Cavendish was no exception, and her trains of thought are often hard to follow. Yet Henry More's cabbalistic rantings and his extended accounts of aerial demons did not displace him from the history of philosophy, as far lesser offenses against literary economy and mental discipline did "mad Madge."[3] Pure antifeminism is an especially tempting explanation for Leibniz's and Cavendish's different standing in the historical record. But to leave the question there is lazy, as Leibniz would say. Beyond the obvious, what precisely in the situation and character of both philosophers accounts for their different reputations as critics of the mechanical philosophy?

Answering this question can help to shed light on the formation of the scientific and philosophical *persona* in the seventeenth century. Leibniz's stature as a metaphysician was recognized only posthumously. Yet it was not unrelated to his mathematical and physical accomplishments in his lifetime, his express commitment to truth and demonstration, and his theologico-political ideals and ambitions. Leibniz passionately desired to be the author of a transcendental system, capable of resolving all sectarian disputes. He viewed himself as a successor to Democritus, Plato, Aristotle and Descartes, building up his case with a sure, if unconscious touch. Cavendish's ambition to be a famous philosopher was no less exalted, but what she did not say and do was more decisive in determining her later reputation than what she did say and do.

1. ANTI-ATOMIC DOCTRINES IN CAVENDISH AND LEIBNIZ

The Cavendish salon in Paris in the mid 1640s, overseen by the genial William Cavendish, Margaret's husband, and his brother, the mathematician Charles Cavendish, was the centre of a revival of Epicureanism led by Hobbes and Gassendi. In occasional attendance were Descartes, Mersenne, Mydorge and Roberval.[4]

The "new philosophy" was a revival of pagan atomism, long excoriated by Christian writers who found Aristotle and Plato far easier to assimilate than Democritus and Epicurus. Both Hobbes's *Elements of Philosophy* and Descartes's *Principles of Philosophy* can be considered neo-Epicurean. While Descartes dissociated himself from materialism and denied the existence of atoms – indivisible least corpuscles – he and Hobbes were agreed that explanations involving the purposeless motion of subvisible particles were intelligible, unlike explanations according to which an active element possessed of an analogue of intelligence, intention, or foresight, worked on a passive element. All generation and corruption of substances and alteration of their qualities was nothing more in their view than the movement and recombination of elementary material particles. These doctrines, along with that of the plurality of worlds, atheism, and the mortality of the soul, were well known, thanks especially to the many editions of Lucretius *De rerum natura* published in the sixteenth and seventeenth centuries. The Objectors to Descartes's *Meditations* (among them Hobbes and Gassendi) were preoccupied with two Epicurean themes: that the soul is material and therefore mortal, and that "God" is merely one of its ideas.

Though Descartes and Hobbes looked back to Lucretius and presumably to what was known through Diogenes Laertius of Democritus and Epicurus, Gassendi's publication of his *De vita et moribus Epicuri, libri octo* in 1647, brought Epicureanism forward. It began to advance in England, with a cautious reference to the "pure and rich Metall" hidden amongst detestable doctrines in Walter Charleton's *Darkness of Atheism* of 1652. Lucy Hutchinson had already begun to translate Lucretius into English in the 1640s, but she did not publish her version. Sincerely or not, she later represented her motive for the translation as her horror that "men should be found so presumptuously wicked to studie and adhere to his and his masters ridiculous, impious, execrable doctrines, reviving the foppish, causall dance of the atoms, and deniing the Soveraigne Wisedom of God in the greate Designe of the whole Universe."[5] Margaret Cavendish had no such scruples and was in on the ground floor with respect to the Epicurean revival. Her *Poems and Fancies* and her *Philosophicall Fancies*, published directly after Charleton's book in 1653, were the first English presentation of the reviving doctrine. Charleton's publication of his *Physiologia Epicuro-Gassendi* of 1654 and *Epicurus's Morals* of 1656, followed, along with John Evelyn's translation of the first book of Lucretius, prefaced by a partisan introduction (Evelyn 1656). The third volume of Thomas Stanley's *History of Philosophy*, dealing with Epicurus appeared in 1660, and Robert Boyle began to publish corpuscularian treatises beginning in 1663.

Echoing Lucretius's unforgettable opening passage on the murder of Iphigenia by Agamemnon, Cavendish went on to say in *The World's Olio* of 1655 that it was better to be an atheist than superstitious; atheism fostered humanity and civility, whereas superstition only bred cruelty. The *Poems and Fancies* are unapologetically Copernican. There are many worlds and the stars may be suns of other planetary systems. Worlds are inside worlds:

Just like unto a *Nest* of *Boxes* round,/ *Degrees* of *Sizes* in each *Box* are found;/ *So* in this *World* may others be,/ Thinner and less, and less still by degree;/ Although they are not subject to our *Sense*,/A *World* may be no bigger than *Two-pence*. (PF 44)

The tiny worlds in a lady's earring may have their own houses, cattle, sun, moon and stars, and wars. The sounds of rushing air and water are the summation of a multitude of small atomic noises, like the rumble made by a crowd of "People rude". Moreover,

Small *Atomes* of themselves a *World* may make,/For being subtile, every shape they take;/ And as they dance about, they places find,/ Of *Forms*, that best agree, make every Kind. (PF 5)

Cavendish's early system was eclectic, positing differently figured fire, air, water, and earth atoms; and not only "matter," but "Motion", "Figure" and "Life", directed by Nature, are said to co-operate to make the world. Consumption, colic, dropsy, palsy, and apoplexy are all atomic diseases. Unlike More and Descartes, Cavendish recognized no spirits or incorporeal substances. There is "attraction," however, of their own particles, to the sun and the earth respectively. Consciousness depended in her view on a material substrate: Nature makes a brain out of matter so that there can be perception and appreciation of the material world.

Where Cavendish derived her knowledge of atomism and how she acquired the ideas for her poem has not been fully explained, especially as she could not read Latin. Sarah Hutton presents good evidence (Hutton 1997) that Cavendish's source was Hobbes, but Hobbes's version was perhaps less likely to inflame the imagination than a peek into his own sources. Another, more compelling possibility is that Lucy Hutchinson showed Cavendish some passages from her secret Lucretius translation, for the two women knew each other.[6] In any case, by later in 1655, Cavendish had abandoned atomism, again under the influence of texts or persons whose identity is unknown. The foppish, casual dance of atoms, she maintained, seemed to describe the political world in its worst moments, but not the natural world. Politics was chaotic, whereas nature was orderly. Not a democrat, she inferred that civil societies and nature both ought to be ruled in a hierarchical manner and that nature evidently was.[7] "If Every and Each Atome were of a Living Substance, and had Equal Power, Life and Knowledge ... they would hardly Agree in one Government"; and even their "Consent and Agreement" would not prevent "Alterations and Confusions" (PPO c2r–c2v). Her opposition to atomism strengthened with time. In her *Observations on Experimental Philosophy* of 1666 (OEP), she alleged that atomism shows a want of depth in the theorist.[8]

There can be no commerce or intercourse, nor no variety of figures and actions; no productions, dissolutions, changes, and the like, without perception; for how shall parts work and act, without having some knowledge or perception of each other? (OEP 15)

Cavendish nevertheless retained her materialism, denying incorporeal substances, and, fearless of the theological implications, insisted that nature had an intrinsic power of movement.[9] In her later systems, she ascribed perception and vitality to all natural entities, denied that perception can be a mechanical or corpuscular process involving pressure and reaction, and posited an innate capacity to "pattern out"[10] in animate substance. Everything is alive and aware.[11]

Turning to Leibniz, we know that he too was excited by atomism, which he encountered in Hobbes and Gassendi in his youth, but then turned away from it in favour of what he considered to be an improved version of the theory of substantial forms. He told Nicholas Remond:

Since the atomic theory satisfies the perceptual imagination I gave myself to it and it seemed to me that the void of Democritus or Epicurus, together with their incorruptible atoms, would remove all the difficulties. It is true that this hypothesis can satisfy mere physical scientists, and assuming that there are such atoms, and giving them suitable motions and figures, there are few material qualities which they could not explain if we knew enough of the details of things [...][12]

Leibniz too came to the conclusion that material atoms are but "the incomplete thoughts of philosophers who have not inquired sufficiently well into the natures of things,"[13] and that the phenomena imply universal perceptive faculties. "Since the universe is regulated in a perfect order, there must also be an order in the representing being, that is, in the perceptions of the soul."[14] Leibniz denied that any part of nature was inert and lifeless.[15] Everything is animated, and

the multitude of souls should not trouble us, any more than does the multitude of Gassendi's atoms, which are as indestructible as these souls. On the contrary, it is a perfection of nature to have many of them.[16]

Perception, he thought, must be a primitive capability of these animated substances, not a mechanical effect.[17] Both writers subscribed to the doctrine of qualitative plenitude, insisting that identical corpuscles are impossible if variety extends to the smallest parts.[18]

   Cavendish and Leibniz both targeted a position that, technically, none of their predecessors held, an ontology of passive, inert material *least* elements and separable Cartesian immaterial souls. But they agreed in what they asserted; that the power of perception is distributed throughout the plant, animal, and mineral worlds, that perception cannot be explained mechanically, that matter cannot be passive or "moveless." Their common objections to Cartesianism go well beyond the issues raised by the Objectors to the *Meditations*. They point to a common source, most likely in Renaissance Neoplatonism or Stoicism, of the doctrine of universal perception and animation. This position, in other words, was not one that only a genius of exceptional logical powers and deep classical erudition could arrive at. A shy woman, without knowledge of any foreign language, who probably derived most of her knowledge of philosophy from Stanley's *History*, came to it a number of years before the well-travelled polymath and voracious reader, gifted in mathematical analysis and accustomed to conversing with the best minds of his generation, did.

   In another sense, their common opposition to material atomism (with adjoined Cartesian minds) was superficial, for the underlying systems of the two critics are in fact very different: Leibniz treated "individual substances" or monads as playing the same role in some respects as material atoms. They are indivisible entities that persist through all phases of the universe and that are the ground of all appearances. At the same time, Leibniz acknowledged the usefulness of material corpuscles in natural philosophy and supposed that they behaved in law-governed ways. It is for Leibniz as if we are minds in machines and everything in nature happens mechanically according to simple and universal laws. He even appeared to agree with Descartes and Locke that perception occurs through corpuscular action and reaction, at least from the perspective of physical science (A VI vi, 121/ RB 121ff.). Descartes, in Leibniz's view, got mechanism and mind-body parallelism more or less right, but he failed to understand the true basis of immortality; the indivisible, indestructible, and imperishable nature of *all* substances and the perceptual capacity of the smallest living creatures. Descartes failed to grasp that inanimate matter is so only in appearance. Cavendish, by contrast, rejected immaterial substances, denied that nature was regulated by laws, and accorded the mechanical philosophy no respect, even for the purposes of mere physical science.

2. CAVENDISH'S ONTOLOGY COMPARED WITH LEIBNIZ'S

When Cavendish gave up atomism, she did not revert to matter and form as components of substances, but proposed that there were three grades of matter that were always found together. One type was inanimate and served as a "ground or grosser substance to work on"; the second type was animate and sensitive and worked on inanimate matter like a "labourer or workman," forming it into various figures. A third type of matter had a "designer" and "surveyor" function and was "animate rational matter" (OEP 157–8). Within the smallest pebble or dust mote was located an entire employment hierarchy.

The creative and transformative powers of nature were salient for Cavendish. "Human sense and reason perceives, that the parts of the earth do undergo continual alterations; generations, dissolutions: some do change into minerals, some into vegetables, some into animals, etc. and these change again into several other figures, and also some into earth again, and the elements are changed into one another [...]" (OEP 132). She denied that all creatures come "by way of seeds or eggs" (OEP 67–8), patching in from William Harvey a reference to "the growth of moss, and the like vegetables that grow on stones, walls, dead animals' skulls, tops of houses, etc." (OEP 68). She found Harvey's *omnis ex ovo* doctrine unacceptably constraining of nature who "hath many more ways of productions than by seeds or seminal principles, even in vegetables" (OEP 68). Cavendish ignored the Galilean-Cartesian demand to conceive of bodies as constrained to move in mathematically describable pathways. "Particular parts are not bound to work or move to a certain particular action, but they work according to the wisdom and liberty of nature, which is only bound by the omnipotent God's decree, not to work beyond herself, that is, beyond matter" (OEP 139).

By contrast, Leibniz emphasized that, while effects and phenomena are varied, their underlying principles are simple, mechanical, and few in number, and that "everything is in conformity with the universal order."[19] Both writers rejected Epicurean mortalism, but Cavendish's objection was doctrinaire. "I have said before that nothing is perishable or subject to annihilation in nature, and so no death."[20] Her claim that nothing in nature perishes was not however, intended, as the verbally similar doctrine of Leibniz was, to support the thesis of personal immortality. Leibniz's notion of natural immortality was altogether different. "There is no dissolution to fear," he says, "and there is no conceivable way in which a simple substance can perish naturally." "For the same reason," he adds, "there is no conceivable way a simple substance can begin naturally, since it cannot be formed by composition."[21]

A third difference between these two critics of neo-Epicureanism, in addition to their incompatible ontologies and views of the laws of nature, consisted in their respective attitudes towards experimental science. Cavendish abandoned her interest in the tiny, nested worlds of the *Poems and Fancies*, though not in multiple worlds and imaginary worlds, when she abandoned atomism. Her *Observations on Experimental Philosophy* were critical of microscopy, which she regarded as both deceptive and useless:

The art of augury was far more beneficial than the latterly invented art of micrography [...] The eclipse of the sun and moon was not found out by telescopes; nor the motions of the loadstone, or the art of navigation, or the art of guns and gunpowder, or the art of printing, and the like, by microscopes [...] [I]f microscopes do truly represent the exterior parts and superficies of some minute creatures, what advantageth it our knowledge? For unless they could discover their interior, corporeal, figurative motions, and the obscure actions of nature, or the causes which make such and such creatures, I see no great benefit or advantage they yield to man (OEP 8–9).

She complained of "poring and Peeping through Telescopes, Microscopes and the like boyish Arts, which neither get Profit, nor improve their Understanding."[22] Cavendish was not the first English critic of the microscope, for, as Hutton notes, Hobbes expressed similar doubts (WME I, 446). Yet she can be considered a vociferous representative of the tradition of British Naked Eye Empiricism, to which Locke and Newton both gave some, and Berkeley considerable allegiance, and in much the same terms. Though she recognized that "The truth is, that all or most artificial experiments, are the best argument to evince, there is perception in all corporeal parts of nature ..." (OEP 113), she did not develop this point as Leibniz, famously enthusiastic about optical instruments and their ability to confirm his pananimist doctrines, did.

How might we compare the philosophical merits of the two? Can we discern *qualitative* differences in the cogency of the two philosophers' anti-Cartesian arguments and the grounding for their rival ontologies, in virtue of which Leibniz was clearly the superior metaphysician? If so, what made one syncretistic, anti-Epicurean, animal-friendly system so much more significant than the other? Cavendish's references to three grades of matter might seem obscure and arbitrary. If all matter is active and percipient, why is there an intermediate grade of matter that is especially like a workman or labourer and how can it perform its function without the foresight of the designing part of matter on another kind of matter? These questions are not answered. Cavendish's mode of argument consists of citing salient phenomena, such as the ubiquity of generation. She insists that three grades of matter, self-knowing and perceptive, are required to explain them and order generally. Relevant alternatives are not explored in detail. Yet are Leibniz's "simple substances" less obscure and arbitrary? Is his idea that individual substances "ground" phenomena but do not causally interact with one another so much more cogent and philosophically satisfactory?

Taken sentence-by-sentence, Leibniz's objections to neo-Epicureanism cannot be considered more original, or his rival ontology more credible in what it asserts, than Cavendish's. The reception of a philosopher's writings is nevertheless determined by more than his sentences; and the reception of sentence X may depend on the sentences Y and Z. Indeed, for meaning-holists, the precise meaning of every sentence – the particular thought expressed – might be held to depend on the meaning of all other sentences asserted by writer or speaker, along with other features of his or her context. This might seem to imply the paradox that no two persons (perhaps not even one person over a temporal interval) could ever mean the same thing by the same words; then no utterance would be exactly understood, perhaps even by the utterer himself. But it follows only that sentences do not

have precise meanings, that tolerances are large; and this helps to explain why
the reception of very similar sentences can be so different.[23] If certain passages
from Cavendish's *Observations on Experimental Philosophy* had been inserted into
the *Essay* of John Locke; others into Newton's *Optics*, and still other passages
from Cavendish's *Philosophical Letters* into the writings of Leibniz, scholars today
would quote mad Madge's trenchant formulations as pointed criticisms expressing,
with beautiful economy, the deficiencies of corpuscularianism, mechanism, and
Cartesianism. In the context of Margaret Cavendish's *oeuvre*, these very sentences
seem to have a different meaning, or little meaning at all. This pathetic situation
deserves further explanation.

3. EXTRA-DOCTRINAL CUES

For a variety of reasons, Cavendish did not provide her readers with the same cues
as to her competence, veracity, and good motives that Leibniz provided in such
abundance.

First, there was a *theological* cue. Leibniz related the significance of his work
to the significance of God, whose power, wisdom, and benevolence he considered
to be knowable. His later view that natural religion "itself seems to decay very
much [in England]"[24] was based not only on his disapproval of Newton's posit
of a God who needs to adjust his astronomical clockwork from time to time, but
on his disapproval of English materialism and the broader pattern of disregard for
theological certainty and divine regulation exemplified by Cavendish and later by
Locke.

The opening of Leibniz's *Discourse on Metaphysics* stated: "The most widely
accepted and meaningful notion we have of God is expressed well enough in these
words that God is an absolutely perfect being [...]".[25] This set the tone and topic
for what followed. Cavendish, by contrast, informed her readers that we could not
know much about God (OEP 47), and that natural philosophy was independent
of theology. In fact, God is rarely mentioned and plays little role in her system.
Cavendish's more Hobbesian stance differentiates her sharply from the pious class
of English vitalists represented by More and Conway. Her neglect of divinity and
her antinomian sentiments contrast with Leibniz's frequent references to God as
"regulating the whole."[26] Indeed, one of her objections to Cartesianism was that it
assigned an authoritarian role to God, who was supposed to lay down invariable
laws of nature. Nature, in her view, is not subject to God, for, "if she were bound to
certain actions, and had not liberty to move as she pleases" she could not bring about
her effects. God's role is restricted to ordaining Nature to "work to the continuation
of creatures" (OEP 138–9).

A second cue is competency in *formal reasoning*, establishing credibility with
respect to the assertion of speculative propositions lying outside human experience.
Leibniz's insistence that all given quantities are divisible was not itself a highly
original or technical objection to material atomism. The argument that the infinite

or indefinite divisibility of matter – its insubstantiality – precludes it from a foundational role is Platonic and was repeated in neo-Platonic texts.[27] Yet Leibniz was the author of an original and highly technical mathematical device, the calculus, and he made important conceptual innovations in mathematical physics and, as was discovered only later, in logic. Like Descartes, who published his *Geometry* and his *Optics* to prove his competence before publishing a metaphysics, Leibniz came to the learned world's attention with his *Hypothesis Physica Nova*, and his objections, addressed to the Royal Society, to the Wren-Wallis collision rules, followed by his "Brief Demonstration" of Descartes's mistaken view of the conservation of motion.

A third, related cue is *truth-commitment* and commitment to *demonstration*. Leibniz articulated both. He says of the despised Scholastic philosophers that "if some exact and thoughtful mind took the trouble to clarify and summarize their thoughts after the manner of analytical geometers, he would find there a great treasure of extremely important and wholly demonstrative truths."[28] In the Preface to the *New Essays*, he claimed that "Logic, together with metaphysics and morals, of which the one shapes natural theology and the other natural jurisprudence, are full of [necessary] truths," like those found in Euclid, whose proof "does not depend on instances, nor, consequently, on the testimony of the senses." (A VI vi, 292–3/ RB 292–3; ibid., 50) Leibniz conveyed the seriousness of what he wished to present by referring frequently to "realités," including truths about supersensible objects and about goodness, justice, and perfection. He elevated Hooke's causal observation, *a propos* of the seeds of the corn violet, that it does not *seem* that there are any two things exactly alike in nature to a principle that can be known a priori through reflection on the nature of the divine power. (A VI vi, 333) Cavendish asserted a commitment to impartial reason. Yet she did not offer to demonstrate, prove or establish truths and principles. Her prefaces detailed frankly, and at great length, her changes of mind and indecision.

A fourth cue is *self-assessment*. Cavendish's *Philosophical and Physical Opinions* of 1655 were prefaced by a cringing "Epistle to the Condemning Reader." Eight years later, she was still on the defensive, expecting the worst. Rather than attempting to gain the reader's confidence in the Preface to her *Observations* eight years later, she remarks,

I confess, there are many useless and superfluous books, and perchance mine will add to the number of them; especially as it is to be observed, that there have been in this latter age, as many writers of natural philosophy as in former ages there have been of moral philosophers; which multitude, I fear, will produce such a confusion of truth and falsehood as the number of moral writers formerly did, with their over-nice divisions of virtues and vices, whereby they did puzzle their readers so, that they knew now how to distinguish between them (OEP 8).

Leibniz did not offer apologies for the state of philosophy, or the frailty of his own intellectual powers, or suggest that human beings ought not to overestimate their importance in the cosmos or the importance of their future fates. He gave to understand that the issues he dealt with were of the greatest significance.[29] Cavendish did not trouble to exalt her species. "Wherefore I, for my part, will rather believe as sense and reason guides me," she declared, "and not according to interest, so as to extol my own kind above all the rest, or above nature herself" (OEP 112).

As her biographer Douglas Grant notes, Cavendish "could have made up for her deficiencies in language and letters by paying attention to what she read, but she read for the spirit only and neglected the form." She could have asked, or paid someone to edit her essays. Instead, she flaunted her literary deficiencies as an accusation against the society that refused her the advantages of learning, and, at the same time, she confabulated plausible-seeming reasons to explain why they were not regrettable. She insisted that her lack of a methodical education was conducive to the formation of her own opinions and that conversation with her brothers, her brother-in-law, and her husband were more than sufficient to instruct her. Torn between two hypotheses that seemed equiprobable to her, that she was the victim of a learned culture that ignored, denied, and repressed her aspirations to be a famous intellectual and that women were intellectually inferior to men and had no real place in that culture, she vacillated. She voiced the opinion that it was against nature for a woman to spell correctly (Grant 1957: 112). She complained that the conventions of grammar were "stricter than need be," defended her right to use a "natural grammar," and insisted that "language should be like garments" whose "trimmings may be different and yet not go out of the fashion" (Grant 1957: 112). She explained her want of proofreading by saying that she feared "lest [it] should disturb my following Conceptions." In short, Margaret Cavendish was lazy, but aware of her own faults and the impediments they constituted. She knew that she could do better, but her sense of futility, her resentment – since no one was helping her, or supplying her with the materials she needed – and finally her aristocratic insouciance prevented her from taking more trouble than she did.

The four cues just mentioned – theological commitment, competence in formal reasoning, truth-commitment, and positive self-assessment – appear, more decisively than the quality and quantity of the arguments themselves, to separate Leibniz's celebrated critique of material atomism and his presentation of a rival system, from the less well-known critiques of Cudworth, More, Conway, and Cavendish. Their absence puts in perspective Pierre Duhem's unforgettable contrast between the orderly French mentality and disorganized English empiricism in his *Aim and Structure of a Physical Theory*. One mode of presentation was just as calculated, however, as the other. The experimental philosophy, according to Stephen Clucas, called for modes of writing that reflected the way in which the inquirer was led by nature, was not in thrall to past authorities, did not distort the presentation of nature by imposing prejudices, and aimed only at establishing the probability and not the certainty of his conclusions (Clucas 2003: 205).[30] Thus Boyle, in the Preface to his *Free Inquiry* (note title!) of 1685, claims that his treatise is "but an *Apparatus* or Collection of Materials." He apologizes for losing his notes and mixing up his papers and his hasty reconstruction. "I hope it will be thought but a venial Fault," he says, "if the Contexture of the whole Discourse do not appear so Uniform, nor all the Connections of its Parts so apt and close, as if no Papers had been lost."[31]

The apologetic stance, in other words, is a deeply-rooted English characteristic, a component of good manners, and both Boyle and Cavendish assumed at the same time a kind of aristocratic indifference to appearances that was perhaps not available to the self-made man, Leibniz. Though Cavendish considered herself a critic of experimental philosophy, she, like Boyle, wanted to make clear that she was led by nature and not in thrall to great authors of the past.

4. ATTITUDES TO THE TRADITION

Cavendish's appeals to nature and nature's authority were remarkably ineffective in establishing her authoritative role as a natural philosopher. Though she and her husband were early users of microscopes, William having a particular fondness for "optic glasses,"[32] she could not align herself with the experimental philosophy that depended upon controlled observation and manipulation of nature with artificial instruments. Excluded, like her presumed mentor, Hobbes, from the Royal Society, except as a one-time observer, she turned her anger against it. *The Blazing World*, a fantasy appended to the *Observations on Natural Philosophy*, incorporated a revenge fantasy reminiscent of Brecht's Pirate Jenny story, in which an Empress, stranded in another world after a shipwreck at the North Pole, gains control of the globe with fire-bombs, forcing "all the rest of the world to submit," and scientific societies are abolished as punishment for their "perpetual disputes and quarrels."

An appeal to solitary inspiration was effective for Descartes, who presented all the cues of importance – theological, mathematical, demonstrative, truth-seeking, and personal – and who was able to announce that he was turning his back on pointless disputations and quarrels, but Cavendish had not "earned" this right. The frontispiece to her *Philosophical Opinions* carried the following motto:

Studious she is and all Alone
Most visitants, when She has none.
Her Library on which She looks
It is her Head, her Thoughts, her Books
Scorninge dead Ashes without fire
For her owne Flames doe her Inspire

Cavendish illustrates Hegel's dictum that women acquire knowledge by a form of osmosis, though why Hegel found this surprising and worth remarking on is unclear. As creatures deprived of effective use of a limb or a sensory organ will compensate by strengthening another capability, Cavendish's vivid pictorial imagination enabled her to transform bits of text and scraps of conversation into philosophical tomes, but the learned world demanded more. Though conversation can deepen understanding when texts are few, Cavendish was limited in this respect, perhaps not so much from her self-professed bashfulness as from her difficulty engaging educated men outside the family circle. Hobbes positively avoided her, and, since she did not understand French (and Descartes did not understand English), it is unlikely that her salon participation brought much illumination. Even to deal with Descartes, she had to have "some few places translated to me out of his works" according to the preface to her *Philosophical Letters.*

Leibniz, by contrast, was naturally social and fitted by his quick grasp of languages for cosmopolitan interaction. He genuinely tried to learn from his inter-locutors. He was allied, until the calculus debacle, with the Royal Society, and with the Parisian Académie des Sciences, and he even founded the Berlin Academy. He was unfazed by the disputes and quarrels of academicians, was able to thrive on controversy, and to accommodate and to tie in with theology not only the new academy science of microscopy, but chemistry, paleontology, and natural history.

Cavendish's hostility to experiment, her unfamiliarity with mathematical modes of argumentation, and her atheistic impulses were fatal to her philosophical ambitions. She could prop herself neither on her record in the exact sciences, nor on a commitment to truth and demonstrability, nor on evocations of God and morals, nor on the recovery of the wisdom of the past. Every cue that could be supplied to the reader to convince him of the significance of her view of nature was missed, and the contrast with Leibniz's deployment of each of these cues is striking. Cavendish's all too evident scornfulness and vanity contrast markedly with Leibniz's posture of commitment. They reflect her exclusion and her self-imposed exile – it is both – from the world of letters, the sense of alienation that led her to trivialize the enterprise at which she so much wanted to succeed. Cavendish's ambitions were at least equal to Leibniz's. She claimed that she wanted to be taken as a natural philosopher on the level of those she wrote about: Descartes, Hooke, Charleton, Harvey and Boyle. She enunciated a "transcending desire to live in the world's memory" – an aspiration she described as common to all men. Yet she knew she was not a great figure to her contemporaries and that she could never fulfill this aspiration. She wanted to replace Aristotle in the University curriculum – but not to have to proofread.

Another consequential difference between Cavendish and Leibniz consisted in their attitudes towards the philosophical enterprise. What were the motivations of these two natural scribblers for putting forward original "systems?" Both were aware that philosophy is a historical and reactive activity, but Cavendish's perspective was aloof and skeptical. The moderns, she said dismissively, put ancient opinions into a new dress or patch them up with some of their own, and "so make a gallimaufry in natural philosophy."[33] With what is either shocking cynicism, or perhaps the most disarming perspicuity, she represented philosophy as a fashionable game played by poseurs:

Since it is now A-la-mode to Write of Natural Philosophy, and I know nobody Knows what is the Cause of anything, and since they are all but Guessers, not knowing, it gives every Man room to Think what he lists, and so do I mean to set up for myself; and play at their Philosophical Game as follows, without Patching or Stealing from any Body.[34]

We have to admit that this is what we do in philosophy, including the patching and the stealing, and that the great metaphysicians of the past were, and most of our own now are "Guessers" of a sort. Yet Leibniz was able to throw a more flattering light on the sense in which philosophical innovation involves building on the past and its authoritative texts, and to recast guessing as strict deduction, or as the decoding of the many informational hints and signs planted by God in the creation. Following a recitation to Foucher of all the philosophers he has been reading, including Bacon, Gassendi, Galileo, Descartes, Plato, Aristotle and the Academicians, Leibniz observes that complete originality is impossible, for "we must necessarily enter through the entryways that nature has made. Moreover, one person alone cannot do everything at once" (GP I, 370–1). Leibniz took time to situate his ontology against the history of philosophy by showing how his own system incorporated some elements of famous past systems and dispensed with others. Modestly, he claimed that he never wished to be the founder of a sect. Immodestly, though not untruthfully, he represented his metaphysical system as equal in profundity to the systems of Democritus, Aristotle, and Descartes.

[W]ith Aristotle and Descartes, and *against* Democritus and Gassendi, I admit no vacuum, and even though, *against* Aristotle, and with Democritus and Descartes, I consider all rarefaction or condensation to be only apparent, nevertheless, *with* Democritus and Aristotle, and *against* Descartes, I think that there is something passive in body over and above extension [...] Furthermore, *with* Plato and Aristotle, and *against* Democritus and Descartes, I acknowledge a certain active force or entelechy in body [...] However, I agree *with* Democritus and Descartes, *against* the multitude of Scholastics, that the exercise of motive power and the phenomena of bodies can always be explained mechanically, except for the very causes of the laws of motion [...].[35]

The tyro might well come away from Leibniz's statement with the following impression: To become an original philosopher, one should assemble a table of systems, decompose them into their doctrinal elements, and reassemble a composite doctrine that will be unprecedented. Provided a number of eligible combinations are not yet attached to great names, one might even have some choice as to which system to invent. Yet this is not exactly how Leibniz proceeded. Though he perhaps entertained occasional doubts about whether defending his system was more than a kind of game, his truth-commitment precluded combinatorial system-assembly. Leibniz's more wholesome perspective reflected his sense that he was a participant in an ongoing enterprise of truth-disclosure. His access to his father's library and the great library at Wolfenbüttel enabled him to seat himself literally amongst the old great thinkers, which Cavendish could not do. He saw himself as a participant in a conversation of minds-across-centuries.

5. CONCLUSIONS

By comparing Cavendish and Leibniz as critics of the Epicurean revival of the mid-seventeenth century, I hope to have brought out some features of English natural philosophy and its relation to the experimental science of the time that are comparable to but that also contrast with Leibniz's own intentions and purposes. I have tried to show how important certain penumbral features of Leibniz's critique of materialism and atomism, some philosophical, others rhetorical or situational, were in determining the later reception and influence of his metaphysics.

It is unfortunate that Leibniz did not peruse Cavendish's *Observations on Experimental Philosophy* with the same curious attention with which he read More's *Antidote Against Atheism*, Ralph Cudworth's *True Intellectual System*, or Anne Conway's *Principles of the Most Ancient and Modern Philosophy*, works that appealed to him (despite his reservations) for their vitalistic sentiments and their rejection of Hobbism and Cartesianism. He would assuredly have praised Cavendish's thesis that there is life and perception everywhere, her remarkable "perspectivalism," (Smith, S. 1998: 131) and her witty accounts of other worlds, even while, in his usual even-handed way, deploring her atheism, her antinomianism, her mistrust of microscopes, and her recourse to spiritistic architectonic agents. For all her faults of *persona* and presentation, Cavendish from time to time acquires a genuine *majesté* in her appeals to impartiality and reason that belies her social snobbery, and Leibniz could not have failed to approve. At the same time, as a philosopher committed to the permanence of substances and the invariability of the laws of nature, he would have found her Heraclitean sentiments disconcerting, especially when she writes that her surroundings prove "the infinite variety in nature, and that nature is a perpetually self-moving body, dividing, composing, changing, forming, and transforming herself by self-corporeal figurative motions" (OEP 84–5).

Cavendish saw this "infinite variety" in the coloration of birds, the differences in human understandings, fancies, conceptions, imaginations, judgments, wits, memories, affections, passions, flesh, gems and skies. Her rejection of anthropocentrism, as well as of laws of nature and clockwork organisms, was just as distinctive. The same features of her situation and character that led her to protest – probably uniquely amongst seventeenth century philosophers – against not only an authoritarian God, but the supposition of human superiority over the rest of creation, were anything but conducive to fame and fortune.

NOTES

[1]   Susan James (1999) emphasizes Cavendish's role as an exponent of English vitalism.

[2]   The view that Cavendish was completely ignored is receiving correction. Leni Robertson, in an unpublished paper, notes that More did engage strenuously with Cavendish's views without, however, naming her. Her influence on the rhetoric surrounding the microscope may also turn out to be anonymous but substantial.

[3]   More has earned a respectable place in the history of science as an influence on Newton, thanks to Edwin Burtt. See Burtt 1932: 127ff.

[4]   See Battigelli 1998: 46–7.

[5]   Lucy Hutchinson, "Dedication to the Earl of Anglesea." In Firth ed. 1885. Reprinted in De Quehen ed. 1996: 25. See Barbour 1997.

[6]   On Hutchinson, see MacCarthy 1946: 3ff. and Barbour 1994 and 1997.

[7]   "I am absolutely against the opinion of senseless and irrational atoms, moving by chance: for, if nature did consist of such atoms, there would be no certain kinds and species of creatures, nor no uniformity or order [...]" (OEP 169).

[8]   "And therefore the corpuscularian or atomical writers, which do reduce the parts of nature to one certain and proportioned atom, beyond which they imagine nature cannot go, because their brain or particular finite reason cannot reach further are much deceived in their arguments, and commit a fallacy in concluding the finiteness and limitation of nature from the narrowness of their rational conceptions" (OEP 199).

⁹ "No part of nature can be inanimate; for, as the body is, so are its parts; and as the cause, so its effects ... Some learned ... are so much afraid of self-motion, as they will rather maintain absurdities and errors, than allow any other self-motion in nature, but what is in themselves: for, they would fain be above nature, and petty gods, if they could but make themselves infinite; not considering that they are but parts of nature, as all other creatures" (OEP 112).

¹⁰ "Perception," she says, "is properly made by way of patterning and imitation, by the innate, figurative motions of those animal creatures, and not by receiving either the figures of the exterior objects into the sensitive organs, or by sending forth some invisible rays from the organ to the object; nor by pressure and reaction" (OEP 15). On "patterning out," see James 1999: 235ff.

¹¹ "[T]here is no part of nature that has not sense and reason, which is life and knowledge; and if all the infinite parts have life and knowledge, infinite nature cannot be a fool or insensible" (OEP 82).

¹² Letter to Remond, 14 July 1714 (L 657/ GP III, 620).

¹³ Leibniz to de Volder, 20 June 1703 (AG 175/ GP II, 250).

¹⁴ Leibniz, *Monadology* 63 (GP VI, 618/ AG 221); Cf. *Principles of Nature and of Grace* 3 (AG 207/ GP VI, 599): "Each monad is a living mirror, or a mirror endowed with internal action, which represents the universe from its own point of view [...]".

¹⁵ "If some defender of the new philosophy which introduces inertness and inactivity into all things were to go so far as to deprive God's commands of all lasting effects [...] he himself may judge how worthy he thinks this is of God [....] [T]he very substance of things contains a force for acting and being acted upon." (AG 159/ GP IV, 508). "I [...] take for granted that every created being [...] is subject to change, and even that this change is continual in each thing [...]" (*Monadology* §10: AG 214/ GP VI, 608).

¹⁶ Letter to Arnauld, 30 April 1687 (AG 87–8/ GP II, 99).

¹⁷ "[I]magine [...] that there is a machine whose structure makes it think, sense, and have perceptions [...] Assuming that, when inspecting its interior, we will only find parts that push one another, and we will never find anything to explain a perception. And so, we should seek perception in the simple substance and not in the composite or in the machine" (Leibniz, *Monadology* §17: AG 215/ GP VI, 609).

¹⁸ Perhaps both Leibniz and Cavendish were prompted by Hooke's remark in the *Micrographia*, quoted by Cavendish, that the seed of corn violets has a skin "very irregularly shrunk and pitted, insomuch that it is almost an impossibility to find two of them wrinkled alike, so great a variety may there be even in this little seed" (OEP 70). Cf. Hooke 1665: 28.

¹⁹ Leibniz, *Discourse* §6 (AG 39/ A VI iv, 1537).

²⁰ Cavendish, *Philosophical Letters*, 221, quoted in Hutton 2003: 193.

²¹ Leibniz, *Monadology* §§5, 6 (AG 213/ GP VI, 607).

²² Cavendish, *Grounds of Natural Philosophy*, 1668, quoted in Hutton 1997: 429.

²³ Consider, in this connection, another English philosopher: Newton observes in the "Queries" appended to the 4th edition of his *Opticks* that "Nature [...] seems delighted with transmutations [...] Eggs grow from insensible Magnitudes, and change into Animals; Tadpoles into Frogs; and Worms into Flies. All Birds, Beasts, and Fishes, Insects, Trees and other Vegetables, with their several Parts, grow out of Water and other watry Tinctures and salts." He asks "And why may not Nature change Bodies into Light and Light into Bodies?" (*Opticks* 4th ed., NY: Dover, 1952, Quest 30, p. 375). Newton's intimation of the secret processes of generation, fermentation, and renewal is lauded by historians of science as prognostic of an eighteenth century chemistry far richer than the Cartesian mechanical philosophy to which Leibniz remained wedded, in which Nature is envisioned as a "perpetual worker". Cavendish makes similar comments regarding nature's power to transform and transmute (OEP 132). Having no hands-on experience with chemistry, she is not considered to have had a profound idea, that shattered the Cartesian paradigm.

²⁴ Leibniz, First Letter to Clarke (AG 320/ GP VII, 352).

²⁵ Leibniz, *Discourse* 1 (AG 35/ A VI iv, 1531).

²⁶ Leibniz, *Monadology* §60 (AG 220/ GP VI, 617).

²⁷ See Wilson, C. 1989: 169–70. Cf. Plato, *Phaedo* 78cff.

²⁸ Leibniz, *Discourse* §11 (AG 43/ A VI iv, 1544).

[29] "Ever since we made mention of establishing a *New Science of Dynamics*, many distinguished persons have requested a fuller explanation of this doctrine in various places [...] Therefore, we shall here present some things that will shed light on it, light that will perhaps return to us with interest [...]" (Leibniz, *Specimen of Dynamics* (GM VI, 234/ AG 118). Cf. *On Nature Itself* (AG 155/ GP IV, 504). "Christopher Sturm, that celebrated gentleman, distinguished in mathematics and physics [...] I too pondered the same question [...] letters that passed between me and the distinguished author [...] in a respectful way [...] publishing several of the transactions [...] I applied my mind and attention to that question [...] important in and of itself [...]". Compare the Preface to the *New Essays* (A VI vi, 43–5/ Langley ed. 1896: 118): "Since the *Essays on the Understanding*, published by an illustrious Englishman, is one of the finest and most esteemed works of our age... I resolved to comment on it ... to procure a more favourable reception for my thoughts by putting them in such good company."

[30] Clucas interprets both Cavendish and Boyle as emphasizing deliberately "the peremptory and artless composition of their respective works" (Clucas 2003: 200). "Boyle's casual essayistic style," he says, "is the perfect vehicle for a mode of natural philosophy which seeks to authorize its own principles of investigation, paradoxically, by denying the authoritative nature of its statements" (Clucas 2003: 201).

[31] Boyle 2000: 440.

[32] See Meyer 1955: 3–7.

[33] Cavendish, OEP 275; Cf. OEP 249: "[M]ost of the opinions of our modern philosophers, are patched up with [the ancients]; some whereof do altogether follow either Aristotle, Plato, Epicurus, Pythagoras, etc., others make a mixture of several of their opinions; and others again take some of their opinions, and dress them up new with some additions of their own."

[34] Cavendish, *Philosophical and Physical Opinions*, 1663, quoted in Bowerbank 1984: 406.

[35] Leibniz, *On Body and Force* (AG 250/ GP IV, 393, my emphasis).

4. DALGARNO, WILKINS, LEIBNIZ AND THE DESCRIPTIVE NATURE OF METAPHYSICAL CONCEPTS

1. INTRODUCTION

Seen from the perspective of his explicit statements, Leibniz's attitude towards the artificial languages developed by George Dalgarno and John Wilkins seems to have been dismissive. For example, he objects to Dalgarno's alphabetical symbolism that it does not display the logical multiplicity required to represent the whole range of simple, indefinable concepts.[1] Similarly, he observes that Wilkins's system of a graphical notation following the model of early chemical notations with its great number of symbols is difficult to memorize and therefore contributes more to confusion than to clarification.[2] As Jaap Maat has pointed out (Maat 2004), even in the details of the linguistic analysis of the grammar of ordinary language Leibniz almost never follows Dalgarno or Wilkins's suggestions.

However, from the perspective of such a dismissive attitude, it is puzzling why Leibniz nevertheless makes frequent use both of Dalgarno's *Art of Signs* and Wilkins's *Essay Towards a Real Character and a Philosophical Language* to structure his own work on the *characteristica universalis*. The present paper argues that Leibniz's persistent interest in both works is situated not so much on a linguistic but rather on a metaphilosophical level. To be sure, the simple concepts identified in Wilkins's and Dalgarno's artificial languages naturally lend themselves to the project of an art of invention that proceeds synthetically by combining the semantic atoms. Indeed, Francesco Piro interprets Leibniz's interest in the work of Dalgarno and Wilkins from the perspective of the applicability of artificial languages for the purposes of an axiomatic metaphysics.[3] Nevertheless, there is a complementary – analytic and descriptive – side to the projects of Wilkins and Dalgarno. In particular, Leibniz's attention focused on Wilkins and Dalgarno's views on the nature of metaphysical concepts. According to Wilkins, the task of philosophy is not the construction of metaphysical theories, but rather a description of the role these concepts play as an implicit part of everyday language. A comparable view can be found in Dalgarno's theory of categorial concepts or "predicaments." For Dalgarno, categorial concepts are implicitly contained in our everyday concepts. In a similar vein, Leibniz conceives of metaphysical concepts as constituents of ordinary concepts that only have to be made explicit. This lends a strongly descriptivist aspect to Leibniz's view of metaphysical concepts, which explains why Leibniz took a particular interest in Dalgarno's and Wilkins's views on the nature of metaphysical concepts and why their views subsequently influenced Leibniz's own work on the *characteristica universalis*.

51

P. Phemister and S. Brown (eds.), Leibniz and the English-Speaking World, 51–61.
© 2007 *Springer*.

2. LEIBNIZ AND THE DESCRIPTIVE NATURE OF METAPHYSICAL CONCEPTS

There can be little doubt that by the time he finished his university studies, Leibniz held that propositions of metaphysics are purely hypothetical. As reading notes written around 1663/64 in his personal copy of Daniel Stahl's *Metaphysical Compendium*[4] show, Leibniz regarded this as a common view shared by Fabri and Hobbes:

> *Metaphysics*, i.e. First Philosophy is a *system of theorems*, a *theorem* in turn is a proposition that is true even if nothing would exist; i.e. a merely hypothetical proposition, or one that can be reduced to hypothetical propositions. In this way Honoratus Fabri defines First Philosophy ... and Th. Hobbes who divides his *De Corpore* in two parts, into First Philosophy, i.e. abstracted from existence; and Physics, i.e. dealing with the causes of the things in the world. Metaphysics is the work of mere *reason*, and derives from definitions; *sense* provides the foundations of physics. (A VI iii, 22)

Interestingly, Leibniz in this note connects the view of metaphysics as a purely hypothetical discipline with the view that metaphysics is derived from rational construction of definitions and does not have to do with causal knowledge. As we will see shortly, his view of the role of a purely hypothetical procedure is soon supplemented by a more pluralistic view of the method of metaphysics. In fact, Leibniz's picture of the nature of metaphysics begins to change quite early on. Already in another early piece, *On Transsubstantiation* [1668–1669 (?)], his portrayal of metaphysical concepts is far more complex. On the one hand, he there uses a hypothetico-deductive type of argument that purports to show the possibility of the Eucharist. For example, he characterises the starting point of his argument as follows: "This proof depends on the explication of the terms 'substance', 'species' or 'accident', and 'numerical identity'; which we will develop on the basis of the notions accepted by the Scholastics, which we will only explicate clearly" (A VI i, 508). On the other hand, this starting point is not purely hypothetical; it also is deliberately conciliatory in the sense that it rests on concepts that are common to different scholastic philosophies. As Leibniz points out later in the text, the scholastic concepts he has chosen here have counterparts in "modern" philosophy. This common conceptual scheme not only serves as an (putatively) uncontroversial starting point. Leibniz also thinks that the rational core of several ancient metaphysical doctrines can be reduced to what is expressible in terms of these concepts, and therefore also in the conceptual framework of the moderns. Moreover, although he uses a hypothetico-deductive model of explanation, he joins the idea that the conceptual basis of this explanation is common to different philosophical traditions with the idea that, in principle, the adequacy of the definitions is accessible to proof. In this sense, a little later in the text he says that

> it is to be proved through the consensus of philosophers that the substance of a thing is not accessible to our eyes. Therefore, another notion of mind is necessary than the one usurped today by sense, otherwise it would be accessible to sense perception. (A VI i, 512)

Thus, metaphysical concepts (such as the concept of substance), which function as the basis for hypothetico-deductive arguments, are not only a part of a conciliatory strategy, but at the same time are capable of being proved themselves.

This complex view of the nature of metaphysical concepts is expressed already in the *Dissertation on the Art of Combinations* (1666). The whole enterprise of a universal characteristic there is portrayed not only as something that aims at the production of discourse, but also (and primarily) as something that rests on an adequate analysis of the categorial structure of our language:

> Truly, I miss much in Lull's terms. Because his whole method is more directed at the art of extemporaneous discourse than at the pursuit of full knowledge of a given subject ... He determines the number of terms arbitrarily, there are nine in each class. Why does he include among the absolute predicates, which have to be the most abstract, will, truth, wisdom, virtue, glory, why does he omit beauty, or figure, or number? To the relational predicates, there have to be added many more, e.g. cause, whole, part, requisite, etc. (Problema II, § 60: A VI i, 193)

Leibniz's own intent to provide a basis for metaphysical concepts that goes beyond their merely rhetorical, discourse-productive use is supplemented in the *Preface to Nizolius* (1670) by an analogous view of the nature of logical concepts:

> True logic is not only an instrument, but also contains somehow the principles and the true reason for doing philosophy, because it hands down those general rules, through which the true and the false can be discerned, and by means of which through the mere application of definitions and experiences all conclusions can be proven. But they also are not the principles of philosophy, or of the propositions themselves, and they do not make the truth of things, but rather show it; nevertheless they make the philosopher, and are the principles of the right way of doing philosophy, which – as Nizolius has observed – is enough. (A VI ii, 408)

Interestingly, in this passage Leibniz does not regard the principles of reasoning as something that is constitutive of philosophy as a particular theoretical discipline. Principles of reason, in his opinion, are not a tool of theory construction. Rather, they are only made explicit in philosophical analysis. In this sense, making principles of reason explicit only "shows" the truth that already is contained in our ordinary way of thinking about things. This view of the descriptive nature of philosophical knowledge leads Leibniz to the claim that philosophers do not know other things than ordinary people but rather the same things in a different way:

> And it is very true that there is nothing that cannot be explicated in popular terms, only using more of them. Therefore, Nizolius rightly urges at various places that what does not possess a general term ... in common language should be regarded as nothing, as a fiction, and as useless. For philosophers do not always surpass common men in that they sense different things, but that they sense them in another way, that is with the eye of the mind, with reflection or attention, and comparing things with other things. (A VI ii, 413)

Although the example of a "comparing things with other things" mentioned at this place concerns Joachim Jungius's attempt at classifying birds through a comparison of their external features, the point Leibniz has in mind here seems to more general. The function of comparing things with each other in this context does not have the function of arriving at empirical generalisations based on an inductive procedure. Rather, using a comparative method leads to an insight into a conceptual structure that, due to the fact that it is shared by all rational beings, can be regarded as a kind of implicit knowledge that only has to be made explicit. This interpretation of shared conceptual structures as implicit knowledge has the consequence that in writing philosophy the following rule has to be observed:

Whenever there are popular terms available that are equally comprehensive, technical terms should not be used. And indeed this is one of the fundamental rules of philosophical style, which should be followed everywhere, in particular by metaphysicians; because most of the dialectical and metaphysical matters themselves occur frequently even in popular speeches, writings, and thoughts, and are used everywhere in normal life. This is why people, guided by this frequent occurrence, have designated them by specific, common, most natural and comprehensive words; in case these are available, it is a sin to obscure things through new, and in the most cases even less convenient, invented ones ... (A VI ii, 415)

If one compares these remarks with the view of metaphysical concepts expressed in the reading notes on Stahl's *Metaphysical Compendium*, it becomes immediately clear that by time around 1670–1671 Leibniz's view of the nature of metaphysics has become far more complex. In particular, the framework of a hypothetico-deductive approach to metaphysics has been supplemented by an interpretation of metaphysical concepts in the framework of a theory of implicit knowledge. This implicit knowledge is understood as something that is common to all rational beings. "Common" notions not only comprise notions of arithmetic and geometry but also structure all areas of ordinary discourse. They are not common because they are abstract, Platonic, entities. Rather, mathematical and geometrical notions are common in the same way as other, non-mathematical, notions are common impli-cations of everyday language. Metaphysics is not only a matter of the construction of adequate explanatory hypotheses, but also a matter of the description of common conceptual structures.

3. WILKINS, DALGARNO, AND THE DESCRIPTIVE NATURE OF METAPHYSICAL CONCEPTS

Leibniz's views as to the nature of metaphysical concepts and their role in the universal characteristic were developed quite far, when in spring 1671 he read John Wilkins's *Essay Towards a Real Character*[5] and when in 1673, during his stay in London, he purchased copies both of this book and of George Dalgarno's *Art of Signs*.[6] Both books contain statements about the nature of the Universal Characteristic and the function of metaphysical concepts that come surprisingly close to those of Leibniz. Wilkins tells the reader about the origins of his book that the basic idea goes back to conversations with Seth Ward, the Bishop of Salisbury. As Ward pointed out to him, previous authors of artificial languages did generally mistake in their first foundations; whilst they did propose to themselves the framing of such a *Character*, from a *Dictionary of Words*, according to some particular Language, without reference to the *nature of things*, and that common Notion of them, wherein Mankind does agree, which must chiefly be respected, before any attempt of this nature could signifie any thing, as to the main end of it. (ERC "To the Reader")

From the outset, the strategy inspired by Ward ties the idea that a universal character should represent the real order of things to the suggestion that in order to achieve this goal the conceptual framework common to all humans has to be analysed. That this type of analysis has more to do with the description of concepts that are actually used than with the introduction of hypothetical definitions becomes apparent in the terminology chosen by Wilkins. About the second part of his book, he says that it

shall contein that which is the great foundation of the thing here designed, namely a regular *enumeration* and *description* of all those things and notions, to which marks or names ought to be assigned according to their respective natures, which may be styled the *Scientifical* Part, comprehending *Universal Philosophy*. It being the proper end and design of the several branches of Philosophy to reduce all things and notions unto such a frame, as may express their natural order, dependence, and relations. (ERC I i, 1: 1)

The research program pursued by Wilkins does not start with arbitrary definitions, but rather aims at specifying concepts that represent the causal structure of reality. This type of an "enumeration and description" of notions that express the "natural order" of things, in Wilkins's opinion, is not only a tool for facilitating communication and of helping memory by a "natural method". It is also an expression of the common nature of rational beings, because it expresses the structure of the language of thought:

As men do generally agree in the same Principle of Reason, so do they likewise agree in the same *Internal Notion* or *Apprehension of things*.
   The *External Expression* of these Mental notions, whereby men communicate their thoughts to one another, is either to the *Ear*, or the *Eye*. ...
   That *conceit* which men have in their minds concerning a Horse or Tree, is the Notion or *mental Image* of that Beast, or natural thing, of such a nature, shape and use. The *Names* given to these in several Languages, are such arbitrary *sounds* or *words*, as Nations of men have agreed upon, either casually or designedly, to express their Mental notions of them. The *Written word* is the figure or picture of that Sound. (ERC I v, 2: 20)

Because the goal of a "philosophical language" is to achieve a correspondence between the order of mental concepts and order of arbitrary signs, Wilkins claims that we "by learning the *Character* and the *Names* of things, be instructed likewise in their *Natures*, the knowledg of both which ought to be conjoyned" (ERC I v, 3: 20–1). The resulting view of the nature of metaphysics is that its aim "should be to enumerate and explain those more general terms, which by reason of their Universality and Comprehensiveness, are either *above* all those Heads of things stiled Predicaments, or else *common to several of them*. And if this Science had been so ordered, as to have contained a plain regular enumeration and description of these general terms, without the mixture of nice and subtle disputes about them; it might have been proper enough for learners to have begun with." In particular, Wilkins regards metaphysical concepts as something that belongs to "such matters as are *prima nota*, and most obvious" and that are therefore most hard to define. (ERC II i, 1: 24) In fact, the tables Wilkins sets forth in the second part of his book do not give any explicit definitions of general terms at all. Rather, they outline a hierarchy of concepts following the model of subordination of concepts of species under concepts of genera, thereby providing a sort of implicit definition of concepts through their place in the hierarchy.

Dalgarno expresses similar intuitions about the role of metaphysical concepts for the foundations of the Universal Characteristic. In a way akin to Wilkins (and probably also inspired by Ward, who was – together with Wilkins – one of the supporters of Dalgarno's work),[7] Dalgarno connects the idea of identifying elements of the symbolism of an artificial language with the idea of expressing thereby the natural order of things:

The absolute doctrine of the first elements of signs, as far as the requirements of the present treatise demand, and brevity suggest: Before I come to *entire signs*, which can be composed from them, and given to the things themselves; it will be necessary to inspect the nature of the *things* themselves ... Because *signs* are taken by us as standing for *things* themselves, it is wholly conforming to reason that the art of *signs* follows the art of *things*. And in the same way as I think that *metaphysics & logic* constitute only a single art; so does *grammar* differ not otherwise, or more, from these, as the *sign* from the *signified*: because these are correlated, the knowledge of both has to be entirely one and the same. (AS 17–8)

The grammar of an ideal artificial language would express the logical structure of reality, and in this sense, for Dalgarno, logic and metaphysics form a single discipline. In the context of such a conception of philosophical grammar, Dalgarno explicitly defends a theory of categorial concepts or "predicaments" against objections such as those in Thomas Hobbes' *On Body*.[8] For Dalgarno, the rejection of a doctrine of predicaments is "absurd and unworthy of a philosopher" exactly because it is the aim of philosophy to "lay bare the natures of things by investigating the differences & similarities; and thus, through method & order to locate & situate them among each other". By contrast, the rejection of the doctrine of predicaments, according to Dalgarno, explains such blatant philosophical errors as the claim that there are "two highest genera of things, *Body* namely & *Non-body*." As he notes, there is "no more absurd & insignificant term than *non-body*" (AS 18–9). However, his reservations go beyond the problem of how a negative concept can function as a foundation of the conceptual structure of everyday language. He also argues that predicaments are implicit presuppositions of ordinary concepts such as that of proof and description:

And I ask those who regard no use for the *predicament*, what do these terms signify, *genus, species, difference, definition*, &c? Certainly, without the supposition of the predicament they are whole absurd & signifying nothing; because all *demonstration* supposes *definition*, a *definition genus & species, genus & species* and ordered *series of predicaments*. And if we want to speak properly, there is no *definition* or *demonstration* (and the writings of these authors abound with these terms) because no *series of predicaments* is constituted: from this follows that what is taken to be a *definition* by someone does not deserve the name of a *description* (as the distinction is commonly made) by someone else; so that what is a *demonstration* for the one, is a *sophistry* for the other. (AS 24–5)

The view of categorial concepts as necessary conditions of ordinary discourse leads Dalgarno to the claim that the nature of categories is inadequately represented in a conceptual "tree" expressing a hierarchy of concepts in the order of progressing abstraction. (AS 27) The alternative picture suggested by Dalgarno – that of a conceptual "genealogy" – captures the fact that categories play a role in concept formation. The role of reason is to discover the role categorial concepts play in ordinary concept formation: "As we through *faith* believe that all men descend from a first parent; we prove through *reason* that all particular notions derive from a first *notion of a being*" (AS 27). In Dalgarno's view, categorial concepts are what gives ordinary concepts the structure they have. Ordinary concepts and discourse cannot be thought without supposing that there are categorial concepts because they are – as Dalgarno puts it – "derived" from them. The contrast Dalgarno has mind can be described as the contrast between a view of categorial concepts as outcome of a process of abstraction and a view of categorial concepts as playing a role in structuring everyday language. This second view is – as we shall presently see – one of the aspects of Dalgarno's work that attracted Leibniz's interest over many years.

4. LEIBNIZ'S RESPONSE TO WILKINS AND DALGARNO

Leibniz's comments on Dalgarno's and Wilkins's writings begin in the early 1670s, and continue during the time of his renewed interest in the project of a Universal Characteristic during the early 1680s. In an early remark on a separate sheet added to his copy of the *Art of Signs*, Leibniz writes: "Dalgarno saw something through a mist p. 33, but horrified by the difficulty, and not seeing sufficiently how the thing could be effected, went wrong in all the rest" (A VI iii, 170). This short note does not tell us exactly what Leibniz thought that Dalgarno saw, and in which respect exactly he thought him to have gone wrong. Jean-Baptiste Rauzy has made the interesting suggestion that Leibniz here echoes Hobbes's view that the series of predicaments does not tell anything about the nature of things and natural species (2001: 219–20, note 6). In fact, Leibniz's objection seems to have something to do with the fact that the categorization as proposed by Dalgarno does not reflect the order of things. However, Leibniz's doubts rather have to do with the specific strategy Dalgarno pursues in the chapter treating the relation between predicaments and philosophical grammar than with the general project of an analysis of categories per se. Such an interpretation is suggested by the place where he disagrees with Dalgarno. Interestingly, the disagreement does not concern Dalgarno's theory of the predicaments in the third chapter of the *Art of Signs*. Rather, it concerns Dalgarno's corollaries relating to the prospects of the application of this theory to the construction of a philosophical grammar in the fourth chapter of the *Art of Signs*, entitled "Some Grammatical Corollaries following from the Exposition of the Predicament." There, Dalgarno claims that the order of the predicaments "is not an adequate foundation for the Art of Grammar" (AS 32). The argument to which Leibniz responded is that "analysis does not sufficiently lead to this notion seen under the form of a single composite, instantly by means of a single act of the mind, graspable without a long discourse" (AS 33). According to Dalgarno, a possible alternative would be to use a purely naturalistic taxonomy, e.g. 6000 species of plants etc.; however, as he points out, such a fine grained taxonomy could not describe adequately what is common to several species of things. (AS 34–5) As a solution, Dalgarno proposes that "a selected number of primary notions should be chosen from the first & and most important sciences; of those namely which in respect to things are called the more general ones; & these should be supposed in the place of the first concepts, and the radical signs should be used to signify them" (AS 35). In addition, Dalgarno is explicit about the fact that he does not offer the tables of predicates and the "Lexicon Philosophico-Grammaticum" as a perfect series of things, but something that has a strongly arbitrary component. In this sense, he holds that the "Art of Signs does not allow for strict philosophical laws" (AS 36). Leibniz criticises this view by pointing out that it is "one thing to separate parts, another to consider distinctly, and there is no need to draw attention to all details at once; it suffices that the character is composed in a way that it can be divided as it pleases" (A VI iii, 174–75, note 14).

Leibniz's objection is not directed at the general plan of outlining a theory of categorial concepts. Rather, the thrust of Leibniz's argument is that, in matters of detail, Dalgarno did not use his theory of the predicaments in an adequate way for the construction of his artificial language. This also is the point of a retrospective remark in a letter to Thomas Burnett of 24 August 1697:

I have considered with attention the great work on *Universal Character and Philosophical Language* of Monsieur Wilkins; I find that he has put there an infinity of nice things, and we never have had a more accomplished table of predicates; but the application to characters and language is not at all conform to what one could and should have done ... The objections of Monsieur Dalgarno and Monsieur Wilkins against the truly philosophical method have only the purpose to excuse the imperfection of their essays, and only indicate the difficulties they were not able to overcome (GP III, 216).

In fact, Dalgarno and Wilkins were aware of the discrepancy between their programmatic intentions and the concrete proposals at constructing a system of signs underlying an artificial language. Nevertheless, despite his own reservations, Wilkins seems to have felt that, in principle, an artificial language expressing the categorial structure of thought that matches the structure of reality could be formulated:

For the accurate effecting of this, it would be necessary, that the *Theory* it self, upon which such a design were to be founded, should be exactly *suited to the nature of things*. But, upon supposal that this Theory is *defective*, either as to the *Fulneß* or the *Order* of it, this must need add much *perplexity* to any such Attempt, and render it *imperfect*. And that this is the case with that common Theory already received, need not much be doubted; which may afford some excuse as to several of those things which may seem to be less conveniently disposed of in the following Tables ... (ERC I v, 3: 21).

A similar attitude can be found in Dalgarno's work. Despite his own qualms about the applicability of predicaments to grammar, Dalgarno characterizes the "Lexicon Philosophico-Grammaticum" as containing "tables of things, and of all simple and general notions ... ordered according to the predicamental order". According to his view, notions formed through the combination of such simple notions "contain descriptions of things that are in agreement with their natures" (AS, "Lexicon Philosophico-Grammaticum", without pagination [following p. 115]).

In notes probably written between October 1677 and September 1680, Leibniz makes use of the Lexicon under exactly this perspective, when he tries to develop his own definitions of metaphysical concepts listed by Dalgarno. For example, Leibniz defines "Ens, Res" as "what can be conceived of distinctly" or, alternatively, as "what can be known" (A VI iii, 182). In entries which he crossed out again, Leibniz defines "substance" as "active and passive being, it is a being that involves all other existing beings in its notion, a persisting being", and "accident" as an "attribute of a substance" (A VI iii, 182, notes). He also makes a similar use of the tables of concepts in Wilkins's *Essay*. Again, Leibniz's thought circles around problem of finding adequate definitions of metaphysical concepts. For example, in a list of definitions following the arrangement of Wilkins's tables, he writes: "A *substance* is what has some action or passion. Or rather: whatever is thought absolutely or completely"[9] (in a first version he had written: "A *substance* is what has some action. Or rather: whatever is thought" [A VI, 2, 488, notes]). In a similar vein, Leibniz's subsequent work on the *Characteristica Universalis* focuses on categorial concepts. In an extensive collection of pieces concerning Wilkins's *Essay*, Leibniz tries to give definitions of metaphysical concepts, e.g.: "*Something* is whatever can be thought. *Nothing* is whatever cannot be thought. A *Thing* is what can be thought distinctly. ... A *Substance* is whose individual cannot be said about another. An *Accident* is whose individual can be predicated of another."[10] In *On the Classes of Things*, he compares the views of philosophers such as Aristotle and Becher on the number and order of categories, and it is in this context that he makes again use of the work of Dalgarno and Wilkins.[11] Finally, in a note probably from the summer of 1688, Leibniz writes:

There is a need for definitions such as my own, namely palpable ones, and with the help of characters bound to something sensible.

  The best method to get an analysis of notions, a posteriori, is to demand the demonstration of the most axiomatic propositions, which seem to others known by themselves. Therefore, the best should be excerpted from the *Regulae Philosophicae* by Stahl and Thomasius[12] [...] In addition, the writings of Plato, Aristotle, Cardano, Galilei, Jungius, Descartes, Fabri, Hobbes [...] Spinoza should be run through [...].

  Both those authors who have notable propositions, which most lead to the principles; and those who have many terms arranged in a real order, such as those who deduce predicaments to even prior concepts.[13]

And among the authors belonging to this last category, Leibniz again mentions Wilkins. These observations point to the conclusion that Leibniz's persisting interest in the work of Wilkins and Dalgarno has to do with his investigation of categorial concepts. He shares with Wilkins and Dalgarno the view that categorial concepts belong to the conceptual framework of our ordinary way of thinking about the world. This distinguishes them, e.g. from concepts underlying propositions about sensible qualities. In *On the Alphabet of Human Thoughts*, he writes: "Whatever has a cause, cannot be conceived by itself; rather, it is conceived through its cause, from which its possibility can be demonstrated."[14] He admits that it might turn out to be difficult to specify the causes for a given sensible quality; in this case, concepts for sensible qualities can "provisionally be taken as primitive ones" (A VI iv, 270). Yet, he distinguishes between primitive concepts that derive from sensible qualities, and primitive concepts that only are perceived by means of an "internal sense", or which are common to several senses. (A VI iv, 271) He provides the following evidence for the existence of this second kind of simple concepts:

> Children who have little experience nevertheless are able to understand almost everything that a prudent teacher explains to them, even if he does not reveal them anything, but only describes it. It is therefore necessary that the concepts of all these things are already hidden in them, and, for this reason, arise from the few things that they had experience of.
>
> In fact, a gifted and attentive child, even with very little experience, can perfectly understand a teacher talking about mathematics, morals, jurisprudence, and metaphysical matters ... for us it suffices that the teacher can be understood by the child, to make it obvious, that the seeds of all these concepts were already in the child, and that therefore form the very few concepts the child had yet, the infinitely many, which the teacher explicated, are necessarily composed. (A VI iv, 271)

This passage bears analogies with Leibniz's later theory of innate ideas, and integrates metaphysical concepts into the realm of concepts accessible to "internal sense." Interestingly, the conception of internal sense at stake here does not presuppose any metaphysical theory, e.g. about the nature of substance. Rather, it is a genuinely epistemological notion that can serve as an explication for the methodological foundation of metaphysical concepts. The kind of knowledge accessible to "internal sense" not only comprises mathematical knowledge, but also metaphysics, ethics, and the theory of law. Because concepts belonging to these areas of philosophical knowledge are accessible to an internal sense understood in purely epistemological terms, they are seen as something that only need to be described by the teacher (or the philosopher) to be made known explicitly. In this sense, metaphysical concepts belong to a kind of knowledge that is accessible on descriptive grounds.

5. CONCLUSION

Comparing Leibniz's early views on the nature of metaphysical concepts with those of Dalgarno and Wilkins, and looking at the way Leibniz responded to their views, one might conclude that for all three philosophers there is more to the method of metaphysics than the axiomatic-deductive side. Although the artificial languages envisaged by Dalgarno, Wilkins, and Leibniz naturally lend themselves to the purposes of a deductive exposition starting with basic definitions and axioms, the project of a universal characteristic in all three philosophers is tied to a view of metaphysical concepts as expressions of the structure of thought and reality. As do Wilkins and Dalgarno, Leibniz regards metaphysical concepts as categorial concepts or "predicaments" as something enters into the formation of our everyday concepts and, therefore, in an implicit fashion, is commonly known. This genuinely epistemological account of metaphysical concepts foreshadows aspects of Leibniz's later theory of metaphysical concepts as innate ideas. According to Leibniz, a comparative method can be used to bring out the implicit knowledge contained in our everyday language. In this sense, he thinks that philosophers do not know different things than non-philosophers but rather the same things in a different way. What different philosophers can know is always the same, and this common knowledge constitutes the rational core of various philosophical traditions. In this way, Leibniz's descriptive strategy in metaphysics serves as the basis for a conciliatory mode of thought that supplements an axiomatic-deductive approach to metaphysics, and at the same time provides an argumentative foundation for a conciliatory strategy that integrates elements stemming from different philosophical traditions.

NOTES

[1]   *Zur Ars Signorum von George Dalgarno* (February–March 1673 [?]); A VI iii, 175, note 6.

[2]   *De lingua philosophica* (end 1687–end 1688): A VI iv, 907.

[3]   See Piro 1990: esp. 40–7.

[4]   Daniel Stahl, *Compendium Metaphysicae In XXIV. Tabellas redactum, Nuncque post Auctoris obitum emendatiùs et auctiùs editum …*, Jena: Georg Sengenwald, 1655.

[5]   See Leibniz to Henry Oldenburg, 29 April / 9 May 1671: A II i, 104.

[6]   See the entry in his travel diary (A VI iv, 169).

[7]   See the acknowledgements in AS, unpaginated page [fol. 8v].

[8]   See Thomas Hobbes, *De corpore. Elementorum philosophiae sectio prima*, ed. Karl Schumann with Martine Pécharman, Paris: Vrin, 1999, I, 2, §§15–16.

[9]   *Vorarbeiten zur Characteristica Universalis* (second half of 1671–spring 1672 [?]): A VI ii, 488.

[10]   *Collectanea tentamen Wilkinsii de charactere universali concernentia* (October 1677–March 1686): A VI iv, 27–8.

[11]   *De rerum classibus* (autumn 1677–summer 1680 [?]): A VI iv, 1009–1010.

[12]   See Daniel Stahl, *Regulae philosophicae*, 2 vols, Jena 1657; Jakob Thomasius, *Dilucidationes Stahlianae in partem priorem regularum philosophicarum Danielis Stahlii*, Leipzig 1676.

[13]   *De definitionibus characterisandis et propositionibus demonstrandis*: A VI iv, 924–5.

[14]   *De alphabeto cogitationum humanarum* (April 1679–April 1681 [?]): A VI iv, 270.

5. "UN DE MES AMIS"

*On Leibniz's relation to the English mathematician and theologian John Wallis**

I. INTRODUCTION

At the end of a long letter dated 17 April 1699 and primarily containing instructions on the creation of a uniform alphabet for the Slavonic languages, Leibniz informs the Swedish historian and linguist Johan Gabriel von Sparwenfeld (1655–1727) of another concern with which he had lately been pre-occupied. Moreover, it was a concern he had recently addressed to the privy council of the house of Brunswick-Lüneburg, to the minister of state to the Elector of Brandenburg, and to the crown prince of Tuscany. Having had no success with either of the former and the latter still presenting an open question, Leibniz felt that Sparwenfeld, who was under master of ceremonies in Stockholm might be able to exert some influence in the direction he was hoping at the Swedish royal court:

It is necessary, sir, that I communicate to you a thought that has come to mind. As my ideas are firmly rooted in the public good, and particularly in the advancement of science, I am always concerned to prevent the loss of useful discoveries. The art of deciphering is one of the greatest examples of the human spirit. I have a friend, who is assuredly among the foremost experts in this field in Europe and who on numerous occasions has given proofs of this which have caused my astonishment. (A I xvi, 726)

Since, as Leibniz goes on to explain, his request to this friend that he set out the precepts of his art had not met with a favourable response, the only option remaining to prevent the disappearance of what he considered to be so useful would be to send a suitable young man with a natural inclination to assiduity and numbers to be trained by him personally. But this would, as Leibniz recognises, require royal patronage:

I think it is necessary that a notable prince have some young man chosen and instructed in this art, with which he will thereafter be able to serve him, it being a matter of sufficient importance to princes. Our court does not care too much for these things, and so yours came to mind. (A I xvi, 726)

The friend, to whom Leibniz refers, is none other than John Wallis (1616–1703), Savilian professor of geometry in the University of Oxford since the heady days of the revolution in 1649, founder member of the Royal Society, and one of his more important correspondents in England.[1] The themes dealt with in their letters ranged from linguistics to the proposal for a Protestant mission to China, from calendar reform to historical and current questions in mathematics.[2] Nevertheless, if we consider that Leibniz never met Wallis and that their exchange of correspondence

---

*All dates in the text are given new style, i.e. according to the Gregorian calendar.

P. Phemister and S. Brown (eds.), Leibniz and the English-Speaking World, 63–81.
© 2007 *Springer.*

only began at the end of 1695, one would be well justified in asking where exactly the basis of the friendship between the two men might lie.[3]

The answer to this is without doubt to be found many years earlier in 1671 when Wallis, as one of three referees,[4] provided a glowing report on the then young philosopher's *Hypothesis physica nova* (1671),[5] which Henry Oldenburg (?1618–1677) subsequently published,[6] together with Wallis's altogether much shorter account of the *Theoria motus abstracti* (1671),[7] in the journal he owned and edited, the *Philosophical Transactions*. Oldenburg, who as secretary to the Royal Society alongside John Wilkins (1614–1672) conceived and transformed this office in the spirit of scientific co-operation along the lines of ideas laid out and practised by Jan Amos Comenius (1592–1670) and Samuel Hartlib (d.1662),[8] sought particularly to give support to his promising and in many ways like-minded young compatriot.[9] After all, Leibniz had in his first letter to Oldenburg of 23 July 1670 not only outlined his then still incomplete new physical hypothesis, but had also spoken positively of Wilkins's and Kircher's (1601–1680) work on universal language schemes, mentioned his plan to reduce jurisprudence to a demonstrative system and deplored the state of politics in Germany as hindering progress in the new science.[10]

Now, with Wallis's backing, Oldenburg had no difficulty in persuading members of the Royal Society to allow the *Hypothesis physica nova* and the *Theoria motus abstracti* to be reprinted under its auspices in London.[11] This, together with the favourable impression Leibniz created during his first visit to the English capital in January/February 1673 was decisive in his being elected fellow of the then most important scientific institution in Europe on 19 April the same year.[12] In short, Wallis, with Oldenburg pulling the strings in the background, is one of the central figures in Leibniz's ascent to the European scientific elite in the 1670s.

Appropriately, Leibniz was called upon by Oldenburg following his election to engage forthwith in the exchange of scientific intelligence and in particular "to bring before the public those matters which either you shall have yourself pursued by reflection and experience in physics and mechanics, or others in Germany shall have thought out on the same philosophical topics".[13] And, indeed, the young philosopher did not disappoint Oldenburg in this respect. Having already provided him with information on Georg Christoph Werner von Memmingen's (d.1672) hydraulic machine[14] and Johann Joachim Becher's (1635–1682) experiments on metals,[15] Leibniz soon obliged with news from Paris on the papers left behind by Gaston Pardies (1636–1673)[16] after his death and on the chemical experiments of Jacques Agar (1640–1715).[17] But this was not a one-way exchange. Not only did Oldenburg frequently send Leibniz details of new publications in England by men such as Robert Boyle (1626–1691) and Francis Willughby (1635–1672), he also happily acted as mediator to the Savilian professor. Thus, the German philosopher and now also budding mathematician had no qualms in engaging Wallis's assistance in investigations on the manuscript holdings in Oxford of authors such as the astrologer Vettius Valens (second century)[18] and the astronomer and mathematician Geminos (fl. 70BC).[19] Even in the 1690s, long after the death of Oldenburg, Leibniz found it perfectly natural to ask Wallis to conduct a search in Oxford for publications by the Slovenian philologist Adam Bohorič (c.1520–1600).[20]

But this was not a friendship based solely on the ideals of scientific co-operation. Leibniz was fascinated by Wallis's acclaimed accomplishments in the deciphering of encoded letters, since first becoming aware of these during his Paris sojourn (1672–1676). Indeed, this is the topic with which Wallis's name is more constantly associated in Leibniz's writings and letters than any other. In the following paper, I shall consider some of the reasons for this, beginning with the systematic importance of the art of deciphering within the context of the *Ars inveniendi*. I shall then proceed to look at the political background to Wallis's work and discuss how this coloured the Savilian professor's response to Leibniz's repeated exhortations to be more forthcoming on the methods of deciphering he employed.

2. LEIBNIZ'S EARLY RECEPTION OF WALLIS AS MATHEMATICIAN AND CRYPTOGRAPHER

Although Leibniz already claimed in his *Theoria motus abstracti* that through the innovative concept of point which he presented in this early work he had been able to save not only Cavalieri's (?1598–1647) method of indivisibles but also Wallis's arithmetic of the infinites from philosophical criticisms which had been levelled against them,[21] there can be little doubt that at this time he had seen nothing in print by the Savilian professor and that his source was instead one of numerous diatribes which Thomas Hobbes (1588–1679) wrote against Wallis in the course of their long drawn out war.[22] This changes only in Paris. From the countless manuscripts which document Leibniz's growth to mathematical maturity during his stay there we know that he read Wallis's most important contribution to the development of modern analysis, the *Arithmetica infinitorum* (1656).[23] And as will become evident when the corresponding material has been edited, his reception of Wallis's *Mechanica sive de motu* (1670–1671) at this time plays a pivotal role in the development of his theory of dynamics. It was from this work that Leibniz acquired important insights into the question of the application of mathematics to physics, particularly with regard to causal relations;[24] indeed, his reception of the *Mechanica* appears to have played a decisive role in his derivation of the principle of sufficient reason.[25] However, it is an indication of the momentous strides in mathematics which Leibniz made over these four years that he was soon able to characterise Wallis's approach to quadratures as being still firmly within the ancient tradition and in this way to contrast it with his own. While he acknowledged that certain modern mathematicians, among whom he numbered Wallis, Cavalieri, and Guldin (1577–1643), had through the careful study of Archimedes's work enriched tetragonistic methods, he nevertheless maintained that what he called the analysis of infinites was entirely different from the geometry of indivisibles of Cavalieri and the arithmetic of infinites of Wallis, then

this geometry of Cavalieri, which is very restricted otherwise, is bound to figures, where it looks for the sums of ordinates. And Mr Wallis, in order to make his investigations easier, gives us by means of induction the sums of certain rows of numbers, whereas the new analysis of infinites considers neither figures nor numbers but quantities in general, as does ordinary algebra.[26]

Wallis's approach relies heavily on his natural mathematical intuition both in respect of the use of induction and of interpolation: on the one hand his ability to recognize that an established pattern in a few cases could reasonably be assumed to continue indefinitely, and on the other hand his ability to interpolate between triangular, pyramidal and other figurate numbers.[27] Thus despite all the credit which accrues to Wallis for having effectively arithmeticized the geometry of Cavalieri, there is still an unmistakably visual aspect to his own method. And this is something which on Leibniz's opinion only his own infinitesimal calculus had been able to overcome. "My arithmetic of the infinites is pure," he writes, "that of Wallis is figurate."[28]

There is a certain irony here, however. As Leibniz himself recognised,[29] precisely Wallis's skill in interpolation stood him in good stead in his work on deciphering, particularly where numerical ciphers or nomenclators were involved, since these involve the decipherer in being confronted with line upon line of numbers in which he has to divine some kind of meaning. Leibniz was well aware that the inspection of tables of data had a central role to play not only in the projected *ars inveniendi* but also in mathematics where he was certain that analytical tables would allow considerable advances.[30] In other words, what he set out to achieve in trigonometry, namely the overcoming of the use of tables,[31] should not be taken as a general rejection of the visual in respect of the perfection of scientific knowledge.

As we know, Leibniz in Paris through what he calls his discoveries in the "secrets of algebra"[32] came to recognise once more the importance of the combinatorics he had learnt in Leipzig and with which he had dealt in his dissertation of 1666. In what represents a substantial advance over the geometrical model of thought he had developed in the *Theoria motus abstracti*, he now conceives all our thinking as "nothing else but the connection and substitution of signs, whether these be words, symbols, or even images".[33] Accordingly, all composite human concepts can on Leibniz's view be expressed by precise characters of simple notions and thus can be manipulated just as with numbers or in algebra. From this concept of course emerged the plan to create an alphabet of human thought, with the help of which it would be possible not only to express all already known propositions and truths, but also to discover new ones. In this broadly-understood sense, combinatorics is all-embracing; it is the general qualitative science dealing with similarity, dissimilarity, and forms, under which the quantitative science of algebra as dealing simply with the relations of equivalence and non-equivalence is to be subsumed.[34]

An inseparable part of Leibniz's conception of combinatorics is the art of invention,[35] the perfection of which he describes on one occasion as being his greatest task.[36] In the most general terms, the *ars inveniendi* is characterised as the art which directs thought to some unknown truth which is to be elicited or by which the means of achieving a certain end are to be ascertained.[37] As such, it pertains both to the synthetic and to the analytic mode of enquiry within Leibniz's combinatorial framework. And it pertains also to mathematics in a narrower sense, namely to analysis. Of the two basic approaches, the analytical is on Leibniz's view the more difficult to pursue, often leading to no conclusion.[38] As an example of this he refers to the problems that can be incurred in deciphering. The synthetic approach, by contrast, which relies less on mental finesse[39] and more on systematic deduction, takes longer but always arrives at a conclusion.

An instance of the role played by the *Ars inveniendi* in analysis and at the same time the first occasion on which Wallis is mentioned by Leibniz in the context of deciphering is to be found in the manuscript *De methodi quadraturarum usu in seriebus* (August/September 1673). Leibniz compares the search for the rule of a series, or of a table, with the search for the key to a cipher. After noting that one series may be part of another and that in such cases it is necessary to choose that which is simplest and which best accommodates the data, he goes on to describe this as being the doctrine of discovery or hypothesis, "of which no-one up to now has dealt with accurately".[40] For at least part of this doctrine, namely that concerning the construction or solving of ciphers, however, Leibniz makes clear that he already has someone in mind for the job: "I should like this to be accurately dealt with by Wallis", he writes.[41]

Not surprisingly, the criteria which Leibniz gives for choosing the most suitable law of construction in mathematics are precisely those to which he appeals in the physical sciences, when confronted by competing hypotheses. On his view the procedures involved are largely identical. Indeed, he often describes the search for hypotheses to explain phenomena in terms of deciphering the secrets of nature.[42] We start out from a certain set of data and conjecture laws or causes from which in a second demonstrative stage the original data can be deduced. Such a method of hypothesis, Leibniz writes, is "like the key to a cryptograph, as it is the more probable the simpler it is and the more that can be explained by its means".[43] Just as it is easier to solve a cryptograph if many letters of hidden sense are written in the same key[44], so too is it easier to investigate the cause of a natural phenomenon common to many things.[45] Nevertheless, on occasion Leibniz admits that there are significant differences. Thus, whereas a physical hypothesis can achieve no more than moral certainty – it is in effect a fiction which suffices for everyday use – it is possible with a cryptograph containing sufficient data to reach solutions for which demonstrative truth can be claimed.[46] However, even this he relativizes in a letter to Hermann Conring (1606–1681), where he suggests that a hypothesis can be considered physically certain when it satisfies absolutely all phenomena that occur, just as a key in cryptography should do.[47]

As has already been mentioned, an essential part of the comparison which Leibniz draws in this respect is to be found in the role of tables, whose significance for combinatorics in general cannot be stressed too highly.[48] Just as he sees the tabular arrangement of data as having an important function in empirical investigations such as those carried out in the field of astronomy or in the study of winds and tides,[49] so too in the case of combinatorial mathematics. The fundamental idea is that we are able to construct tabular arrays on the basis of known magnitudes or values and that we are then able to guess hitherto unknown values within them.[50] Leibniz refers in this context to the information which he and his contemporaries obtained through observing Jan Hudde's (1628–1704) mortality tables and which he especially used for his important work on the mathematics of insurance.[51]

Despite repeated criticism[52] of Wallis's employment of interpolation in mathematics, he was aware that in cryptography this approach constituted the successful use of the Savilian professor's natural mathematical intuition.[53] Similarly, outside the immediate sphere of mathematics Leibniz was able to put a positive line on induction whose use by Wallis in the context of analysis, for example in guessing the continuation of arithmetic series, he also rejected[54] as being less than rigorous. As numerous comments by Leibniz on the importance of the inductive method make clear, he saw in this a central aspect of human inventiveness.[55]

3. PUBLISHING THE ART OF DECIPHERING: *LEIBNIZ'S REQUESTS AND WALLIS'S RESPONSE*

If Leibniz already in Paris had expressed the wish that Wallis provide an accurate account of the art of deciphering, he did not direct this wish personally to the Savilian professor until their correspondence began in December 1695. Nevertheless, in numerous letters beforehand to possible intermediaries such as Henri Justel[56] (1620–1693) or mutual friends such as Thomas Smith (1638–1710),[57] Leibniz sought to convey his desire that Wallis be forthcoming on the methods he employed. He also used the opportunity of his anonymous review of Wallis's *Treatise of Algebra* (1685) for the *Acta eruditorum* in June 1686 for this purpose. Towards the end of the review, Leibniz points out that much in the book had an affinity to the deciphering of cryptograms, and that the precepts of this art which had previously been supplied were very imperfect.[58] Referring to Jacques Auguste de Thou's (1553–1617) testimony to François Viète's (1540–1603) skill as a decipherer, Leibniz suggests that Wallis would equal or even surpass the praises poured on the French mathematician if he were to provide posterity with a specimen of his own accomplishments.[59] It would seem that Leibniz at this time was still basing much of his knowledge in this respect on what Hobbes had written in the *Examinatio et emendatio mathematicae hodiernae* (1660).[60] There, the English philosopher, clearly aware of the rivalry which existed between Wallis and certain French mathematicians, had mentioned Thou's testimony alongside remarks on the collection of letters which Wallis had deciphered during the Civil Wars and later deposited in the Savilian Library in Oxford,[61] knowing full well also that Wallis was suspected of having deciphered King Charles's (1600–1649) cabinet captured at the battle of Naseby.[62]

But by the 1690s Leibniz would have been aware that the Savilian professor had in the meantime deciphered literally hundreds of sheets of cipher for the Elector of Brandenburg. These were communications between Louis XIV (1638–1715) and his ambassador in Poland and concerned political undertakings directly threatening the existence of Prussia. Although the German states naturally had their own black chambers with skilled decipherers,[63] it is a reflection both of England's newly-achieved standing within the Protestant alliance and Wallis's reputation as a decipherer that the intercepted letters went to government officials in London who then forwarded them to Wallis in Oxford. In the light of what he felt to be insufficient recompense for his efforts – he eventually received a gold medal and chain from Berlin,[64] Wallis was able to point out to one of the officials concerned, William Harbord (1635–1692), in August 1691 that the deciphering of some of the letters had "quite broke all the French King's measures in Poland for that time; and caused his Ambassadors to be thence thrust out in disgrace".[65]

Soon after Leibniz began his correspondence with Wallis, he used the exchange of letters to impress upon the Savilian professor the need that he publish something of the art of "divining that which is secretly written",[66] even going as far as to quote the words of the anonymous reviewer of the *Treatise of Algebra* in the *Acta eruditorum*, who as we have mentioned was none other than Leibniz himself. Wallis, who was clearly disinclined to give away any secrets as far as his own methods were concerned, was quick to reply that the art of deciphering could not be reduced to certain rules "on account of the infinite variety of ways in which ciphers can be applied" and because of their difficulty "which is already great and grows from day to day".[67] Admittedly, he does make a general comment on his approach, but this does not go beyond the obvious: the need to start with conjectures and then to proceed "according as they are perceived to succeed or not to succeed" and correspondingly either to continue with or change the conjectures made "until something of reliable meaning is established".

Wallis goes on in his reply to mention[68] that he had sent an example of a cipher with its solution to the editor of the *Acta eruditorum*,[69] evidently hoping in this way to bring the discussion on the matter to an end [Figures 1 and 2]. However, Otto Mencke (1644–1707) was less than enthusiastic at the sight of the package he received from Oxford, containing as it did over two folio pages of nomenclator, the deciphered letter itself (two pages), the intermediate stage with nomenclator and part solution entered between the lines (over three pages), and finally the key, written in the form of a table (one page).[70] Quite apart from the problem of finding someone to print the material, Mencke pointed out in a letter to Leibniz the danger of compromising the primate of Poland. But perhaps more pertinently, he was unable to discern any use in what Wallis had sent, suggesting that if it had any, it would surely have been printed beforehand in the *Philosophical Transactions*.[71] In fact, the cipher and its solution did finally appear in print: Wallis published the whole content of his package to Mencke together with immeasurably more valuable correspondence in the third volume of his monumental *Opera mathematica* (1693–1699).[72]

Leibniz, who had no option but to accept Wallis's claim that there were no general precepts to deciphering,[73] clearly felt that the Englishman could have been more forthcoming and not only sent Mencke the solution to a numerical cipher but also the means he had employed, believing that it would not have been possible from a single encoded letter of such complexity to find its key.[74] In fact, for Wallis it was. Since Leibniz recognised that it was no coincidence that minds that excel in algebra, "the pinnacle of calculus"[75] also excel in deciphering,[76] and was thus convinced that Wallis would in this respect be able to make a considerable contribution to human knowledge, he now pursued another line of approach and

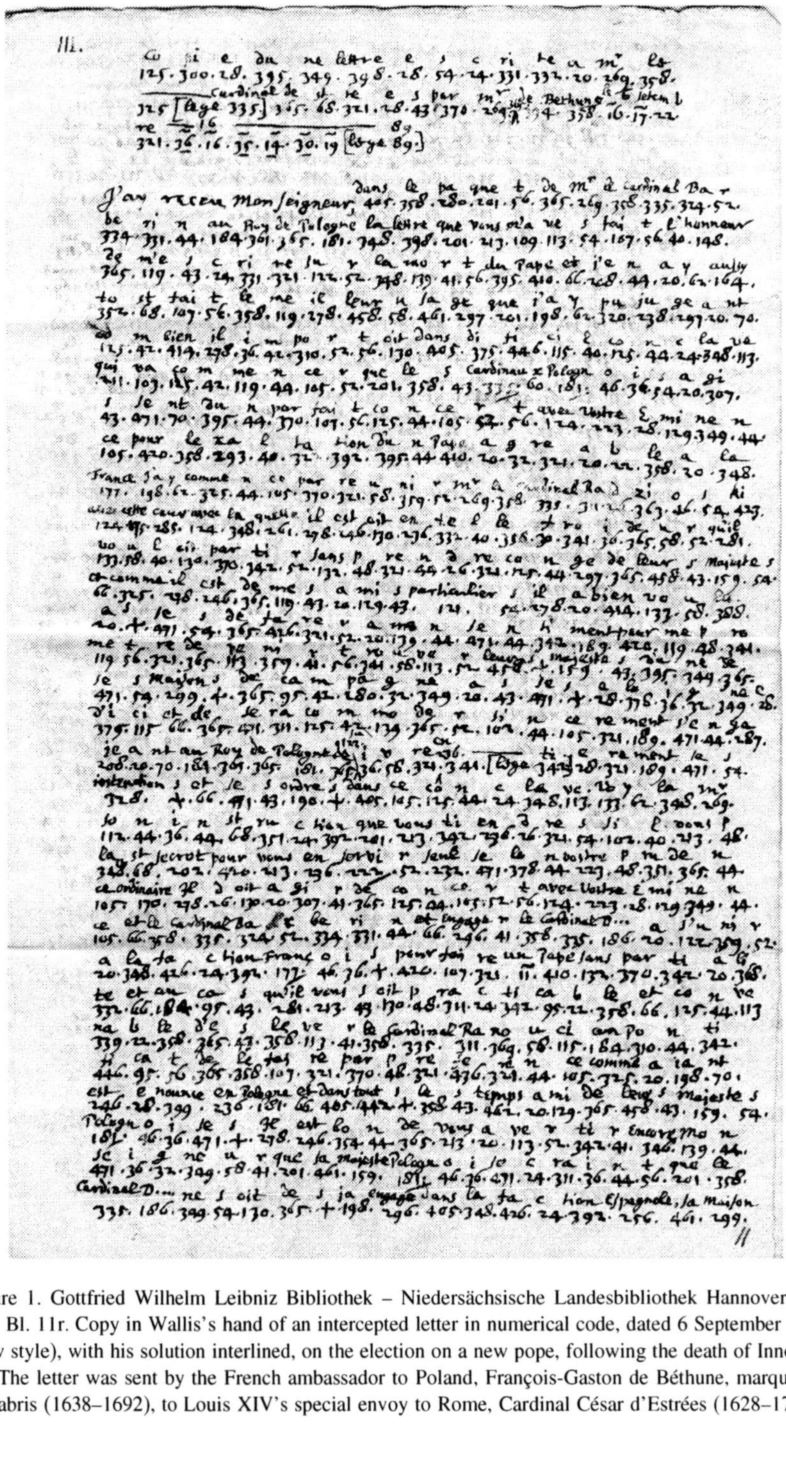

Figure 1. Gottfried Wilhelm Leibniz Bibliothek – Niedersächsische Landesbibliothek Hannover LBr 974, Bl. 11r. Copy in Wallis's hand of an intercepted letter in numerical code, dated 6 September 1689 (new style), with his solution interlined, on the election on a new pope, following the death of Innocent XI. The letter was sent by the French ambassador to Poland, François-Gaston de Béthune, marquis de Chabris (1638–1692), to Louis XIV's special envoy to Rome, Cardinal César d'Estrées (1628–1714)

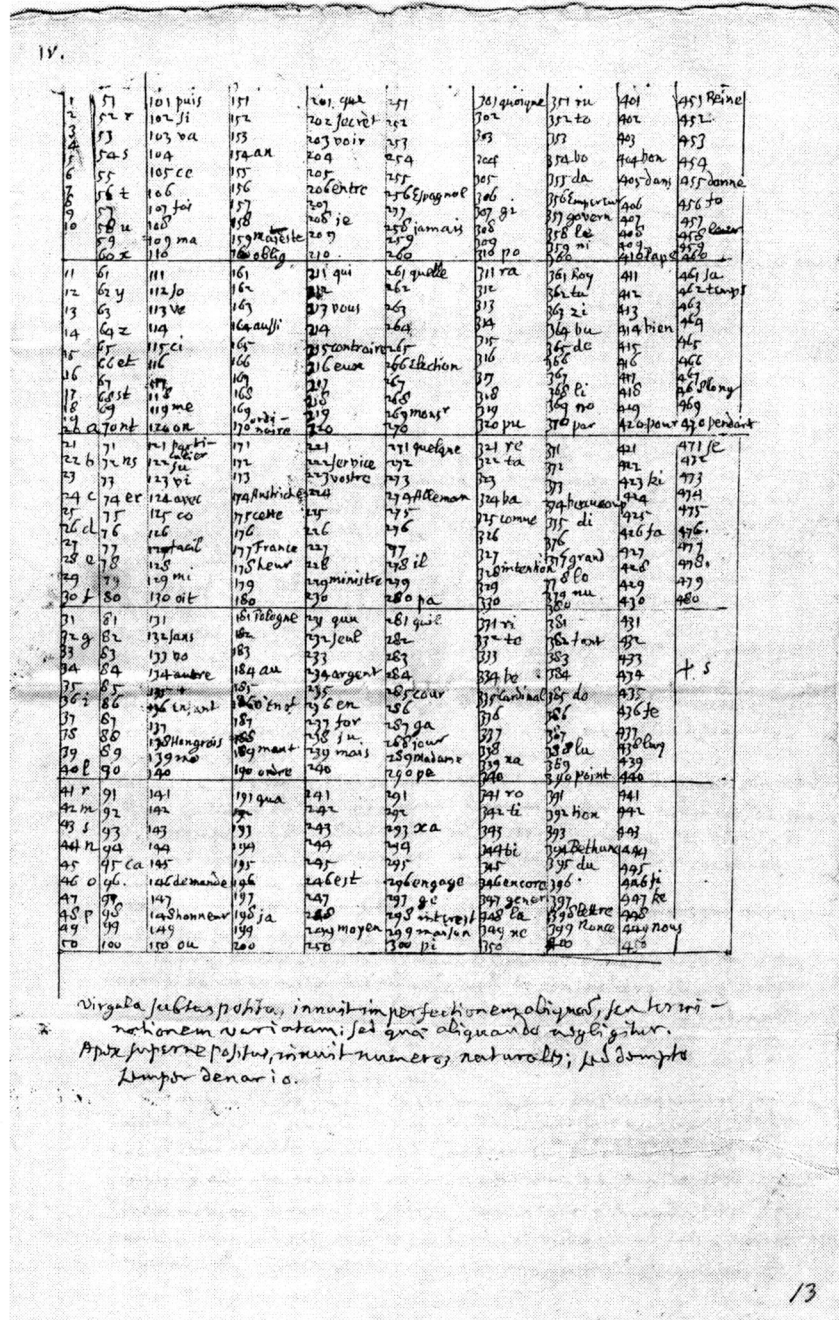

Figure 2. Gottfried Wilhelm Leibniz Bibliothek – Niedersächsische Landesbibliothek Hannover LBr 974, Bl. 13r. Wallis's key to the previous letter

sought to persuade him to outline the computational foundation to his art. In this context he refers explicitly to the importance of this information for furthering the *ars inveniendi*:

I acknowledge that the *Ars cryptolytica* cannot be reduced to certain methods, and, if it were capable of this, would be less ingenious than it is; and for this reason I wish perhaps that the theory be set out, and so to speak the calculus of the problem explained. Nor do I judge this to be of value in itself, but rather on account of our being able from this source to promote the art of invention.[77]

4. LEIBNIZ'S FINAL INITIATIVES TOWARDS WALLIS

It might in many ways seem hard to understand why a philosopher and mathematician of Leibniz's ability should have been so apparently dependent on receiving help from another on so important a topic. Part of the answer to this might be that he lacked the practical experience of regular deciphering, as he suggested on one occasion in a letter to Franz Ernst von Platen (?–1709),[78] or simply a lack of time. Then, asked by Eusebius in the Introductory Dialogue on Arithmetic and Algebra why he himself, or another under his direction, should not begin to undertake such a pleasant and useful task, Charinus, alias Leibniz, replies: "You know, Eusebius, how much I do and perhaps, even if it be possible for one person to perform everything, when many people join their plans together perhaps something even greater can be carried out".[79]

But it is not inconceivable that it also reflects his recognition that his own work on the topic lacked any real insight [Figure 3]. The precepts of the art of deciphering which he wrote sometime between 1682 and 1688 and therefore possibly before he published the review of the *Treatise of Algebra*, move solely in the sphere of mono and polyalphabetic ciphers, and contain nothing which could not have been gathered from countless publications on deciphering which had appeared since the Renaissance from authors such as Porta (1540–1615), Trithemius (1462–1516), Selenus (1579–1666), Kircher, Schwenter (1585–1636), and Harsdoerffer (1607–1658).[80]

Although Leibniz already in his youth spoke of the construction of an arithmetical machine[81] for encoding and deciphering official letters, and clearly throughout his life held an interest in the topic, this interest was by no means uncritical. Thus, when his correspondent Johann Sebastian Haes, an associate of Papin, repeatedly outlines his plans[82] for a tract on steganography, which would evidently be in much the same mould as so many others, Leibniz's response is decidedly reserved. In fact, rather disregarding the ambitions of the author, Leibniz remarks to Haes on one occasion how he would like to see someone suitable provide an account of the art of ciphers, thereby quoting the examples of Viète and Wallis.[83] This was precisely the point. Previous contributions to the topic had, in Leibniz's words, been very imperfect. As an accomplished mathematician and logician who could also boast skills in linguistics and deciphering, Wallis promised so much more.[84] "With what is the whole art of secret writing concerned, if not with formulae and combinations?"[85] asks Charinus in the Introductory Dialogue on Arithmetic and Algebra. And just as Leibniz abhorred the empty words of dilettantes on questions

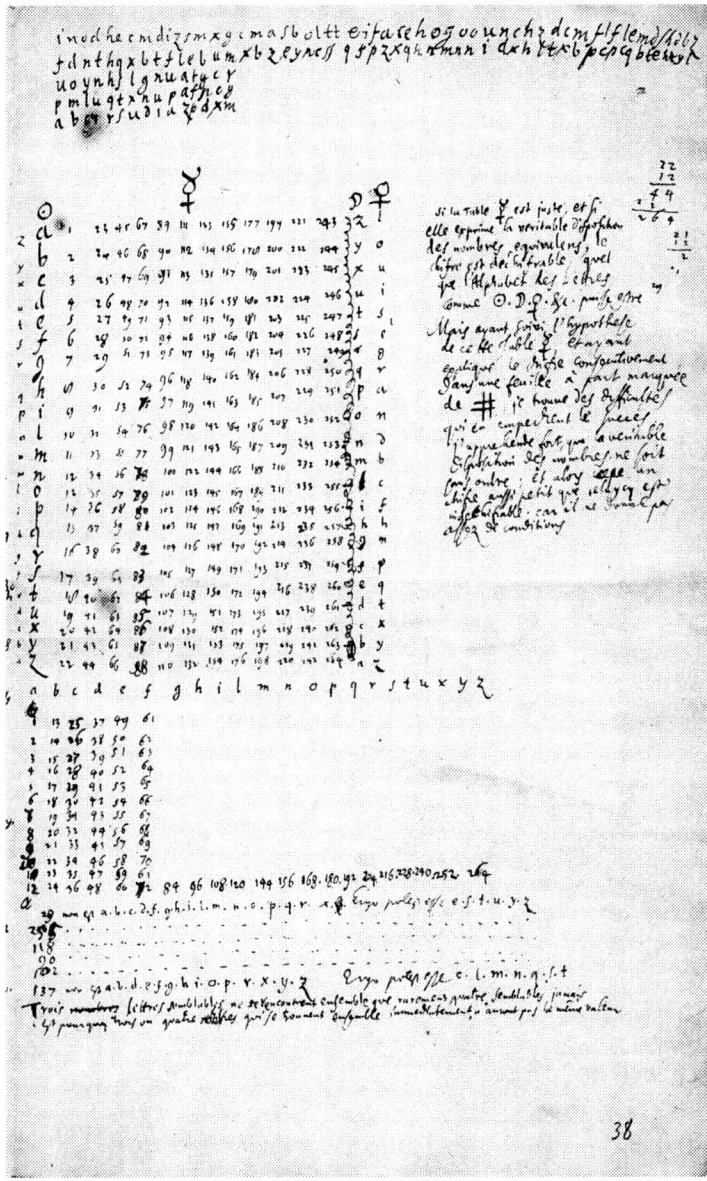

Figure 3. Gottfried Wilhelm Leibniz Bibliothek – Niedersächsische Landesbibliothek Hannover LH V, VI, 4, Bl. 38r. Deliberations, by Leibniz, on decipherable and non-decipherable ciphers. On the right-hand side of the page he has written: "If the table ♀ is correct, and if it expresses the true disposition of the equivalent numbers, the cipher is decipherable whatever alphabet taken is taken for ☉. ☽. ♀. etc. But having followed the hypothesis of the table ♀ and having explained the cipher consecutively on a separate page marked #, I find difficulties which prevent success in this. Moreover, I fear that the true disposition of numbers be without order. And thus that a cipher as small as this one is not decipherable, because it does not supply enough conditions."

in jurisprudence, geometry, and the Cabbala, extolling in his later years the praises of acroamatic knowledge,[86] so too he rejected popular writings on deciphering. "The *ars deciphrandi*", he writes to Johann Bernoulli (1667–1748) in March 1697, "deserves to be dealt with by a mathematician."[87]

In the face of Wallis's denial of the existence of precepts to deciphering and his failure to respond to Leibniz's exhortation to contribute to the promotion of *ars inveniendi*, Leibniz's focus of action finally switched to the possibility of the Savilian professor training suitable young men in the art he mastered so well. In fact, Leibniz brought up this possibility in one of his earliest letters[88] to Wallis, who in his reply certainly did not appear to rule it out, noting only that "the matter means so much work that there is scarcely anyone who would wish to learn it".[89]

Encouraged by this response, Leibniz repeated his suggestion that "certain shrewd and studious young men" be sent to Wallis "to be guided through the steps" of his discoveries.[90] This would, he writes, enable such an important art to be propagated, adding that the work would be undertaken discretely "for a generous prince." Not unwisely, he sought at the same time to prepare the ground for this project financially. The first opportunity for this presented itself in the course of his correspondence with crown prince Ferdinand of Tuscany (1663–1713), where he sought to build on the latter's interest in acquiring knowledge on the art of memory.[91] As this had yet to produce a satisfactory result and feeling the pressure of time in view of Wallis's age,[92] Leibniz turned to his home country. On 24 February 1699, he set out his detailed proposal in a letter[93] to Paul Fuchs (1640–1704), minister of state to the Elector of Brandenburg, and just three weeks later on 17 March he addressed the conference of the house of Brunswick-Lüneburg on the same topic:

> It will be well known that the most famous decipherer now living in Europe, is to be found in England. He is a first-rate mathematician and stands with me in correspondence. Since he is now a man of eighty years and it is to be feared that the great things he has achieved in this art will be lost with him, I have remonstrated with him for the public good on many occasions that he finally be prepared to instruct in this one or other young man who may be found here and who is blessed with similar inclination to calculation and effort.[94]

Recounting the progress of his discussions with the Savilian professor, Leibniz goes on to claim that Wallis had approved of his proposal. But, as with Florence and Berlin, all this was apparently to no avail, thus explaining the approach he made to Stockholm later in the year.

In fact, Leibniz's claim did not quite represent the truth. Wallis, whose career had been set in motion by his cryptographical skills and who had succeeded in finding in his grandson, William Blencowe (1683–1712),[95] a suitable successor, was far from willing to make knowledge of his methods available to others. In his letter to Leibniz of 8 April 1700, he makes clear that both political considerations and the nature of cryptography itself preclude the wide dissemination of techniques. "It could," he writes, "be of great inconvenience both to us and to our friends – no less than to our enemies – if the art of disclosing secret writings becomes indiscriminately known."[96] Here, finally, was the crux of the problem. Not for the first time, Leibniz's insatiable appetite for knowledge in order to promote the public good through the advancement of science was thwarted by the demands of politics. But it was thwarted also by the very nature of the knowledge he sought to acquire. As Wallis makes clear, allowing his methods to become widely known would effectively endanger the very institution of secret diplomatic communication. But equally if not more important was a consideration which he for understandable reasons fails to mention: that from a personal point of view the value of his skills lay precisely in the fact that he alone possessed them. As such they had not only played a decisive role in his being able to maintain his posts as Savilian professor of geometry and Keeper of the Archives of the University of Oxford during the turbulent period of the Restoration, but also represented a secure source of income for the future. Wallis therefore had every reason to ensure that the art of deciphering remained in the family, just as was the case with his counterpart in France, the cryptologist Antoine Rossignol (1600–1682).

Wallis would no doubt have been flattered by Leibniz's repeated attempts to find out more about his methods of deciphering. But the Savilian professor sought to turn the very fact that these requests had come from abroad to his own personal advantage, by suggesting that his willingness to reject such approaches should be traded against what on his view was long outstanding: proper compensation for his services. This becomes clear at a time when the question of financial or other reward was once more up for discussion. In an opportune letter to the Archbishop of Canterbury, Wallis let it be known that "he hath been sollicited more than once, by Letters from Myn Heer Leibnitz, on behalf of the Elector of Hannover; who is willing to send some persons hither, whom he is very desirous the Doctor would instruct in this Art".[97] Diplomatically avoiding any suggestion of disloyalty, he indicated that while he was willing to help the Elector, he did not feel it would be proper to make the art public without his majesty's permission. Although Wallis was himself evidently concerned that his skills might die with him, he felt that not allowing knowledge of his techniques to go abroad was "preferable to any personal advantage which he may receive from a forraign Prince". The true meaning of his remarks was nevertheless clearly understood by those in power: the following year Wallis was awarded a yearly pension of one hundred pounds by the King.

Leibniz, too, played the diplomatic card, though with less success. In his efforts to gain support for his plan to send suitable young men to England to be instructed in the art of deciphering, he emphasized in particular the political significance of Wallis's skills. But his own genuine interest was not so much of a political as of a philosophical nature. As we have seen, Leibniz promised himself greater insight into his projected *ars inveniendi* through the analytical methods applied by Wallis to the encrypted letters he sought to explain. But in the absence of the hoped for information from his English friend, much for him necessarily remained a mystery. And we are no better off: like Leibniz, we can now only surmise on the significance of what the Savilian professor might have had to say. Wallis's secret art was, in effect, destined to remain a family secret.

NOTES

[1] For biographical accounts of Wallis see Scott, J. F. 1938, Scott, J. F. 1960 and Scriba 1966.

[2] The best account of Leibniz's relation to Wallis, although focussed almost exclusively on mathematical topics, is still Hofmann 1973.

[3] There are numerous other references to Leibniz's friendship with Wallis. See for example Smith to Leibniz, 13/23 December 1694 (A I x, 654); Smith to Leibniz, 23 September / 3 October 1696 (A I xiii, 281); Leibniz to crown prince Ferdinand of Tuscany, 20/30 September 1699 (A I xvii, 527).

[4] At the meeting of the Royal Society on 2/12 April 1671 Boyle, Hooke, Pell, and Wren were requested to examine the *Hypothesis physica nova*. However, only Hooke, Pell, and Wallis are actually recorded as having done this. It would thus appear that either Boyle or Wren simply passed the work on to Wallis for consideration. See Birch 1756–57, II, 173.

[5] Wallis to Oldenburg, 7/17 April 1671 (HH VII, 559–62/562–4).

[6] [J. Wallis], *Dr. Wallis's Opinion Concerning the Hypothesis physica nova of Dr. Leibnitius*, in: *Philosophical Transactions*. No. 74 (14 August 1671), 2227–31. In addition, Oldenburg also sent Wallis relevant extracts of Wallis's letters in Oldenburg to Leibniz, 12/22 June 1671 (HH VIII, 99–103/103–4). Leibniz's delight at Wallis's judgment can be recognised from his remarks in Leibniz to Oldenburg, 15/25 October 1671 (A II i, 166) and Leibniz to Fogel, 5/15 October 1671 (A II i, 154).

[7] Wallis to Oldenburg, 2/12 June 1671 (HH VIII, 72–3/73–4).

[8] See Hill 1965: 106; Webster 1975: 501–2.

[9] For a more detailed account of Oldenburg's support for Leibniz see Beeley 2004.

[10] Leibniz to Oldenburg, 13/23 July 1670 (HH VII, 64–6/66–7).

[11] Leibniz's treatise was reprinted by John Martyn, the printer to the Royal Society under the title *Hypothesis physica nova, sive Theoria motus concreti, una cum Theoria motus abstracti*, London 1671. See also Oldenburg's advertisement of the reprinting in *Philosophical Transactions* No. 73 (17 July 1671), 2213–4.

[12] Birch 1756–57, III, 82. Oldenburg informed Leibniz of the decision in his letter of 10/20 April 1673 (HH IX, 582/583).

[13] Oldenburg to Leibniz, 10/20 April 1673 (HH IX, 582/583).

[14] Leibniz to Oldenburg, 18/28 September 1670 (HH VII, 166/170).

[15] Leibniz to Oldenburg, 29 April / 9 June 1671 (HH VIII, 25/29).

[16] Leibniz to Oldenburg, 16/26 April 1673 (HH IX, 594/598).

[17] HH IX, 596/600.

[18] This emerges from Leibniz to Oldenburg, 26 February / 8 March 1672/73 (HH IX, 491/495). The request had in fact originated from Pierre-Daniel Huet. The Savilian professor sent the results of his investigations to Oldenburg; they eventually reached Huet after first being forwarded to Leibniz. See Huet's letter to Oldenburg of 26 March / 5 April 1673 (HH IX, 538/539).

[19] In a postscript to his letter to Oldenburg of 18/28 November 1676 (A III v, 11), Leibniz asks the Secretary of the Royal Society to inform him of the existence of Apollonius manuscripts in England and suggests that he employ the assistance of Wallis in Oxford.

[20] See Leibniz to Wallis, 18/28 May 1697 (GM IV, 29), and Wallis to Leibniz, 30 July / 9 August 1697 (GM IV, 39). See also Wallis to Leibniz, February–April 1699 (LBr 974, Bl. 37a).

[21] Leibniz, *Theoria motus abstracti*, preface (A VI ii, 262).

[22] On the topic of the disputes between Hobbes and Wallis see Jesseph 1999 and Probst 1997.

[23] The evidence suggests that his intensive study of the *Arithmetica infinitorum* began in mid-1674. See Eberhard Knobloch's and Siegmund Probst's introductory remarks to A VII iii, xx–xxi.

[24] For example, in manuscript notes on Wallis's *Mechanica*, Leibniz remarks "Effectus sunt causis suis adaequatis proportionales. Hanc propositionem ait transitum aperire a mathematica ad physicam". See Niedersächsische Landesbibliothek, LH 35 XIV 2, Bl. 117r.

[25] See Duchesneau 1994: 100–1; Fichant 1978: 229.

[26] Leibniz, *De la chainette* (GM V, 259). See also *De arithmetica infinitorum perficienda* (A VI iii, 408).

[27] See Whiteside 1960–62 and Prag 1931.

[28] Leibniz, *De progressionibus et de arithmetica infinitorum* (A VII iii, 102): "Arithmetica infinitorum mea est pura, Wallisii figurata." See also Leibniz to Laloubère, 5/15 October 1691 (A I vii, 400).

[29] See Leibniz 1686: esp. 289.

[30] See Leibniz, *De arte combinatoria scribenda* (A VI iv, 426): "Characteristica vera et tabulis et analysi auxiliatur. De Tabulis ita condendis ex cognitis, ut ex interpretatione vel continuatione seriei divinentur incognita"; *De arte inveniendi in genere* (A VI iv, 81); *De arte characteristica inventoriaque analytica combinatoriave in mathesi universali* (A VI iv, 324). See also Leibniz to Foucher, January 1692 (GP I, 404). "C'est que j'avois un projet de certaines Tables Analytiques ou de Specieuse fondées sur les combinaisons, lesquelles si estoient faites, seroient d'un secours merveilleux en Analyse, en Geometrie et en toutes les Mathematiques, et pousseroient l'Analyse à une grande perfection"; Leibniz to Duke Johann Friedrich, 16/26 March 1673 (A I i, 488): "Zu geschweigen wie allerhand Tabulae in obgedachten Scientien, einmahl vor allemahl zu erleichterung Menschlicher arbeit."

[31] See Leibniz to Duke Johann Friedrich, February (?) 1679 (A I ii, 124): "et pour la geometrie j'avois trouvé le premier le secret des tables des sinus, et supplée ce defaut de geometrie practique, en sorte qu'on peut maintenant resoudre aisément les problemes de trigonometrie par regle sans avoir les livres et Tables"; *De republica literaria* (A VI iv, 438); *Elementa nova matheseos universalis* (A VI iv, 523); Leibniz to Arnauld, beginning of November 1671 (A II i, 180). See also Leibniz to Huet, 1/11 August 1679 (A II i, 482), where he refers to his *De quadratura arithmetica circuli ellipseso et hyperbolae cujus corollarium est trigonometria sine tabulis*. The first complete edition of this text is Knobloch ed. 1993.

[32] Leibniz, *Aufzeichnung für die Audienz bei Kaiser Leopold I* (A IV iv, 26): "[...] bis ich profundissima Analyseos Speciosae Mathematicorum arcana nicht nur begriffen sondern auch höher getrieben, denn darinn stecket der rechte usus characterum et artis inveniendi [,] ich halte dieß inventum vor das allerhochste so in Scientiis humanis pro tempore geschehen kan."

[33] Leibniz, *De modis combinandi characters* (A VI iv, 922): "Omnis ratiocinatio nostra nihil aliud est quam characterum connexio, et substitutio. Sive illi characteres sint verba, sive notae, sive denique imagines."

[34] Leibniz, *De synthesi et analysi universali seu arte inveniendi et judicandi* (A VI iv, 545): "Caeteroqui Ars Combinatoria speciatim mihi illa est scientia (quae etiam generaliter characteristica, sive speciosa dici posset), in qua tractatur de rerum formis sive formulis in universum, hoc est de qualitate in genere sive de simili et dissimili, prout aliae atque aliae formulae ex ipsis *a*, *b*, *c* etc. (sive quantitates sive aliud quoddam repraesentent) inter se combinatis oriuntur, et distinguitur ab Algebra quae agit de formulis ad quantitatem applicatis, sive de aequali et inaequali, itaque Algebra subordinatur Combinatoriae, ejusque regulis continue utitur, quae tamen longe generaliores sunt, nec in Algebra tantum, sed et in arte deciphratoria, in variis ludorum generibus, in ipsa geometria lineariter ad veterum morem tractata, denique in omnibus ubi similitudinis ratio habetur locum habent." See also Leibniz to Tschirnhaus, end of May/beginning of June 1678 (A III ii, 449–50); *De ortu, progressu et natura algebrae, nonnullisque aliorum et propriis circa eam inventis* (GM VII, 206); Knobloch 1973: 57.

[35] See Knobloch 1973: 56–7.

[36] Leibniz, *Aufzeichnung für die Audienz bei Kaiser Leopold I* (A IV iv, 26): "Das groste so ich vorhabe ist perfectio Artis inveniendi so in Analysi et Arte Combinatoria bestehet."

[37] Leibniz, *Consilium de encyclopaedia nova conscribenda methodo inventoria* (A VI iv, 345): "Quarta est Topica seu ars inveniendi, id est ars dirigendi cogitationes ad aliquam veritatem ignotam eruendam, vel media finis cujusdam reperienda."

[38] Leibniz, *De arte inveniendi in genere* (A VI iv, 80).

[39] On occasion, Leibniz likens algebra and deciphering to the mental finesse involved in a game of chess. See for example *Zu Prestets Elemens des mathematiques* (A VII ii, 806); *Elementa nova matheseos universalis* (A VI iv, 513); *De synthesi et analysi universali seu de arte inveniendi et judicandi* (A VI iv, 545).

[40] Leibniz, *De methodi quadraturarum usu in seriebus* (A VII iii, 253): "Potest autem eadem series data esse pars aliarum diversarum, ex his eligenda est simplicissima aut rebus praesentibus accommodatissima, quod aliunde dignosci potest. Posse esse differentium partes, sic probo: Quia si v.g. unus adhuc terminus adderetur nullae ad alios terminos relationis, opus foret ad altiorem forte ire aequationem regulae seriei

reperiendae causa. Est haec ipsissima doctrina divinandi seu de hypothesibus, quam nemo accurate tractavit."

[41] Ibid.: "Huius pars est doctrina de chiffris construendis solvendisque, quem vellem a Wallisio accurate tradi."

[42] See for example Leibniz's preliminary study for his letter to von Hessen-Rheinfels, 28 November / 8 December 1686 (GP II, 70); Leibniz to Basnage, after 2/12 September 1695, GP III, 121; Leibniz to Burnett, 11/21 June 1695 (GP III, 161).

[43] Leibniz, *Praefatio ad libellum elementorum physicae* (A VI iv, 1999): "Methodus conjecturalis a priori procedit per Hypotheses, assumendo quasdam causas licet sine ulla probatione, atque ostendendo quod ex illis positis ea quae nunc contingunt, sint eventura. Talis hypothesis est instar clavis cryptographicae, et eo magis est probablilis, quo est simplicior et quo plura per ipsam possunt explicari." See also *Nouveaux essais* IV, 12, §13 (A VI vi, 454–55): "[Theophilus] L'Art de decouvrir les causes des phenomenes, ou les hypotheses veritables, est comme l'Art de dechiffrer, où souvent une conjecture ingenieuse abrege beaucoup de chemin"; Leibniz to Conring, 19/29 March 1678 (A II i, 399).

[44] Leibniz, *Praefatio ad libellum elementorum physicae* (A VI iv, 2001): "[…] semper enim facilius est causam investigare phaenomeni quod pluribus commune est; perinde ac facilius est cryptographemata solvere, si plures literas occultato sensu secundum eandem clavem scriptas, nanciscamur." See also *Introductio ad scientiam generalem modum inveniendi demonstrandique docentem* (A VI iv, 371–2); *De arte combinatoria scribenda* (A VI iv, 425).

[45] Sometimes Leibniz makes a direct comparison between the formation of hypotheses and the explication of a cryptograph. See for example *Schediasma de arte inveniendi theoremata* (A VI iii, 426): "Ars faciendi Hypotheses, sive Ars conjectandi diversi generis est, huc pertinet ars explicandi Cryptographemata, quae pro maximo haberi debet specimine artis conjecturandi purae et a materia abstractae, unde regulae duci possunt quas postea etiam materiae applicare liceat."

[46] Leibniz, *Praefatio ad libellum elementorum physicae* (A VI iv, 1999): "Quanquam non negem tantum esse posse numerum phaenomenorum quae per hypothesin aliquam feliciter explicantur, ut pro moraliter certa haberi queat." See also *Praecepta Artis Deciphratoriae* (A VI iv, 1203): "Deciphrare est Epistolam ignotae significationis characteribus scriptam explicare. Haec semper possumus, quando est aliquod significationis Alphabetum, et sufficientia sunt data"; *Introductio ad scientia generalem modum inveniendi demonstrandique docentem* (A VI iv, 371–2); *De arte combinatoria scribenda* (A VI iv, 425).

[47] Leibniz to Conring, 19/29 March 1678 (A II i, 399): "Et contingere potest ut hypothesis aliqua haberi possit pro physice certa; quando scilicet omnibus omnino phaenomenis occurrentibus satisfacit, quemadmodum Clavis in Cryptographicis."

[48] See *De arte inveniendi in genere* (A VI iv, 80–1).

[49] Leibniz, *Schediasma de arte inveniendi theoremata* (A VI iii, 426).

[50] *De arte combinatoria scribenda* (A VI iv, 424): "De arte observandi aliquid curiosum ex oblatis Tabulis."

[51] Leibniz, *Loss- und Leibrenten* (A IV iii, 433); *De reditibus ad vitam* (A IV iii, 440); *De arte combinatoria scribenda* (A VI iv, 423–4, 425).

[52] See for example Leibniz, *De geometria recondita*, GM V, 231; Leibniz to Wallis, 28 September / 8 October 1697 (GM IV, 41).

[53] See Leibniz 1686: 289.

[54] See for example Leibniz 1696: 252.

[55] See for example Leibniz, *De Synthesi et analysi universali seu arte inveniendi et judicandi* (A VI iv, 544); Knobloch 1973: 58.

[56] Leibniz to Justel 10/20 October 1690 (A I vi, 267). See also Leibniz to Justel for Halley 24 May / 3 June 1692 (A III v, 314).

[57] Leibniz to Smith, 6/16 October 1696 (A I xiii, 300). See also Leibniz to Burnett, 14–18/24–28 April (?) 1695 (A I xi, 432); Leibniz to Burnett, 1/11 February 1697 (A I xiii, 551).

[58] Leibniz 1686: 289: "Caeterum cum celeberrimus Autor (quemadmodum intelleximus) excellat in solvendis, sive, ut vulgo loquuntur, deciphrandis Cryptographematibus, eaque scientia magnam cum illis, quae in hoc opere traduntur, affinitatem habeat, orandus magnopere est, ut praecepta ejus tradat, praesertim cum ea, quae hactenus prostant, valde sunt imperfecta. Ita in hoc quoque genere Vietae laudes

aequabit, imo vincet, si duraturo ad posteritatem specimine ostendat, quod illum fecisse soli Thuani testimonio credere cogimur. Sed nunc promissam paulo ante meditationem subjiciemus."
[59]   Ibid. See also Leibniz for Burnett, 14–18/24–28 April (?) 1695 (A I xi, 432): "Je souhaitte qu'on puisse porter M. Wallis, à publier quelque chose de ses pensees cryptographiques. Car on sçait qui'il y excelle. Mons. de Thou dans son Histoire loue le celebre Viete, pour avoir reussi merveilleusement aux dechifremens. Mons. Wallis ayant egalé la gloire de Viete dans les Mathematiques pourroit l'egaler ou meme sur passer encor en cela."
[60]   See T. Hobbes, *Examinatio et emendatio mathematicae hodiernae*, London 1660: 36 (WML IV, 55). See also *Dialogus physicus de natura aeris*, London 1661: 35 (WML IV, 290).
[61]   The transcript, which Wallis deposited in 1653, is now Bodleian Library, MS e. Mus. 203. A further autograph copy, now also in the Bodleian, is MS Eng. misc. e. 475.
[62]   See *The King's Cabinet Opened: or certain pacquets of secret letters and papers. Written with the King's own hand, and taken in his cabinet at Nasby Field, June 14, 1645, by victorious Sir Thomas Fairfax* […], London 1645. Reprinted in *The Harleian Miscellany* 7 (1811), 544–76, 544 (note). See Smith, D. E. 1917.
[63]   See for example the account of diplomacy and secret service in the state of Brunswick-Lüneburg in Schnath 1938–82: II, 348–58; Strasser 1988: 249–50.
[64]   This present from the Elector of Brandenburg was promised him towards the end of 1690. However, on its arrival in England the medal and chain was found to be of inferior quality and was sent back. Wallis evidently later received a replacement. See Pawling to Wallis, 31 March / 10 April 1692, British Library, Add. Ms. 32499, f. 308r.
[65]   Wallis to Harbord, 15/25 August 1691, British Library Add. Ms. 32499, f. 283r–283v, 283r. See also Wallis to Pawling, 21/31 December 1691, British Library Add. Ms. 32499, f. 302r.
[66]   Leibniz to Wallis, 19/29 March 1697 (GM IV, 14): "[…] ut de Arte Divinandi occulte scripta."
[67]   Wallis to Leibniz, 6/16 April 1697 (GM IV, 18–9): "Quod memoras de Arte divinandi Occulte Scripta, est ea res non certis regulis coercenda propter infinitam varietatem Ciphras ponendi (et quarum difficultas, jam satis ardua, quotidie crescit) quae a conjecturis principio positis inchoanda est, quae prout succedere vel non succedere deprehenduntur, vel prosequendae sunt vel mutandae, donec quid certi constat."
[68]   Ibid.: "Misi tamen (ex multis) Exemplar unum Epistolae Ciphris scriptae, prout ea ad manus meas pervenit intercepta, cum ejusdem Expositione a me praestita, ad Dn. Editorem Actorum Lipsicorum."
[69]   Wallis to Mencke, 1/11 January 1697 (Wallis 1693–99: III, 659–60).
[70]   The basis of the enclosure was the letter of the French emissary to Poland François-Gaston de Béthune to Cardinal d'Estrées of 27 August [6 September] 1689. After perusing the material, Mencke sent it as an enclosure to his letter to Leibniz of 22 May / 1 June 1697 (A I xiv, 244–46). The original manuscripts are now Niedersächsische Landesbibliothek LBr 974, Bl. 8–13.
[71]   Mencke to Leibniz 22 May [1 June] 1697 (A I xiv, 245): "Ich sehe auch nicht, cui bono; sonst würde Ers wol in die *Transact.* gegeben haben."
[72]   Wallis 1693–99: III, 660–7.
[73]   See for example Leibniz für die Geheimen Räte in Celle und Hannover, 7/17 March 1699 (A I xvi, 121).
[74]   Leibniz to Mencke, August – beginning of September 1697, A I xiv, 439: "Es wäre zu wündschen daß H. Wallisius nicht nur solutionem Epistolae cryptographicae, sondern auch modum solvendi geben hätte. Ich glaube aber daß er aus diesen einzigen brief clavem also wie er sie hier gegeben nicht finden können."
[75]   Leibniz to Schmidt, 10/20 March 1699, A I xvi, 639: "Nam Algebra est calculi apex."
[76]   Ibid.: "Putem autem qui ad calculos sit aptus, etiam istis Cryptolyticis parem fore: praesertim si in Algebra vel possit aliquid vel aliquando se praestare posse sperare nos jubeat ". See also Leibniz' remarks on the rules (*artificia*) of the *ars cryptolyticae* in his letter to Wallis, 28 September / 8 October 1697, GM IV, 42: "Est enim in his velut fastigium quoddam subtilitatis simul industriaeque humanae." Similarly in Leibniz to Wallis, 28 March / 7 April 1698 (GM IV, 44–5); Leibniz to Sparwenfeld, 7/17 April 1699 (A I xvi, 726).

[77] Leibniz to Wallis, 28 September / 8 October 1697 (GM IV, 42): "Agnosco certis methodis comprehendi non posse [sc. Ars cryptolytica], et, si posset, minus foret artificiosa; et vel ideo velim ipsa exponi artificia, et quasi calculus problematis soluti. Neque ego ista per se, sed potius ob artem inveniendi hinc promovendam, aestimanda censeo." See also Leibniz to Wallis, 28 May / 7 June 1697 (GM IV, 27): "Itaque, licet facile agnoscam Cryptographematum solutionem certa methodo absolvi non posse, specimina tamen ejus aliqua a Te extare proderit, quibus ipsa ars ratiocinandi occultaque pervestigandi augeatur."

[78] Leibniz to Platen, c.1700, Niedersächsische Landesbibliothek, LBr 731, Bl. 30r: "Gleichwohl dafern aus denen mir bekandten regeln die deciphration zu wege zu bringen [...] und sonderlich dafern nur die in Zahl alphabet gegen ein ander überstehend zahlen solchen Alphabet gemäß gleicher bedeutung haben. So habe ich noch einige hofnung daß wiewohl ich in dieser materi mir groß exercitium [nicht] anmaßen kann [...]."

[79] Leibniz, *Dialog zur Einführung in die Arithmetik und Algebra*, ed. E. Knobloch, Stuttgart-Bad Cannstatt 1976: 57/59, "[Charinus] [...] Tota ars cryptographica quid aliud quam formulas ac combinationes tractat, licet nulla illic quantitatis ratio habeatur [...] [Eusebius] Praeclara dicis, mi Charine, et quae miror ac doleo non satis observari [.] itaque optarem vel te vel ex sententia tua te monente alium quendam opus tam jucundum tamque utile attentare. [Charinus] Non ignoras Eusebi, quam multa moliar, et fortasse possim, quae praestare uni omnia non vacat. Sed si plures consilia conjungerent agi posse etiam multo majora, quam quisquam facile suspicetur."

[80] See Leibniz, *Praecepta artis deciphratoriae* (A VI iv, 1206). There are a number of papers in the Leibniz-Archiv in Hanover which provide evidence of Leibniz having carried out investigations of his own on the topic of deciphering. See for example LH 5 VI 4, Bl. 38–40. Already in the *Dissertatio de arte combinatoria*, Leibniz refers to Gustavus Selenus (a pseudonym employed by Duke August of Brunswick-Lüneburg) *Cryptomenytices et Cryptographiae libri IX*, Lüneburg 1624. See *De arte combinatorial* (A VI i, 204). See also Leibniz for von Strattmann, May to Autumn 1689 (A I v, 444).

[81] *Aufzeichnung für die Audienz bei Kaiser Leopold I*, August/September 1688 (A IV iv, 27); *Kurzfassung einiger Ausführungen vor Kaiser Leopold I*, August/September 1688 (A IV iv, 45); *Ausführliche Aufzeichnung für den Vortrag bei Kaiser Leopold I*, second half of September 1688 (A IV iv, 68); Leibniz to Duke Johann Friedrich, February (?) 1679 (A I ii, 125); Leibniz to Duke Johann Friedrich, October 1679 (A I ii, 223); Leibniz to Mertz von Quirnheim, 18/28 February 1678 (A I ii, 319).

[82] See for example Haes to Leibniz, 9/19 November 1691 (A III v, 204); Haes to Leibniz, 21/31 January 1692 (A III v, 251).

[83] Haes to Leibniz, 28 March / 7 April 1692 (A III v, 287). "[...] Vous me dites dans vôtre derniere en citant Viete et Wallis que Vous souhaiteriés que quelque habile autheur traitast à fond l'art des chifres."

[84] See Leibniz to Fuchs, 14/24 February 1699 (A I xvi, 577–8): "J'adjouteray seulement que M. Wallis m'ecrit du 16/26 du mois passé qu'il a reconnu qu'il n'y a que certains esprits propres à ce travail et à cette espece de divination. Et en effect on trouve que ce sont ceux qui ont du genie pour le calcul et pour l'Algebre, comme l'exemple de feu M. Viete maistre des requestes de l'hostel du Roy de France grand Algebriste et merveilleux dechifrateur, et celuy de M. Wallis luy même le font connoistre." The passage to which he refers in Wallis's letter of 16/26 January is GM IV, 60–1.

[85] Leibniz, *Dialog zur Einführung in die Arithmetik*, 57: "Tota ars cryptographica quid aliud quam formulas ac combinationes tractat, licet nulla illic quantitatis ratio habeatur."

[86] See Leibniz to von der Hardt, 9/19 October 1707, Niedersächsische Landesbibliothek LBr 366, Bl. 320v–321r: "Apud Theologos inter arcana Acroamatica esse deberit doctrina irenica; apud philologos Cabala; apud jurisconsultos doctrina juris naturae; apud medicos chymia; apud Philosophos sublima de deo scientia."

[87] Leibniz to Bernoulli, 5/15 March 1697 (GM III, 377): "An Dnus. Frater tuus aget etiam de arte, quam vocant, deciphrandi, quae utique a Mathematico tractari meretur: ea quae hactenus in eam rem extant, parvi sunt momenti."

[88] See Leibniz to Wallis, 19/29 March 1697 (GM IV, 14): "Si qui tamen adessent Tibi juvenes ingeniosi et discendi cupidi, possent coram paucis verbis a Te multa discere, quae interesset non perire."

[89] Wallis to Leibniz, 6/16 April 1697 (GM IV, 19): "Sed tanti laboris res est, ut vix sit qui velit ediscere."

[90] Leibniz to Wallis, 24 November / 4 December 1699 (GM IV, 74): "Et cum interroganti mihi atque hortanti respondens non videreris recusare operam, ingeniosos aliquos et studiosos juvenes ad Te mittendos ducendi per inventionum Tuarum vestigia, ut tanta ars propagaretur, jussus nempe sum ex Te quaerere, quibus legibus conditionibus subire laborem non recuses, ut mysteria illa candide discipulis paucis et selectis aperiantur. Erit autem Tibi res cum Principe generoso, et dum illis satisfacies, poteris simul utilitati publicae et gloriae Tuae velificari."

[91] See for example Leibniz to crown prince Ferdinand of Tuscany, 24 October / 3 November 1698, where after discussing the memory skills of a certain Libbes (Lübbert) from Hanover he turns to the topic of deciphering and the abilities in this respect of his friend Wallis (A I xvi, 250–51): "Il m'est venu dans la pensée à cette occasion un autre Effort de l'Esprit humain non inferieur à cela. C'est ce que je sçay une personne merveilleuse pour le déchiffrement, de sorte que je suis presque étonné moy même de ce que j'en ay vû. Mais c'est un homme extremement âgé, et qui ne sçauroit plus vivre long temps. Quand il sera mort, nous regretterons de l'avoir laissé mourir sans avoir fait instruire par luy quelque jeune homme propre à conserver cette science dans un si haut degré. Ainsi mons tres humble avis seroit de faire instruire un même jeune homme chez ces deux excellens Maistres, et cela au plustost." See also Leibniz to crown pince Ferdinand of Tuscany, 20/30 September, 1699 (A I xvii, 527); Leibniz to crown prince Ferdinand of Tuscany 18/28 December, 1699 (A I xvii, 727).

[92] Leibniz expresses his fear that Wallis's skills might be lost forever when he dies on numerous occasions. See for example Leibniz to Justel for Halley 24 May / 3 June 1692 (A III v, 314); Leibniz to Justel, 10/20 October 1690 (A I vi, 267).

[93] Leibniz to Fuchs, 14/24 February 1699 (A I xvi, 577–8).

[94] Leibniz, *Promemoria für die geheimen Räte in Celle und Hannover*, 7/17 March 1699 (A I xvi, 120–1): "Es wird bekand seyn, daß der berühmteste Dechifrateur so iezo in Europa lebet, sich in England finde. Es ist ein treflicher Mathematicus und stehet mit mir in Correspondenz. Weil es nun ein 80 jahriger Mann, und zubesorgen, daß ein großes so er gethan dieser Kunst hohes zubringen mit ihm verlohren gehen werde, so habe ihn mit vielen remonstrationen pro bono publico dahin vermocht, daß er sich endtlich erbothen, einen und andern hier zu bequemen mit einem zu dergleichen calculis und laboribus geneigten Genio begabten jungen Menschen darinn zu informiren, wo bey als er sich anfangs entschuldiget, daß die Kunst in praecepta generalia nicht zubringen, ich vorgeschlagen, daß die information durch exempla geschehen kondte, in dem der discipulus durch die vestigia solutionum jam factarum gefuhret, und ihm wie man dahinter kommen gewieß[en], mithin dadurch das liecht angezundet, und der methodus beybracht wurde, welchen vorschlag er auch guth gefunden."

[95] Blencowe, who became fellow of All Souls, Oxford in December 1702, was officially appointed decipherer, together with Wallis, during the reign of William and Mary in April 1701.

[96] Wallis to Leibniz, 29 March / 8 April 1700 (GM IV, 76): "Nostris utique Amicis non minus quam Inimicis magno fore posset incommodo, si Ars, occulte scripta recludendi, passim innotesceret. Nam in negotiis magni momenti transigendis magno usui esse solet, posse secreto res communicare." Referring to Leibniz's request, Wallis reiterates this argument in his letter to Ellis of 30 April / 10 May 1700, British Library Add. MS. 28927, f. 115r–116v, 115r.

[97] [Charlett] to Tenison, 22 September / 3 October 1700, Bodleian Library MS Ballard 24, f. 9r–10v, 9r. Although copied by Arthur Charlett and sent in his name, this letter is in fact from Wallis. See also Wallis to Tilson, 20/31 March 1700/1, British Library Add. MS. 32499, f. 373r.

6. LEIBNIZ AND ROBERT BOYLE

Reason and faith: Rationalism and voluntarism

1. INTRODUCTION

Robert Boyle was nearly 20 years older than Leibniz and was in his mid-40s on the only occasion on which the two men are known to have met, during Leibniz's visit to London in 1673. By that stage Boyle had done much of his important work in chemistry and was established as one of the leading lights of the Royal Society. When Leibniz went to visit Boyle on 12th February, he also met the mathematician John Pell, who exposed his ignorance of the latest developments in mathematics, specifically the work of François Regnauld that had already been published by Gabriel Mouton.[1] Though Boyle's opinion of Leibniz is unknown, the latter probably appeared as a rather brash young man given to making claims to be an innovator in mathematics he could not substantiate. Whether for that or some other reason, there were no seminal exchanges between the two men and they did not correspond.

Nonetheless Boyle had been, and remained, quite an important figure for Leibniz, as one of the leaders of the first generation of Modern philosophers. The younger man invoked Boyle, for instance, in one of his own early declarations of support for the new philosophy, in his *Confession of Nature against the Atheists* of around 1668. Leibniz stated that:

...we must agree with those contemporary philosophers who have revived Democritus and Epicurus and whom Robert Boyle aptly calls corpuscular philosophers, such as Galileo, Bacon, Gassendi, Descartes, Hobbes and Digby, that in explaining corporeal phenomena we must not unnecessarily resort to God or any incorporeal thing, form or quality ...but that so far as can be done, everything should be derived from the nature of body and its primary qualities – magnitude, figure and motion. (A VI i, 489–90/ L 110)

But, though Leibniz wanted to endorse the corpuscular philosophy or what he sometimes called the mechanical philosophy,[2] at least as a methodology for physics, he was aware of its tendency to naturalism. He sought to resist the view that everything could be explained in naturalistic terms and indeed to stress the need for a deity to make sense of the mechanical philosophy. According to Leibniz, the origin of the primary qualities themselves can only be found by supposing an incorporeal principle which, as it turns out, must also be an intelligence. Such, in outline, is the argument of Leibniz's *Confessio Naturae*.[3] It is not clear whether the "naturalists" he believed himself to be refuting included all the people he had listed as "corpuscular philosophers." Probably not. No doubt he meant to include Democritus and Epicurus. And he would have probably included Hobbes, as well as Descartes (and Spinoza), whom he was later to accuse of naturalism.[4] Whether

83

P. Phemister and S. Brown (eds.), Leibniz and the English-Speaking World, 83–93.
© 2007 *Springer.*

at that stage he suspected Boyle of naturalism is not clear. He may not, in 1668, have had any inkling of Boyle's enthusiasm for natural theology. And indeed he may not have become aware of it until 1675, when he first read Boyle's defence of theological studies, though Boyle had written his *Excellence of Theology* ten years earlier. This work, or so Leibniz claimed in a letter to one of the secretaries of the Royal Society, Henry Oldenburg, made a deep impression on him. Indeed, he went on, it confirmed him in the intention he had formed some time before, of "treating the science of mind through geometrical demonstrations" (GM I, 83/ L 165). The *Elementa de mente* project was intended to provide what Leibniz saw as a much-needed complement to Hobbes's *Elementa de corpore*. It would certainly have included some defence of belief in an incorporeal deity.

Between late 1675 and early 1676 Leibniz read and made notes on four of Boyle's apologetic writings, beginning with *The Excellency of Theology* (1674) and its appended treatise on the *Excellency and Grounds of the Mechanical Hypothesis*. Leibniz also wrote notes on *Some Motives and Incentives to the Love of God* (1670), *Some Considerations about the Reconcileableness of Reason and Religion* and *Some Physico-Theological Considerations about the Possibility of the Resurrection* (1674). An excellent introductory overview of these notes and indeed of Leibniz's relation to Boyle is to be obtained from Leroy Loemker's ground-breaking paper "Boyle and Leibniz" (Loemker 1955). Loemker worked on the manuscripts that were later published as "Auszüge aus Schriften Boyles" (A VI iii, 218–41) in the Akademie Edition. His paper contains many suggestions and reflections that are worth further consideration and it remains the obvious starting-point for further work on the connections between the thought of Boyle and that of Leibniz.

As Loemker observes, Leibniz and Boyle were both Modern philosophers with a strong commitment to the organised advancement of the sciences. Leibniz had read Boyle's *Origin of Forms and Qualities* and made a reference to it in a letter to Herman Conring in 1678:

...I take to be demonstrated what [Boyle] stressed continuously, and took such great care to prove. I believe that no prudent man will doubt that the apparatus of forms and faculties is useless in giving the reasons for things. (A II i, 386)

Despite the substantive agreement there is more than a hint of criticism of Boyle here, as Loemker points out. Leibniz was impatient with Boyle's method of arguing by the enumeration of examples, claiming he could get to the heart of the matter in a more direct way. A similar criticism and boast appeared in a short paper of February 1676 (not discussed by Loemker) in which Leibniz comments on his own and on Boyle's work on the Resurrection. Here too Leibniz acknowledged a "notable agreement" with his own views. But, in his opinion, Boyle "spent too long on chemical illustrations" whereas Leibniz himself "followed up the difficulties with more precision" (A VI iii, 478). These criticisms seem to reflect differences in philosophical method (to which I will return) and should dispel any suggestion that Boyle was some kind of hero for the young Leibniz.

One of the many interesting suggestions in Loemker's paper concerns the probable influence of Boyle who, it is claimed, "forced [Leibniz] to make place for experiment and hypothesis in his method of analysis and synthesis, and so to develop a logic of truths of fact or empirical or synthetic propositions in which a priori and *a posteriori* components are combined" (Loemker 1955: 39). Loemker's paper attaches particular importance to a then unpublished conspectus and preface for an *Elementa physicae* which he later translated in his important edition of Leibniz's *Philosophical Papers and Letters*.[5] In his editorial introduction Loemker claims that, in this prospectus, "the influence of Francis Bacon, and particularly of Robert Boyle, is obvious" (L 267). This conspectus and preface, now published in the Akademie Edition,[6] show Leibniz to be well aware of sophisticated empirical methods for the discovery of natural causes and even slightly on the defensive so far as concerns a priori methods. He supports a priori methods since he thinks we should be able to make inferences about the world from the fact that "God works in the most perfect way" (A VI iv, 1999/ L 283). But he comes close to confining such methods to metaphysics and suggesting that knowledge of the interior constitution of bodies based a priori upon the known nature of God is not something that can be attained in this life and is better left for the hereafter.

In his 1955 paper, Loemker goes on to suggest that Boyle "probably encouraged" Leibniz's shift from the ontological argument for God's existence which at one time was "the keystone of his logic and metaphysics" to the argument "from an immanent teleology in a mechanistic order" (Loemker 1955: 39). Loemker cites the arguments in Leibniz's *Tentamen Anagogicum* (1696) as an example of his later tendency to argue that we can only explain the way nature is by assuming an intelligent cause (GP VII, 270/ L 484n). This turn to teleology was, he suggests, influenced by Boyle's argument from design. More generally, Loemker suggests Boyle may have influenced Leibniz away from "the ideal of philosophic certainty" and to the much greater emphasis on probability that is notable in his later philosophy. These are topics that would be worth pursuing for a larger view of Boyle and Leibniz and perhaps for a better view of Leibniz. But, as they lie outside the scope of this paper, I shall not pursue them here.

More directly relevant to the topic of this paper are Loemker's remarks on the differences between Boyle and Leibniz concerning faith and reason. Both believed in the possibility of natural theology – indeed they both favoured some kind of teleological argument – and both held that faith and reason should not positively conflict. These are important points of agreement. At the same time Boyle tended to stress the autonomy of religion and reason, effectively assigning to reason what Loemker calls "the field of scientific analysis and explanation." Reason, however, is limited for Boyle when it comes to matters of religion in a way it is not for Leibniz. Loemker writes: "Leibniz, mathematician and Platonist, believed that the realm of divine order and purpose is itself accessible to [reason]" (Loemker 1955: 38).

Loemker's remarks about Boyle and Leibniz on faith and reason, though on the right lines, are rather abridged, and his discussion is not wholly clear. His account will certainly admit of amplification and on some points it calls for qualification. In this paper I will also pay attention to two topics Loemker did not consider: the writings of Boyle and Leibniz on the possibility of the Resurrection and the more recently-favoured dichotomy between theological "voluntarism" and "rationalism." I will try to bring out, firstly, how the different ways in which Boyle and Leibniz sought to answer a contemporary problem posed for belief in the Resurrection illustrates their differences over the relation of faith and reason. I will then consider whether the differences between the two philosophers are well brought out by the contrast between theological "voluntarism" and "rationalism."

2. REASON AND BELIEF IN THE RESURRECTION

Boyle and Leibniz held contrasting views of faith and reason. Both regarded reason and revelation as alternative sources of religious belief: but for Boyle it was, as we might put it, a strong (exclusive) disjunction whereas, for Leibniz, it was a weak (inclusive) one.

In his *Reason and Religion* Boyle suggests that reason is an inferior source of truth to revelation. My own reason, for Boyle, is like the use

of my watch to estimate time when ever the sun is absent or clouded; but when he shines clearly forth, I scruple not to correct and adjust my watch by his beams cast on a dial. *So,* when no other light is to be had, I estimate truth by my own reason, but where divine revelation can be consulted, I would willingly submit my fallible reason to the sure informations afforded by celestial light. (HD VIII, 261)

For all his commitment to the progress of the natural sciences and to the project of natural theology, Boyle thought that the knowledge humans can achieve through the exercise of reason was very limited.

We can see how different Leibniz's view is if we look, for instance, at his *Discourse on Metaphysics*, which seeks to provide a philosophical basis for a number of important religious truths. Amongst these is that God will preserve all minds in a perfect republic where happiness is assured to those who love Him (§§35–36). Leibniz concludes his *Discourse* by claiming that the ancient philosophers had "very little knowledge" of these truths: "Jesus Christ alone expressed them divinely well and in such a clear and familiar way, that the most simple minds came to understand them" (§37). The implication is that, for less simple minds, these important truths are established by (Leibniz's) philosophy. If humankind made proper use of their reason there would be no need for revelation. The roles of reason and revelation are thus, for Leibniz, complementary rather than competitive.

Of course Leibniz did acknowledge "mysteries" that reason could not penetrate, such as the Incarnation. Those who believe in those mysteries go beyond reason. But such is the universal harmony, as Leibniz saw it, that we may suggest analogies for the Kingdom of Grace based upon our knowledge of the Kingdom of Nature. One example where he does this is in his theory of the resurrection.[7]

Boyle and Leibniz both wrote about the resurrection in the 1670s. Leibniz had written a memorandum on the subject in May 1671 at the instigation of his patron Johann Christian von Boineburg.[8] He had already formed a view of his own by the time he received, via Knorr von Rosenruth, a copy of Boyle's little book (HD VIII, 299–313) on the resurrection in February 1676. He gave an account of this himself in one of the Paris writings included by Parkinson in his edition of the *De summa rerum*, under the title "On the Seat of the Soul." As was usually his practice, Leibniz prefaces his criticism of Boyle by saying that "there are many things [in Boyle's book] which agree admirably with my views" (A VI iii, 478/ P 33).

They do indeed address many of the same problems and come to the same broad conclusion that the difficulties can be overcome and so resurrections should not be dismissed as impossible. Their conclusions are philosophically modest compared with the brash claims almost standardly made at the time, especially by less careful Christian philosophers and sometimes even by Leibniz, for demonstrations of the immortality of the soul.[9] Both Boyle and Leibniz accepted that belief in resurrections was a matter of religious faith. And, perhaps for that reason, little interest has been taken by students of either Boyle or Leibniz in what they had to say about the topic.

But, as is particularly clear in Boyle's treatment, the question whether resurrections are possible raises general questions about the conditions that are necessary and sufficient for a material substance identified at one time to be denominated the same substance as one identified at another. Boyle refuses to take the easy way out of saying that the human soul is the *form* of the person and so will constitute the same person with "whatever duly organized portion of matter" it is united to (HD VIII, 311). He takes the resurrection to involve the restoration of the soul, after what he nicely calls its "widowhood", to the very *same body*. This seems to be the common Christian belief, at least in earlier centuries, and is linked with popular superstitions about how, at the sound of the Last Trumpet, all the graves will open and the revivified bodies rise up in the direction of Heaven. This common belief is sometimes referred to as "the resurrection of the flesh" and it is the tenability of this belief about which Duke Johann Friedrich appears to have sought Leibniz's opinion: Leibniz himself refers to it as the "*resurrectionem carnis*" (A VI iii, 478/ P 33).

Boyle's work was written for publication and intended to survive critical scrutiny. And perhaps for this reason it is Boyle who treats this topic in a way more likely to please an analytical philosopher. His project is "to determine what is absolutely necessary and but sufficient to make a portion of matter, considered at differing times or places, to be fit to be reputed the *same* body" (HD VIII, 300). By a careful consideration of examples he argues persuasively that something may remain the same body even though it is very different in size and has undergone major changes in appearance. The general objection is put that, when a person dies, some of the parts of their body will,

according to the course of nature, resolve themselves into multitudes of steams that wander to and fro in the air; and the remaining parts ...undergo such a corruption and change, that it is not possible so many scattered parts should be again be brought together, and reunited after the same manner wherein they existed in a human body whilst it was yet alive. (HD VIII, 304)

And, if this objection seems merely to reflect a feeble idea of omnipotence, there is a sharper objection, at least to the idea of a general resurrection. For, in some cases, a dead person will be eaten by cannibals, their bodies presumably becoming part of several other bodies. It seems then absolutely impossible for each to have their very own bodies restored to them at the same time, as those who believe in a general resurrection are committed to supposing. For there will not be enough bodies to go round.

Boyle conceded that this was a "weighty objection" (HD VIII, 304). For him it was indeed necessary for a body to be correctly demominated the same body at different times that it should retain at least a quorum of its distinctive particles. However the particles could still exist even though a body had been eaten. Boyle gives a number of examples, such as that of the pigs on the Irish coast, that were so much fed with shell fish as to acquire a distinctive fishy taste. The suggestion is that the distinctive shell fish particles are retained in the body of the pigs and that an omnipotent being who saw any point in doing so could re-constitute the shell fish whose particles had thus been scattered. His general conclusion, to miss out much detail, is that there is no reason why an omnipotent being should not be able to "so order and watch over the particles of a human body" that

he may re-unite them betwixt themselves and, if need be, with particles of matter fit to be contexed with them, and thereby restore or reproduce a body which, being united with the former soul, may, in a sense consonant to the expressions of Scripture, recompose the same man whose soul and body were formerly disjoined by death. (HD VIII, 311)

Boyle does not claim that this story is at all probable, given the natural course of things. He admits it would never have occurred to him to think that the dead might be raised if he had not read in the Bible that it was God's purpose:

...neither do I know how to prove that it will be, but by flying not only to the veracity but the power of God, who having declared that he will raise the dead, and being an almighty agent, I have reason to believe that he will not fail to perform his purpose. (HD VIII, 299)

Boyle is not concerned to argue that the Resurrection is philosophically probable but only to refute the claim of some philosophers to show that it is absolutely impossible. It is possible to believe in the Resurrection as something that is within God's power and, for Boyle, God's omnipotence "extends to all that is not truly contradictory to the nature of things, or to his own" (HD VIII, 311). The force of what is sometimes called "the Cannibals objection" may be taken to be that the Resurrection is contrary to the nature of bodies. And so Boyle thought it a weighty objection that called for a reply.

Boyle's approach is an empirical one. There is evidence, he considers, that the particles of various foodstuffs survive in the bodies of those who eat them, since those bodies take on the distinctive taste, colour or whatever of those foodstuffs. Leibniz was not happy with this approach. His own approach, indeed, has a strong a priori component, since he does not think anything is a true substance unless it is a true unity and in theory indestructible except by a miracle. He is led to explain how a substance can be denominated the very same substance at different times by postulating an essence – what he called a "*Kern*" or "seed" in his memorandum for Duke Johann Friedrich and what he elsewhere calls a "flower of substance" (*flos substantiae*)[10] – that remains the same throughout all changes. Unlike Boyle, he does not treat the soul and the body as separate substances. For Leibniz, as

I understand him, every soul (except God, at least) has a body. What happens when people die is indeed that the soul is parted from its gross body. But it always retains a "subtle body." In a later writing he explains in what sense he believes we will become like Angels in the future state and in what sense we will be *mentes incorporatas*:

We shall put off the body, it is true, but not entirely: and we shall retain the most subtle part of its substance (quintessence), in the same way as chemists are able to sublimate a body or mass, the defecated part alone remaining. (OH 411)

That any such thing will happen is, for Leibniz, a matter of religious faith. It goes beyond what philosophy can strictly hope to establish. At the same time it is a philosophical assumption that all genuine substances are true unities and are therefore indestructible. It is true that, for Leibniz, though we may be indestructible, our memories are certainly not and our ability to retain our sense of our own identity (necessary for anything worth calling immortality) depends on God's goodness. But here too philosophical arguments can also come into play to support the view that God will reward the virtuous and punish the wicked. Furthermore, Leibniz's belief in a general harmony of things leads him to see in the Kingdom of Nature analogies from which he could speculate about the Kingdom of Grace. Thus he thought it relevant to invoke certain familiar facts of nature to refute the freethinker who claimed that death was total extinction. In the *New Essays* he invokes the transformation of caterpillars into butterflies and the preservation of thought in sleep (A VI vi, 58) as evidence that an afterlife is at least conceivable. And I think, though it could not be demonstrated from that text alone, that such examples were also intended to make an afterlife more plausible. That certainly seems to be the relevance of the examples Leibniz draws from the natural sciences to support his claim that substances all have a *flos substantiae*.

Their discussions of the Resurrection illustrate some of the ways in which Boyle and Leibniz differ about faith and reason. For Boyle, the positive belief in the Resurrection comes entirely from revelation and the role of philosophy is only to counter the claim that it is absolutely impossible. Faith and reason are thus made consistent. Leibniz certainly agreed that they must indeed be consistent. But philosophy, for him, has a more wide-ranging role in supporting religious belief. Faith is not, for him, separate from reason, and, though it goes beyond what reason can establish, it does have some rational support. The positive belief in the Resurrection is supported by Scripture and the "motives of credibility" that underpin, or so he claimed, the acceptance as revelation of what is plainly taught in scripture.[11] But, as I have argued, belief in the possibility of resurrections and, to that extent of the Resurrection is positively indicated by a variety of philosophical considerations drawn from Leibniz's philosophy. His philosophy can admit either the view of some Christians that individual humans are resurrected as they die or the view of others that they will sleep until the Day of Judgment when the dead will be raised all together. So it leaves some matters undetermined by philosophy. Thus he can truthfully say, as he sometimes did, that not much is known much about the details of the after-life except what is revealed to us in the Bible.[12]

Revelation still has a role to play, therefore, in two ways: it has a relatively minor role to play in filling out details that philosophy cannot provide: and a major role for the bulk of humanity who cannot benefit from the insights of philosophy. For many of the truths of religion, including the broad view of the after-life, revelation provides, for Leibniz, a complementary way of arriving at belief to that provided by reason. But he was never happy about depending entirely on revelation for any of the cardinal truths. Indeed he was later inclined to suspect those who took such a fideistic stance of disguising their own scepticism.[13]

3. VOLUNTARISM AND RATIONALISM

It has become a commonplace for students of Boyle to refer to him as a theological "voluntarist." This view is well summarized and explained by John Henry:

...Boyle's theology, as McGuire and others have shown,[14] was undeviatingly voluntarist. For Boyle, it was God's supreme power and His arbitrary will which were paramount. The idea that the complexity of the world system could be reduced to a few simple laws of nature was associated in Boyle's mind with intellectualist theologies in which, as far as Boyle and all other theological voluntarists were concerned, God's power was circumscribed by the need to conform to the dictates of man-made reason and the expectations of man's ethical assumptions. The rational reconstruction of the system of nature, which Descartes no less than scholastic philosophers indulged in, seemed to imply that God could not have done things otherwise. Boyle's anti-rationalist experimental philosophy went hand in hand with his theological voluntarism. Whatever regularity there was in the system of the world was imposed by God arbitrarily by His absolute power, not as a result of God following the dictates of reason. Accordingly, we could only discover the regularities of the world by experience. (Henry 1994: 132)

It is tempting to see the differences between Boyle and Leibniz in the light of this dichotomy. And this temptation may be increased when we realise that this is the only issue on which the eirenic Leibniz, in his extensive notes on Boyle's writings, seems to have been provoked into outright disagreement. Boyle, in *Reason and Religion*, quotes with approval Descartes's well-known reply to Arnauld: "je n'ose pas dire, que Dieu ne peut pas faire une montaine sans vallée, our que 1. et 2. ne fassent pas 3. mais q'il m'a donné une ame, faite on sortie, que je ne puis pas le concevoir autrement."[15] And this elicited from Leibniz the response: "This does not satisfy me. Whatever implies a contradiction is impossible, for it is to say nothing" (A VI iii, 236). Leibniz's objection here is to Descartes's voluntarism about eternal truths, which he later expressed vigorously in his *Discourse on Metaphysics*:

...if we say that things are good by no rule of goodness beyond the will of God alone, we thoughtlessly destroy, I think, all the love and glory of God. For why praise Him for what He has done if He would be equally praiseworthy for doing the opposite? Where will His justice and His wisdom be, if all that remains of Him is some kind of despotic power, if His will takes the place of reason, and if, by the very definition of tyranny, what pleases the Almighty is *ipso facto* just? Besides, it seems that every act of willing presupposes some reason for willing, and that reason is naturally prior to will. That is why I still find rather strange the expression of [Descartes[16]] who says that the eternal truths of metaphysics and geometry[17] are no more than the effects of God's will. It seems to me, rather, that they are no more than the consequences of His understanding, which certainly does not depend on His will, any more than His essence does. (§2: A VI iv, 1532/ MB 40)

Leibniz might appear, then, to belong squarely on the side of theological "rationalism" and Boyle on the side of "voluntarism." The dichotomy, however, needs to be refined if it is to be other than confusing. It is clear, in the first place, that Descartes cannot both be the proto-typical "rationalist" (or what John Henry calls an "intellectualist") he is commonly supposed to be and, at the same time, an up-holder of what appears to be an extreme voluntarism, as attacked by Leibniz.[18] And, even if commitment to one kind of voluntarism ought to have implications for the other, it is useful to distinguish voluntarism with respect to eternal truths from voluntarism with respect to laws of nature. Once we do this, however, Leibniz and Boyle do not appear as quite so opposed as they may have appeared at first.

In particular, it becomes clear that Boyle is not committed to voluntarism in relation to eternal truths and Leibniz is not committed to opposing it for laws of nature. Boyle's enthusiastic quotation of Descartes's refusal to say that God could not vary the eternal truths is misleading.[19] He was concerned to praise Descartes for opposing philosophers who make human reason the measure of God and what He can do. He was not concerned to claim that God's will is absolutely unlimited. On the contrary, as we have seen, he holds that God's omnipotency "extends to all that is not truly contrary to the nature of things, or to his person" (HD VIII, 311). It seems reasonable to interpret this qualification as excluding from God's power anything that would involve a contradiction. And, since the principle of contradiction was, for Leibniz, the highest principle of eternal truths, he and Boyle seem to be broadly in agreement as to what is not subject to God's will. Moreover, for Leibniz as for Boyle, the laws of nature are dependent on, indeed are expressions of, God's will. Leibniz's remark, in the *Discourse*, that "'nature' is no more than a custom of God from which he can exempt Himself" (§7) expresses a kind of voluntarism about laws of nature.

There remain, however, important areas of disagreement between Boyle and Leibniz in relation to the intelligibility of the world and indeed of God's purposes. Leibniz was committed to the view that the world is in principle intelligible to us. Indeed it is part and parcel of the mechanical philosophy as he understood and accepted it.[20] He began a paper of 1677 "On a method of arriving at a true analysis of bodies [....]" by declaring:

First of all, I take it to be certain that all things come about through certain intelligible causes, or causes which we could perceive if some angel wished to reveal them to us. And since we may perceive nothing accurately except magnitude, figure, motion, and perception itself, it follows that everything is to be explained through these four. (A VI iv, 1971–72/ GP VII, 265/ L 173)

Leibniz did not claim, of course, that nature was wholly intelligible to us and so he could agree with Boyle that empirical methods were needed to discover the laws of natural science. But, as we saw earlier, he did not agree that these were the only methods. Again, Leibniz did not claim that the laws of grace were actually known to us or even that they could be. It was common ground with Boyle that the workings of Providence were a mystery to us. Nonetheless, with his commitment to eternal truths of goodness and justice and, moreover, with his belief that these are

known to us, Leibniz was committed to elevating human reason to an extent that
Boyle could not accept. His way of thinking seems to be a clear example of what
Henry calls an "intellectualist theology" in which, from Boyle's point of view, God
is limited by the creations of human reason.

There is a further fundamental issue between Boyle and Leibniz that makes it
misleading to refer to them as "voluntarists" in the same sense, in respect of the laws
of nature. Both would have agreed that God freely chose to institute the laws by
which our universe is governed. But they have mutually opposed views of freedom.
Boyle held that the laws of nature were "arbitrary",[21] by which he seems to have
intended that God enjoyed a "liberty of indifference" with regard to them. Leibniz
rejected these notions as inconsistent with his principle of sufficient reason. He, for
his part, is accused of embracing, without admitting it, a system in which, because
of the place of the sufficient reason in it, things cannot be other than they are and in
which there is no room for God to make genuine choices. Leibniz was, of course,
familiar with this accusation and denied it strenuously. From his point of view a
choice that was not wholly rational would not be an expression of genuine freedom.
This is not the place to enter into this controversy. It is sufficient to note that Boyle
and Leibniz are on opposite sides of it.

4. CONCLUDING REMARKS

The two broad issues in Boyle's and Leibniz's philosophies of religion with which I
have been concerned in this paper – faith and reason, on the one hand, a voluntarism
vs rationalism, on the other – are closely connected. Boyle's voluntarism, which
emphasises the arbitrariness of the divine will, makes the ways of God inscrutable
to human reason and so places more emphasis on the importance of faith. Leibniz
objected to such emphases on the arbitrariness of God's will, insisting on its wisdom
and so rationality. Whereas Boyle makes God distant and mysterious, Leibniz insists
that humans are made in the image of God and so can have some knowledge of
God's motives. God is thus by no means inscrutable to human reason, according
to Leibniz. There are, then, some important differences between the philosophies
of science and religion of Boyle and Leibniz notwithstanding the fact that they
were both committed to the defence of natural religion and the advancement of the
natural sciences. But it is easy to misrepresent these differences by underplaying the
importance of reason and logic in Boyle's philosophy of religion or the importance
of empirical considerations in Leibniz's philosophy of science.

NOTES

[1] See Aiton 1985: 44 for an account of this incident.
[2] He used the phrase "the mechanical philosophy", for instance, in *Discourse on Metaphysics* §18
and the phrase "the corpuscular philosophy" in a similar context when writing to Arnauld in 1687
(GP II, 78).
[3] A VI i, 489–93/ GP IV, 105–10/ L 109–15.

⁴   He accused Descartes and Spinoza of reviving a form of Stoicism (A VI iv, 1385–6/ AG 280). The piece in which he does so is sometimes referred to as "Two Sects of Naturalists" following a phrase that Leibniz used in the first sentence, when he also referred to the fashion for Epicureanism, though without mentioning names.

⁵   Chicago University Press, 1956. 2nd edn., Dordrecht: Reidel, 1969, referred to here by the abbreviation "L".

⁶   A VI iv, 365–6 respectively.

⁷   Both Leibniz and Boyle tended to write about "the Resurrection of the dead" as a singular event occurring at the time of the Last Judgement. And that is how it is presented in the Creeds. But some of the philosophical questions about the possibility of "the resurrection" are just as much questions about the possibility of "resurrections" of many bodies.

⁸   See A II i, 105–10.

⁹   Leibniz's *Confessio Naturae* contained a claimed demonstration of the immortality of the soul but he later denied, for instance in his criticisms of Descartes (e.g. GP IV, 300–1), that any immortality worth having (i.e. with consciousness of continued identity) could be demonstrated.

¹⁰   See, for instance, his 1676 note on the possibility of the Resurrection (A VI iii, 478).

¹¹   See, for instance, his *Examination of the Christian Religion*, A VI iv, 2361 and *Theodicy*: Preliminary Discourse, §29.

¹²   In these terms Leibniz expressed scepticism about the detailed account of the after-life offered by his friend Francis Mercury van Helmont. See, for instance, his letter to the Electress Sophie of 3 September 1694: K VII, 304.

¹³   For instance, in his Preface to the *New Essays*, he wrote: "It has long been known that those who have sought to destroy natural religion and reduce everything to revelation, as if reason had nothing to teach us in this area, have been under suspicion, and not without reason" (A VI vi, 68).

¹⁴   Henry refers to McGuire 1972, Klaaren 1977 and Henry 1990. Jan Wojcik has claimed that Boyle is a clear, even a "paradigmatic", example of a voluntarist (Wojcik 1997: 190ff.).

¹⁵   Quoted in Leibniz's notes, A VI iii, 236. Cf. AT V, 224.

¹⁶   Descartes's name is dropped in later drafts, as is also the earlier reference to Spinozists. The latter are referred to vaguely as "the latest innovators" and, instead of Descartes, Leibniz refers to "certain other philosophers." I take these changes to be diplomatic and not the correction of mistakes.

¹⁷   Leibniz added in an early draft "and consequently also the rules of goodness, justice and perfection."

¹⁸   This problem is discussed in Wojcik 1997: 197–9.

¹⁹   It misled me for a while but, thanks partly to comments on my paper in discussion at the Liverpool Conference, in particular by Martha Bolton, I have come to see that it is a mistake to treat Boyle as a follower of Descartes at this point. It is not entirely clear whether Leibniz thought he was or was not.

²⁰   There is some irony in this, since the mechanical or "corpuscular" philosophy was a matter on which, as I indicated at the beginning of the paper, he agreed with Boyle. But his agreement with Boyle was expressed negatively as refraining in physics from invoking incorporeal principles and deriving everything from the primary qualities of matter. See the extract from Leibniz's *Confession of Nature* quoted at the beginning of this paper.

²¹   Appendix to *Christian Virtuoso*.

7. LEIBNIZ AND THE CAMBRIDGE PLATONISTS

The debate over plastic natures

By his own account, Leibniz first encountered the *True Intellectual System of the Universe* of the Cambridge Platonist Ralph Cudworth during his visit to Rome in the spring of 1689, although the work itself had been published just over a decade earlier in 1678. Leibniz would later report to Cudworth's daughter, Damaris Masham, that he had been delighted to see the wisdom of the ancients "accompanied by solid reflections".[1] He had certainly taken the book seriously, devoting sufficient attention to make copious critical notes to the first part.[2] Some years later, towards the end of 1703 or early in 1704, Masham sent Leibniz a copy of her father's *True Intellectual System* [TIS]. So began a two-year correspondence between Leibniz and Masham.

On his side, Leibniz believed that Masham was in the habit of discussing his letters with her paying houseguest, the most prominent English philosopher of the age, John Locke,[3] and he frequently urged her to engage with Locke on the topics they covered. But Cudworth's views are not far from Leibniz's thoughts at this time either. In fact, Lady Masham's gift was timely, for it was around this time that Jean le Clerc, editor of the journal *Bibliothèque choisie*, asked Leibniz to explain the relation between his theory of pre-established harmony and Cudworth's doctrine of plastic natures. Le Clerc had recently published excerpts from Cudworth's *True Intellectual System*. Bayle had responded in his *Continuation des pensées diverses sur la comète*, published in 1705, that in his opinion the immaterial plastic natures proposed by Cudworth and the vital principles favoured by Henry More opened the door to atheism and thus posed a threat to traditional religion.[4] In the meantime, Le Clerc wanted to know how these doctrines were viewed from Leibniz's perspective. Leibniz answered him in 1705 by publishing a letter to the editor of the *Histoire des ouvrages des sçavans*, Basnage de Beauval. Accordingly, the letter entitled *Considerations on Vital Principles and Plastic Natures, by the author of the system of pre-established harmony* details the points of agreement and disagreement between Leibniz and the proponents of vital principles and plastic natures and shows why Leibniz's doctrine of pre-established harmony, far from encouraging atheist tendencies, in fact provides a persuasive proof of the existence of God.

We believe that Leibniz's response to his Cambridge contemporaries, and most notably to Cudworth, can help shed new light on the metaphysical and theological issues at stake in the latter half of the seventeenth century in the debate between those who believed it necessary to invoke immaterial principles of growth and development to explain natural phenomena, and those who thought everything in nature could be explained in terms of matter in motion alone. While Leibniz

95

P. Phemister and S. Brown (eds.), Leibniz and the English-Speaking World, 95–110.
© 2007 *Springer.*

and Cudworth's respective positions represent varying degrees of deviation from the austerity demanded by the Cartesian explanation of natural phenomena, their theories differ dramatically from one another. Cudworth's position may be seen as a creative attempt to synthesise a version of atomism with his Platonic conviction that the workings of nature must be guided by some spirit superadded to nature's material parts. Leibniz's particular response to the Cambridge Platonist's conception of plastic natures is rooted, in turn, in his conception of organism and in the dynamical notion of derivative force,[5] which Leibniz, in response to Cudworth's doctrine of *immaterial* plastic natures, presents as a theory of *material* plastic natures. This theory, together with a doctrine of preformation, enables Leibniz, in his view, to avoid the threats of encroaching atheism that he and Cudworth alike believed to have arisen from the new mechanistic picture of nature.

1. CUDWORTH ON PLASTIC NATURE AND PLASTIC NATURES

In his *True Intellectual System of the Universe*, Cudworth understands either of two quite different things by the notion of plastic nature. One is something more or less the same as Henry More's notion of *archeus*, namely, a singular plastic or animating faculty belonging to a world-soul, which, as Leibniz would describe it, "animates ... bodies wherever it meets them, just as the wind produces music in organ pipes" (D II, 225). In this first sense, Cudworth's plastic nature of the world is nothing other than an "Inferior and Subordinate Instrument" of God, which "doth Drudgingly Execute that Part of his Providence, which consists in the Regular and Orderly Motion of Matter" (TIS I, iii, 37, art. 5: RC 150). This universal plastic nature is what keeps the inanimate or inorganic parts of the world moving in accordance with natural laws. Cudworth writes for instance that "there is a *Mixture* of *Life* or *Plastick Nature* together with *Mechanism*, which runs through the whole Corporeal Universe" (TIS I, iii, 37, art. 3: RC 148).[6] The other conception is of particular plastic nature*s* belonging to individual creatures, that is, to those entities in the universe commonly thought to be living. On this second conception, akin to Leibniz's own account of the entelechy of an animal, each individual substance is endowed with its own plastic nature, the "Inward Principle" of its motion (TIS I, iii, 37, art. 4: RC 150). Cudworth draws explicitly on the Platonic tradition in elaborating his theory of plastic natures. "The Platonists seem to affirm both these together," he writes, "namely that there is a *Plastick Nature* lodged in all particular Souls of Animals, Brutes and Men, and also that there is a General *Plastick* or *Spermatick Principle* of the whole *Universe* distinct from their Higher Mundane Soul, though subordinate to it, and dependent upon it" (TIS I, iii, 37, art. 21: RC 165). François Duchesneau has rightly noted that it is the first of these two notions that would come to predominate among the Cambridge Platonists, as "the followers of More and of Cudworth ... passed from the singular of the *plastic nature* to the plural of the *plastic natures*" (1998: 181). It is against the background of this notion of a plurality of plastic natures that Leibniz elaborates his own conception of organism within his mature metaphysics of corporeal substance.

The individual living being has two aspects for Cudworth: the immaterial active force and the matter or body upon which this active force works and with which it forms a living being. Each individual plastic nature is an inner force that moves its own particular body. In this way, there arises no further need to resort to God's influence in either moving or changing the direction of a body. Acting as God's instruments, plastic natures unconsciously bring about changes in extended matter, just as minds or souls do consciously (TIS I, iii, 37, art. 15: RC 158–9). The unconscious powers within each individual living thing bring it about that each moves in accordance with God's will without being moved directly by God.[7] Once created, the natural world is capable of forming and moving bodies on its own. God becomes extraneous to the enterprise. We will return to this aspect of Cudworth's theory in the final section. It is sufficient to note here that, in moving from the concept of a singular plastic nature to that of a plurality of plastic natures, Cudworth is seeking to avoid hylozoism, which he sees as the variety of atheism characteristic of a metaphysical system such as Spinoza's, according to which nature as such is ensouled.[8]

In appearing to lend preference to particular spiritual forces over a singular universal soul, Cudworth might be taken as rejecting the Platonic tradition of cosmological thinking, rooted in the *Timaeus*, according to which God is conceived, not as a detached father, but rather as an active and immanent craftsman. But in fact, Cudworth sees his account as a return to true ancient wisdom, simultaneously Mosaic and Platonic. He considers these ancient traditions as providing the kernels of a sort of atomism, and thus as a partial anticipation of modern mechanism. On Cudworth's view of "Platonist atomism," even in natural phenomena spirit is prior to matter, for without the animating force of spirit in nature, modern mechanism will be unable to account for growth and change.

Common to all the Cambridge Platonists is a concern to attribute the responsibility for the execution of "the Regular and Orderly Motion of Matter" (TIS I, iii, 37, art. 5: RC 150) not to a primal God, nor even to some soul of the universe or *anima mundi*, but rather to the individualised, invisible powers of which some ancient Platonists spoke. For Cudworth, matter is in itself inert, but everywhere animated, not by one common soul that pervades the universe, let alone directly by God, but rather by individual spirits. The first part of this agreement, concerning the essential inertness of matter, cannot be stressed too much. According to the Platonic tradition, matter is not so much an ingredient of the world – "stupid" matter cannot be a first principle, as Cudworth insists throughout the *True Intellectual System* (e.g. TIS I, iii, 34: RC 142) – let alone the basic ingredient, but rather the very opposite of that which is, namely God. The extent to which something is material is a measure of the extent to which it *is not*. It would make no sense, then, to attribute a capacity for sensation or thought to matter, as Cudworth thinks the hylozoists would like to do. Matter, as the principle of non-being, can limit or hinder the mental activity of a spirit mixed up with it, but certainly cannot itself engage in mental activity.

Like Leibniz, the Cambridge Platonists are revisionists with respect to what was perhaps the most radical innovation of the mechanical revolution: they wish to bring back the ends or final causes that Descartes had sought to banish from the new scientific ontology. Also like Leibniz, Cudworth regards the reintroduction of plastic natures as part of an effort to salvage an important component of the now antiquated philosophy of Aristotle. Cudworth even believes that Aristotle had his own doctrine of plastic natures, explaining that the Greek philosopher "concerns himself in nothing more zealously than this, That Mundane things are not Effected, merely by the *Necessary* and *Unguided Motion* of *Matter*" (TIS I, iii, 37, art. 6: RC 151). Cudworth believes that it is the individual plastic nature that constitutes the immediate efficient cause of any natural phenomenon, but that, insofar as it is operating in accordance with divine command, it ensures that all such phenomena proceed "*for the sake of something*, and *in order to Ends*, Regularly, Artificially, and Methodically" (TIS I, iii, 37, art. 2: RC 147). Without the plastic natures or divine command, everything would happen simply fortuitously. With divine command, but without plastic natures, things would happen according to God's ends, but God would have to see to them directly.

Leibniz happily embraces certain views Cudworth would find occasion to ridicule *avant la lettre*. Cudworth, ignorant of course of what would eventually emerge as Leibniz's mature metaphysics, describes the view that matter itself might be endowed with perception in terms remarkably similar to Leibniz's theory of individuals nested one within the other in the composite substance:

> If *Matter*, as such, had *Life*, *Perception*, and *Understanding* belonging to it, then of Necessity must every *Atom* or *Smallest Particle* thereof, be a *Distinct Percipient* by it self; from whence it will follow, that there could not possibly be, any such *Men* and *Animals* as now are, Compounded out of them, but every Man and Animal, would be a *Heap* of *Innumerable Percipients*, and have Innumerable *Perceptions* and Intellections; whereas it is plain, that there is but one *Life* and *Understanding*, one *Soul* or *Mind*, one *Perceiver* or *Thinker* in every one. And to say, that these innumerable *Particles* of *Matter*, Do all *Confederate* together; that is, to make every Man and Animal, to be a *Multitude* or *Common-wealth* of *Percipients* and Persons as it were clubbing together; is a thing so Absurd and Ridiculous, that one would wonder, the *Hylozoists* should not rather chuse, to recant that their *Fundamental Errour*, of the Life of *Matter*, than endeavour to seek Shelter and Sanctuary for the same, under such a Pretence. For though Voluntary *Agents* and *Persons*, may Many of then, resign up their wills to One, and by that means, have all but as it were One *Artificial Will*, yet can they not possibly resign up their *Sense* and *Understanding* too, so as to have all but one Artificial Life, Sense, and Understanding. (TIS I, v: RC 839)

In other words, in Cudworth's view, Spinoza inevitably leads to Leibniz. The attribution of perception or mental activity to nature itself entails a metaphysics of nested individuality. Leibniz indeed embraces such a metaphysics, according to which every individual corporeal substance involves a "clubbing together" of infinitely many other corporeal substances. Leibniz embraces what Cudworth had deemed the absurd conclusion that every portion of every body consists in "*Innumerable Percipients*" and their "Innumerable *Perceptions* and Intellections," although this is not for Leibniz the same as to say that matter as such has perception attached to it. To appreciate how Leibniz could accept the position denounced by Cudworth, while at the same time rejecting many of what Cudworth takes to be its implications, we must look in some detail at Leibniz's concept of organism.

2. LEIBNIZ ON THE ORGANIC STRUCTURE OF BODIES

Prior to Leibniz and his contemporaries, an organ was regarded simply as a tool, or as something that functioned toward an end greater than itself. The term "organism", as far as we can tell, was not in use much at all prior to Leibniz, and in any case it did not mean for him what it would come to mean in the following centuries. As Duchesneau has observed, in Leibniz's usage "organism" is not to be understood as inviting an indefinite article; there are for Leibniz no particular organisms, as there are particular dogs and horses and men.[9] "Organism," rather, is a term complementary to "mechanism." This meaning comes through, for example, when Leibniz asserts that "organism, that is to say order and artifice, is something essential to matter, produced and arranged by the sovereign wisdom" (GP III, 340). Just as "mechanism" in the seventeenth century does not refer to some particular machine, but to the nature of a broad class of entities, so too "organism" is for Leibniz meant to describe a class of entities.

But which class, exactly? Leibniz's contemporary, Anne Conway, uses the term "organism" to describe that paradigm machine of the seventeenth century, the humble clock. Thus she writes that nature is not "simply an organic body like a clock, which has no vital principle of motion in it" (1996: 64). For Leibniz, an organic body is distinct from a clock with respect to the complexity of its consti-tution, but – and this is something that has not been adequately noted concerning Leibniz's conception of organism – Leibniz *does* agree with Conway insofar as he holds that an organic body can be considered only in itself, without further reference to its single, dominant vital principle. Thus for example in the famous letter to De Volder of 20 June 1703, Leibniz distinguishes between the "organic machine" which is the mass or secondary matter of a corporeal substance, on the one hand, and, on the other, the animal itself, which is this organism considered as united into one in virtue of the presence of a dominant monad (GP II, 252/ AG 177). While it is true that the dominant monad is "in the machine" (GP II, 252/ AG 177), and its presence is required if the other monads are to be regarded as "subordinate" monads, nevertheless, the organic machine itself operates as any other mechanism. Its motion and resistance are explicable solely in physical terms without reference to any animating dominant force. For Leibniz, an organic body is distinct from a mere mechanical body in that it is infinitely complex, not because it possesses an immaterial vital principle, even though it does. Metaphysically, an organic body is always dominated by the soul or form of the animal or corporeal substance to which it belongs, but physically, the difference between an organic body and an inorganic body is found in the complexity of the organic body: it and all of its parts and the parts of the parts, *ad infinitum*, are machines, that is to say, mechanisms, of nature.[10]

Leibniz, then, like Conway, understands "organism" not as synonymous with "animal", but rather as picking out things – whether artificial, as in Conway's case, or natural, in Leibniz's – that, though organised, can nonetheless be scientifically accounted for without appeal to any principle of animation in them. An animal, for Leibniz, is a natural being considered as having a soul, an *anima*, while the generic term "organism" is used in relation to the same natural being, but considered only as an organic body, that is as an infinitely complex machine of nature. As Leibniz explains as late as 1714 in the *Principles of Nature and Grace*: "this body is organic when it forms a kind of automaton or natural machine, which is not only a machine as a whole, but also in its smallest distinguishable parts" (GP VI, 598/ AG 207).[11]

Leibniz introduces his theory of organism specifically in order to be able to account for the organisation of natural bodies without any appeal to the life or – what is the same thing – the capacity for perception characteristic of mind-like entities. According to this theory, everything that happens in nature can be explained without introducing immaterial principles of activity. Hence, his oft-repeated lesson about rushing to immaterial principles *too soon*, when mechanical explanations will do just fine. All that is needed is to appeal to the organic structure of all matter, a structure wherein everything is mechanical, and everything continues to be mechanical at any given level of analysis. We could say that there is order or structure "all the way down," although this is not quite correct, since there is in fact no "all the way" to be spoken of: analysis proceeds *ad infinitum*. It is, we suggest, the mechanism of the infinitely complex organic body – *pris à part*, as Leibniz sometimes puts it – that is what he has in mind when he speaks of the organism. That is to say, for Leibniz, "organism" refers to natural mechanisms. The organic body is in turn a mechanism or machine of nature, which remains mechanical in its least parts, and which does not require the introduction of the capacity for perception that would be required in an exhaustive account of the corporeal substance whose body it is. The organic body is that which does not require any consideration of the capacity for perception characteristic of the simples constituting the composite in order to understand how the composite is composed. We might thus say that "organism" and "organic body" are physical concepts, rather than metaphysical concepts. No metaphysical immaterial principle of activity need be introduced in order to understand the physical notion of an organic body, although it would be required to understand the notion of the animal to which this body belongs. These remarks are not surprising given that for Leibniz "organism" is really just a further elaboration of the concept of mechanism, which he very famously claimed could be fully understood without invoking any immaterial principles.

It is with respect to the question at what point such principles must be invoked in order to account adequately for natural phenomena that Leibniz departs most drastically from Ralph Cudworth. Leibniz regards the use of particular immaterial principles in the explanation of natural phenomena as no more satisfying than the occasionalist theory or the doctrine of a world soul. As he explains in the *Critical Thoughts on the General Part of the Principles of Descartes* of 1692:

[I]t is as vain [in the explanation of natural phenomena] to introduce the perceptions and appetites of an Archeus, operative ideas, substantial forms, and even minds, as it is to call upon a universal cause of all things, a *deus ex machina*, to move individual natural things by his simple will. (GP IV, 391/ L 409)

In Leibniz's opinion, the dominant monad of a corporeal substance or animal does not need to be invoked in the course of explanation of the motions of bodies. As he had noted in the previous paragraph, he agrees entirely with Descartes that "all the particular phenomena of nature can be explained mechanically if we explore them enough and that we cannot understand the causes of material things on any other basis" (GP IV, 390/ L 409).

So it is that, according to Leibniz, the motion of the animal's body can be explained without invoking the presence of a soul. The animal's organic body is indeed no less a machine than is a clock, even though it is infinitely more complex than a clock. For this reason, he can declare in 1705 that he has "no need to resort, as does Cudworth, to certain immaterial *plastic natures*," since "preformation and this infinitely complex organism provide me with material plastic natures that meet the need" (*Considerations*: GP VI, 544/ L 589). All that is needed for an adequate explanation is a consideration of the infinitely complex structure or pre-established infinite divisions within the animal's body. These allow the motions of the larger parts to be explained in terms of the motions of the smaller parts. Since the division of parts proceeds to infinity, there is no motion within the whole that cannot be explained mechanically in terms of the motion of its parts. Of course, it is an essential part of Leibniz's unique variety of pananimism that each of the infinitely many parts of an animal's body, as well as each of the parts of all material bodies, is endowed with some soul or soul-like principle. But these immaterial principles are not implicated directly as causally efficacious in the motion of bodies. The physical explanation of motion is the same whether the body is an inanimate entity, such as a billiard ball, or an organic body, such as the body of an animal. The mechanical explanation of the motion of the billiard ball refers to the external bodies that impose themselves on the ball and the internal forces in the ball whereby it either resists the motion of the others or gives in and is moved by them. The motions of the organic bodies are explained mechanically in similar fashion, that is, by reference to the body's internal forces and their relations in collisions with the forces in external bodies. The physical causes of the motions and resistances in any body are its internal derivative forces. The metaphysical sources of these internal forces are the primitive, monadic forces that exist as souls, substantial forms and primary matter, but these are never to be used in scientific explanations. In scientific explanations, bodies' sizes, shapes, motions, resistances and underlying derivative forces are quite sufficient.

Leibniz judges that Cudworth's soul-like, immaterial plastic natures are similarly of no use in scientific explanation. Accordingly, he advises replacing them with a notion of organicity which avoids appeal to incorporeal principles and which views the soul or life of a living creature as co-existing with its material body, but as playing no scientifically explanatory role in the motion of its body. Despite his protestations to Masham that he is not averse to the plastic natures of her father –

As far as plastic nature is concerned, I admit it in general, and I believe, along with Mr. Cudworth, that animals are by no means formed mechanically by something that is not organic, as Democritus and M. Descartes believed ... Matter is plastic or organic throughout, even in those portions that are as small as can be conceived. (GP III, 368)

–in fact, he adjusts them to suit his own concept of the organic. While Leibniz tells Masham that he "in general" admits the plastic natures of her father, he adapts the notion to his own concerns in two important respects. First, he asserts that all matter, everywhere, is governed by individual plastic or organic natures. This means that there is nothing inanimate that is kept in motion by a world soul or universal plastic nature alone.[12] Second, he opposes any use of incorporeal plastic natures in the explanation of natural phenomena on the ground that he simply has no need of them (*Considerations*: GP VI, 544/ L 589). For Leibniz to be governed by plastic nature is simply to be organic, and this plasticity or organicity is material, residing in the preformed, infinite complexity of the composition of the corporeal substance's organic body.

In this way Leibniz treads a middle path between the Cartesian mechanists and the vitalists. He agrees with the mechanical philosophers that "no other principles are necessary for the explanation of natural phenomena than those taken from abstract mathematics, or from the doctrine of size, figure, and motion" (*Critical Thoughts*: GP IV, 390/ L 409). He thinks they are wrong, though, to the extent that they fail to realise that a metaphysical explanation is required to explain the mechanical principles and general laws of nature used in the explanations of natural phenomena (*Critical Thoughts*: GP IV, 390/ L 409). Metaphysical considerations based on final causes and taking into account principles of fitness and perfection must be invoked at a metaphysical level. Ultimately, we can explain the laws that govern the operations of bodies only through appeal to God's wisdom and benevolence. In this respect, the vitalists were right. The action of incorporeal mind cannot be left out of the complete explanation of physical phenomena. All the same, insofar as vitalists such as Cudworth believe that an incorporeal principle is needed to describe the proximate causes of particular things in nature, they overstep the bounds of the intelligible causes and abandon mechanism too readily. Cudworth's shortcoming is not that he holds to immaterial forms – such a criticism would be a suitable one for Descartes to make, but not Leibniz – but rather that he, in company with the Scholastics, "appl[ies] them where [he] ought rather to have sought the modifications and instrumentalities of substance ... that is, mechanism" (*Critical Thoughts*: GP IV, 391). In the same vein, Leibniz writes in the *New Essays* that "the movement of the plant, which we call sensitive, arises from mechanism, and I do not at all approve of taking recourse to the soul when it is a matter of explaining the details of the phenomena of plants and animals" (A VI vi, 139).

As we noted earlier, Cudworth believed that the view that every part of matter is ensouled amounts to the absurd claim that every part of matter itself has life. For Cudworth, matter is not alive, but the living force of plastic natures works upon matter to bring about its motion and development. Cudworth had worried that if life were not superadded to material things in nature, but were rather intrinsic to it, then the absurd consequence would follow that every part of nature would be a perceiving subject. Leibniz accepts both that all of nature is in itself living, and that every part of nature is home to a perceiving subject. This is not to say however that for Leibniz matter itself perceives. Rather, souls perceive and bodies move.

These simple truths ground the distinction between the two different kingdoms of final and efficient causes (*Monadology* §79: GP VI, 620). In the kingdom of final causes, souls have appetites, desires, volitions and perceptions just as they would even if bodies did not exist. Meanwhile in the kingdom of efficient causes, bodies move and resist as if there were no souls (*Monadology* §81: GP VI, 621). Appetitions and perceptions in souls unfold without any causal input from bodies and their sequences are explained in terms of final causes, not efficient ones. Similarly, neither perceiving souls nor Cudworth's immaterial plastic natures are required to explain physical phenomena through the system of efficient causes. However, although each particular bodily phenomenon is explicable in terms of efficient causes alone, by nothing other than geometric and quantitative principles, the reason why these principles obtain in the world rather than any other requires us to appeal to the Principle of Sufficient Reason and to the metaphysical principles of goodness and perfection. In effect, final causes explain the general principles of efficient causation. They do not explain particular efficient causes on a one by one basis, but they do explain why the system of efficient causation operates in the way it does and not otherwise. To repeat the point made earlier, Leibniz steers a middle course between Descartes and Cudworth by rectifying their respective errors: Descartes relies too heavily on mechanism alone and fails to appreciate that, ultimately, higher metaphysical principles must be adduced to explain natural or physical phenomena; Cudworth resorts to vitalism and its accompanying metaphysical principles *too quickly* and fails to appreciate that mechanical explanations suffice for the explanation of particular physical phenomena.

3. LEIBNIZ ON PRE-ESTABLISHED HARMONY AND PREFORMATION

What takes the place of the immaterial plastic nature in Leibniz's philosophy, then, is simply the motion of physical bodies acting in accordance with the laws of motion to which all bodies in the physical universe are subject. But he still needs to explain how new organic bodies are formed out of the mass of bodies already existing. Change does occur and new organic bodies appear, but they do not appear from nowhere. They come from what is already there, that is to say, from pre-existing corporeal substances and their pre-formed organic bodies. New formations arise entirely through the pre-established laws of nature and without recourse to any influence on the part of an immaterial soul or an immaterial plastic nature. The motions of each organic body and the larger combinations of which it will be part have been set in advance from the very beginning. Each animal or corporeal substance already exists and will continue to exist. The apparent generation of a new creature or its apparent death "is only the transformation of the same animal, which is sometimes augmented and sometimes diminished" (*Considerations*: GP VI, 543/ L 589). The mechanism by which its organic body will be transformed, as in the transformation from caterpillar to butterfly, is already active in the mechanical collisions and motions of the organic bodies of the creatures that exist in even the smallest parts of matter. As Leibniz declares, "the mechanisms of nature are mechanisms down to their smallest parts" in such a way that "smaller machines are enfolded in greater machines to infinity" (*Considerations*: GP VI, 543/ L 589). What we wrongly assume to be the birth of an entirely new creature is only the augmentation of a living creature which has existed, as it were as a seed, since the creation of the world. It would go beyond the limits of the possibilities of mechanism to propose that an organic body could ever come into being where there was not one before. "The mechanism", Leibniz notes, is "incapable of producing *de novo* these infinitely diverse organs" (*Considerations*: GP VI, 544). However, the mechanical operation of bodies in accordance with the laws of nature may bring about the transformation of creatures through the physical transformation of their organic bodies. Thus, mechanism "can very well attain them from the development and transformation of a pre-existing organic body" (*Considerations*: GP VI, 544).

All the same, an organic body can be considered *pris à part* from the animal of which it is the body. This pre-existing organic body including all its ensuing transformations, and the fact that it may be considered apart from the corporeal substance as a whole, is of tremendous importance for our effort to understand the position Leibniz assumes in the debate over causation triggered in the first half of the seventeenth century. Cartesian interactionism had been discredited. No intelligible explanation was possible that would explain how souls could bring about by causal influence any changes in bodies. Leibniz had realised that the soul can neither move nor change the direction of any body and had suggested that, given conservation of force rather than motion, the equivalence of forces in interacting bodies means that, to all intents and purposes, each body moves only by its own force and not on account of any other. So, whereas Descartes had to introduce motive force into bodies either from souls or ultimately from God, both Leibniz and Cudworth advanced upon the Cartesian position in realising that bodies move by their own inner forces and not by any external force, divine or otherwise.

Nevertheless, Leibniz holds that Cudworth's doctrine has not in fact succeeded in overcoming all the deficiencies of Cartesian mechanism. Like the doctrine of Cartesian interaction, plastic natures too can offer no intelligible explanation as to how something immaterial can bring about any physical changes in material bodies. Cudworth has not avoided the problems faced by Descartes over the interaction of the unextended soul and the extended body. In fact, Cudworth simply removed the problem of interaction to a microscopic level. Unexplained interaction is still supposed to occur, but among plastic natures and unseen bodies rather than at the level of souls and their visible, larger-scale bodies. We no more understand how an incorporeal plastic nature can act on the physical body than we can understand how an incorporeal soul can cause changes in its body. The mechanism by which immaterial plastic natures act and that by which Cartesian souls act remain equally unexplained.

Leibniz's doctrine of pre-established harmony is postulated precisely to replace interactionism between the immaterial and the material. In its place, he substitutes a theory of the agreement and exact correspondence, without mutual influence, between the soul's perceptions and appetites and the body's motion. Supposedly causally influential immaterial plastic natures are therefore irrelevant to him. In *Considerations on Vital Principles and Plastic Natures*, he remarks that he neither needs Cudworth's immaterial plastic natures, nor do they fulfil his need: *"non mi bisogna, e non me basta* [I do not need it, and it does not meet my need] because this preformation and this infinitely complex organism provide me with material plastic natures that meet the need" (GP VI, 544/ L 589; L 591, note 8).

We have found one reason – namely, the doctrine of pre-established harmony – why he does not need Cudworth's doctrine of immaterial plastic natures. Cudworth's doctrine of plastic natures was invoked to explain the formation of plants and animals from unintelligent matter. As we have seen, however, they do not fulfil this purpose since they fail to provide an adequate explanation of the immaterial action on the material. Leibniz does not need them because he is not concerned to explain any interaction of the material and the immaterial. There simply is none. Nevertheless, the question of the formation of plants and animals remains. That requires an explanation. This is Leibniz's "need". He requires an explanation of the physical construction of living organisms from what had been supposed to be an inorganic universe. And to explain this, he has at hand the doctrine of preformation and the "infinitely complex organism" that together give him "material plastic natures" that do fulfil his need in a way that Cudworth's plastic natures cannot.

Cudworth had resorted to the doctrine of immaterial plastic natures because he had assumed that organisms did not previously exist. Something therefore had to be introduced in order to create living beings. In this, Leibniz likens Cudworth's doctrine to those who believe that it is the soul that is responsible for making its own body:

I have no need to resort, as does Cudworth, to certain immaterial *plastic natures*, though I recall that Julius Scaliger and other Peripatetics, as well as certain adherents of Van Helmont's doctrine of the archeus believed that the soul makes its own body. (GP VI, 544/ L 589)

Leibniz, on the contrary, has animals or corporeal substances that are neither generated nor destroyed, but only transformed in accordance with the pre-established harmony, and whose transformations are explicable by a theory of material, as opposed to immaterial, plastic natures, as the next section will show.

4. MATERIAL PLASTIC NATURES AND DERIVATIVE FORCE[13]

The second reason why preformation and the infinitely complex organic body provide material plastic natures lies in the fact that the infinitely complex organic body has its own physical derivative forces embedded within it. To this extent, Leibniz's derivative forces do the same work as Cudworth's immaterial plastic natures. Cudworth regards his plastic natures as the causes behind the motions and resistances of bodies. They obviate the need to resort to God to explain the motion of bodies. This is the very role that Leibniz assigns to the derivative forces of bodies. He notes at the beginning of his *A Specimen of Dynamics* that there must be something over and above extension in corporeal things. There must be a "force of nature" implanted everywhere by the Creator (GM VI, 235/ AG 118). That this force is a derivative force, not a primitive force, is clear from Leibniz's description of it as endowed with "conatus or nisus" (GM VI, 235/ AG 118) that attains its full effect "unless it is impeded by a contrary *conatus*" (GM VI, 235/ AG 118). Derivative forces are forces of acting and resisting in physical bodies. They are the forces within bodies "by which bodies actually act on one another or are acted upon by one another" (*A Specimen of Dynamics*: GM VI, 237/ AG 120).

Each derivative force is metaphysically grounded in its being a modification of monadic primitive active and passive forces. Such primitive forces, taken individually, give rise to the sequences of perceptions and appetitions that constitute each individual creature's mental life. Aggregated together as the organic body of a creature, these same primitive forces are modified as physical derivative forces in the body. And so, derivative forces belong to the corporeal substances only insofar as the corporeal substances possess organic bodies in which the derivative forces reside.

Thus, as do Cudworth's immaterial plastic natures, Leibniz's material derivative forces operate at the level of phenomena. In his *Correspondence with De Volder*, which dates from around the same time as he was writing *Considerations on Vital Principles and Plastic Natures* for Le Clerc, Leibniz informs the Leiden professor that his derivative forces are to be "relegated to the phenomena" or to the "corporeal mass":

I show that corporeal mass [*massa*], which is thought to have something over and above simple substances, is not a substance, but a phenomenon resulting from simple substances, which alone have unity and absolute reality. I relegate derivative forces to the phenomena ... (To De Volder, 1704 or 1705: GP II, 275/ AG 181)

The phenomenal bodies to which derivative forces are relegated are aggregates of corporeal substances or animals, whose own organic bodies are also aggregates of corporeal substances with organic bodies. In relegating derivative forces to phenomena, Leibniz is assigning derivative forces to organic aggregate bodies. They are assignable to inorganic bodies only insofar as each inorganic aggregate is a composite of organic ones.

Like the phenomenal aggregate bodies themselves, derivative active and passive forces are divided into "lesser phenomena" (To De Volder, 30 June 1704: G II, 268/ AG 179). In other words, they are divided across the smaller organic bodies that comprise larger organic bodies. Derivative forces are infinitely complex. Each is composed of an infinite number of smaller derivative forces in the organic bodies of the subordinate corporeal substances that comprise the parts of the organic body of the larger corporeal substance. The motion of a body over time "derives from an infinite number of impetuses" and each momentary impetus itself "arises from an infinite number of increments successively impressed on a given mobile thing" (*A Specimen of Dynamics*: GM VI, 238/AG 121).

Derivative forces, as well as being either active or passive, are also either living or dead forces. The dead forces are mere "solicitations" to motion. They have not yet given rise to motion in a body. Accumulation of dead forces, however, gives rise to the actual living forces from which the motion of the body does arise: "living force ... arises from an infinity of continual impressions of dead force" (GM VI, 238/ AG 122). Living force itself is also either total or partial. Partial living forces are either relative or directive. The relative partial living forces are those by which the subordinate organic bodies within a larger aggregate body act upon each other. The directive partial living forces are the forces by which the whole aggregate itself acts on other bodies outside of itself. Total force Leibniz conceives as comprising both the relative and directive partial living forces. What Leibniz is developing in *A Specimen of Dynamics* is a complex system of (seemingly) interacting forces in which the parts of a body act on the other bodies in the aggregate and the body as a whole acts on other bodies external to it. Each organic body is in this way a machine, acting by means of its own derivative active and passive forces, but also composed of smaller machines, each of which is itself divided into increasingly smaller and smaller machines of nature.

This is not at all dissimilar to the way in which Cudworth conceives immaterial plastic natures as present in matter in all its infinite divisions. Leibniz's theory of derivative force, however, is potentially more useful as the basis of a sound dynamical philosophy, capable of describing and even explaining the motions and resistances of bodies in physical terms in ways that neither Cudworth's immaterial natures, nor of course, Leibniz's correlative primitive active and passive forces, could ever hope to emulate. The differences, of course, are crucial. The only plastic natures that Leibniz admits are material ones. As physical, not metaphysical, forces, derivative forces may be regarded as *material* plastic natures. Material plastic natures have the advantage over immaterial ones in that they do not introduce metaphysical forces into physical explanations. As noted earlier, Leibniz had criticised Cudworth's doctrine on the ground that it resorted too soon to metaphysical notions that are out of place within a purely mechanical system of explanation. In Leibniz's dynamics, derivative forces, operating within the pre-established harmony among bodies, eliminate the need to appeal to primitive metaphysical forces in scientific explanations. While it is indeed the case that each derivative force is a modification of a metaphysical primitive force from which it springs, the way in which the modification arises and the nature of the ultimate source of the modification, do not need to be, and cannot be, explained in scientific terms.

Each derivative force is like an individual moment in the unfolding of the more general law that governs the whole corporeal substance, but, because the derivative forces are "relegated to the phenomena", each can occur only given the presence of the corporeal substance's infinitely divided organic body. Appeal to derivative forces, however, is all that is required in a physical explanation of the phenomena. To go beyond these to the foundational primitive forces is to appeal to metaphysical concepts that are out of place in the mechanistic explanation and which indeed serve no physically relevant explanatory purpose. Cudworth's plastic natures do not fill Leibniz's need because they too, like the primitive forces of the monads, are metaphysical rather than mechanical. What *is* needed are the derivative forces of bodies themselves, together with the doctrine of preformation and the infinite complexity of organic bodies.

It is our contention, therefore, that the material plastic natures that Leibniz brings into play in relation to Cudworth are already present in part in his dynamics as bodies' derivative forces. The equivalence is not exact. Material plastic natures are "natures" or "essences". Derivative forces, on the other hand, are mere modifications of primitive essences or natures. Strictly speaking, as modifications of primitive forces, derivative forces are not natures at all. But they do reside within corporeal substances and these, as substances, have their own natures or essences. The natures of preformed corporeal substances and the physical derivative forces that reside in their organic bodies together provide Leibniz with a material alternative to Cudworth's immaterial plastic natures.

5. THE SPECTRE OF ATHEISM

We will do well to conclude by drawing out some of the theological import in what otherwise might appear a rather recondite controversy in early modern natural philosophy. Cudworth worried that two different ancient varieties of atheism threatened to resurge within modern philosophy. There was, first of all, "*Anaximandrian* and *Democritick*" atheism, which had it that "the First Principle of all things… be *Stupid Matter* devoid of all manner of Life, and contending that all *Life* as well as other Qualities is *Generable* and *Corruptible*, a mere Accidental thing" (TIS I, iii, 34: RC 142). The other genus of atheism was for him the "*Stoical* and *Stratonical*," which founded everything on the principle "That there is a *Life* and *Natural Perception* Essential to *Matter, Ingenerable* and *Incorruptible*" (TIS I, iii, 34: RC 142). According to Cudworth's theory in contrast, as we have seen, life and perception do guide natural phenomena, while nonetheless not being intrinsic to matter.

Cudworth does not, for the most part, accuse his contemporaries of overt atheism. Rather, he believes that they allow atheistic ideas to seep into their systems unawares. Cartesian mechanism without some supplementary role for spirit is patently atheistic, since it allows nature, given a fixed quantity of motion, to function altogether on its own, without any perceived need for phenomena to be explained by non-material causes. Cudworth understands occasionalism, the theory according to which "every thing in Nature should be done immediately by God itself," to be no less atheistic than the other alternative, that of chance, in so far as "it would render Divine Providence Operose, Sollicitous and Distractious, and thereby make the Belief of it to be entertained with greater difficulty, and give advantage to Atheists" (TIS I, iii, 4: RC 149). For God to have to see to everything is effectively for God to be demoted to a station in the world whose occupant is unworthy of the name "God" and atheism again prevails. Thus Cudworth thinks that both Cartesian interactionism and Malebranchean occasionalism open the door to Godlessness, while only a theory of nature underlain by plastic natures can avoid such encroachment. What is needed instead is "some other Immediate *Agent* and

Executioner...., for the producing of every Effect; since not so much as a Stone or other Heavy Body, could at any time fall downward, merely by the Force of a *Verbal Law*, without any other *Efficient Cause*" (TIS I, iii, 37, art. 2: RC 147).

Cudworth's answer to Descartes and Malebranche – not to mention Spinoza, who in collapsing God and nature into one promotes a view no better for Cudworth than materialism – is a novel synthesis of mechanistic atomism with a Platonic metaphysics of spirit and matter. Spirit itself is an approximation of God, thereby allowing God to retain a role neither as – to use Robert Boyle's phrase – a "vicegerent,"[14] nor as an internal animating force, but instead as the epitome of spiritual nature to which particular plastic natures approximate.

Leibniz contends that his philosophy too is able to avoid atheism. In the first instance, Leibniz is excused from atheism for exactly the same reasons as is Cudworth. Leibniz is rescued from the atheistic threat that comes with the attribution to God of direct responsibility for the motions of bodies. Only the motions and resistances of bodies, arising from their derivative forces, bring about changes in the speed and direction of other bodies' motions. Neither souls nor God effect these changes immediately. Leibniz is also rescued from the similar threat that comes from the removal of God-like (because mind-like) principles from nature altogether. Substantial forms and souls are everywhere throughout the material world, each dominating its own organic body.

But whereas in Cudworth's view, immaterial plastic natures effect physical changes on material bodies, Leibniz's spiritual principles, unlike Cudworth's, do not so much "Drudgingly Execute" (TIS I, iii, 37, art. 5: RC 150) the work that must needs get done in nature, as they underlie nature itself. The primitive forces of the simple substances are the metaphysical foundations whose modifications are the derivative forces present in aggregate, extended bodies. But the primitive forces do not actually interfere in the everyday causal interactions of bodies. This non-interference is made possible by pre-established harmony, which guarantees that even without plastic natures everything will unfold as if God always had a hand in it, while keeping the transcendent Creator's hands free from those calluses that would afflict a lesser demiurge.

Moreover, Leibniz believes that this doctrine of pre-established harmony, and the associated theory of the preformation of corporeal substances and of the infinite complexity of the mechanism of each organic body, not only avoids atheism but serves as a powerful counter against it insofar as it provides positive reason to assert the existence of God. The mechanical organisation present in the arrangement of the organic bodies that comprise the extended material world is so intricate that it can only have been so arranged by divine wisdom (To Masham, September 1704: GP III, 362).[15] As he would later explain in the *Theodicy*, and as we have outlined above, mechanical operations suffice to "produce the organic bodies of animals", but they do so only because the seeds of present organic bodies were already "contained in those of the [organic] bodies whence they spring, right back to the primary seeds" (GP VI, 40/ HF 64). The preformation of creatures depends upon God's infinite power and wisdom. Only God could have pre-established the order of nature right from the very beginning (GP VI, 40/ HF 64). Leibniz's account of a world in which "[t]here is no chaos in the inward nature of things, and there is organism everywhere in a matter" (GP VI, 40/ HF 64) is a description of a world explicable only as the handiwork of God.

NOTES

[1]   'Je vis ce livre la premiere fois à Rome, où M. Auzout, Mathematicien François de grande reputation, l'avoir apporté, et je fus charmé de voir les plus belles pensées des sages de l'antiquité mises dans leur jour, et accompagnées de solides reflexions: en un mot beaucoup d'erudition, et autant de lumiere, jointes ensemble' (To Masham, early 1704?: GP III, 336).

[2]   A VI iv, 1943–55. The editors note the watermark dated July–August 1689 (A VI iv, 1943).

[3]   "Je considere la correspondance que j'ay avec Mylady Masham, comme si je l'avois avec Mons. Lock luy même en partie, car puisqu'il estoit chez elle à la campagne à Oates, lorsque cette dame m'écrivoit et me repondoit sur mon hypothese philosophique et marquoit même que Mons. Lock voyoit nos lettres, il y a apparence qu'il y a quelque part, au moins par le jugement qu'il en faisoit sans doute, et qu'il ne dissimuloit pas apparemment aupres de cette dame" (To Burnett, 2 August 1704: GP III, 297–8).

[4]   L 590, note 1.

[5]   For a fine, earlier discussion of Cudworth's role in the development of a philosophical conception of force in Leibniz, see Wilson, C. 1990.

[6]   This and related features of Cudworth's theory of innate principles of development in nature are treated in Smith, J. E. H. 2006.

[7]   Cudworth's view of the natural world is described in Jacob 1991: 110–14.

[8]   Cudworth describes hylozoism at TIS I, iii, 2: RC 105.

[9]   In personal conversation.

[10]   See also Fichant 2003. We agree with Fichant that the reality or actualisation of the organic body or natural machine requires the activity of the dominant monad (2003: 19).

[11]   As far as we can determine, the first occurrence of the term "organisme" in Leibniz is in May 1704, in the correspondence with Masham (GP III, 340). See also Leibniz's letters of 30 June 1704 (GP III, 356) and September 1704 (GP III, 362). Masham uses the term "organism" in her letter of June 1704 (GP III, 350) and it appears again in her letter to Leibniz of 8 August 1704 (GP III, 358). From this point, it appears Leibniz uses the term "organism" is used to describe the mechanism of the body of the corporeal substance, not the corporeal substance itself and the correlate term "organic body" to refer to particular instantiations of this mechanism. Thus in the passages cited from the De Volder correspondence and the *Principles*, what is organic is the body itself, while an animal is this same body regarded as ensouled.

[12]   Of course, Leibniz admits there are inanimate bodies, but their motion is a result of the animated parts and is not caused by their being moved by a World Soul.

[13]   The interpretation of derivative force assumed in what follows is defended in Phemister 2005: 187–207.

[14]   Boyle 1996: 13.

[15]   Masham insists to Leibniz that her father's plastic natures do not lead to atheism because they too are dependent on God's intellect (20 October 1705: GP III, 371).

8. LEIBNIZ'S *NOUVEAUX ESSAIS*

A contest by dialogue

The most conspicuous feature of *Nouveaux Essais* (NE) is the form in which it is written – a dialogue between Philalethes, a follower of Locke, and Theophilus, a follower of Leibniz, or rather Leibniz himself.[1] One might expect the exchange to exhibit a form that indicates and implements the overall purpose of the piece, as one finds with Leibniz's other works in this genre.[2] But the point of dialogue in NE is unclear, and its effect is disappointing.[3] At least in part, this is because Philalethes' speeches are limited largely to rehearsing the content of Locke's *Essay*. While Theophilus is responsive to his companion's reports, Philalethes generally replies with little more than the next point in his source. This, alone, prevents discussion from developing a thesis, unravelling a problem, or guiding a novice from ignorance to knowledge. Since these are the familiar philosophical purposes of dialogue, its use in NE seems sterile to many readers. Ceding control of the agenda to Locke fosters other seemingly unsatisfying aspects of the work. Although there are many points on which the philosophers disagree, and Philalethes is converted on a number of them, Leibniz's method of arguing is elusive. Exposition of his position is unsystematic and inevitably diffuse. There is no attempt to demonstrate the metaphysical claims that, as we know, Leibniz was most anxious to establish against Locke – despite his insistence that these doctrines are capable of rigorous demonstration. His contentions are generally based on a handful of principles that he makes little effort to prove.[4] To many readers, the exchange seems to provide scant reason to credit Leibniz's philosophy overall, or to dismiss that of Locke.

This paper proposes, however, that the exchange has a form productive of philosophical results. Perhaps the dialogue's peculiar structure, rather than stifling debate, is the key to Leibniz's mode of engagement with Locke. Its unusual features may enable a method of evaluating the two philosophers' doctrines that serves in place of the sort of argumentation commentators expect, but fail to find. This is the thesis of the present paper. Many factors affected how Leibniz proceeded with respect to his English counterpart. My concern is not with his motivation, but just with the dialectic device he deploys.[5] A better understanding of the role of dialogue in NE may, at least, bring readers' expectations more in line with the author's intentions.

1. PURPOSES OF THE DISCUSSANTS: INFORMATION SHARING AND PROBATION

Leibniz apparently made a strategic decision to use dialogue to frame his remarks. Manuscripts show that Books I and II were initially drafted in a format that interspersed extracted portions or summaries of the *Essay* with Leibniz's comments.

111

P. Phemister and S. Brown (eds.), Leibniz and the English-Speaking World, 111–132.
© 2007 *Springer.*

It was only when starting Book III that he shifted to dialogue, later returning to adjust the two earlier books. The change of style caused little disruption. The Preface was added, as were the first several conversational exchanges; none of this material was drawn from the previous draft.[6] For the rest, the earlier version was easily converted to conversation since it already distinguished two voices: one Locke's; the other Leibniz's. From this, it appears that dialogue does not so much affect what Leibniz says about his opponent's views, as the context in which he says it. The switch turns a series of comments into a fictional event, in which the participants do not just give voice to the views of the two philosophers, but also reflect on them. Leibniz may well have thought this allowed a type of philosophical exchange that would be difficult, if not impossible, in the original format.

Conversation is governed by canons of rationality; as Paul Grice observed, the purpose for which people converse determines, in a general way, what they ought to say at each stage.[7] We might, accordingly, look to the aim of the conversation depicted in NE to understand its implicit rules. In fact, the characters reveal their purposes at the outset. Reunited after a long absence, the friends find their philosophical views have grown in different directions, and Theophilus anticipates: "we have what we need to give each other a long period of mutual pleasure by explaining our positions to one another" (NE: A VI vi, 71).[8] In addition to updating each other on their philosophical thoughts, they also intend to compare them for truth. The truth deciding aim is soon made explicit. Reporting that he disagrees with his friend's opinion "that we can acquire all our knowledge without aid of innate impressions," Theophilus says: "what follows will make us see which of us is right" (NE: A VI vi, 75).

Theophilus mentions another purpose. While he "found fine things" in the *Essay*, he adds, "it seems to me that we should go further into things, and even part company with [Locke's] opinions when he adopts ones that limit us unduly, and somewhat lower not only the condition of man but also that of the universe" (NE: A VI vi, 73). Two aims are thereby announced: treating things less abstractly and redressing demoralizing opinions. With the former in view, a number of Theophilus' speeches, which otherwise seem tiresome digressions, make conversational sense, that is, contribute to the speaker's ends.[9] And Theophilus takes every opportunity to promote plans for increasing our knowledge and to admire the infinite fineness of the universe. For his part, Philalethes hopes he will find "something solid" in his friend's views and expresses willingness to be taught in that case.[10] In context, this pointedly signals reluctance to accede to doctrines seemingly favorable to religion and morality without solid evidence of their truth. We know what "Theophilus" means. The Lockean explains that he sometimes adopts the name by which he goes in the dialogue, for it means "one who sincerely seeks to know the truth" (NE: A VI vi, 73, 386). Truth-seeking is one explicit purpose of the dialogue; correcting demoralizing opinions is another, but subordinate to the first.[11] Also at the outset, Philalethes announces the peculiar conversational rule: to "take care to follow" the *Essay*, which he claims to remember almost *verbatim*.

As depicted, the discussants make some progress in the search for truth. On rough count, there are more than twenty speeches in which Theophilus states that he has shown some thesis to be true. Philalethes claims no such successes, but there are several places where he says, in effect, that he has come to see that his former opinions are false. At the same time, they speak of a vague, but unpretentious, degree of probation. Theophilus claims to show [*montre*] things, to make it seen [*faire voir*] that claims are true, to have established [*déterminé*] some things, removed [*levé*] problems, refuted his friend's opinions and disabused him. Different terms are used in NE when a high degree of certainty is in view: *prouver, démontrer, connoissance certaine*; but these words are not applied to results of the discussion.[12] Some letters of Leibniz provide further evidence that he takes NE to have probative force, but in moderate degree. Several times, he writes that his aim is to "clarify" things, which at least implies progress toward truth.[13] To Jacquelot, he says more specifically that he aims, above all, to vindicate the immateriality of the soul; that he justifies innate ideas and truths, as well as the utility of maxims; and that he shows several other doctrines.[14]

Leibniz ascribes probative power to the discussion staged in NE. But so far, this is not to say that dialogue is integral to this result, that the form gives rational credibility to the outcome. It remains to be seen whether the exchange is conducted in a manner capable of justifying one or the other party's views. My thesis is that the rules of the fictional conversation are, in effect, the logical form in which Leibniz's philosophy is tested against Locke's.

Background for this interpretation is found in Leibniz's studies in logic, including (*inter alia*) the art of discussing a question well. Rooted in Artistotle's *Topics*, this branch of logic was developed in several directions by the medievals, reformed by humanist authors, and reconstituted, again, in the universities of the early modern era.[15] It had special interest for Leibniz, who hoped to cultivate a discursive art of resolving controversies on the basis of reasons. Toward this end, he studied ways of organizing discussion for the purpose of deciding a disputed question with a degree of certitude appropriate to the available data. Leibniz's work in this multi-faceted area has recently received sustained attention from Marcelo Dascal and his colleagues.[16] They are, I think, the first to observe that Leibniz's research in theory of discourse is, or might be, portrayed in NE. This paper follows the general idea, but develops it along rather different lines. To put it briefly, the scholars mentioned suggest the dialogue illustrates Leibniz's ideal of conflict resolution, which they take to be a conciliation of positions held going into the discussion, a synthesis drawn from opposing views.[17] On the account urged in this paper, however, the friends come to agree as a result of an amicable competition between their original views. The initial position of one wins out, and the opinion of the other is consequently revised.[18] In the event, Locke's follower alters some of his views, but there is scant indication that Theophilus does the same.

2. HOW TO HEAR A DISPUTE PRODUCTIVELY: *AVOID DISTORTION,*
PRESENT THE ECONOMY

In many papers and letters, Leibniz complained that disputes in important areas – practical and theoretical, religious and secular, public and private – are badly managed.[19] Either they arrive at no decision or, a bad one (NE: A VI vi, 418). From the 1670s on, he was writing on questions such as the value and purpose of hearing disputes, appropriate rules and procedures for conducting a hearing, the proper judge of controversies. Naturally his focus shifted over time; it issued in several formal projects, which were never realized – a balance to weigh reasons, a calculus of probabilities, a complete juridical logic.[20] It also produced a number of practical proposals for managing effective discussion.[21] Much of this material on organizing discourse for problem solving purposes finds its way into NE. But two themes are especially important for my purpose: (i) that strict procedures are needed to avoid inter-personal pitfalls and (ii) that rules of contesting are indispensable for securing an outcome.

To begin with the first, Leibniz notes that the discussants' self-promoting behavior usually keeps them from settling anything.[22] An essay *Des Controverses* (1680) names devices which we all realize we unthinkingly deploy in the heat of debate. For one thing, "each of the disputants chooses his own style of ordering, and arranges the reasoning of his adversary to suit himself, just as he does his own." Moreover, "in reporting the opponent's arguments, one conceals or weakens them. This is often without malice due to pressure to turn everything to one's advantage." Another invention is "the repetition of one's purported reasons without taking account of the responses that the adversary has given, which happens either due to forgetfulness or due to caution, for often the responses seem to one pitiful and unworthy of being reported. Yet the adversary is persuaded of just the contrary." Finally, "there is digression, when we loose our heads and throw ourselves at some incidental difficulty … which always gives rise to new questions" (A IV iii, 210).[23] The same essay proposes a remedy for such evasions, namely, a prescription for recording the discussion. A person is to be charged with the difficult task of presenting all sides of the debate in such a faithful and neutral way that no reader will be able to tell which side the reporter favors. The report must expunge extraneous speech, eliminate all hint of emotion, identify the several reasons put forward on each side and the corresponding replies, and present the whole in an orderly way "so that one can see the entire economy" of the dispute. From this, "it will ordinarily be easy for a man of good sense to judge what has been accomplished on the basis of the report without the reporter needing to state it" (A IV iii, 212).[24]

We can see in this a basis for the most conspicuous rule in NE: that Philalethes's speeches should generally follow the *Essay*. We might say this is a precaution meant to guard against distorting the order of Locke's reasons, for the practice conforms to Leibniz's theory in this respect. Yet if this is the author's intention, he should be equally concerned to prevent other abuses, such as omitting or enfeebling his opponent's arguments. In fact, Locke's reasoning is very often altered; this could hardly be avoided, because it is rendered by Leibniz already working from

Coste's translation. In any number of places, Locke's point is missed, blunted, or misdirected.[25] Even so, one could argue, Leibniz aims to depict a successful discussion, which requires that Locke's position be faithfully represented.[26] If he does not manage to avoid distortion altogether, he may still take measures toward that end. It is not unlikely that the conversational rule, which seems to stifle fruitful debate, has a theory-based function.

There could be no objective reporter depicted in NE because the author is one of the disputants, but the participants themselves keep a record. Theophilus, in particular, regularly notes when he or his friend repeats an earlier point.[27] Both parties note, now and then, that Theophilus has been digressing.[28] As mentioned, they signal, in various ways, that certain doctrines are shown or refuted.[29] The fact that the discussants are keeping track of their claims, responses, and progress toward truth implies, pragmatically, that readers should do the same.

We do, in fact, understand that points relevant to the search for truth must be extracted from their immediate conversational context. Philosophically inclined readers take the dialogue in two ways – (i) as conversation for the purpose of mutual exchange of the participants' views; Philalethes tends to say what comes next in the *Essay* and Theophilus responds with his own view on the topic, in accord with Grice's basic rule for co-operative information-sharing exchange: say what is relevant to the immediately prior speech, in view of the agreed upon purpose of the conversation; and (ii) as a competitive exchange for the purpose of seeing which party's views are correct; the operative rule calls for making contributions with an eye, not just to the immediate stage, but to a score to be tabulated at the end of the conversation on the basis of all contributions and regardless of order.[30]

A reader who wants to follow the competition must assemble statements from scattered portions of the dialogue. To illustrate, Leibniz clearly intends to make a case that the necessary truths of logic, mathematics, etc. are innate in the human mind; the thesis is enunciated in Book I, where it is plainly relevant, but supported by an argument that hardly seems worth considering. The argument delivered in Book I comes to this: we have basic knowledge of the necessity of general truths in arithmetic, etc.; the only truths known by our senses are singular; singular propositions cannot justify the necessity of a general proposition (at most, they are evidence of the truth of a generalization); so our basic knowledge of the necessity of general truths comes, not from our senses, but from principles that are innate (NE: A VI vi, 49–51, 77, 85; also NE: A VI vi, 446–7). Of course the discussion is subtle, complex, and suggestive, but this is the bare-bones argument. To those familiar with the *Essay*, it seems a flagrant failure to engage, for Locke agrees that the particular truths known by the senses are insufficient to justify the mathematical knowledge we have. Yet Locke avoids Leibniz's conclusion, because he has a non-innatist account of a priori knowledge. Such knowledge is founded on the immediate self-evidence of basic truths, from which other truths are demonstrated by self-evident steps. Locke contends that we immediately accept, say, that $2 + 3 = 5$, when we first understand it, not because the truth is innate, but rather because we have a general capacity to recognize self-evident truths.[31] Since Locke has, after all, a theory of a priori knowledge, Leibniz's contention that necessary truths are known a priori – and therefore innate – seems entirely irrelevant. The failure of logical contact is local to this part of the dialogue, however. It is explained, I suggest, by the parties' adherence to a Gricean co-operative information sharing conversational rule.

The characters use the whole conversation to decide whose view is right. The account of the epistemology and metaphysics of necessary truths, which Theophilus eventually puts on the table, directly challenges Locke on a priori knowledge. It involves the following claims, again stated only in outline: (a) axioms of geometry, e.g. may be allowed to be self-evident, but they do not have the highest degree of certainty; such axioms should be accepted only provisionally until they are demonstrated by principles that are still more certain;[32] (b) the metaphysical ground of necessary truths, i.e. their necessity, is not found in human ideas, but rather in the understanding of God, the source of all possible being; (c) mathematical ideas in human souls express, correspond to, and are caused by ideas in the understanding of God – hence, innate.[33] For Leibniz, a priori knowledge is warranted in part by consciously grasped connections among ideas; but Lockean self-evidence is less certain than evidence of another sort. Moreover, a priori truths have an external warrant in virtue of the correspondence between our ideas and the eternal archetypes of all that can possibly exist. The additional warrant is in effect even if those who assent to necessary truth are unaware of its presence. This theory of Leibniz plainly engages Locke's anti-innatist epistemology. For the present, my point is just this. In Book I, Theophilus gives an argument for his innatist thesis consisting of just what is topically relevant there, and it has no force against his friend. Substantive engagement is achieved, but only later on, when Philalethes arrives at matters that make it relevant for Theophilus to expound his theory of a priori justification (NE IV, ii) and the metaphysical ground of necessary truth (NE IV, xi).

We are forced to piece together Leibniz's position on a number of topics because the dialogue follows the order of Locke's thought. Although many readers consider this a fault, it has ground in Leibniz's theory. No party engaged in a dispute speaks to the case systematically; all participants order things for their advantage. Only a neutral reporter can reconstruct all sides of the issue in the objective way that permits it to be decided well. Since Leibniz, both author and character, is an interested party, how is the fundamental economy of the dispute to be recorded? How else, if not by readers, themselves.[34]

3. RULES THAT ENABLE A DECISION

In an early paper (1677?), Leibniz developed the thesis that the hearing of a controversy is a sort of contest: "A hearing [*judicium*] is a state of contesting [*certantium*] with reasons under the expectation of a conclusion" (A VI iv, C 2163–7).[35] Some contests are by physical force, but a *judicium* is a contest by reasons, yet still under the expectation of a decision. At the end of a war, it is usually clear who won, but when combat by reasons ends, it is seldom evident which side is holding the truth. How, then, can there be a realistic expectation of a conclusive outcome? Leibniz begins to answer this question:

> Thus a hearing [*Judicium*] differs from a dispute [*Disputatione*] in this, that in a hearing under the start of the contest there is the expectation that it is possible to arrive at a conclusion; and when a dispute is begun without a judge or rule, nothing important is accomplished, but the condition of the issue at the start remains the same at the end; as does the condition of souls. (*De controversiis sacris generalibus*; A VI iv; C 2163)

Continuing this line of thought:

> The expectation of an exit consists in the contest's having a nature that, one judges, obliges one to expect a conclusion. ... Thus in order that we thoroughly understand controversies, which can arise in legal, sacred, or civil affairs, we should consider the persons doing the contesting, the expectation of a conclusion due to the rules of the contest itself, and finally the reasons by which the issue is contested. For treatment of a judge or a rule is contained under treatment of the expectation of a conclusion. (A VI iv, C 2164)

In this paper, nothing more specific is said about appropriate rules, but the idea is clear enough. In a successful discussion of a controversial matter, the participants' contributions must have a logical shape capable of deciding on which side truth lies. Without that, there is mere dispute and no one's mind is changed.

For this purpose, Leibniz places great store in the established process of arguing in form. A letter to Gabriel Wagner (1696) describes what happens when people try to reason with each other: "... in free discourse, we think more of skill, eloquence, and subtlety, of approval and esteem, than of the foundation of truth. The result is that when both sides are defended by able and alert people, no decision is reached, but both sides are merely stiffened" (GP VII, 521/ L 467). The solution is regulation. Leibniz illustrates with a favorite anecdote, an experiment he made while disputing with a scholar on a question of dynamics:

> ... we exchanged letters which, though courteous, were not without mutual complaints that each unintentionally distorted the meanings and utterances of the other. So I proposed the syllogistic form, ... We carried the matter beyond the twelfth pro-syllogism, and from the time we began this, complaints ceased, and we understood each other ... (GP VII, 522/ L 467)[36]

There are definite rules for arguing in form: one party produces a valid syllogism to prove the proposition in dispute; the other party either accepts it, and the matter is concluded, or challenges a premise; in the latter case, the first party produces a pro-syllogism to prove the premise; the second party has the same options as before, and so on; the procedure ends if the second party agrees with the first or the first party admits lack of proof.[37] To Leibniz's mind, the experiment confirms the effectiveness of form-governing rules: "For the very nature of our procedure will eliminate all repetition, irrelevance, unnecessary prolixity, ... deficiencies and omissions, whether intentional or unintentional, and ... all disorder, misunderstanding, and dishonest conduct of the argument as well" (GP VII, 522/ L 467). But, as he elsewhere allows, the procedure is mind-numbingly tedious.[38]

Other rules of contesting are promoted. A brief allusion to a familiar set of rules is made in the following passage taken from a long tract on the reunion of the western Church:

> ... the way of dispute or discussion is ineffective, as long as there is no judge, and no regular form that the disputants are obliged to follow exactly. Because of this, in conferences, as well as written controversies, ... one conceals the objections or solutions of the adversary, ... one does not distinguish the office of the respondent [*respondant*] or that of the opposent [*opposant*], any more than that of the one that must prove or not prove [*doit prouver ou non*]. (*Des Methodes de Reunion*, n.d.: FCO II, 2)

Lack of a judge and lack of regular form are two sides of the same coin; the form determines how the contest is decided. Here Leibniz complains that discussants ignore the rules of scholastic disputation, which assign the responsibility to prove to one party and different responsibilities, to the other party.

The uses of disputation in medieval universities were several, and the purpose of some forms of the practice is now obscure. In the seventeenth century, however, its official purpose was to determine the truth, or falsity, of a thesis.[39] In fact, it was mainly an exercise for students although more serious disputations were required for the baccalaureate, and faculty disputed as well. The basic rules are simple. Any number of speakers could take part, but two sets of duties are to be performed, those of respondent and opposant:

> The respondent began by making known his affirmative or negative response to some thesis or question. The opponent then produced a series of arguments designed to show the falsity of the respondent's position. The respondent had to repeat these arguments, analyze them, and reply to each appropriate part by granting it, denying it, or making a distinction. The opponent then attacked the respondent with further arguments and with counter-examples. Both parties were supposed to uphold truth as far as possible, ... The respondent had also to avoid contradicting himself, whereas the opponent hoped to induce him to do just that. (Ashworth ed. 1985: li–lii)

Evidently the respondent wins if she neither contradicts herself nor affirms a known falsehood; we need not go into a full account of conditions for winning, losing, or halting without decision.

In so-called "public disputations," the rules require (or allow) the respondent to state reasons for answering as she does; the reasons are added to the list of propositions the opponent can attack.[40] Conditions sufficient for victory were not changed under these more demanding rules – the respondent wins provided she affirms nothing known to be false, including mutually contradictory propositions. From the point of view of probation, a skilfully conducted disputation can indicate whether a thesis can, or cannot, be defended against objections, but nothing more. The opponent is obliged to prove *against* the thesis. The respondent's evidence-giving arguments come into play only because the opponent, by raising objections to their soundness, might force the respondent to affirm something known to be false. Disputation is plainly not a significant test of truth for some theses; the old example of a thesis unsuited for disputation is that the number of stars is even. Still, in disputation of some theses, loss on the part of a skilful respondent makes their falsity highly credible. And the truth of a thesis supported by antecedent evidence could gain additional rational credibility if successfully defended against an able opposent.

Philalethes complains that the practice does nothing but encourage students to cavil and deny the obvious. But although Theophilus admits that school disputations are sloppily run and hardly concerned with truth, he insists the procedure can be useful; for instance, "... at the start of the Reformation the Protestants challenged their adversaries to conferences and disputes, and sometimes upon the success of these disputes the public decided in favor of reform." Still he goes on in a critical vein: "The art of disputing, or of combat with reasons, ... is very great and important; but unfortunately it is very badly regulated, which is why often no decision is reached, or a bad one. ... In short, the art of conferring and disputing needs to be totally reorganized" (NE: A VI vi, 418).

Still Leibniz trusts the model for some purposes. In his published *Discours Préliminaire de La Conformity de la Foy avec la Raison* (1710), he uses disputational rules to defend the rationality of assent to Christian mysteries against Pierre Bayle's attack. In this case, both parties agree that items of faith are backed by "motives of credibility," such as reports of miracles associated with their delivery. Bayle contends it is nevertheless irrational to assent to mysteries because they are inconsistent with known truths. Leibniz, on the contrary, denies that faith and reason conflict. To show this, he casts the Christian believer in the role of respondent *vis à vis* an opposent who raises Bayle's objections. It is a well conceived strategy. By rules of the contest, the respondent is not prevented from winning by the incomprehensibility of the mysteries: "... he who maintains a thesis (the *respondens*) is not bound to account for it, but he is bound to meet the objections of an opponent." Faced with an objection, the defendant need only deny one of its premises or deny its force against the mystery, without contradicting himself. Stressing the probative value of this procedure, Leibniz notes its use in legal hearings: "A defendant ... is not bound (as a general rule) to prove his right or to produce his title to possession; but he is obliged to reply to the arguments of the plaintiff" (§58: GP VI, 82/ HF 105).[41] Leibniz trusts disputation enough to rest his case against Bayle on its rules. Of course, the outcome has probative force only because there is independent basis for accepting the contested thesis, the motives of credibility.

Some stretches of the exchange in NE plainly conform to disputational rules, as we will see. But without independent basis for accepting the doctrines defended, this has little or no truth-deciding value. Moreover, several doctrines said to be shown, in the dialogue, are not tested by these rules. It seems likely, then, that other rules of contesting are in play. Leibniz's thesis, that unregulated discussion has no expectation of reaching a conclusion (it changes nothing), strongly suggests that the dialogue instantiates a logical form capable of showing which of the parties is right.

There are at least two such rules abroad in NE, I suggest. Each character's claims are tested against those of the other by comparison on two grounds: explanatory power and capacity for solving metaphysical problems. If one character's doctrine does better than the other's by either measure, it thereby gains a certain rational credibility in the eyes of the discussants. Both modes of establishing truth are well rooted in Leibniz's thought. The first is drawn from his view on the methodology of natural science. A hypothesis about the causes of observed phenomena is confirmed in proportion to its explanatory success: "... a hypothesis becomes more probable as it is simpler to understand ... and the greater the number of phenomena that can be explained by it, and the fewer the further assumptions" (GP I, 195–6/ L 188). Leibniz proceeds to defend the principle against the ancient objection that true propositions (phenomena) can be deduced from a false premise. An essay promoting natural science also endorses the "conjectural method," which is to accept a hypothesis that can explain many phenomena until a more fruitful or intelligible one is found (A IV iii, 1999–2000/ L 283–4). The method is endorsed again in NE and scholars have found that it generally shapes Leibniz's treatment of questions in natural science.[42] The second test – that of problem-solving ability – was introduced in the *Systeme nouveau* (1695) in support of an anti-Cartesian account of the "nature and communication of substance." The basic argument made in this article consists of three points: the hypothesis of inter-substantial harmony is possible; it has advantages for religion and morals; and "... we may say that it is something more than a theory, since it hardly seems possible to explain things in any other intelligible way, and because several serious difficulties which have perplexed men's minds up till now seem to disappear of themselves when we fully understand it" (§§15–7: WF 19–20).[43] The last point hints at a contest, for the serious difficulties in view are presented as consequences of the Cartesian theory of substance.[44] Leibniz's alternative theory is, then, to be accepted largely because it solves difficulties internal to its main competitor. In NE, Locke is the competitor and his principled scepticism is a source of problems that, it is said, can be resolved by Leibniz's metaphysics.[45]

To sum up my argument so far: Leibniz's theory of discourse implies that productive discussion of disputed matters should be regulated and recorded in ways that are reflected in some of the peculiarities of the dialogue in NE. Moreover, in addition to theorizing that discussion of a controversial issue changes no minds unless conducted by rules capable of producing an outcome, Leibniz proposes several regulative structures. Among others, he overtly relies on rules of disputation to defend doctrines that have independent rational credibility in *Discours Préliminaire*. His characters rely on disputational form in NE, as well. But how is antecedent credibility bestowed in the dialogue? Still arguing from the theoretical demand for rules of contesting, I propose that credibility is assigned by the outcome of two bases of comparing the respective views of the discussants: their ability to explain agreed upon phenomena and their capacity to solve, as opposed to generate, mutually recognized problems. The doctrine that does better enjoys a degree of rational support, as a result; and its credibility is increased, if it can be defended by disputation. None of these three rules of contesting is explicit in the dialogue, but they implicitly determine the outcome, or so I suggest.

4. CONTESTING BY RULES OF DISPUTATION

A detailed argument from the text cannot be made here, but it is possible to illustrate how the suggestion works in a few prominent cases. To do this, I will once again need to describe positions and arguments broadly; although this ignores a great deal that is important and interesting, I think it sufficiently accurate to confirm my proposal. To start with the first rule, long stretches of the dialogue conform to the rules of disputation. At least three theses Theophilus is said to show are tested by disputation: (i) that we have innate knowledge of principles of logic, arithmetic, geometry, etc.; (ii) that the soul always thinks, "... even in sleep, it has some perception of what is happening around it" (NE: A VI vi, 115); (iii) that axioms and maxims are useful for demonstrating other truths.[46] Because I intend to illustrate another rule with the case of innatism, I focus on this example here. After a few sets of exchanges, both the first and second chapters of Book I fall into a pattern: Philalethes poses objections, many explicitly labelled objections, challenges, or phrased with the "but" of objection. Theophilus precisely performs the office of respondent. He either accepts the point but denies its force against his position, or introduces a distinction that deflects its force, or denies a premise of the objection. Sometimes he elaborates or provides reasons, as permitted under rules of public disputation. A look at the text will confirm this, but what does it show? One might say it shows nothing about tacit scholastic rules; it is merely the natural response to Locke's attack on innatism. After all, Book I, chapter 2 of the *Essay* is an extended objection to innatism in trilemma form: the theory of innate knowledge is either false – because it states that innate propositions are imprinted so that even children and idiots assent to them; or it is meaningless – because it makes no sense to say we know propositions of which we have never been aware; or it is no different from what Locke maintains – that humans have the innate capacity to perceive (some) truths and acquire knowledge. The tripartite objection must be reported and deflected, if Leibniz hopes to make a convincing case for innatism.[47] This is true, but it does not count against the proposal that he cast this phase of the discussion in disputational form. The crucial question is whether the exchange is *judged*, in the dialogue, by disputational rules.

If it is judged this way, it is fair to say that Theophilus wins – as he does in the dialogue. The respondent prevails if he neither affirms a known falsehood nor contradicts himself, and Theophilus manages that. More important, no more rigorous standard is applied to his responses. Indeed, critics of Leibniz complain that his replies to Locke invoke unclear or untenable distinctions: "implicit" or "potential" knowledge, as opposed to "actual" or "explicit" knowledge; innate tendencies, as (supposedly) distinct from innate capacities; propositions or ideas "drawn from the senses", in (alleged) contrast to their being "brought to mind" by the senses.[48] Theophilus makes some effort to explain these differences, but he is not challenged in the way many readers would like. In effect, they want a standard of adequacy for response more demanding than that in force in the dialogue, that is, rules different from those the discussants are playing by. The less demanding standard, which is operative, fits the rules of disputation.

5. CONTESTING ON THE BASIS OF EXPLANATORY POWER:
THE CASE OF INNATE IDEAS AND TRUTHS

Success under disputational rules has probative value only if the innatist theory has antecedent credibility. This comes, my suggestion is, from a comparison of the explanatory power of Locke's blank slate and that of Leibniz's innate tendencies. Theophilus claims to show "... there are ideas and principles which do not come from the senses, and which we find in ourselves without having formed them..." Ideas and truths are "in us implicitly," before we become aware of them.[49] I take this to mean that a mind has, and utilises, modifications that represent certain propositions before the mind consciously entertains them. Roughly speaking, NE contains three lines of reasoning in support of implicit (innate) principles: (i) one to the effect that various human cognitive performances indicate that some principles are in us implicitly: (ii) another, that the ideas we have by inner reflection are innate because "we are innate to ourselves"; (iii) finally, a priori knowledge of general necessary truths implicates innate ideas.[50] My suggestion is that each consideration is accepted (shown) on the ground that Leibniz's position affords a better explanation of agreed upon phenomena than does Locke's.

The first line of argument is readily construed as proposing a hypothesis to explain facts about human cognition; it belongs to the science of pneumatology (NE: A VI vi, 56). Theophilus links the innatism controversy directly to undeniable facts about our mental performance: "... even if they [sc. the laws of identity and non-contradiction] were not known, they would still be innate because *they are accepted as soon as they have been understood.* But ... fundamentally everyone does know them; ... *we use the principle of contradiction (for instance) all the time, without distinctly considering it, and there is no barbarian who, in a matter he takes seriously, is not offended by the conduct of a liar, who contradicts himself*" (NE: A VI vi, 76, italics added). Further, we constantly make inferences without thinking of the principles that validate them; an untutored Swedish boy does amazing arithmetical calculations in his head, and so on. These are, in effect, phenomena that Theophilus purports to explain. For him, an innate principle takes the form of a causally active mental modification, a constant tendency to form thoughts in accord with the principle, to make inferences licensed by it, to sort particular cases in accord with it, to assent to it when it comes explicitly to mind.[51] According to his hypothesis, we have innate tendencies to think and reason in accord with principles of logic and arithmetic (*inter alia*), which explain why we perform in the ways described. Accordingly Theophilus claims: "some [instincts] contain theoretical truths, and the internal principles of ... reasoning are like that, when we use them through a natural instinct without knowing the reasons for them. *You cannot avoid acknowledging some innate principles, in this sense ...*" (NE: A VI vi, 90, emphasis added). Indeed, Philalethes cannot deny that we often reason in accord with general truths without explicitly thinking of them, and before having entertained them; but he makes no attempt to explain how the mind constructs a cogent inference. Like Locke, he avoids hypotheses about hidden causes of conscious phenomena.[52] If explanation is the goal, he is forced to yield to his friend's hypothesis, all the more when it prevails in disputation against his Lockean objections. It must be said, however, that Theophilus' explanation is nearly trivial: we make inferences that conform to the law of non-contradiction because we have an in-born disposition to do so. While this does rule out other causes by identifying the type of mechanism that (purportedly) accounts for the fact that children make cogent inferences long before they assent to abstract principles, it cannot explain the fact that children sometimes reason illogically.

Theophilus's hypothesis does not win entirely by default, however. By and large, Locke tries to discredit innatism by charging it with obscurity, but this leads him to challenge its explanatory pretensions. In the effort to clarify the position, Locke anticipates, an innatist might say that a proposition is in-born in the human mind just in case humans assent to the proposition – not at birth, which Locke takes to be patently false – but rather as soon as it is proposed and understood. Locke retorts that this makes innatism useless. To explain the fact that humans assent, say, to the law of non-contradiction immediately upon understanding it, we need only note the principle's intrinsic self-evidence. Innate knowledge has nothing to do with it; assent is merely an exercise of the broad human capacity to acquire knowledge, in this case, by perceiving an evident truth.[53] As Philalethes puts it, "the unhesitant assent the mind gives certain truths depends on the capacity of the human mind [*la faculté de l'esprit humain*]." To which, his friend opines: "Very well. But it is the particular relation the human mind has to these truths that makes the exercise of this capacity easy and natural in regard to them, and this makes us say they are innate" (NE: A VI vi, 80). That is, self-evidence is not an intrinsic property of a proposition, but rather a property it has in relation to one or more minds. What is self-evident to one mind may not be, to another. The suggestion that humans immediately assent to a principle because of its evidence is no explanation at all; on the contrary, a proposition's being self-evident to humans is explained (or defined) by the general human disposition to give immediate assent. Theophilus's innatist explanation, thin as it is, has a fair claim to be better than that of Philalethes.

The second line of pro-innatist reasoning is summarized by the remark that ideas of being, substance, duration, action, etc. are innate, since "we are innate to ourselves" (NE Preface: A VI vi, 52).[54] This rather puzzling thesis deserves careful discussion.[55] Broadly speaking, though, I suggest that, at least in part, the claim is that the theory that ideas of being, substance, etc. are innate explains several (purported) facts about our existential statements and self-regarding behavior. With regard to the idea of being, Theophilus says: "... we are, so to speak, innate to ourselves, and as we are beings, being is innate in us, and the knowledge of being is comprised in the knowledge we have of ourselves" (NE: A VI vi, 102).[56] Later speeches apparently elaborate. Statements to the effect that things other than oneself exist are analyzed as predications. They express propositions formed from the idea of an object and the idea of existence: "And the existence of the object of the idea can be conceived as the concurrence of that object with myself" (NE: A VI vi, 358). In regard to innatism, the point seems to be that I cannot conceive x's existence as concurrence with myself unless I am disposed to assume that I exist, or to form thoughts in accord with this proposition. Further, Theophilus maintains, to ascribe any attribute to oneself is to assert (*inter alia*) that one exists; e.g. to say *I am thinking* is already to say *I am*. Thus "… we can be confident that [*I am*] is … one of the first known statements – in the natural order of our knowledge, that is, since it may never have occurred to a man to form this proposition explicitly, even though it is innate in him" (NE: A VI vi, 411). What supports the innatist conclusion here is, I take it, that children typically make existential and self-attributive assertions before it occurs to them that they, themselves, exist; yet the cogency of the former depends on the truth of the latter, as Theophilus has it. This developmental fact is purportedly explained by the hypothesis that humans are innately disposed to form thoughts governed by what is expressed by "I exist." The blank slate hypothesis offers no competing explanation. Nor does the *Essay* propound alternative analyses of existential and self-predicative statements, as far as I can see.

As for other ideas "innate to oneself," Theophilus claims that the uninterrupted sequence of a person's thoughts conveys a sense of genuine, substantial identity. This is so strong that we are naturally deceived, if our successive thoughts do not belong to the same enduring substance (NE: A VI vi, 236).[57] Perhaps he would say something similar about deliberations that lead to action, namely, that we are victims of deception if the substance that thinks these thoughts is not the cause of the intentional actions that follow. But a person may live long without explicitly assenting to the propositions expressed by "I am a substance, an enduring thing, a cause, etc." and this may be explained by the theory that, prior to our explicitly thinking such propositions, they influence our conscious thoughts.

A crucial question for my thesis is this: is rational support for innatism derived solely from the competition with Philalethes or, alternatively, does Theophilus adduce evidence sufficient to make the innatist hypothesis probable, independently of anything said by his friend? Two considerations count against the latter. In some passages, Leibniz is plainly urging innatism as an explanatory hypothesis, and such hypotheses are usually assessed in relation to all the available alternatives; yet although Gassendi, Hobbes, and others propound non-innatist cognitive theories, only Locke's views are considered; nevertheless Leibniz's theory is said to be shown. Moreover, the case for the innatist hypothesis, as Theophilus states it, is meager. As mentioned, it comes uncomfortably close to vacuity, and is quite unable to explain anything other than rudimentary facts about the chronological order in which children typically assent to various propositions. Still, it is fair to say, Theophilus fields a theory with more explanatory potential than any put forward by Philalethes.

The third line of pro-innatist argument concerns the proper account of a priori knowledge. This, too, is a contest between explanations, I suggest. Both Locke and Leibniz intend their theories of a priori knowledge to say what justifies us in assenting, for instance, to mathematical truths and to explicate the sense in which those truths are "necessary," or "eternal." On the Lockean account, a priori knowledge is evidentially founded on the perception that the ideas that form a proposition stand in a necessary relation; e.g. the idea of the sum of 2 and 3 joined with the idea of 5 plainly exhibits the relation of equality. The knowledge is intuitive if the relation is immediately self-evident and demonstrative if apprehended by a series of individually evident intermediary relations among ideas. As for the metaphysical status of propositions known on the evidence of such inter-ideal relations, they are eternal truths: "This is not because ... they are engraved on the mind after some patterns that always existed, but because we can be certain that any creature endowed with the ability and means to consider these ideas will find the truth of these propositions" (NE: A VI vi, 446).

Leibniz might have faulted Philalethes's epistemology on the ground that self-evidence is not, after all, a reliable criterion of truth; self-evidence is variable among individuals and unstable over time in a given individual. In several places, including a short study inspired by the *Essay*, he urges this objection, but it is never explicitly voiced and only rarely implied in NE.[58] Theophilus seems to grant that immediate evidence is a species of a priori justification, but insists that more certain means of justification are used by the most rigorous mathematicians. Textbook geometry, for instance, consists of proofs based on axioms that seem evidently to be necessarily true; indeed, on his view, the fact that we find these axioms evident is explained by the theory that they are innate. But in strictness, evident axioms should be accepted only provisionally until such time as they have been reduced to identities with the aid of definitions.[59] Nor is this all that warrants our knowledge in mathematics. Certainty with regard to necessary truths is "grounded in the linking together of ideas," Theophilus grants. But responding to Philalethes's remark that eternal truths are dependent on the existence of ideas like ours, he asks, "what would become of the real foundation of this certainty of eternal truths" if there were no minds or ideas? Unlike his friend, he has an answer: necessary truths "must be grounded in the existence of a necessary substance. That is where I find the pattern for the ideas and truths which are engraved in our souls" (NE: A VI vi, 447). This explicates the metaphysical ground of the necessity of truths known a priori and, at the same time, provides an additional warrant, external to the evident relations among ideas. Innate ideas track metaphysical necessity, because those ideas are directly caused by, and represent, ideas in the understanding of God, which determines all possible being.

With this account in the offing (it comes later in the dialogue), Theophilus says, "... it cannot be denied that the senses are inadequate to show [the] necessity [of truths], and that therefore the mind has a disposition ... to draw them from its own depths"; the mind is "the source of necessary truths, as I have just shown" (NE: A VI vi, 80). In other words, innatism about truths known a priori is established by the standards at work in the dialogue. What entitles this account to prevail over Philalethes's anti-innatist theory of a priori knowledge? The former can fairly claim to offer a more satisfactory account of the evidential support for mathematical claims (evidence stronger than self-evidence), the overall warrant for accepting such claims (the external component), as well as the metaphysical source of the necessity of truths known a priori. To be sure, there may well be an account of these matters superior to Leibniz's but the contest is between him and Locke. Let me turn to a different issue, and the second mode of competing.

6. CONTESTING BY PROBLEM SOLVING POWER: *SCEPTICISM ABOUT THE SOUL'S IMMATERIALITY*

Sometimes the conversation focuses on problems engendered by Lockean views. The *Essay* opens the door by apologizing for the limited scope of human knowledge. Our cognitive powers fall short of what we might wish, Locke admits, but they suffice for our physical and moral needs. Still higher spirits, with superior ways of knowing, are surely happier than we are. And limits on our understanding cause confusion, uncertainty, and disputes, he admits.[60] When Philalethes faithfully mentions problems with which Locke's theory leaves us, Theophilus picks them up.

The dialogue takes this turn, for example, when it comes to Philalethes's scepticism about whether matter thinks. Leibniz aims, above all, to vindicate the immateriality of thinking substance, as we know. And in the course of the dialogue, Philalethes gives up his scepticism: "I ... see that as you handle the matter, one can reasonably settle [*déterminer raisonnablement*] the present question ..." (NE: A VI vi, 380); that is, we have reason to answer the question, whether matter thinks, in the negative. Commentators have had great difficulty understanding the dialogue at this point.[61]

Theophilus' speeches frustrate attempts to find a clear line of argument. Nevertheless one can discern a logical shape in the conversation: Theophilus proposes a hypothesis that removes a problem that gives rise to Locke's scepticism. This gives the hypothesis credibility: an essential part of this hypothesis is that the soul is immaterial. That is, the immaterialist hypothesis receives a sort of proof by virtue of removing a problem in Philalethes's position. A quick look at the sort of logical relations in play helps to bring this out.

The discussants' vocabulary signals that they are not trading in premises and conclusions, as we might expect, but rather in problems, explanations, and hypotheses. Philalethes introduces the topic by saying: "Another *problem* is to know, whether any purely material being thinks, or no" (NE: A VI vi, 378, emphasis added). Theophilus notes the problem and sets out to relieve it: "I hope you will at least admit that I can make some *progress with the problem*, ... without pronouncing magisterially as a substitute for good reasons; ..." (NE: A VI vi, 378, emphasis added). A long, tangled speech follows, in which Theophilus rushes through many points: that we must distinguish between confused and obscure ideas; that there is a difference between primary and secondary matter, the latter being an aggregate; that a real aggregate presupposes real unities; the nature of a real unity is to perceive and act; real unities constitute the inner nature of matter; every body capable of expressing reasoning has an immaterial soul, in accord with the natural harmony of substances. He goes on to state that "there cannot be matter without immaterial substance, i.e. without unities"; and more (NE: A Vi vi, 378–9). Now some of these points are explicated elsewhere in NE, but others allude to doctrines elaborated only in other places. If there is an *argument* for the conclusion that "there cannot be matter without immaterial substances" adumbrated here, it is surely obscure. In fact, Philalethes does not take his friend to be giving an argument, but rather proposing a hypothesis. To Philalethes's mind, the hypothesis addresses and solves the difficulty that vexed him at the outset: "These *explanations* of yours have rather taken me by surprise ..." (emphasis added). He goes on to speak the line about realizing now that the question can be settled rationally. And Theophilus's next speech confirms that hypothesis-proposing is what he has been doing: "Indeed there is *nothing unintelligible in this new hypothesis* ..." (NE: A VI vi, 380, emphasis added). There are, then, signs that the immateriality of the soul is part of a hypothesis that derives rational credibility from its ability to remove problems.[62]

Getting down to particulars, what *is* the problem that has been solved? Philalethes starts by saying there is an epistemic problem, namely, to know whether matter thinks; but he later reveals, in conformity with Locke, that the epistemic problem arises from a conceivability problem:

Body as far as we can conceive is able only to strike and affect body; and motion is able to produce nothing but motion, so that when we allow body to produce pleasure or pain, or the idea of a colour, or sound, it seems that we are fain to quit our reason, go beyond our own ideas, and attribute it wholly to the good pleasure of our Maker. What reason shall we find, then, to conclude that it is not the same with perception and matter? (NE: A VI vi, 381)[63]

That is, bodily motions cause sensations, but we cannot *conceive* how they do so; for that reason, we cannot *know* how sensation is related to matter, or in particular, whether matter does the sensing (thinking). Theophilus's hypothesis addresses the conceptual blank. In his next speech, he makes clear that on his hypothesis of pre-established harmony, matter does *not* produce pleasure, pain, or sensations – that would indeed be inconceivable; but "... given my view, nothing unintelligible happens ..." (NE: A VI vi, 381). Philalethes referred to our inability to conceive how nature (supposedly) performs a certain causal operation as a problem. He accepts the hypothesis of harmony, in the dialogue, because it obviates the problem. So far so good, perhaps. But both parties agree, with less apparent cogency, that Theophilus has solved the *epistemic* problem, that he has given "good reasons" to say the soul is immaterial. No reader could think Theophilus has offered premises from which this conclusion might seem to follow, nor does Philalethes suppose that he has. It is rather that the immateriality of spiritual substance is an integral part of the hypothesis of inter-substantial harmony, which, as a whole, removes the problem of inconceivable causal interaction. This success, plus its intelligibility and simplicity, apparently give the immaterialist hypothesis a degree of rational credibility in the eyes of the speakers. This is, I suggest, how the dialogue reaches the result it does on this central issue.

This is an example of several problems generated by Locke's scepticism and solved by the theory of immaterial substance, as the characters agree.[64] Nevertheless, the case at hand involves a relatively meager display of problem solving power. Outside NE, Leibniz claims the system of pre-established harmony allays several different, more formidable, problems: questions about the conservation of force, the scope of laws of motion, inter-substantial causality, mind-body union, etc. Theophilus/Leibniz could have made a more impressive case for his theory of immaterial substance in connection with the doctrine of substantial harmony it underwrites. The fact that he does not reinforces the suggestion that NE depicts a contest between exactly two philosophers. Theophilus's theory of substance solves a problem that, as both discussants agree, stems from the Lockean stance initially taken by Philalethes.

7. CONCLUSIONS

To conclude: what did Leibniz gain by setting his remarks in dialogue form? I would urge that the dialogue instantiates rules essential to Leibniz's mode of engaging Locke. Perhaps it is not necessary that the contest be conducted in conversation. Any device for reporting Locke's position and juxtaposing Leibniz's views that allows for a comparison of their explanatory, problem-solving, and disputational resources would suffice. But the fictitious event is a neat device. Without a heavy-handed statement of regulations, it suggests a rule-governed contest between the speakers' views, especially to readers trained by disputation. Moreover, Philalethes's distance from Locke allows him to participate in judging the outcome when it goes against Locke. And Theophilus' judgment is distanced from that of Leibniz. The results flow from the rules. If the characters simply act with intellectual honesty in matters affected by the rules, and it is plausible that they do, they make the case. The onus of doing so does not fall on the author.

NE might, then, be seen as an experiment in which philosophical debate is cast in an interesting mold – philosophers are brought to agree by honestly assessing the relative explanatory and problem solving prowess of their views, then exposing them to objections drawn from the opposite side. Leibniz's doctrines gain rational credibility in NE because they win a carefully delimited contest – a competition between exactly two systematic philosophers in accord with procedures adopted precisely for their capacity to decide between them on rational grounds. This accounts, I suggest, for features of the dialogue that are somewhat unsatisfying to many readers, lack of systematic development, absence of demonstration, reliance on unargued principles, tolerance of underdeveloped distinctions, and the like. Such ways of characterising the exchange assume a style of philosophising different from that portrayed. The dialogue *has* only modest pretensions to establish truth, but it is fair to say that, by virtue of its implicit rules, the exchange achieves the degree of probation it claims.[65]

NOTES

[1]   See Brunschwig ed. 1966: Introduction.
[2]   See Dooren 1975.
[3]   See the interesting article by Marsh 1989–2001. On the classical Platonic, Ciceronian, and Lucian models of dialogue and their development in the renaissance and early modern period, see Schaffer 1988.
[4]   "We must not, indeed, expect to find in the work of Leibniz an attempt to lay bare the fundamental principles of the philosophy he criticizes, or to show in what respects these need correction, ... The aim of Leibniz is rather to develop and set forth his own views on the questions which arise, under the stimulus afforded by the thought of another" (Gibson 1917: 267). Also see Gibson 1917: 275.

"As a work of literature, the *New Essays* is rambling, and in its handling of dialogue conspicuously maladroit; as an objective commentary on Locke's ideas it is marred by polemical distortion; even as an exposition of Leibniz's own system of thought it fails to satisfy, for Leibniz tends to assume many of his principles without fully explaining them" (Jolley 1984: 9).

"... Leibniz's handling of the dialogue form is disappointing. ... Instead of two real people seriously arguing, we have a mechanical spokesman for Locke (Philalethes) who dutifully serves up portions of the *Essay* so that Leibniz's spokesman (Theophilus) can pass judgment on them. ... The gravest defect is that Leibniz does not try to give a comprehensive understanding of the main outlines of Locke's way of thinking, or of his own. Although he sometimes criticizes Locke on internal grounds of inconsistency, Leibniz does not try to enter into the Lockean manner of thinking. Nor does he properly introduce the reader to his own" (RB x–xi).

⁵   For information about the circumstances that led up to the drafting of NE, see the introduction in the Akademie edition (A VI vi, xvii–xxvii); also RB vii–x. Jolley (1984) urges that Leibniz's correspondence with Thomas Burnett made him suspect Locke's sincerity and thus to attack the *Essay* obliquely and promote his own views in a round about way. The present paper proposes a different explanation of the seeming absence of direct argument in terms of the sort of dialectic carried on in the dialogue. This explanation does not address Leibniz's broader motives for writing NE in this form, but it ought to be factored into any account of them.

⁶   A VI vi, xxiv. Also see critical apparatus, A VI vi, 40–79.

⁷   Grice 1975.

⁸   Citations and quotations from NE are based on the Berlin Akademie edition (A VI, vi); translations mainly follow RB although with some changes.

⁹   No doubt there are several ways in which Leibniz regards Locke's philosophy as superficial. I have in mind especially his sense that Locke's theories often abstract from the social and historical context in which human cognitive activity takes place. For instance, Locke's theory of knowledge is propounded with little attention to the state of the various sciences, their accomplishments, current problems, useful techniques, and so on. In Leibniz's view, this distorts Locke's account of the basis of scientific knowledge and its potential scope; e.g. to Burnett (GP III, 176). Speeches that detail the state of theoretical and applied mathematics, legal theory, physics, theology, and even gossip about living and dead practitioners, counteract this sort of superficiality. A similar point about Locke's philosophy of language, as compared to Leibniz's, is made by Hacking 1988.

¹⁰   In a specimen of his reflections on the *Essay* (1698), written with encouragement of Burnett, Leibniz explains that he holds that the soul always perceives and that this confutes the lamentable opinion that the soul is material. He then adds: "I acknowledge, however, that our interest is not governed by anything but the truth, and here I do not want to mix theological reasons with philosophical ones" (*Echantillon de Réflexions sur le II. Livre*: A VI vi, 16). See Jolley 1984: 34.

¹¹   These goals accurately reflect the opinion Leibniz expressed in a letter contemporary with the writing of NE: "I am persuaded that this able author's intentions are extremely good, and that he believes what he says: but, at the same time, I hold that the contrary is more in conformity with the truth and more agreeable to religion and morality" (To Jacquelot, 29 April 1704: GP III, 473–5). Translations are by the present author unless a published translation is cited.

¹²   For these terms in NE, see A VI vi, 370–5; A VI vi, 383 contrasts what the discussants have established [*déterminé*] with what can be demonstrated [*démontré*]; A VI vi, 362–73 notes weaker and stronger sorts of *connoissances* and *preuves*, but neither term is applied to results of the conversation. This is not to deny that in other works, Leibniz's use of epistemic terms such as *démonter, montrer*, etc. varies considerably.

¹³   Soon after Locke's death, Leibniz wrote to Coste that his aim was more to clarify things than to refute Locke's opinions (GP III, 392; also to Sophie Charlotte, 25 April 1704: KSC 230).

¹⁴   "I engage above all to vindicate [*vindiquer*] the immateriality of the soul, which Mr. Locke leaves in doubt; I also justify [*justifie*] innate ideas and innate truths, by showing that [*faisant voir que*] eternal or necessary truths cannot be proven [*être prouvées*] by the senses, and that we draw knowledge of them from the depths of our own understanding; Mr. Locke's mistake seems to come from his not having considered sufficiently the nature of demonstrations [*démonstrations*]. I also justify [*justifie*] axioms or

maxims, the use of which Mr. Locke misunderstands. I show [*montre*], again against the opinion of this author, that the individuality of a man, which makes him remain the same, consists in the duration of the simple immaterial substance that is in him. That the soul is never without thought, that there is neither a void nor atoms, that matter or what is passive cannot think unless God adds to it a substance that thinks. And there is an infinity of other points on which we differ. ..." (To Jacquelot, 29 April 1703: GP III, 473–4).

[15]   For background see Stump 1982 and references in note 39, below. See also Marsh 1989–2001.

[16]   Dascal, Racionero and Cardoso, eds. Forthcoming. I am grateful to Marcelo Dascal for allowing me to see an early draft of the introduction and the table of contents in pre-publication version. See also Dascal 2001; also Olaso 1975.

[17]   Dascal et al. eds. forthcoming: "Introductory Essay", section 5. Other scholars ascribe to Leibniz a rather similar method based on the thesis that all rational minds represent the same domain of truths, although with more and less confusion. The underlying truth and basis of potential agreement is to be brought to light by techniques of clarification, such as definition of terms. Berlioz (2002) traces Leibniz's use of this method in a precis of letters exchanged by Locke and Stillingfleet. Rutherford (1996) argues that Leibniz adopted this procedure in philosophical articles and correspondence for mainly ethical reasons. The technique is sometimes at work in NE, e.g. A VI vi, 107.

[18]   Theophilus could hardly be depicted as revising his views without implying that Leibniz's views were significantly altered by reading the *Essay*. This would be factually inaccurate. At the time of composing NE, he wrote to Jacquelot: "Perhaps, Sir, you will be surprised to see me write that I worked on this as a project that does not demand application. But it is because I have, long ago, settled these general philosophical matters in a manner that I believe to be demonstrative or as near to that as is necessary, so that I have hardly need to meditate on them anew" (GP III, 474).

[19]   E.g. Letter to Gabriel Wagner on the Value of Logic (1696): GP VII, 514–27; L 462–71; also GP VII, 476–9; A VI iv, 2245–83.

[20]   On the balance of reason, see A I vi, 118; C 211–4; also Olaso 1975. On the calculus of probabilities, see e.g. A III ii, 230; for background, see the introduction to Parmentier, ed. 1995: 239–50. On juridical logic, see Kalinowski 1977. The famous universal characteristic is a purely formal device intended to serve this aim; see Couturat 1901: 96–103.

[21]   See Dascal 2001.

[22]   E.g. *Des Methodes de Reunion*: FCO II, 1–21.

[23]   See also NE: A VI vi, 182.

[24]   The piece indicates Leibniz's willingness to undertake the reporter's task, and he may do so in *Systema Theologicum* (FCO I, 81n). Also see A VI iv, 2250.

[25]   Some cases are more egregious than others. But examples are not confined to any particular topic: e.g. Philalethes's brief report makes Locke's technical account of the reality, adequacy, and truth of ideas look fatuous. I suspect this falls in the class of arguments so pitiable, in Leibniz's eyes, that he is loathe to report them. On the topic of thinking matter, (NE: A VI vi, 63) misstates the conclusion of Locke's argument in a passage to Stillingfleet; but it seems unlikely that the misrepresentation is intentional because the passage itself has just been quoted, its line of reasoning is less then clear, and Locke's position on the issue is correctly reported nearby.

[26]   Parmentier (2006) identifies several techniques Leibniz uses to reformulate Locke's position in terms more favorable to his own, but still concludes the mis-representation is unintentional.

[27]   E.g. " I have answered that already" (NE: A VI vi, 83); "You keep facing me with an objection that I have already refuted" (NE: A VI vi, 91); "You are reverting again to the same assumption ..." (NE: A VI vi, 96); "I am very pleased that you are now correcting the contrary claim which you seemed to make ... above" (NE: A VI vi, 208); "I have already said something about this ..." (NE: A VI vi, 189); "I have already said to you that essences are everlasting because ..." (NE: A VI vi, 296); "I have already pointed out to you that I have reasons ..." (NE: A VI vi, 353); "We have already given too much attention to this. I am surprised that you should return to it ..." (NE: A VI vi, 395); "I fail to see why you return to a topic about which we have argued a great deal ... But it gives me the opportunity to set you right once again" (NE: A VI vi, 400).

[28] E.g. "That is not what we are concerned with now, since we are discussing ..." (NE: A VI vi, 338); "But let me get back to my main point. Thinking about harmful beliefs and our right to criticize them has led me to digress" (NE: A VI vi, 463); "Your digressions are enjoyable and instructive. But let us turn ..." (NE: A VI vi, 471).

[29] E.g. "[the mind] would not be the source of necessary truths, as I have just shown that it is" (NE: A VI vi, 80); "You are returning to your assumption that what is not known is not innate, inspite of my having refuted it so often" (NE: A VI vi, 96); "I have shown how even when asleep the soul has some perception ..." (NE: A VI vi, 115); "I have shown you the basis of true physical identity, and have shown that ..." (NE: A VI vi, 247); "So you do see that 'gold' signifies not just what the speaker knows ..." (NE: A VI vi, 354); Philalethes: " ... but now that I grasp your theory of the pre-established harmony, that difficulty – which we had despaired of solving – appears to me to have vanished as if by magic" (NE: A VI vi, 390); "Have you forgotten that I have shown that ideas are inherently in our minds and come from its own depths" (NE: A VI vi, 392); Philalethes: "I had thought that axioms did not have much influence on other parts of our knowledge, but you disabused me by showing ..." (NE: A VI vi, 411).

[30] For the contrast between the logic of co-operative and strategic, or competitive, conversations, see Grice 1975 and Hintikka 1986.

[31] See Essay I, ii, 21 (59: 19–27); Essay I, ii, 16 (55: 32–56: 5); Essay IV, ii, 1.

[32] NE: A VI vi, 108, 406–15. The unreliability of alleged self-evidence is plainly implied at 409 and 362. It is also implicit in Theophilus' handling of primary truths of reason, which he allows to have the "immediacy of ideas", but nevertheless delimits by more objective criteria (NE: A VI vi, 367–71).

[33] NE: A VI vi, 447; also NE: A VI vi, 452.

[34] A short essay on the judge of controversies concludes: "Speaking absolutely, no one is the judge of controversies, if not each one himself" (A VI iv; C 2156). Some sixteenth century writers on dialogue urged that the issue discussed in a dialogue should be left to the reader to decide; see Marsh 1989–2001.

[35] Also see other pieces on *De Judice Controversiarum*: A VI iv, 2155–67.

[36] Also see NE: A VI vi, 482. For other mentions of this incident involving Denis Papin, see Couturat 1901: 2n1.

[37] The passage goes on to say that depending on the nature of the matter in dispute, other outcomes are possible.

[38] NE: A VI vi, 260–1, 415–23.

[39] On the history of dialectical disputation, in general, and the particular type of medieval disputation called *obligatione*, see Stump 1982; Yrojonsuuri 2000; on later forms of disputation, see Ashworth 1986 and the editor's introduction (Ashworth ed. 1985).

[40] Ashworth ed. 1985: liii

[41] Also see §72.

[42] NE: A VI vi, 450, 484. See Couturat 1901: 265–8; Duchesneau 1993: esp. 384–7.

[43] See also letter to Lady Masham: GP III, 354. Writing to De Volder (1699), Leibniz presents his theory of substance as an explanatory hypothesis in context of the physical problems De Volder found with the Cartesian theory of material substance (e.g. GP II, 168/ L 515).

[44] See Brown, S. 1996. Brown 1984 urges that Leibniz's mature philosophical method is akin to hypothetical-deductive reasoning; cp. Rutherford 1996.

[45] The importance of problem solving power briefly surfaces in the following, which was struck, along with the surrounding material, in drafting the Preface: "... for I think that I have resolved several difficulties that he (Locke) left in their entirety" (A VI vi, 46). To D'Ausson, whose pessimistic view of human knowledge was influenced by the *Essay*, Leibniz writes that "most of the problems of which Locke treats are capable of solution" (Jolley 1984: 163–4, n1 & n2).

[46] NE: A VI vi, 111, 161, 411.

[47] The same goes for Locke's objections to the doctrine that the soul always thinks and the received dictum that knowledge proceeds from maxims that are already known (*praecognita*), both closely associated with innatism.

[48] See e.g. Scott, D. 1988: 124; also Scott, D. 1987; Jolley 1990: chs. 2 and 9; Cowie 1999: 3–26.

[49] NE: A VI vi, 74, 76, 77.

[50]   Leibniz's defence of innate knowledge and ideas is discussed more thoroughly in my unpublished paper "Leibniz's Innatism".

[51]   "For knowledge, ideas, and truths to be in our mind, it is not necessary that they ever actually be thought; they are only natural habits, that is dispositions, active and passive attitudes, and more than a *tabula rasa*" (NE: A VI vi, 106). See NE: A VI vi, 110, against "inactive faculties"; also NE: A VI vi, 112.

[52]   See Essay I, i, 2. Theophilus accordingly hints that his companion's difficulty making sense of innate knowledge stems from his overlooking the fact that even memory depends on hidden structures that store and retrieve propositions when needed (NE: A VI vi, 140, 77, 78).

[53]   Essay I, ii, 21 (59: 19–27); Essay I, ii, 16 (55: 32–56: 5); Essay IV, ii, 1.

[54]   See also NE: A VI vi, 86, 102.

[55]   Critics charge that Leibniz's argument is deeply flawed, among other reasons, because it hangs on an ambiguity between properties that are innate to a soul (substantiality, etc.) and ideas, or intentional contents of dispositions, that are innate; see e.g. Jolley 1990:181–7. McRae (1976: 93–102) urges that there is an ambiguity in Leibniz's notion of innateness in connection with metaphysical ideas and mathematical/logical ideas. On the interpretation proposed here, Leibniz's notion of innateness is subject to neither ambiguity, but the issue deserves closer attention than I can give it here.

[56]   See also NE: A VI vi, 129.

[57]   Philalethes says as much (NE: A VI vi, 238), as does Locke (Essay II, xxviii, 13).

[58]   See *Réflexions sur la Second Réplique de Locke* (1699–1700): A VI vi, 29–30. Here the criticism is offered to explain Stillingfleet's opposition to the way of ideas. See also *Meditations on Knowledge, Truth and Ideas* (1684): L 293–4; *Critical Thoughts on the General Part of the Principles of Descartes* (1692): L 389; NE: A VI vi, 82, 409; NE: A VI vi, 361–7.

[59]   NE: A VI vi, 77–8, 85, 360, 406–7, 413–7, 451–3. The highest degree of certainty is achieved by showing that a proposition has the logical form of an identity. Theophilus suggests his friend has been prevented from recognizing certainty of this sort because of his tendency to conflate images and ideas; only the latter are constituents of propositions and capable of analysis. See NE: A VI vi, 137, 261–2, 449–531.

[60]   E.g. Essay I, i, 4–8; I, iii, 18; II, xv, 8; II, xxiii, 2–5, 12, 23–9; II, xxvii, 13; III, vi, 14–27, 48–50; IV, iii, 6, 11–6, 24–6, 28–30.

[61]   See Jolley 1984: 102–5, 116; see also Jolley 1984: 124.

[62]   The title page of the dialogue is inscribed: "*NOUVEAUX ESSAIS SUR L'ENTENDEMENT par l'auteur du Systeme de l'Harmonie préetablie.*" The suggestion is that the dialogue continues to advocate the theory of harmony, and perhaps by the method employed in his public presentation in *Systeme nouveaux*.

[63]   Also see the end of the previous speech.

[64]   For example, it solves several problems arising from Locke's handling of personal identity.

[65]   I am grateful to the participants in the "Leibniz and the English" conference held at Liverpool in 2003 and the Leibniz Symposium at the APA meeting in Pasadena, 2004 for helpful questions and discussion, especially Nicholas Jolley, George McDonald Ross, and Maria Rosa Antognazza.

NICHOLAS JOLLEY

9. LEIBNIZ, LOCKE, AND THE EPISTEMOLOGY OF TOLERATION

It is not surprising that, as two highly intelligent and socially responsible thinkers, Leibniz and Locke were both deeply troubled by the problem of religious conflict which disfigured their age.[1] Yet characteristically, they adopted very different approaches to solving the problem. Leibniz believed that the best hope for peace lay in promoting schemes for the reunion of the churches; to this end he devoted enormous amounts of time and energy to defining contested articles of faith in such a way that reasonable people could assent to them. Locke, by contrast, believed, more realistically perhaps, that the best hope for peace lay in accepting disagreement as inevitable and in seeking to persuade his readers of the case for religious toleration, somewhat narrowly construed. This stark contrast between the two philosophers may stand in need of some qualification. In the case of Leibniz Professor Antognazza has recently shown that he defended the principle of religious toleration (at least on the part of churches) in his correspondence with Pellisson (Antognazza 2002). And in the case of Locke we need to remember that in some of his writings he promoted credal minimalism in the spirit of the Latitudinarians; in *The Reasonableness of Christianity* Locke's insistence that there is only one essential article of the Christian faith seems designed to persuade men of good will who disagreed on various articles of faith that they could conscientiously co-exist within the same broad church. Nonetheless, despite these qualifications, the essential contrast remains: Leibniz was an ecumenist, Locke was a tolerationist.

My intention in this paper is thus not to challenge this essential contrast but rather to question how far it is reflected in the philosophical debate between Leibniz and Locke. There has been a tendency in some recent writing to see the *Essay* as a contribution to what might be called "the epistemology of toleration"; that is, Locke's analyses of the nature of knowledge and belief and his account of the limits of knowledge are in the service of showing that toleration is justified. In this paper I argue that although the *Essay* tends to support the principle of toleration, it is less clear how far it contains specific arguments for the principle. And in the light of this fact we can see that it is a mistake to suppose that in the *New Essays* Leibniz actually rejects Lockean tolerationist arguments. Indeed, there is little in the work to suggest that Leibniz saw Locke's *Essay* as a major document in the epistemology of toleration.

I. LEIBNIZ'S ECUMENISM

How far Leibniz saw the *Essay* as a contribution to the epistemology of toleration may be controversial, but one thing about Leibniz's response to Locke is clear: Leibniz's own ecumenist strategy makes its presence strongly felt in the *New Essays*

133

P. Phemister and S. Brown (eds.), Leibniz and the English-Speaking World, 133–143.
© 2007 *Springer.*

on Human Understanding.[2] This strategy emerges in a striking and ironic way in one place (among others) as a result of some misguided tinkering on the part of Pierre Coste, the French translator of the *Essay*. Consider the fact that in the chapter "Of wrong Assent, or Error" (IV, xx) Locke characteristically offers a Roman Catholic ("intelligent Romanist") as an example of how subscription to false principles may seduce people into further error:

> Take an intelligent *Romanist*, that from the very first dawning of any Notions in his Understanding, hath had this Principle constantly inculcated, *viz.* That he must believe as the Church (*i.e.* those of his Communion) believe, or that the Pope is infallible; and this he never so much as heard questioned till at forty or fifty years old he met with one of other Principles; How is he prepared easily to swallow, not only against all Probability, but even the clear Evidence of his Senses, the Doctrine of *Transubstantiation*? This principle has such an influence on his Mind that he will believe that to be Flesh, which he sees to be Bread. (Essay IV, xx, 10)

But Coste is producing a translation aimed at a mainly Roman Catholic readership whom he does not wish to offend; accordingly, when he comes to this passage he changes Locke's "Romanist" to "Lutheran" and Locke's "transubstantiation" to "consubstantiation". Confronted with a text whose corruption he does not suspect, Leibniz moves at once into high ecumenical gear; the speech which he gives to Theophilus is a masterly and characteristic example of Leibniz's writing in this vein. With some heat Theophilus proceeds to complain that the Lutherans, or rather Evangelicals as he prefers to call them, have been victims of a caricature. Properly interpreted, as it is by Theophilus, the doctrine of the Lutherans with regard to the "real presence" is far from absurd; it emerges as a doctrine to which any rational Christian of good will should be able to subscribe. Indeed, through the mouthpiece of Theophilus Leibniz suggests that other churches and sects really do already agree with the Lutheran doctrine of real presence. Not merely is the Lutheran doctrine essentially the same as Calvin's teaching on the issue; it is also said to be the same as that of "some highly capable Anglican theologians" (NE IV, xx/ RB 514). This last point is articulated not by Theophilus but by Locke's spokesman Philalethes who is made to apologize for buying into a caricature of Lutheran teaching; presumably the Lockean spokesman is himself intended to be a member of the Church of England. Quite possibly there is a political dimension to this instructive discussion. By the time that Leibniz wrote the *New Essays on Human Understanding* the Lutheran Elector of Hanover, Georg Ludwig, had become legally recognized as the next in line of succession to the English throne. But in some quarters his status as heir was none too popular. Leibniz the diplomat would have seen no harm in taking the opportunity to persuade an English readership that Lutheran beliefs were not at all outlandish; in fact they were close to those of the Anglican Church itself.

As a result of Coste's meddling the issue which Leibniz addresses is consubstantiation, not the distinctively Catholic dogma of transubstantiation. But it seems reasonable to speculate that even if Coste had not meddled with Locke's text, Leibniz's ecumenical instincts would still have been aroused on this occasion. True, the tone would probably have been different: Leibniz would have responded, not with exasperation to a perceived caricature of the teachings of his own church, but rather with a much milder attempt to put the best face on a Catholic dogma which he was not obliged to accept. This speculation gains credit not just from Leibniz's partial defenses of Catholic dogma elsewhere in the *New Essays*,[3] but also from his well-known dealings with the dogma of transubstantiation in other writings. In his correspondence with Des Bosses, for instance, Leibniz seeks to show how this dogma can be accommodated by the theory of monads.

2. TOLERATION AND LOCKE'S *ESSAY*

There is no doubt, then, that Leibniz's ecumenical strategy makes its presence felt in the *New Essays on Human Understanding*. But in the *New Essays*, as we have seen, Leibniz is responding to a philosopher who is famous for pinning his hopes, not on ecumenism, but on securing assent to the principle of religious toleration narrowly construed. It is natural to ask, then, whether Leibniz takes a philosophical stand on toleration in the *New Essays*. But before addressing this question it is necessary to ask whether Locke's *Essay*, as opposed to his other writings, actually contains a philosophical case for toleration.

Among recent writers it is John Rogers who answers this question most clearly in the affirmative. In his paper "Locke and the Latitude Men" Rogers claims in general that there are strong connections between Locke's advocacy of toleration and the basic project of the *Essay*, namely, that of charting the limits of human knowledge: Rogers even detects in the *Essay* an explicit argument for toleration which he terms the "Argument from Ignorance" (Rogers 1998). It is possible, I think, to be sympathetic to Rogers's general thesis that there is a link between Locke's commitment to the principle of toleration and the project of the *Essay*, while remaining sceptical as to how far the work gives actual arguments for the principle. In this section I shall cast my net widely and seek for evidence of other epistemological arguments for toleration than the one discussed by Rogers.

According to Rogers, it is the Argument from Ignorance which constitutes the main bridge between Locke's project in the *Essay* and his advocacy of toleration. In Rogers's words, the argument is simply that "unless you know that you what the truth is on some matter, you have no business attempting to force others to accept your opinion or of [sic] suppressing those who propound a view contrary to one's own" (1998: 113). In fact, what Rogers states here is not an argument, but rather a general principle which serves as the conditional premise of an argument: to complete the argument it seems that a further, categorical premise needs to be supplied. Presumably, then, the Argument from Ignorance, when fully stated, would take the following form:

(1) There are many issues (e.g. in religion) with respect to which we do not know that we know the truth.

(2) On any issue with respect to which we do not know that we know the truth, we have no right to employ coercion.

(3) Therefore, there are many issues with respect to which we have no right to employ coercion.

So stated, the Argument from Ignorance calls for some comment. For one thing, it is important to draw attention to the fact that the second premise is equivalent to only a necessary condition of justified coercion: coercion with respect to matters such as religious doctrines is justified only if you know that you know the truth. Yet in places Rogers suggests that he envisages a biconditional premise: knowing that you know is not only necessary but also sufficient for the justified use of force (1998: 130). But such a sufficient condition for legitimate coercion is of course not required to derive the conclusion, and there is no ground for attributing it to Locke; indeed, Rogers's doing so seems to be based on a mistake. It is true of course that in the *Letter on Toleration* Locke is notoriously willing to deny toleration to atheists. It is also true that the existence of God, for Locke, is an issue with respect to which demonstrative knowledge can be shown to be possible: at least those who follow his own version of the cosmological proof may be said to come to know, in the strict sense, that God exists. It may of course be doubted whether Locke is committed to holding that they thereby come to have the second-order knowledge which is at issue in the alleged sufficient condition, but this is a side issue. The important point is that Locke's case for denying toleration to atheists turns not on the demonstrative certainty of God's existence; it turns rather on the alleged fact that, by denying that God exists, atheists do not recognize an obligation to keep their agreements (GK 134–5). Nowhere does Locke suggest that either the intuitive or demonstrative certainty of a proposition is a ground for persecuting those who refuse to assent to the proposition. Thus it would be muddying the waters to convert the second premise of the argument into a biconditional.

There is a further issue which is raised by Rogers's statement of the principle which forms the second premise of the argument. On Rogers's formulation it is not clear to whom the "you" refers. Rogers's main concern is with the issue of religious toleration on the part of the state of the kind that was established, at least in a limited form, by the Toleration Act of 1689. In the *Letter on Toleration* Locke is explicitly concerned to set out a principled case for limits on the coercive authority of the state with respect to religion. It is thus natural perhaps to suppose that the premise ought to be understood as a strong thesis: unless you know that you know, you – that is, neither the state nor private citizens, individually or collectively – have the right to coerce others into accepting your opinions. But it is always possible to understand the premise in a weaker way so that it is only coercion on the part of private individuals that is at issue. In that case the argument would have nothing specifically to do with the legitimacy of toleration on the part of the state. As we shall see, this ambiguity will return to haunt us.

Rogers thus claims that Locke stated at least one explicit argument for toleration in the *Essay*. But is this claim justified? There is no doubt that some of the materials for the Argument from Ignorance are to be found in the *Essay*; it is surely uncontroversial that Locke is committed to the first premise of the argument which simply summarizes the agnostic thrust of his epistemology in Book IV of the *Essay*. Indeed, Locke is arguably committed to a stronger thesis than the first premise: there are many issues (e.g. in religion) on which we know, or at least can know, that we do not know the truth. But the presence of the Argument from Ignorance in the *Essay* proves harder to document than might be inferred from Rogers's account. Certainly there is one prominent place early on in the *Essay* where Locke makes a suggestive connection between toleration and the project of charting the limits of knowledge. In the Introduction to the *Essay* Locke offers an informal argument which turns on the premise that, once we recognize the limits of human understanding, "we shall not peremptorily, or intemperately require demonstration" (Essay I, i, 5) where probability only is to be had. This argument certainly offers an important clue to the motivation of Locke's project in the *Essay*: Locke's hope is that by reading and being persuaded by the arguments of the work people will be cured of their intolerance of other views. But this is a purely descriptive argument which does nothing to establish the duty of religious toleration; indeed, it seems rather to presuppose that toleration is something to be valued.

Perhaps the closest that Locke ever comes to stating explicitly a version of the Argument from Ignorance is in a passage of IV, xvi, 4 which, even by Lockean standards, is singularly prolix and inelegant:

Since therefore it is unavoidable to the greatest part of Men, if not all, to have *several* Opinions, without certain and indisputable Proofs of their Truths, and it carries too great an imputation of ignorance, lightness, or folly, for Men to quit and renounce their former Tenets presently upon the offer of an Argument, which they cannot immediately answer, and show the insufficiency of: It would, methinks, become all Men to maintain *Peace*, and the common Offices of Humanity *and Friendship, in the diversity of Opinions*, since we cannot reasonably expect, that any one should readily and obsequiously quit his own Opinion, and embrace ours with a blind resignation to an Authority which the Understanding of Man acknowledges not. (Essay IV, xvi, 4)

At first sight it might seem open to doubt whether the issue of coercion is even broached in this passage: Locke's interest appears to be in questions about good manners or etiquette. It may seem, then, that the issue of coercion is raised only obliquely insofar as if I have a duty to maintain friendship with others who disagree with me, then *a fortiori* I have a duty not to coerce them into accepting my opinion. But in fact a little later Locke does explicitly discuss the use of coercion: we must not treat others ill because they will not "receive our opinions, or at least those we would force upon them". Moreover, we should take more care to "inform our selves, than constrain others" (Essay IV, xvi, 4). Thus it does seem fair to say that Locke here is committed to claiming that if you do not know that you know the truth on some issue, then you have no right to employ coercion.

Yet we can then go on to ask the question: Coercion on the part of whom? As we have seen, in the *Letter on Toleration* Locke is explicitly concerned to set limits to the coercive authority of the state. But there is no mention of the state in this passage from the *Essay*. It is tempting perhaps to say that in the light of the *Letter on Toleration* Locke should be read as advancing the strong thesis discussed above: unless they know that they know, then neither the state nor private citizens, individually or collectively, have the right to coerce others. But where the

Essay is concerned it is dangerous to make explicit what Locke left vague, perhaps intentionally. It must be remembered that toleration was still a sensitive issue when the work was written, and that whereas Locke was prepared to take credit for the *Essay* he never admitted to authorship of the *Letter on Toleration*.

In the *Essay*, then, we find a version of the Argument from Ignorance which leaves its application to the state unspecified. It is tempting to cast our net more widely and ask whether other arguments for toleration are to be found in the *Essay*. Here again it may seem natural to take our cue from the *Letter on Toleration* itself: this work undoubtedly does contain an epistemological argument for toleration which turns not on the limits of human knowledge but on the very nature of belief. Implicitly opposing Descartes's teachings in the Fourth Meditation Locke argues that belief is not under the control of the will: although threats of persecution may be successful in changing people's behavior, they are necessarily futile for the purpose of changing people's beliefs:

> ...The care of souls cannot belong to the civil magistrate, because his power consists wholly in compulsion. But true and saving religion consists in the inward persuasion of the mind, without which nothing has any value with God. And such is the nature of human understanding that it cannot be compelled by any outward force. Confiscate a man's goods, imprison or torture his body; such punishment will be in vain if you hope that they will make him change his inward judgment of things. (GK 68–9)

The Argument from the Involuntariness of Belief, as we may call it, is less directly related to Locke's central purpose in the *Essay* than the Argument from Ignorance. Nonetheless, as an epistemological argument for toleration, it is clearly of the right sort to find an appropriate home in the *Essay*. But is the Argument from the Involuntariness of Belief to be found in the work? Here again it seems that the answer must be somewhat discouraging. Certainly Locke states the anti-Cartesian premise about the nature of belief or inner assent: "As Knowledge is no more arbitrary than Perception, so, I think, Assent is no more in our Power than Knowledge" (*Essay* IV, xx, 16). Yet, in marked contrast to the *Letter on Toleration*, Locke does not draw the conclusion concerning the necessary futility of employing coercion for the purpose of changing people's beliefs.

3. TOLERATION AND LEIBNIZ'S *NEW ESSAYS*

We may say, then, that to the extent that there is a case for toleration in the *Essay* it leads a somewhat subterranean existence. The Argument from Ignorance is stated in a vague way which leaves its application to the state unclear; the Argument from the Involuntariness of Belief is only sketched. It is in the light of this aspect of the character of Locke's *Essay* that we must consider Leibniz's response in the *New Essays*. Certainly we should beware of concluding hastily that Leibniz both detects and rejects a Lockean case for toleration.

The situation is clearest in the case of the Argument from the Involuntariness of Belief, for in this case there is no question of Leibniz explicitly repudiating a Lockean argument. On the contrary, as Professor Antognazza has recently shown,

Leibniz himself was prepared to deploy such an argument in his correspondence with Pellisson. Professor Antognazza writes:

> Moreover, a further philosophical premise becomes apparent in several texts: to change beliefs or opinions is not in the power of the will, but only in that of the intellect. No human being should be punished for believing (or not believing) a certain doctrine, therefore, since to do otherwise is not within the scope of his/her will. (2002: 618–9)

This is precisely Locke's argument in the *Letter on Toleration* in the mouth of Leibniz. It is true that in the *New Essays* Leibniz makes the non-Lockean point that there is a sense in which belief is obliquely under the control of the will; as Leibniz says:

> we can bring it about indirectly that we believe what we want to believe. We can do this by turning our attention away from a disagreeable object so as to apply ourselves to something else which we find pleasing; so that by thinking further about the reasons for the side which we favor, we end up by believing it to be the most likely. (NE IV, xx/ RB 517)

Otherwise, in the *New Essays* Leibniz largely confines himself to a clear endorsement of the anti-Cartesian thesis concerning the nature of belief: beliefs, says Leibniz, are "inherently involuntary" (NE IV, xx/ RB 520).[4] But Leibniz does not draw any conclusions in the *New Essays* from this thesis about the futility of religious persecution for the purpose of changing people's minds.

The *New Essays*, then, furnishes no evidence that Leibniz rejects the Argument from the Involuntariness of Belief; as we have seen, on occasion Leibniz is even prepared to advance this argument himself. John Rogers has argued, however, that Leibniz does reject the Argument from Ignorance, as he terms it. According to Rogers's account, Leibniz seeks to block the argument by rejecting its first premise. As Rogers writes, "Leibniz was already committed to an account of the origins and nature of knowledge which did not have the epistemic implications of Locke's philosophy" (1998: 131). The import of Leibniz's philosophy is that "we can, if we dig deep enough, answer many questions which we at first might believe impossible of resolution" (1998: 132). Thus, on Rogers's account, it seems that Leibniz is not concerned to reject the argument by taking up a hostile stand towards the general principle which forms its second premise; he is concerned rather to challenge the premise which summarizes, as it were, the agnostic or even skeptical thrust of Locke's epistemology in Book IV of the *Essay*.

It seems, however, that we need a more nuanced account of Leibniz's attitude to this premise than Rogers provides. It is true that Leibniz is more optimistic than Locke about the extent of natural theology; he agrees of course with Locke that the existence of God can be proved, but he also thinks, as Locke does not, that the immateriality and natural immortality of the soul can likewise be demonstrated. No doubt there are other issues – for example, concerning divine providence and human freedom – where Leibniz is more optimistic than Locke about the prospects of definitive rational resolution. But of course on debated issues in revealed theology – such as the Eucharist or the Trinity – Leibniz will agree with Locke that knowledge in the strict sense (*scientia*) is not possible. Here, as we have seen, Leibniz will concentrate his efforts not on attempts at demonstration but rather on showing that the doctrines can be interpreted in such a way as to remove the obstacles to assent on the part of rational Christians of good will; in the case of the Eucharist or the Trinity no logical absurdity is involved. According to the traditional formula, the doctrines may be above reason, but they are not contrary to reason. Thus suitably interpreted the thesis which Rogers attributes to Locke as a premise of an argument – there are many (religious) issues on which we do not know that we know – is one which Leibniz can actually endorse.

It may be objected that in the *New Essays* Leibniz sounds a more authoritarian note than Locke. Although Leibniz agrees with Locke in censuring people's readiness to condemn others, he is also capable of writing:

We certainly have the right to protect ourselves against evil doctrines which influence morality and pious observances but we should not malign people by ascribing these to them without good evidence. (NE IV, xvi/ RB 461)

Such a passage is certainly in marked contrast with Locke's claim in the *Letter on Toleration* that "the magistrate ought not to forbid the holding or teaching of any speculative opinions in any church, because they have no bearing on the civil rights of his subjects" (GK 120–1). In fact, however, there is a sense in which Leibniz's authoritarian claim is consistent with at least a version of the Argument from Ignorance. For Leibniz, there are indeed certain evil doctrines against which we have the right to protect ourselves; but as the passage in the *New Essays* suggests, these concern issues in natural theology – such as the immortality of the soul and divine providence – which are capable of definitive resolution; they are not to be numbered among the issues with regard to which we do not know that we know, and thus they are not covered by the categorical premise. But it is still the case that there are many religious issues – such as the Eucharist and Trinity – where we do not know that we know, or even know that we do not know. And on the plausible assumption – which is not challenged by Rogers – that he accepts the conditional premise of the Argument from Ignorance, Leibniz can agree with Locke that coercion in respect of these doctrines is inappropriate.

4. CONCLUSION: ECUMENISM VERSUS TOLERATION

The *New Essays*, then, provides scant evidence for saying that Leibniz rejected a Lockean case for toleration. Yet it would be also misleading to claim that in the *New Essays* Leibniz really engages with a tolerationist case; there is little in the work to suggest that Leibniz saw the *Essay* as a contribution to the epistemology of toleration. In one way Leibniz's response is understandable; the *Essay* contains at most sketches of, or vague statements of, arguments for toleration by the state. We might then say that Leibniz could not be expected to take a stand on arguments that were not fully spelled out. Yet in another way Leibniz's response is a little surprising. The whole tendency of the *Essay* is clearly towards promoting the goal of toleration, and Leibniz might have been expected to detect this tendency: crudely,

Leibniz might have been expected to read between the lines. His apparent failure to perceive the drift of Book IV of the *Essay* is matched by a similar imperceptiveness elsewhere: In the *New Essays*, for instance, Leibniz simply passes over without comment the great introductory chapter of the *Essay* where Locke explains that in his view previous philosophers have been on the wrong track and that in order to make progress philosophy should be reoriented towards a critique of the human understanding.[5] Here, as we have seen, Locke is reasonably clear that one result which he expects from this project is a more tolerant attitude towards the opinions of others who disagree with us on issues which are now recognized as incapable of a definitive resolution.

Some readers may resist the suggestion that Leibniz was guilty of a lack of insight and seek other explanations of the same facts about the *New Essays*. For instance, it might be objected that Leibniz was not so much imperceptive about the drift of the *Essay* as silent for diplomatic reasons: the issue of religious toleration was still controversial at the time when the *New Essays* was composed, and Leibniz was writing not just for an English readership but also for French readers who within living memory had experienced the Revocation of the Edict of Nantes. Moreover, Leibniz may have been cautious because he believed that Locke held convictions – such as the natural mortality of the soul – which were precisely of the sort which should not be tolerated. Yet it is equally likely that Leibniz's failure to comment on the tolerationist tendency of the *Essay* reflects his lack of enthusiasm for this strategy for solving the problem of religious conflict. Although prepared to state tolerationist arguments on occasions, Leibniz was deeply convinced that it was ecumenism, not toleration, which offered the best hope for peace.

At this stage it is natural to press the question: why did Leibniz prefer ecumenism to toleration as a strategy for resolving religious conflict? At least part of the answer to this question emerges from Leibniz's incidental remarks in the *New Essays*. As we have seen in the case of consubstantiation, Leibniz tended to believe that the disagreements between the sects were often more apparent than real: the appearance of serious disagreement had been fostered by those who, either out of ignorance or malice, had caricatured the opinions of rival sects. In such cases there was a key role for a theological diplomat such as Leibniz to play in overcoming the caricatures and persuading the parties to the disputes – at least those of good will – that they were more nearly in agreement than they supposed. In other cases, Leibniz seems to have thought that his more purely philosophical skills could play a role in resolving conflicts. Theological debates often centered on mysteries which were widely understood to involve claims about the impossible, and thus in the eyes of many could not legitimately command assent. As Leibniz observes, the Socinians oppose the Trinity and the Zwinglians the Real Presence on the ground that these doctrines violate "necessary principles" (NE IV, xviii/ RB 499). Here Leibniz believed that progress towards peace could be made by clarifying the nature of the impossibility at the heart of these doctrines. If it could be shown that the impossibility in question was merely physical, and not logical or metaphysical, then the scruples of the Socinians and the Zwinglians could be removed.

Yet it is also tempting to look for a deeper explanation of Leibniz's ecumenism in terms of his basic metaphysical commitments. As a metaphysician Leibniz is famous for reviving the neoPlatonic doctrine that substances are microcosms of the universe: according to Leibniz, every created substance, and *a fortiori* every mind, perceives the whole universe according to its point of view. This doctrine is generally taken to underwrite Leibniz's project of reconciliation in philosophy: Ancients and Moderns, Platonists and Aristotelians have a perception of all the fundamental truths about the universe, even if this perception is in varying degrees one-sided and confused. It is natural to wonder, then, whether these same metaphysical commitments similarly underwrite his project of religious reconciliation.

An explanation of this kind seems generally promising, but it needs to be able to meet two objections. In the first place, it may be thought that the metaphysical doctrine of the microcosm is too limited in its scope to play the assigned role. The disputed issues in theology concern miracles and mysteries, and while miracles are events within the created (though not course natural) order, mysteries typically are not: they concern the nature of God himself who stands outside the realm of creation. Thus from the fact that every mind perceives the whole universe according to its point of view, it does not follow that it perceives the true nature of God, even partially or confusedly. This objection can be met by expanding our account of the Leibnizian metaphysical doctrines which are relevant to grounding his ecumenical project. According to Leibniz, whereas every created substance perceives the whole universe, created minds or spirits have a further privilege: they express God himself. On the assumption that this doctrine holds for those aspects of the divine nature which are disclosed by revelation, as well as those accessible to reason, there will be no truth about God which is not expressed by every mind.

A further objection is inadvertently suggested by Professor Antognazza. In "Leibniz and Religious Toleration" Antognazza invokes such metaphysical doctrines in passing to explain Leibniz's acceptance of the policy of toleration (at least on the part of churches). As she writes, "Leibniz's attitude [i.e. in favor of toleration] seems to be very much in line with [his] general outlook on reality, an outlook characterized by the firm conviction that sparks of truth can be found in every position and that the infinite variety and multiplicity encountered at every level in the universe can and ultimately ought to be traced back to unity" (2002: 612). But if Leibniz's metaphysical commitments explain his acceptance of toleration, they surely cannot also explain his preference for ecumenism over toleration as a strategy for dissolving religious conflicts.

The response to this objection is, I think, clear. Strictly speaking, the metaphysical doctrines we have cited cannot by themselves explain Leibniz's preference for ecumenism over toleration; they need to be supplemented by his further assumption that mental confusion can in many cases be overcome. As a philosopher, Leibniz seeks to reconcile the various sects such as the Platonists and Aristotelians by dissipating such confusion and leading them to an awareness of the one-sidedness of their views; to adapt Leibniz's famous remark to Remond, he will seek to persuade them that while they are generally right in what they assert, they are often wrong in what they deny (GP III, 607). As a theologian Leibniz will seek to end religious conflict in a strictly analogous manner. Toleration would indeed be the preferred strategy only if it were not possible to overcome confusion and one-sidedness in this way. But as things stand, toleration is relegated to the status of a second-best policy. There is a sense in which Leibniz is an optimist in this area in the ordinary, everyday meaning of the term, and not just in the technical sense implied by the doctrine that the actual world is the best of all possible worlds.

It is not inappropriate, then, to seek to explain Leibniz's enthusiasm for the project of ecumenism in terms of his deep metaphysical commitments. But it is also difficult to avoid the impression that other, more nebulous factors were at work. Leibniz's political writings often suggest that he was inspired by the essentially medieval vision of a Europe united in its political and religious allegiances; such a conception was of course never fully realized even in the middle ages, but the conception arguably struck deep roots in the medieval mind. Measured against this vision of unity, the fragmented Europe of his time could only seem a deeply unsatisfactory situation. In this area of his thought it is tempting to compare Leibniz unfavorably with the more realistic Locke who accepted political and religious fragmentation as an inescapable fact of life, and then sought strategies for making the situation tolerable; by the side of Locke Leibniz may seem to us like a reactionary and impractical visionary. But before we dismiss Leibniz in this way we should do well to remember that in our own times the Leibnizian vision of unity has come close to realization, if not in the religious sphere, at least in the political arena.

NOTES

[1]   I am grateful to the participants in the conference, "Leibniz and the English-speaking World", at the University of Liverpool, September 2003, for their helpful comments on an earlier draft of this paper.

[2]   Unlike Locke, Leibniz is even prepared to see something of value in the Enthusiasts. See, for instance, his comments on Jacob Boehme (NE IV, xviii/ RB 507–8): his writings "actually do have something fine and grand about them" (RB 508).

[3]   See, for instance, NE IV, xviii/ RB 500, 502.

[4]   Cf. Leibniz, *Critical Thoughts on the General Part of Descartes' Principles of Philosophy*: L 387.

[5]   Leibniz is not the only distinguished commentator on Locke's *Essay* who ignores the arguments of the Introduction. In his *Locke* (Ayers 1991) Michael Ayers also devotes no space to discussing these arguments.

10. "IS THE LOGIC IN LONDON DIFFERENT FROM THE LOGIC IN HANOVER?"

Some methodological issues in Leibniz's dispute with the Newtonians over the cause of gravity

I. TWO QUESTIONS

Why is Leibnizian Force Intelligible but "Newtonian" Attraction Unintelligible?

In his letter of November 1715 to Caroline, which ignited the controversy with Clarke, Leibniz wrote:

> Sir Isaac Newton, and his followers, have ... a very odd opinion concerning the work of God. According to their doctrine, God Almighty wants to wind up his watch from time to time: otherwise it would cease to move. (GP VII, 352/ HGA 11)

In his second paper, Leibniz added that

> if God is oblig'd to mend the course of nature from time to time, it must be done either supernaturally or naturally. If it be done supernaturally, we must have recourse to miracles, in order to explain natural things: which is reducing an hypothesis *ad absurdum*: for every thing may easily be accounted for by miracles. But if it be done naturally, then God will not be *intelligentia supramundana*: he will be comprehended under the nature of things; that is, he will be the soul of the world. (GP VII, 358/ HGA 20)

When Clarke responded by suggesting that "*natural* and *supernatural* are nothing at all different with regard to God, but distinctions merely in our conceptions of things" (GP VII, 362/ HGA 24), Leibniz was ready with his stock example concerning gravity:

> That which is supernatural, exceeds all the powers of creatures. I shall give an instance, which I have often made use of with good success. If God would cause a body to move free in the aether round about a certain fixed centre, without any other creature acting upon it: I say, it could not be done without a miracle; since it cannot be explained by the nature of bodies. For, a free body does naturally recede from a curve in the tangent. And therefore I maintain, that the attraction of bodies, properly so called, is a miraculous thing, since it cannot be explained by the nature of bodies. (GP VII, 367/ HGA 29–30)

In his fifth and final paper, Leibniz added that if it were held that attractions are not miraculous, then "the assertors of them must ... have recourse to absurdities, that is, to the occult qualities of the schools; which some men begin to revive under the specious name of forces; but they bring us back again into the kingdom of darkness" (GP VII, 417/ HGA 92).

145

P. Phemister and S. Brown (eds.), Leibniz and the English-Speaking World, 145–162.
© 2007 *Springer*.

Whether miraculous or occult, Leibniz held that attractions are unintelligible because they are non-mechanical,[1] which brings me to the first question that I wish to discuss in this paper. For although Leibniz complained bitterly that the Newtonians were guilty of reintroducing scholastic occult qualities, accusing them of employing the subterfuge of calling them "forces," it is well known that he himself had argued for the reintroduction and rehabilitation of scholastic substantial forms and had suggested that they might more intelligibly be termed "forces." In the *New System* of 1695, for example, he explained that he

> had penetrated far into the territory of the Scholastics, when mathematics and the modern authors made me withdraw from it, while I was still young. I was charmed by their beautiful ways of explaining nature mechanically, and I rightly despised the method of those who use only forms or faculties, from which one can learn nothing. But since then, having attempted to examine the very principles of mechanics in order to explain the laws of nature which experience has made known, I perceived that considering extended mass alone was not sufficient, and that it was necessary, in addition, to make use of the notion of force, *which is very intelligible, despite the fact that it belongs in the domain of metaphysics.* (GP IV, 478/ AG 138–9; my emphasis)

But if the notion of force is "very intelligible" according to Leibniz, what are we to make of his later charge that Newtonian gravitational force is obscure to the point of being "unintelligible"? Fairness would seem to dictate that what is good for the goose be good for the gander, so how could Leibniz possibly justify his apparent double-dealing on this head?

Why Not an "Une-Fois-Pour-Toutes" Explanation of Gravity?

Before pursuing this question further, let me turn to a second point that Leibniz made in his letter to Caroline of November 1715, namely, that "according to my opinion, the same force and vigour remains always in the world, and only passes from one part of matter to another, agreeably to the laws of nature, and the beautiful pre-established order" (GP VII, 352/ HGA 12). I am particularly interested in the suggestion that the laws of nature are executed by means of a pre-established harmony, a suggestion strengthened in his second paper, where Leibniz declared that "God has foreseen every thing; he has provided a remedy for every thing before-hand; there is in his works a harmony, a beauty, already pre-established" (GP VII, 358/ HGA 18). It is well known that Leibniz did not allow that force could be transferred from one body to another, writing in *A Specimen of Discoveries* (c.1688), for instance, that "it is evident that no impetus is transferred from one body to another, but each body moves by an innate force, which is determined only on the occasion of, i.e. with respect to, another" (A VI iv, 1620/ RA 310–311/ MP 79). So when in the letter to Caroline he had said that "the same force ... only passes from one part of matter to another," perhaps he added "agreeably to the laws of nature, and the beautiful pre-established order" as an afterthought and as a safeguard.

The particular doctrine of the pre-established harmony between body and soul is discussed explicitly, and at length, in the correspondence with Clarke. Both Clarke and Newton thought that it was Leibniz's doctrine of pre-established harmony that constituted the real miracle, not gravitational attraction.[2] Thus it is significant that in one of his letters to Lady Masham, Leibniz drew a parallel between action-at-a-distance and mind-body interaction in order to illustrate a point about miracles:

> [I]t is no more comprehensible to say that a body acts at a distance with no means or intermediary than it is to say that substances as different as the soul and the body operate on each other immediately; for there is a greater gap between their two natures than between any two places. So the communication between these two so heterogenous substances can only be brought about by a miracle, as can the immediate communication between two distant bodies; and to try to attribute it to I know not what influence of the one on the other is to disguise the miracle with meaningless words. (GP III, 354/ WF 212)

This brings me to the second question that I wish to pose in this paper, namely, if both bodily action-at-a-distance and mind-body communication are miraculous, why didn't Leibniz seek to deal with the former in the same way as he did the latter, rather than insisting on a mechanical explanation of gravitation? To dispense with miracles in the case of mind-body interaction, Leibniz employed a strategy that he often employed in dispensing with apparent miracles, namely, that of offering what was, as he told Queen Sophie Charlotte, only *une fois pour toute* – "only a once-for-all explanation" (GP III, 347/ WF 224). Since the one, truly unavoidable miracle was that of creation, why not, Leibniz seems to have reasoned, simply roll as many apparent miracles as possible into that initial, mega-miracle of creation – and thus the *preformation* of organic bodies, the *pre-establishment* of reason in seed destined to assume human form, the *pre-established* harmony between mind and body, more generally the *pre-established* harmony of final and efficient causes, and ultimately, the *pre-established* harmony of the kingdoms of nature and of grace, all apparent miracles reduced and assimilated to the one great miracle of creation.[3] An *une-fois-pour-toutes* arrangement at the moment of creation made it unnecessary for God to intervene miraculously in the course of nature; so again, why not an elegant, *une-fois-pour-toutes* explanation of the apparent miracle of gravitation, rather than a cumbersome, and ultimately unworkable, mechanical gravitational aether? I will defer attempting to answer this question in favor of returning for the moment to the first question that I posed above.

2. ISN'T WHAT'S GOOD FOR THE GOOSE GOOD FOR THE GANDER?

Can Leibnizian Force be Intelligible if "Newtonian" Attraction is Unintelligible?

Why did Leibniz think that the force he had introduced by way of rehabilitating scholastic substantial forms was "very intelligible," while he argued that Newtonian gravitational force was a "scholastic occult quality," and thus an idol of the "the kingdom of darkness"? Before addressing that question directly, it should be noted that at the time of the correspondence between Leibniz and Clarke, neither Clarke nor Newton held that matter acts at a distance.[4] Both thought of matter as inert, possessing only a passive power of resistance, or inertia, which was proportional to its mass; and thus for both, matter "acted," or rather resisted, only in impact. Furthermore, at the time of the correspondence neither Newton nor Clarke believed that gravity could be explained by a material medium, primarily because, as Newton had argued in the General Scholium added to the 1713 edition of the *Principia*, such a medium could not explain the observed motions of the planets and would in any case impede the motion of comets, whose orbits are oblique to those of the planets.[5] In fact, at the time of the correspondence, both Clarke and Newton appear to have believed that gravity might be due to the action of some incorporeal substance – although by then Newton may have already come to embrace as its cause the quasi-material and non-mechanical aether that he would introduce in the Queries added to the 1717 edition of the *Opticks*.[6] In Query 23 of the 1706 edition of the *Opticks* (Query 31 of the 1717 edition), Newton had allowed himself to speculate publicly that God is "a powerful ever-living agent, who being in all places, is more able by his will to move the bodies within his boundless uniform sensorium, and thereby to form and reform the parts of the universe, than we are by our will to move the parts of our own bodies" (HGA 181). He was generally more cautious, however; and indeed earlier in this same Query he had argued that "how these attractions may be perform'd, I do not here consider. What I call attraction may be perform'd by impulse, or by some other means unknown to me" (HGA 174). Clarke quoted this passage, among others, in his fifth paper to illustrate that by attraction "we do not mean to express the cause of bodies tending towards each other, but barely the effect" (GP VII, 437/ HGA 115); and although Clarke was *relatively* circumspect about the cause of gravity in the correspondence, he had elsewhere made it clear that he believed it to be due to the direct action of God or some other immaterial substance,[7] and the same was at least suggested by these remarks from his fourth paper:

That one body should attract another without any intermediate means, is indeed not a miracle, but a contradiction: for 'tis supposing something to act where it is not. But the means by which two bodies attract each other, may be invisible and intangible, and of a different nature from mechanism; and yet, acting regularly and constantly, may well be called natural ... (GP VII, 388/ HGA 53)

All of this suggests that it is at best misleading to argue, as Dan Garber has, that

the Newtonians are not claiming that God simply moves bodies, but that God has given bodies such a nature that they attract one another in the appropriate way, and that such a nature directly gives rise to the Newtonian law of universal gravitation, without there being any mechanical cause. Their claim is not that the attraction of bodies for one another goes beyond their nature, but that their nature is something different than Leibniz (and other stricter mechanists) think it is. (Garber 1995: 335)[8]

But certainly both Newton and Clarke thought that "the attraction of bodies for one another goes beyond their nature," since for them matter was, by its nature, totally inert, capable only of resistance, and exercising that only in response to an external force. That is why they *did* indeed believe that "God simply moves bodies"; and even when, in the 1717 edition of the *Opticks*, Newton replaced God as the cause of gravity with an active, non-mechanical aether, the latter cause was itself conceived to be *extrinsic* to inert matter. On the other hand, Roger Cotes, editor of the 1713 edition of the *Principia*, seems to have conceived gravity as an inherent and primitive property of matter, writing in the preface to that work that "among the primary qualities of all bodies universally, either gravity will have a place, or extension, mobility, and impenetrability will not" (CW 392). Moreover, whether his judgment was justified or not, Leibniz made it clear in a letter that he wrote to Huygens in 1690 that this was the view of gravity that he attributed to Newton himself, saying that "it seems that, according to him, [attraction] is only a certain incorporeal and inexplicable power" (GM VI, 145/ AG 309). It was this conception of gravity that Leibniz had in mind when he argued that Newtonian gravitational force was an unintelligible occult quality – indeed so occult, as he declared in his letter of 26 January/6 February 1711 to the Dutch philosopher Nicolaus Hartsoeker, "that it can never become intelligible, even if an angel, not to say God himself, should try to explain it" (GP III, 519).[9]

Mechanistic Explanations more Informative than Those in Terms of Forms?

Leibniz initiated his public attack on Newton's natural philosophy in 1710 with some rather innocuous remarks in §19 of the Preliminary Dissertation of the *Theodicy*; and it is perhaps significant that it is difficult to find texts written prior to that time in which he argued that scholastic forms were unintelligible, as opposed to having been merely misapplied. And there was good reason for that; for his own purpose was not to reject the forms of the scholastics, but rather, as he said in the *New System*, "to restore, and, as it were, to rehabilitate the *substantial forms* which are in such disrepute today, but in a way that would render them intelligible, and separate the use one should make of them from the abuse that has been made of them" (GP IV, 478–9/ AG 139). Garber has consequently suggested that Leibniz's criticism of Newtonian gravitational force should be understood, not as a rejection of scholastic forms per se, but rather as a rejection of their use in explaining particular phenomena, on the grounds that the explanations they yield are empty.[10] Garber argues that

mechanistic explanations of the phenomena [on Leibniz's view] are preferable not because they are *truer* than the Scholastics' account, only more informative. When understood properly, Leibniz's mechanical explanations do not *replace* Scholastic explanations, but are *grounded* in them; mechanical explanations are a schematic and partial way of describing what goes on in the form, what *all* forms have in common. It is what we have to fall back on in our ignorance of what specifically God programmed in [to the forms]. (Garber 1985: 99)

Although I believe that there is a great deal to be said for what Garber suggests here,[11] I am not convinced that it helps us much in explaining Leibniz's attitude toward gravitational force in particular. To begin with, it doesn't explain why Leibniz argued, not simply that appeal to gravitational force was uninformative, but that it was, in fact, unintelligible. It might be possible to attribute this claim to rhetorical excess, but if so, it is an excess that seems to undermine Leibniz's own proposed reintroduction of scholastic forms. Furthermore, it is difficult to see how Leibniz's "mechanistic explanation" of gravity could really be "more informative" than the one in terms of form, or gravitational force. A mechanistic explanation would, of course, have to make appeal to impact as the real cause of gravitational motion. But by the 1680s, Leibniz had already adopted the doctrine that substances cannot causally interact and, what is more, had apparently concluded that this doctrine should be extended as well to the material bodies which are aggregates of those substances. Thus in a passage from a piece that the editors of the Akademie edition entitle *Principia logico-metaphysica* and tentatively date between the spring and fall of 1689, Leibniz wrote:

> Strictly speaking, one can say that *no created substance exerts a metaphysical action or influx on any other thing.* For, not to mention the fact that one cannot explain how something can pass from one thing into the substance of another, we have already shown that from the notion of each and every thing follows all of its future states. What we call causes are only concurrent requisites, in metaphysical rigor. This is also illustrated by our experience of nature. For bodies really rebound from others through the force of their own elasticity, and not through the force of other things, even if another body is required in order for the elasticity (which arises from something intrinsic to the body itself) to be able to act. (A VI iv, 1647/ AG 33/ MP 90)[12]

It would thus appear that for Leibniz the post-collision motion of a body requires another body only as a "concurrent requisite," rather than as a real cause; thus the motions of bodies in collision seem to be due to a pre-established harmony of motion rather than to a real causal influence between them. If that is right, then it seems by Leibniz's lights that a purely mechanistic explanation can provide no genuine causal explanation of the motions of bodies in collision and hence no genuine causal account of gravitational motion. On the other hand, it is true that a "mechanistic" account of the concurrent requisites of some phenomenon may at least provide the basis for prediction, and in that sense be more informative than an account in terms of scholastic forms. But the concurrent requisites of gravitational motion on the sort of mechanistic account that Leibniz envisioned, namely, the motions of the particles of a gravitating aether, cannot even provide predictive information, since they are unobservable, theoretical entities. In the case of gravitational motion, prediction is based entirely on the observation of the gravitating bodies themselves. So again, in the case of gravitational motion, it is hard to see how a mechanistic account of the sort that Leibniz envisioned could be more informative than an account in terms of scholastic virtues. Given Leibniz's own, deep account of causal activity, a mechanistic, gravitational aether could be nothing but a superfluous theoretical entity, providing neither an ultimate causal explanation nor a predictive tool.[13]

Appeal to Attractive Force Violates the Methodological Apartheid between Physics and Metaphysics?

Leibniz's belief that explanations in terms of scholastic forms were useless for explaining the particular phenomena of nature led him to adopt a methodological principle almost immediately upon his decision to rehabilitate scholastic forms in 1678,[14] a principle that he invoked repeatedly in his later work. Having reintroduced substantial forms for the sake of saving physics from the follies of Cartesianism, Leibniz began to build what he thought should be an impenetrable wall between physics and metaphysics. Although Leibniz insisted that forms were needed in order to provide a proper metaphysical basis for demonstrating the laws of motion, he also insisted that these forms were to have no place in explaining the particular phenomena of nature, where everything, he thought, not only could be explained mechanically, but ought to be explained in that way, without appeal to metaphysical notions, like his newly resurrected forms.[15] It became clear in later works that he was motivated in large part by a felt need to placate the then ascendant mechanists, who Leibniz must have reckoned would be quick to accuse him of doing precisely what he would later accuse the Newtonians of doing, namely, reintroducing the discredited occult qualities of the scholastics. Anxious to satisfy both scholastics and moderns, Leibniz argued that the methodological apartheid of physics and metaphysics provided, as he put it in the *Specimen Dynamicum*, "the middle way in which one satisfies both piety and knowledge" (GM VI, 242/ AG 126).

Perhaps, then, and quite apart from the question of whether his own, mechanistic account of gravitational motion was really more informative than one in terms of scholastic virtues, Leibniz may have thought that Newton's introduction of a force of gravitation violated what he took to be a sound methodological principle separating physics from metaphysics. Although this would again not explain his charge that such a force is unintelligible, it might nonetheless explain his aversion to what he thought to be Newton's attempt to introduce such a force into the realm of physics. He mistook Newton in this regard, however, since Newton himself had constructed a methodological wall very similar to Leibniz's own, as he explained in perhaps the most well-known passage from the General Scholium of the 1713 edition of the *Principia*:

> I have not yet been able to deduce from phenomena the reason for these properties of gravity, and I do not feign hypotheses. For whatever is not deduced from the phenomena must be called a hypothesis, and hypotheses, whether metaphysical or physical, or based on occult qualities, or mechanical, have no place in experimental philosophy. In this experimental philosophy, propositions are deduced from the phenomena and are made general by induction. The impenetrability, mobility, and impetus of bodies, and the laws of motion and the law of gravity have been found by this method. And it is enough that gravity really exists and acts according to the laws that we have set forth and is sufficient to explain all the motions of the heavenly bodies and of our sea. (CW 943)

If anything, the wall that Newton sought to erect here between "hypotheses" and "what can be deduced from the phenomena" was even more rigid than Leibniz's own wall between physics and metaphysics. Indeed, it is clear from this passage that Newton meant to exclude from experimental philosophy such speculative, "mechanical" hypotheses as the harmonic vortex that Leibniz had introduced to explain planetary motion,[16] as well as such "physical" hypotheses as that gravity is a primary quality of bodies, which Cotes introduced in the Preface to the 1713 edition of the *Principia* and which Leibniz had criticized as a return to scholastic occult qualities.[17] However, Newton did not wish to block the possibility of non-mechanical explanations of gravity, complaining in Query 28 of the 1706 edition of the *Opticks* that while the ancient "philosophers of Greece and Phoenicia ... tacitly [attributed] gravity to some other cause than dense matter, [l]ater philosophers banish such a cause out of natural philosophy, feigning hypotheses for explaining all things mechanically, and referring other causes to metaphysics" (HGA 173). This was, of course, a perfect description of Leibniz's wall; but how Newton could have thought that a non-mechanical cause of gravity might be "deduced from the phenomena" in accord with his own methodological strictures is extremely unclear.

The Experimental Method and the Law of Gravitation

In a post script to his letter to Abbé Conti of 25 November/6 December 1715, and after remarking that Newton's "philosophy appears a bit strange to me," Leibniz seemed to give at least a grudging endorsement of Newton's experimental method:

I ... admire very much the physico-mathematical thoughts of M. Newton, and the public would be greatly in your debt, sir, if you could persuade this capable man to give us his conjectures in physics to this point. I strongly approve his method of deducing from the phenomena what can be deduced from them without supposing anything, though this would sometimes be only to deduce conjectural consequences. However, when the data are not sufficient, it is permitted (as is done in deciphering) to conceive hypotheses, and if they succeed, we accept them provisionally, until some new experiences bring us new data, and what Bacon calls a crucial experiment for deciding between the hypotheses. ... I am very much in favor of the experimental philosophy, but M. Newton errs greatly when he supposes that all matter is heavy (or that each part of matter attracts every other part), which experience does not establish, as M. Huygens has already very rightly determined. The gravitating matter cannot itself have this heaviness of which it is the cause, and M. Newton does not furnish any experience or sufficient reason for the void and atoms, or for universal mutual attraction. And since it is not known perfectly and in detail how gravity is produced, or elastic force, or magnetic force etc., we do not on that account have reason to appeal to scholastic occult qualities or to miracles ... (TSHT VI, 252–3)

In the letter answering Leibniz that he eventually sent to Conti, Newton, being more intent on the calculus dispute, wrote laconically on the philosophical points that Leibniz had raised.[18] But in one of the earlier drafts of the letter, Newton had written at much greater length, as follows:

But Mr Leibnitz insinuates that gravity must be caused by the action or impulse of some bodies or subtile matter & the matter Wch causes gravity cannot gravitate it self. He goes upon the Hypothesis of the materialists viz that all the phaenomena in nature are caused by mere matter & motion ... And his zeale for this precarious hypothesis makes him rail at Mr Newton's universal gravity. He denys none of Mr Newtons experiments. He denys not the third Rule of Philosophy. And yet from the Experim^{ts} & that Rule universal gravity necessarily follows. But he denys the conclusion. And indeed he has a very good faculty at denying conclusions. That Rule is the Rule of Induction. And without it no Proposition can become general in Naturall Philosophy. Without it we cannot affirm that all bodies are impenetrable. And the argument by Induction for universal gravity is as strong as the argument for universal impenetrability. Yet Arguments from Induction are not Demonstrations. They are only to take place till some experimental exception can be found. ... It's not impossible but that an exception may be found in time. But a mere hypothesis or supposition of an exception is no exception. The exception ought to be experimental. The meaning of Conclusions made by Induction is that they are to be looked upon as general till some reale exception appeare. And in this sense gravity is to be looked upon as universal. To make an exception upon a mere hypothesis is to feign an exception. It is to reject the argument from induction, & turn Philosophy into a heap of Hypotheses, which are no better then a chimerical Romance. (Koyré and Cohen 1962: 113–5)

In the covering letter with which he forwarded Newton's reply to Leibniz, Conti wrote:

I will speak to you again of the philosophy of Mr. Newton. It is first necessary to agree upon the method of philosophizing and to distinguish carefully the philosophy of Mr. Newton from the consequences that many draw from it very inappropriately. (TSHT VI, 296)

In referring to "the method of philosophizing," Conti doubtless had in mind the four Rules for the Study of Natural Philosophy that headed Book III of the *Principia* – and especially Rule III, the rule of induction, that Newton had brandished repeatedly by name in the draft of his letter to the Abbé. When Leibniz replied to Conti on 29 March/9 April 1716, he was clearly in no mood to be lectured; and in a postscript intended specifically for the Abbé, he shot back:

I am astonished, sir, that you say that before speaking of the philosophy of M. Newton, it is necessary to agree upon the method of philosophizing. Is the logic in London different from the logic in Hanover? When we reason in good form from well-established facts, or from indubitable axioms, we do not fail to be right. If the opinions of M. Newton are better than they have said, so much the better; I will always be very glad to give him his due. (TSHT VI, 312)

Whatever might be said about differences in logic between London and Hanover, I think it can be said that Leibniz missed, or ignored, the point of Newton's methodological complaints against him. Cleared of the obscurities that surrounded the discussion of this issue, Newton's point seems fairly obvious. In appealing to the inductive principle in Rule III, he was arguing that gravity should be accepted, not as a *primitive quality* of bodies, as Leibniz had charged and Cotes seems actually to have held, but rather as a *primitive law of motion*, at least provisionally, on a par with the other laws of motion, including those governing the collision of bodies. The universal law, he thought, should be accepted based on the observed regularities, in accordance with Rule III; an ultimate explanation of gravitational motion could be hoped for and sought, but only under the constraint of consistency with the observed phenomena. There should have been nothing in this that Leibniz could not have agreed to. He could have accepted the universal law of gravitation as a primitive law of motion, as he had the laws of collision, and he might then have argued, in a way that would have been consistent with his wall between physics and metaphysics, that the law of gravitation itself should be explained metaphysically, in terms of the same force in bodies that he had postulated to explain the other laws of motion. But Leibniz had committed himself in advance to the idea that the law of gravitation was a *derivative law* that was to be explained in terms of the laws of impact. Granted that it is not in the nature of bodies to move in ellipses, it does not follow that such motion needs to be explained by impact. But Leibniz insisted that "through derivative force, primitive force is altered [*variatur*] in the collisions of bodies" (GP IV, 397/ AG 254), apparently believing that the only alternative was action-at-a-distance, which he regarded as unintelligible, as did Newton and Clarke as well.[19]

Attraction is Unintelligible Because it Involves Action-at-a-Distance?

Perhaps, then, that is the final, and obvious, explanation of why Leibniz rejected attraction as unintelligible: because it would apparently have to involve action-at-a-distance. But appearances aside, I think Leibniz had another option, one that could have been underwritten by his own, deep account of causation. Contrary to what

Garber has suggested, it was not the Newtonians – at least not Newton and Clarke – who had introduced a radically new conception of the nature of matter. For them, it was still inert and inactive. Leibniz, on the other hand, *had* proposed a radically new conception of the nature of matter, according to which it was active, and, on his deep analysis, spontaneous. In a very late paper, *Anti-barbarus physicus*, Leibniz chided the Newtonians, saying that

those who, induced by the successful discovery that the great bodies of this planetary system have an attraction for their sensible parts, imagine that every body whatsoever is attracted by every other by virtue of a force in matter itself, whether it is as if a thing takes pleasure in another similar thing, and senses it even from a distance, or whether it is brought about by God, who takes care of this though a perpetual miracle, so that bodies seek one another, as if they sensed each other. (GP VII, 342/ AG 317)

But there appears to be a *tertium quid* that Leibniz fails to mention here, namely, the *une-fois-pour-toutes* explanation, where the apparent miracle of "bodies seek[ing] one another, as if they sensed each other" might be rolled, pre-established, into the original miracle of creation. Here, it seems, was a genuine option. Why didn't Leibniz take it?

3. GRAVITY: WHY NOT PRE-ESTABLISHED HARMONY, *UNE FOIS POUR TOUTES?*

The Une-Fois-Pour-Toutes *Explanation of Gravity would be Miraculous*

In a letter from September 1704 to Isaac Jaquelot, Leibniz wrote:

There is no comparison between the action of one body on another and the influence of the soul on the body. There is immediate contact between bodies, and we understand how that can be, and how, since there is no penetration, their coming together must alter their movement in some way. But we see no such consequences with the soul and the body: these two do not touch, and do not interfere with one another in an immediate way which we can understand and deduce from their natures. All they can do is to be in agreement, and to depend on one another by a metaphysical influence, so to speak, in virtue of the soul's ideas; and that is contained in God's plans, which are in conformity with them. They are related through the mediation of God, not by a continual interruption of the laws of the one because of its relation to the other, but by a harmony pre-established in their natures *une fois pour toutes*. (GP VI, 570/ WF 199)

Here Leibniz draws a contrast between body-body relations and mind-body relations that seems to suggest that the former can, and do, involve genuine causal interactions while the latter cannot and do not. Since bodies occupy space and are impenetrable, they can, unlike the mind and body, "interfere with one another in an immediate way which we can understand and deduce from their natures." But despite appearances, I do not think this passage should be taken as endorsing genuine causal interaction between bodies. I suggested earlier that the deep, metaphysical explanation that Leibniz offers for the laws of collision is really just an *une-fois-pour-toutes* expla-nation. In metaphysical rigor, a proximate body that touches is only the occasional cause of the change in another body's motion – the motion of the one is limited only *ideally* by the proximate presence of the other, but *actually* by the spontaneous activity of the underlying substances. And if the *proximate* presence of a body can be an intelligible, occasional cause of the change in another body's motion, then it would seem that the *remote* presence of a body could do just as well. But even if both the proximate presence and the remote presence of a body could provide an occasional cause for the change in another body's motion, there is a difference for Leibniz; for the mere presence of a body, if it is remote, cannot be understood as providing an occasion that necessitates change of motion in the way that the presence of a proximate body does, which, *by its nature*, is impenetrable. Thus the *occasion* of the change of motion in proximate bodies is natural, and hence comprehensible, in a way that the occasion of the change of motion in remote bodies is not.[20] And so in a letter published in July 1698 addressing Bayle's difficulties with the *New System*, Leibniz wrote:

It isn't sufficient to say that God has made a general law, for in addition to the decree there has also to be a natural way of carrying it out. It is necessary, that is, that what happens should be explicable in terms of the God-given nature of things. Natural laws are not as arbitrary and groundless as many think. (GP IV, 520/ WF 82/ L 494)

For Leibniz, then, the *une-fois-pour-toutes* explanation turns out not to be a genuine alternative to the miraculous after all, since it must assume that the gravitational motion of two bodies is brought about "by a continual interruption of the laws of the one because of its relation to the other" (GP VI, 570/ WF 199)[21] – a continual interruption that does *not* occur in the case of the coordination of mind and body. But it is here, in light of the very real problems that Newton had raised against any purely mechanical account of attraction, that one might have hoped for a more daring proposal from Leibniz. For he might have argued that experience reveals the need for a revised conception of the nature of matter, according to which a body would naturally obey the law of gravitation, just as he had earlier argued that experience reveals a need for a revision in the Cartesian conception of the nature of matter, so that a body might be said to obey naturally the laws of motion. And just as before, his deep metaphysics would have enabled him to provide an elegant, *une-fois-pour-toutes* explanation of the law of gravitation itself.

The Une-Fois-Pour-Toutes *Explanation of Gravity would be Inconsistent with the Conservation of* Vis Viva

But there is a further consideration that might help to explain why Leibniz did not choose this more radical path. In his fifth paper for Clarke, Leibniz wrote:

I say ... 'tis supernatural that the whole universe of bodies should receive a new force; and consequently that one body should acquire any new force, without the loss of as much in others. And therefore I say likewise,'tis an indefensible opinion to suppose the soul gives force to the body; for then the whole universe of bodies would receive a new force. (GP VII, 413/ HGA 86)

If incorporeal things – like those postulated by Clarke, and sometimes by Newton, to explain attraction – were able to generate motion, there would needs be an increase in the amount of force in the world. Indeed, any non-mechanical explanation of attraction – including the *une-fois-pour-toutes* explanation suggested above – would have that result; for it seems that at every moment of the world's existence, at least as Leibniz could have conceived it, there must have existed what we would call "gravitational potential energy," as well as magnetic and electrical potential energy. Over time, such energy would inexorably be transformed, so that the amount of kinetic energy in the world – the energy that Leibniz called *vis viva* or *potentia actrix* – would necessarily increase with time. But Leibniz had argued that *"The foundation of the laws of nature ... should ... be sought in ... the fact that it is necessary that the same quantity of potentia actrix be preserved"* (GP IV, 506/ AG 157).

For Newton, it was quantity of motion, not of force in Leibniz's sense, that was relevant to the question of whether the universe was running down, as he clearly thought that it was: "Seeing therefore the variety of motion which we find in the world is always decreasing," he wrote in Query 23 of the 1706 *Opticks*,

there is necessity of conserving and recruiting it by active principles, such as are the cause of gravity, by which planets and comets keep their motions in their orbs, and bodies acquire great motion in falling; and the cause of fermentation, by which the heart and blood of animals are kept in perpetual motion and heat; the inward parts of the earth are constantly warm'd, and in some places grow very hot; bodies burn and shine, mountains take fire, the caverns of the earth are blown up, and the sun continues violently hot and lucid, and warms all things by his light. For we meet with very little motion in the world, besides what is owing either to these active principles or to the dictates of a will. (HGA 178)

In the 1717 edition, he added that "if it were not for these principles the bodies of the earth, planets, comets, sun, and all things in them would grow cold and freeze, and become inactive masses; and all putrefaction, generation, vegetation and life would cease, and the planets would not remain in their orbs" (HGA 178).

In the supply of active principles that worked to replenish the motion that was always decreasing in the world, Newton saw a sign of God's providence; in his conservation law, Leibniz saw a sign of God's perfect workmanship and the source of the world's order and intelligibility. "My axiom," he said

is not simply *that the whole effect corresponds to the complete cause*, but *that the whole effect is equal to the complete cause*. And I do not use it to explain primitive force (which needs no explanation), but to explain the phenomena of secondary force. It provides me with equations in mechanics, just as the common axiom that the whole is equal to its parts taken together, provides us with them in geometry. (UL VI, 529/ WF 34)

Collision was not only the occasion for the change of motion, but also for the redistribution of forces, in accordance with equations underwritten by the conservation of *vis viva*. If motion could be increased by non-mechanical causes such as attractions, there would be no obvious or principled way to compensate for the gain in force with a corresponding loss elsewhere. Lacking a higher-level conservation law, like the conservation of energy, Leibniz's dynamics would be left without equations, and the world without dynamic order. In any event, it is doubtful whether Leibniz would have tolerated a conservation law in which a term like *potential* energy appeared. "Force of action in bodies," he wrote,

is something distinct and independent of anything else that one can understand in them. Everything else is as though dead without it, and incapable of producing any change. A *faculty*, about which there was a lot of noise in the schools, is nothing but a mere possibility of action; but the force of action is an entelechy or even a positive action. And that is what is needed. Possibility alone produces nothing, unless it is put into action; but force produces everything. (UL VI, 529–30/ WF 35)

The Une-Fois-Pour-Toutes *Explanation would make the Plenum Superfluous*

Given the complexity and integration of his thought, the problem that the *une-fois-pour-toutes* explanation of gravity made for the conservation of *vis viva* was probably only one among many reasons that must have made it difficult for Leibniz to take such an alternative seriously. One additional reason that may have bulked especially large for Leibniz was the fact that an *une-fois-pour-toutes* explanation of gravity would have made the hypothesis of a plenum appear superfluous. In fact, in his *Anti-barbarus physicus* Leibniz had written that the defenders of gravitational attraction

are forced by this view of the essential attraction of matter to defend the vacuum, since the attraction of everything for everything else would be pointless if everything were full. But in the true philosophy, the vacuum is rejected for other reasons. (GP VII, 343/ AG 318)

But if, as appears obvious, Leibniz was referring to the Newtonians here, then he was grossly understating their case in favor of the void. For, as we have seen, Newton had argued, not simply that the plenum was "pointless," but rather that it was positively inconsistent with the observed motions of the planets and comets. If Leibniz had taken this criticism seriously, and had consequently adopted an *une-fois-pour-toutes* explanation of gravity, he, too, it appears, would have been forced to defend the vacuum. But as he suggested in this passage, Leibniz had "other reasons" for rejecting the vacuum. In the correspondence with Clarke, for example, he argued that "one reason, among others, why I maintain that there is no vacuum at all" is that "the more matter there is, the more God has occasion to exercise his wisdom and power" (GP VII, 356/ HGA 16; cf. GP VII, 377/ HGA 44); thus the principle of perfection requires a plenum. Another reason, he argued, was "grounded upon the necessity of a sufficient reason"; for it is "impossible there should be any principle to determine what proportion of matter there ought to be, out of all the possible degrees from a plenum to a vacuum, or from a vacuum to a plenum" (GP VII, 378/ HGA 44). But as his discussion in the postscript to his fourth paper made clear (see GP VII, 377–8/ HGA 43–5), Leibniz also seems to have regarded the doctrine of the void as going hand-in-hand with the doctrine of atoms, against which he also had a host of objections.

In the end, far too many of his systematic doctrines would have been jeopardized by an *une-fois-pour-toutes* explanation of gravity; so Leibniz dug in his heels and resisted attraction.[22]

NOTES

[1] Thus in the Preface to the *New Essays*, he wrote:

So we may take it that matter will not naturally possess the attractive power referred to above, and that it will not of itself move in a curved path, because it is impossible to conceive how this could happen—that is, to explain it mechanically—whereas what is natural must be such as could become distinctly conceivable by anyone admitted into the secrets of things. This distinction between what is natural and explicable and what is miraculous and inexplicable removes all the difficulties. To reject it would be to uphold something worse than occult qualities, and thereby to renounce philosophy and reason, giving refuge to ignorance and laziness by means of an irrational system which maintains not only that there are qualities which we do not understand—of which there are only too many—but further that there are some which could not be comprehended by the greatest intellect if God gave it every possible opportunity, i.e. [qualities] which are either miraculous or without rhyme or reason. (A VI vi, 66/ RB 66).

²   In his fourth paper, Clarke commented with gleeful disdain: "That the soul should not operate upon the body; and yet the body, by mere mechanical impulse of matter, conform itself to the will of the soul in all the infinite variety of spontaneous animal-motion; is a perpetual miracle. *Pre-established harmony*, is a mere word or term of art, and does nothing towards explaining the cause of so miraculous an effect" (GP VII, 386/ HGA 51).

For good measure, Clarke added in his fifth paper that "the harmonical soul, in the hypothesis of an *harmonia praestabilita*, is merely a fiction and a dream" (GP VII, 438/ HGA 116). As usual, Clarke was following Newton's lead here. In his letter of 26 February/8 March 1716 to Conti, Newton had declared that Leibniz

colludes in the significations of words, calling those things miracles wch create no wonder & those things occult qualities whos causes are occult tho the qualities themselves be manifest & those things the souls of men wch do not animate their bodies. His *Harmonia praestabilita* is miraculous & contradicts the daily experience of all mankind, every man finding in himse[l]f a power of seeing with his eyes & moving his body by his will (TSHT VI, 251).

These were sentiments that Newton had expressed repeatedly in the drafts of the letter, writing in one of them that Leibniz's doctrine of pre-established harmony was among those "Metaphysical Hypotheses such as never were and never can be decided by experiments," and which "turn philosophy into a Romance" (Koyré and Cohen 1962: 75). For his part, after suggesting that the Newtonian attractions "bring us back again into the kingdom of darkness", Leibniz commented in his fifth paper for Clarke that "what has happened in poetry, happens also in the philosophical world. People are grown weary of rational romances ... and they are become fond again of the tales of fairies" (GP VII, 417/ HGA 93).

³   On preformationism and the pre-establishment of reason, see Brown, G. 1995: 28–35.

⁴   In his fourth paper, for example, Clarke argued "that one body should attract another without intermediate means, is indeed not a miracle, but a contradiction: for 'tis supposing something to act where it is not" (GP VII, 388/ HGA 53). And in a famous passage from his letter to Richard Bentley of 25 February 1693, Newton wrote:

'Tis inconceivable that inanimate brute matter should (without the mediation of something else which is not material) operate upon and affect other matter without mutual contact; as it must if gravitation in the sense of Epicurus be essential and inherent in it. ... That gravity should be innate inherent and essential to matter so that one body may act upon another at a distance through a vacuum without the mediation of any thing else by and through which their action or force may be conveyed from one to another is to me so great an absurdity that I believe no man who has in philosophical matters any competent faculty of thinking can ever fall into it (TSHT III, 253–4).

⁵   See CW 939; cf. Clarke's fifth paper: GP VII, 438/ HGA 117. Leibniz had written directly to Newton on 17 March 1693, saying: "You have made the astonishing discovery that Kepler's ellipses result simply from the conception of attraction or gravitation and trajection in a planet. And yet I would incline to believe that all these are caused or regulated by the motion of a fluid medium, on the analogy of gravity and magnetism as we know it here. Yet this solution would not detract from the value and truth of your discovery" (TSHT III, 258).

In his reply of 15 October 1693, Newton, even at this early date, had made Leibniz directly aware of the difficulties posed by the resistance of a gravitating medium:

For since celestial motions are more regular than if they arose from vortices and observe other laws, so much so that vortices contribute not to the regulation but to the disturbance of the motions of planets and comets; and since all phenomena of the heavens and of the sea follow precisely, so far as I am aware, from nothing but gravity acting in accordance with the laws described by me; and since nature is very simple, I have myself concluded that all other causes have to be rejected and that the heavens are to be stripped as far as may be of all matter, lest the motions of the planets and comets be hindered or rendered irregular. But if, meanwhile, someone explains gravity along with all its laws by the action of some subtle matter, and shows that the motion of planets and comets will not be disturbed by this matter, I shall be far from objecting (TSHT III, 287).

6   On Newton's belief between 1684 and 1710 that the direct action of God was the cause of gravity, see Dobbs 1991: 191–212. On his later adoption of the non-mechanical aether as the cause of gravity, see Dobbs 1991: 218–30.

7   On this, see Vailati 1997: 187–9.

8   Two pages earlier, Garber had written:

While Newton's own attitude was not altogether clear on this, one could get the impression from Newton, and, indeed, one did get the clear view from some of his followers, that the universal gravitation of the *Principia* was intended to be a basic, irreducible, and inexplicable property of matter as such, something that one need not and could not explain mechanically. (Garber 1995: 333)

Garber does mention Cotes in a footnote (148) as an example of one such follower. But Newton's own attitude was quite clear indeed in *rejecting* gravity as "a basic, irreducible, and inexplicable property of matter as such." Thus, again, it is quite misleading to suggest in general that the Newtonians were trafficking in a new conception of the nature of matter.

9   The letter was published in the *Memoires de Trévoux* in March 1712 and reprinted in the *Memoirs of Literature* of London in May and the Amsterdam edition of the *Journal des Sçavans* in December.

10   See Garber 1995: 332–4.

11   See my discussion in Brown, G. 1992.

12   Similarly, in a short note that the editors of the Akademie edition date between March of 1689 and March of 1690, Leibniz wrote:

The system of occasional causes ought to be partly accepted, and partly rejected. Each substance is the true and real cause of its *immanent* actions, and has a force of acting, and although it is sustained by divine concurrence, it is impossible for it to behave merely passively, and this is true in corporeal substances as well as incorporeal ones. But again each substance (excepting God alone) is but the occasional cause of its own *transient* actions on another substance. Therefore the true *reason for the union between soul and body*, and the cause of one body's accommodating itself to the state of another body, is simply that the different substances of the same world system were so created from the beginning as to harmonize with one another as a result of the laws of their own individual nature. (A VI iv, 1640–1/ RA 312–3/ MP 80–1; cf. A VI iv, 1620/ RA 310–1/ MP 79; GM VI, 251/ AG 134–5; GP II, 116/ HTM 148; GP IV, 486/ AG 145/ WF 20; GP IV, 475–6/ WF 26; GP IV, 557–8/ WF 110–2/ L 576–7).

For an extended discussion of this topic, see Brown 1992.

13   In Section 10 of the *Discourse on Metaphysics*, Leibniz suggests that appealing to forms to explain the operation of things is to act "as if we were content to say that a clock has a quality of clockness derived from its form without considering in what all this consists; that would be sufficient for the person who buys the clock, provided that he turns over its care to another" (A VI iv, 1543/ AG 42). This suggests that mechanical explanations, unlike those in terms of forms, provide information about how we might manipulate things in inventing machines and keeping them in good repair. But, again, such knowledge does not seem to be at issue when it comes to the explanation of gravitational motion.

14   At the beginning of 1678, Leibniz discovered that the Cartesians had erred in their belief that quantity of motion is conserved in collisions, finding instead that it is power that is conserved, where power is to be measured by taking the mass of a body into the square of its velocity (see *De corporum concursu* in Fichant 1994). Close on the heels of this discovery, between the summer and winter of

1678/79, Leibniz composed a conspectus for a little book on the elements of physics. There he postulated a passive power of resistance in body in addition to its active power of motion:

Body is extended, mobile, resistant. It is that which can act and be acted upon insofar as it is extended. It acts if it is in motion, is acted upon if it resists motion. So we should consider: first, extension; next, motion; and third, resistance or collision. ...

Now there follows the subject of incorporeals. There turn out to be certain things in body which cannot be explained by the necessity of matter alone. Such are the laws of motion, which depend on the metaphysical principle of the equality of cause and effect. Here therefore the soul must be treated, and it must be shown that all things are animated. ... Force or power should now be treated; when it is to be known, it must be estimated from the quantity of the effect. But the power of the effect and of the cause are equal to each other, for if that of the effect were greater we would have a mechanical perpetual motion, if less, we would not have physical perpetual motion. Here it is worth showing that the same quantity of motion cannot be conserved, but that on the other hand the same quantity of power [*potentiae*] is conserved. (A VI iv, 1988–9/ RA 233–5)

By the fall of that year, Leibniz was prepared to announce to his Catholic employer, duke Johann Friedrich of Hanover, that "there is something of great import in my philosophy which will give it some admittance among the Jesuits and other theologians, namely, that I restore the substantial forms that the atomists and Cartesians claim to have exterminated" (A II i, 490). The powers that had to be added to the merely geometrical matter postulated by the Cartesians were not really that different, Leibniz thought, from the forms that had been postulated in the scholastic philosophy, lately disdained. Thus in a text dating from somewhere between the summer of 1678 and the winter of 1680/81, Leibniz summed up his discoveries in the following terms:

When I considered how, in general, we could explain what we experience everywhere, that speed is diminished through an increase in bulk [*moles*] as, for example, when the same boat is carried downstream goes more slowly the more it is loaded down, I stopped, and all my attempts having been in vain, I discovered that this, so to speak, inertia of bodies cannot be deduced from the initially assumed notion of matter and motion, where matter is understood as that which is extended or fills space, and motion is understood as change of space or place. But rather, over and above that which is deduced from extension and its variation or modification alone, we must add and recognize in bodies certain notions or forms that are immaterial, so to speak, or independent of extension, which you can call powers [*potentia*], by means of which speed is adjusted to magnitude. These powers consist not in motion, indeed, not in conatus or the beginning of motion, but in the cause or in that intrinsic reason for motion, which is the law required for continuing. And investigators have erred insofar as they considered motion, but not motive power or the reason for motion, which even if derived from God, author and governor of things, must not be understood as being in God himself, but must be understood as having been produced and conserved by him in things. From this we shall also show that it is not the same quantity of motion (which misleads many), but the same powers that are conserved in the world. (A VI iv, 1980/ AG 249–50)

The seeds of the methodological principle separating physics from metaphysics can be detected in the following passage from the beginning of this same text:

There was a time when I believed that all the phenomena of motion could be explained on purely geometrical principles, assuming no metaphysical propositions, and that the laws of impact depend only on the composition of motions. But, through more profound meditation, I discovered that this is impossible, and I learned a truth higher than all mechanics, namely, that everything in nature can indeed be explained mechanically, but that the principles of mechanics themselves depend on metaphysical and, in a sense, moral principles, that is, on the contemplation of the most perfectly effectual [*operans*], efficient and final cause, namely, God, and cannot in any way be deduced from the blind composition of motions. And thus, I learned that it is impossible for there to be nothing in the world except matter and its variations, as the Epicureans held. (A VI iv, 1976/ AG 245).

[15]   See the texts cited in Garber 1995: 332.

[16]   See Leibniz's *Tentamen de motuum coelestium causis*, which was published in the February 1689 issue of the *Acta eruditorum*.

[17]   Alexandre Koyré has suggested with some plausibility that "as to 'physical hypotheses,' ... Newton here has in mind the frequent misinterpretations of his theory of universal gravitation by those who, like Bentley and Cheyne, Huygens and Leibniz, transformed gravitation into a physical force and made it an essential or at least a primary property of bodies – the first pair in order to accept, the others in order to reject, this 'hypothesis'" (Koyré 1965: 39). Cotes' name, of course, could easily be added to those of Bentley and Cheyne, since, as Koyré himself notes Cotes was "convinced ... that attraction was, as a matter of fact, a property of body, and even a primordial one. Accordingly, he said so in his preface [to the 1713 edition of the *Principia*]" (281).

[18]   In the reply he sent to Conti, Newton wrote:

As to Philosophy [it is as little to the purpose]. He colludes in the significations of words, calling those things miracles wch create no wonder & those things occult qualities whos causes are occult tho the qualities themselves be manifest & those things the souls of men wch do not animate their bodies, His *Harmonia praestabilita* is miraculous & contradicts the daily experience of all mankind, every man finding in himse[l]f a power of seeing with his eyes & moving his body by his will. He preferrs Hypotheses to Arguments of Induction drawn from experiments, accuses me of opinions wch are not mine, & instead of proposing Questions to be examined by Experiments before they are admitted into Philosophy he proposes Hypotheses to be admitted & believed before they are examined. (TSHT VI, 285–6).

[19]   See note 4 above.

[20]   On the other hand, although the pre-established harmony provides an intelligible account of the *apparent* interaction between mind and body, there can be no *natural* way of accounting for how they might *actually* interact, since, as Leibniz says, "these two do not touch, and do not interfere with one another in an immediate way which we can understand and deduce from their natures."

[21]   In this case, of course, the laws of the one are the same as the laws of the other, since they are both bodies; but the *une-fois-pour-toutes* explanation would require a constant interruption of the laws of each because of the presence of the other – in particular, a continual interruption of the law that an unimpeded body moves in a straight line.

[22]   It is perhaps worth mentioning that one reason Leibniz defended a vortex theory to account for the motions of the planets is that he thought it could explain something that the Newtonians could not explain, namely, why all the planets move around the sun in approximately the same plane and in the same direction. Thus he wrote to Huygens in 1690:

Although Newton is satisfactory when one considers only a single planet or satellite, nevertheless, he cannot account for why all the planets of the same system move over approximately the same path, and why they move in the same direction, using only impetuosity together with gravity. That is what we observe, not only for the sun's planets, but also for those of Jupiter and those of Saturn. This is good evidence for there being a common reason that determines them to behave in this way; and what other more probable reason can be brought to bear than that some kind of vortex or common matter carries them around? For to have recourse to the decision of the author of nature is not sufficiently philosophical when there is a way of assigning proximate causes; and it is even less reasonable to attribute this agreement among the planets of the same system to good luck, given that the agreement is found in all three systems, that is, in all the systems known to us. (GM VI, 190/ AG 310)

In arguing that it "is not sufficiently philosophical" to have "recourse to the decision of the author of nature" to explain the data in question, Leibniz anticipated Newton's argument in the General Scholium of the *Principia* that the fact that the planets move in approximately the same plane and in the same direction cannot be explained by the laws of mechanics and must therefore be due to "the design and dominion of an intelligent and powerful being" (CW 940). But Leibniz's argument seems underwhelming, since it only delays an inevitable appeal to God; for Leibniz himself would appear obliged to make appeal to God's original designs in order to account for the motion of the harmonic vortex that he postulated to explain the motions of the planets. Furthermore, the claim that Newton has not explained by "proximate causes" the data in question seems an extremely weak point to put against the charge that Newton would later lay to Leibniz's account, namely, that the vortex theory is in direct conflict with the observed motions of the planets and comets (see note 5 above). To suppose that the charge that one has failed to explain everything is as damning as the charge that one's proposed explanation is in conflict with the observational data would seem to put an end to all scientific reasoning.

STEPHEN H. DANIEL

11. THE HARMONY OF THE LEIBNIZ-BERKELEY
JUXTAPOSITION

Historians have often noted that Leibniz and Berkeley share similar views on abstract ideas, the primary-secondary quality distinction, a relational (anti-Newtonian) account of space and time, God's direct involvement in experience, and a worry about materialism's threat to religion.[1] But beginning as early as 1716, commentators have associated Leibniz and Berkeley especially because they both emphasize the role of perceivers in defining reality and provide seemingly phenomenalist descriptions of physical bodies.[2] Not surprisingly, readers often think of Berkeley when they see comments by Leibniz such as "to Exist is nothing other than to be Sensed [*Sentiri*] – to be sensed, however, if not by us, then at least by the Author of things" (*Certain Physical Propositions*: A VI iii, 56/ Adams 1994: 169), and "to be [*esse*] is simply nothing other than being able to be perceived" (*On Matter, Motion, Minima, and the Continuum*, December 1675: A VI iii, 466/ P 11). It is also easy to draw connections between Leibniz's doctrine of self-contained, co-ordinated monads and Berkeley's account of the role of minds in a universe characterized by beauty, perfection, and harmony. No doubt, Leibniz's emphasis on the metaphysical principles underlying such harmony is different from Berkeley's focus on the "experimental" strategies for appreciating the law-governed character of nature. All the same, for both thinkers, hardly anything is more central than their insistence that reality and experience exhibit an order that informs everything we know.

For years, however, scholars have maintained that the similarities between Leibniz and Berkeley are more than offset by their differences. For example, some commentators argue that Berkeley's phenomenalist account of bodies as "mere" mental images or perceptions is inconsistent with Leibniz's metaphysics of monads.[3] Some claim that Berkeley lacks Leibniz's pre-established harmony doctrine.[4] Others contend that Leibniz's concept of monads (the principles of identity and unity) includes much more than Berkeley's notion of mind.[5] Still others assert that Berkeley's identification of reality with perception contradicts Leibniz's views on sub-conscious perceptions and the infinite divisibility of extended bodies.[6] Several propose that Leibniz and Berkeley differ on the nature of substances and on the existence of substantial forms,[7] while a few maintain that Berkeley's description of a contingent universe is at odds with Leibniz's mathematically-determined ontology.[8]

Admittedly, there are differences in the ways that Leibniz and Berkeley present their ideas. But that does not mean that they differ substantially regarding their fundamental insights. Indeed, when we read them as similar to one another, we learn more about their doctrines individually and discover that they are, in fact,

163

P. Phemister and S. Brown (eds.), Leibniz and the English-Speaking World, 163–180.
© 2007 *Springer*.

much more alike than has previously been acknowledged. I propose, therefore, first to show how a juxtaposition of their texts reveals that there is more than simply a *prima facie* case to be made for saying that, despite differences in presentation and emphasis, Leibniz and Berkeley share common beliefs. Second, I indicate how such a juxtaposition can be used to show how the very points mistakenly cited to differentiate them are clarified precisely by appreciating their similarities, particularly in terms of understanding how minds differentiate and relate bodies. Such a strategy, I argue, is especially useful for understanding how their accounts of perception, substance, and contingency depend on their mutual commitment to the harmony of all things and on their sensitivity to distinguishing the different domains of natural philosophy and metaphysics.

1. THE SIMILARITY OF STANCES

To be sure, Berkeley and Leibniz do raise objections about one another's doctrines (or what they think are those doctrines). For example, in Berkeley's view, Leibniz's appeals to infinite divisibility and substantial forms introduce mathematical or metaphysical concepts into what are more properly mechanical or physical discussions.[9] In so doing, Leibniz (according to Berkeley) is at best "abstract and obscure" (*De Motu* §19: LJ IV, 35) and at worst a supporter of the kinds of pantheism, materialism, fatalism, determinism, and atheism found in Hobbes, Spinoza, and Bayle.[10]

According to Leibniz, Berkeley's reluctance to invoke mathematical and metaphysical concepts leads to claims that are unnecessarily puzzling. As he writes in 1715 to Bartholomew Des Bosses, "The Irishman who attacks the reality of bodies seems neither to offer suitable reasons nor to explain his position sufficiently. I suspect that he belongs to the class of men who want to be known for their paradoxes" (15 March 1715: GP II, 492/ L 609).[11] In the margin of his copy of Berkeley's *Principles of Human Knowledge* (PHK) he adds (again probably in 1715):

Much of this is right and agrees with my way of thinking, but it is expressed paradoxically. We need not say that matter is nothing; rather it is enough to say that it is a phenomenon, like the rainbow – not a substance, but what results from substances. Nor need we say that space is no more real than time; it is sufficient to say that space is nothing but the order of co-existing things, and time the order of subsisting things [*subexistentiarum*]. True substances are monads or perceivers [*percipientia*]. But the author should have expanded on these themes to include the infinity of monads out of which, by means of their pre-established harmony, all things are constituted. He unfortunately, or at least needlessly, rejects abstract ideas, restricts ideas to images, and scorns the subtleties of arithmetic and geometry. Most unfortunately, he rejects the division of extension to infinity, even though he might be correct in rejecting infinitesimal quantities. (Robinet 1983: 218/ Berlioz 1999: 437/ my translation)

As Leibniz sees it, Berkeley's treatment of the doctrines on which they otherwise might agree is expressed in a way that can distract readers from the issues at hand. Because that treatment is so much like Leibniz's (and was recognized as such early on), it prompts Leibniz here to reiterate commonplaces in his thought. But contrary to what many of the above-mentioned commentators conclude, that reiteration does not mark points of disagreement between the two thinkers. Rather, it highlights views on which he and Berkeley might otherwise agree *if* Berkeley is understood in a certain way.

No doubt, based on his reading of the anti-Malebranchean reviews of Berkeley's *Principles of Human Knowledge* in the *Journal des sçavans* (September 1711) and the *Mémoires de Trévoux* (May 1713), and the reviews of the *Three Dialogues between Hylas and Philonous* (TDHP) in the *Journal litéraire* (May–June 1713) and the *Mémoires de Trévoux* (December 1713), Leibniz could easily have seen how Berkeley (and by association, he himself) might be misinterpreted. Indeed, according to those reviews, Berkeley is a solipsist or a sceptic who denies the existence of bodies and maintains that the things we perceive are not real (MT 173–90).[12] Leibniz's comments are thus meant to distance himself – at least in his own mind and to Des Bosses – from a way of reading Berkeley that at the time was widespread. It is not surprising, then, that the points to which Leibniz draws attention not only specify topics in Berkeley's thought that resonate with his own ideas but also specify doctrines open to misunderstanding by Cartesian, Lockean, and Scholastic critics such as those who raise the spectres of solipsism and scepticism in the reviews.

For his part, Berkeley is hardly in any better position to evaluate Leibniz, since he relies mostly on secondary accounts for insights into Leibniz's mathematical ideas and the metaphysical underpinnings of mechanics.[13] Even on the rare occasions when he reads Leibniz's work directly (e.g. the first part of *Specimen Dynamicum* as it appears in the April 1695 *Acta Eruditorum*), Berkeley has no access to texts that would suggest Leibniz's phenomenalist views or his cautions about inappropriately extending metaphysics into mechanics. For example, he is unaware of how Leibniz dismisses forces that are "thought to be in extension or mass, yet outside perceivers and their perceptions" as "out of this world" (To De Volder, 19 January 1706: GP II, 282). From Berkeley's perspective (at least as expressed in *De Motu*), Leibniz is as guilty of invoking occult forces as the Scholastics whom he criticizes. Berkeley draws this conclusion because he does not have the full picture of Leibniz's position and thinks of physical (i.e. derivative) forces as occult to the extent that they depend on metaphysical primitive forces.[14]

I suggest that it is a mistake, therefore, to think that Leibniz rejects what *we* know to be Berkeley's doctrines (explained and expanded in works other than the *Principles*), just as it is a mistake to think that Berkeley's criticisms are directed against Leibniz's doctrines (which were largely unpublished and unknown to him). This allows us to be open to the prospect that the two thinkers are much closer to one another than they suspect. If we do not consider this possibility, we risk reading (as is typically done in "standard" or "traditional" accounts) Cartesian, Lockean, or Scholastic ways of thinking about minds, perception, or substances into their views, when in fact it might be more productive to think of them in terms of one another.

Such an approach requires that we acknowledge how comments by Leibniz and Berkeley that highlight the similarity of their ideas are sometimes overlooked by those who want to distance them from one another. For example, when MacIntosh (1970–71: 156) and Berlioz (1999: 448) deny that Berkeley has a position comparable to Leibniz's pre-established harmony doctrine, we should remember Berkeley's comments about "the constant regularity, order, and concatenation of natural things, the surprising magnificence, beauty, and perfection of the larger, and the exquisite contrivance of the smaller parts of the creation, together with the exact harmony and correspondence of the whole" (PHK §146)[15] – all of which God exhibits to us "according to such rules as he himself hath ordained, and are by us termed the *Laws of Nature*" (TDHP: LJ II, 231). Or when Adams (1983: 223–4; 1994: 221), M. D. Wilson (1987: 13–4) and Look (forthcoming) claim that Berkeley identifies real bodies as merely the conscious sense perceptions of finite minds, we need to recall Berkeley's observations that sensible things continue to exist even when no finite mind perceives them (PHK §§6, 48, 147) and that "it is plain [that sensible things] have an existence exterior to my mind, since I find them by experience to be independent of it" (TDHP: LJ II, 230). Or when McRae (1976: 139), S. Brown (1984: 141–2, 148) and Berlioz (1999: 438) say that, in contrast to Leibniz, Berkeley rejects the propriety of speaking about material or corporeal substances, we have to counter with Berkeley's admissions that, in fact, "there are bodies, even corporeal substances, when taken in the vulgar sense" (PHK §82):

If by material substance is meant only sensible body, that which is seen and felt (and the unphilosophical part of the world, I dare say, mean no more) – then I am more certain of matter's existence than you or any other philosopher pretend to be. ... I do therefore assert that I am as certain as of my own being, that there are bodies or corporeal substances (meaning the things I perceive by my senses). (TDHP: LJ II, 237–8)

and

It will be urged that thus much at least is true, to wit, that we take away all corporeal substances. To this my answer is, that if the word *substance* be taken in the vulgar sense, for a combination of sensible qualities, such as extension, solidity, weight, and the like; this we cannot be accused of taking away. But if it be taken in a philosophic sense, for the support of accidents or qualities without the mind; then indeed I acknowledge that we take it away, if one may be said to take away that which never had any existence, not even in the imagination. (PHK §37: LJ II, 87)[16]

In passages such as these, Berkeley appropriates the term *substance* as it applies to bodies or corporeal substances and reformulates it to refer to the distinctive arrangement or organization of qualities. In doing so, he rejects both Descartes' doctrine of substance as a thing in which attributes or modes "inhere" (*Sixth meditation*: CSM II, 54; *Third set of objections with replies*: CSM II, 124) and Locke's substratum concept of "*pure Substance in general*" as the "he knows not what support" (Essay II, xxiii, 2)[17] of qualities in favour of a view in which a body is understood as nothing other than a specific ordering of characteristics. Such an arrangement of *acts* of perceiving (which Berkeley calls perceptions) in understanding and the acts of will (which he calls volitions) constitute what mind is "in the strictest sense" (TDHP: LJ II, 240). Because the organization of qualities into corporeal things is solely the product of mind, only mind can be said to constitute the *substance* of corporeal things. Properly speaking, however, mind itself cannot be considered a *thing*:

Say you the mind is not the perceptions, but that thing which perceives. I answer, you are abused by the words *that* and *thing*; these are vague, empty words without a meaning. ... If you ask what thing it is that wills, I answer if you mean idea by the word *thing* or any thing like an idea, then I say tis no thing at all that wills. This how extravagant soever it may seem, yet is a certain truth. We are cheated by these general terms, *thing, is*, etc. ... It should be said nothing but a will, a being which wills being unintelligible. ... Tis an easie matter for a man to say the mind exists without thinking, but to conceive a meaning that may correspond to those sounds, or to frame a notion of a spirit's existence abstracted from its thinking, this seems to me impossible. (NB §§581, 658, 499a: MA 307, 314, 299; PHK MS version of §98: LJ II, 84n)[18]

To consider a mind as a thing apart from its activity of differentiating and associating ideas would require that we appeal to a principle of differentiation by which it is identified. But such identification is exactly the function of mind itself; so to frame a notion of a mind apart from its activity would require the activity of yet another mind (whose distinct identity would in turn have to be determined by another mind, and so on). Berkeley pre-empts such a regress simply by restricting the use of *substance* to the activity (i.e. mind) that constitutes differentiation and association. In this way, all talk of bodies unerringly implies talk of minds.

Writing five years earlier in the *New Essays on Human Understanding*, Leibniz makes a similar point when he dismisses as an unintelligible abstraction Locke's "I know not what" support-of-ideas view of the mind. There he proposes that the discussion of substance in general cannot fruitfully be modelled on Locke's analysis of material substances. But he does not shift the focus from material substances to spiritual substances without at the same time indicating that a substance simply cannot be conceived apart from the "attributes or predicates" that express its activities:

If you distinguish two things in a substance – the attributes or predicates, and their common subject – it is no wonder that you cannot conceive anything special in this subject. That is inevitable, because you have set aside all the attributes through which details could be conceived. Thus, to require of this 'pure subject in general' anything beyond what is needed for the conception of 'the same thing' – e.g. it is the same thing which understands and wills, which imagines and reasons – is to demand the impossible. (New Essays II, xxiii, 2/ RB 218)

As with Berkeleyan substances, a Leibnizian substance is not a *thing* that just happens to engage in certain activities; rather, its existence *is* its activities. By noting this point and Berkeley's willingness to acknowledge the existence of corporeal substances (properly understood), we are put in a better position to appreciate how Leibniz's treatment of substance combines the themes of perception and existence in a way that explains why his remarks sound so much like Berkeley's. That in turn can cause us to reconsider how we understand the two thinkers' evaluations of each other.

I do not mean to imply that Berkeley was influenced by Leibniz, even though he does refer to him on several occasions in his *Of Infinites* (1707), *Notebooks* (1707–1708), *De Motu* (1721), *Alciphron* (1732), *Theory of Vision Vindicated* (1733), and *Analyst* (1734). Rather, I suggest that Berkeley shares with Leibniz a view of substance that not only differentiates them from Descartes, Locke, or others who think of ideas (in Berkeley's expression) "by way of *mode* or *attribute*" (PHK §49) but also allows them to think of spiritual substances in a way that distinguishes them from their contemporaries. However, because they have limited access to one another's writings, they fail to recognize each other as kindred spirits. Nonetheless, their efforts to clarify their positions (e.g. regarding the phenomenalistic account of bodies and the harmony of creation) identify the issues that unite them and (as in the case of Berkeley's criticisms of Leibniz's notions of infinite divisibility and substantial forms) delineate what, for each, are the proper bounds of natural philosophy and metaphysics.

2. PHENOMENALISTIC SUBSTANCES

The line of argument that both Leibniz and Berkeley develop can be sketched out as follows. To exist means to exist as a determinate thing, that is, as a thing that is perceived to have certain characteristics that distinguish it from other things. Furthermore, for *it* to be perceived as a thing (e.g. a body) having those character- istics requires that it be perceived as having an identity or unity that is intelligible or sensible to some mind. Its meaning or sense (sometimes, "sensibility") can be understood either in isolation (as an imaginary, "incongruent" phenomenon) or as an integral part of the harmony of all perceivers and perceptions (i.e. as a *real* object). Either way, the "substance" of the object – that which differentiates and identifies it as *this* or *that* particular object – cannot be understood in solely material terms, because matter in itself does not contain a principle of differentiation by which corporeal bodies are distinguished.

Appreciating this fundamental rejection of exclusively materialistic doctrines is important for seeing how Leibniz and Berkeley converge in their treatments of infinite divisibility. As I show in the following section, the two thinkers seem to disagree on whether extension can be described in metaphysical terms (Leibniz implies yes, Berkeley no) and thus on whether it is proper to speak of matter as infinitely divided into an infinity of bodies. But even Berkeley is willing to say that, for heuristic purposes, bodies can be treated like geometrical fictions (and thus as infinitely divisible) as long as such mathematical insights are not applied to determinate physical objects (NB §261; *De Motu* §39, and *Of Infinites*: LJ IV, 237). Leibniz likewise advises against applying purely ideal (mathematical) concepts to physical objects. Indeed, Leibniz and Berkeley agree that a real being is a unity that is not infinitely divisible. For Berkeley, the only point of possible disagreement is whether Leibniz's practice of referring to matter (along with space, time, extension, motion) as real, "well-founded phenomena" unnecessarily risks creating the impression that mathematical or metaphysical ways of speaking are appropriate in properly scientific contexts (Leibniz, *First Truths*: L 270; To De Volder, 30 June 1704: GP II, 268–9/ L 536; Berkeley, PHK §§118–25, 133; TDHP: LJ II, 257–8; *De Motu* §§39–46).

However, before discussing the proper limits of metaphysics, I here consider how, for both Leibniz and Berkeley, the meaningful or sensible existence of a thing consists not only in its being perceived but also in its being perceived in harmony with all other things in the universe. Leibniz begins to develop this theme as early as 1671–72. His insight – that to exist is to be sensed or perceived – seems to strike him (just as it later does Berkeley) as unexpected. "I seem to myself to have discovered," Leibniz writes in 1672, "that to Exist is nothing other than to be Sensed [*Sentiri*] – to be sensed, however, if not by us, then at least by the Author of things, to be sensed by whom is nothing other than to please him, or to be Harmonious" (*Certain Physical Propositions*: A VI iii, 56/ Adams 1994: 169).[19] Of course, saying that something is sensed does not necessarily mean that it is sensed only by means of our five senses, for something can be sensible (i.e. meaningful) or "make sense" to God as well, and it is this sensibility that constitutes a particular thing's existence. As Leibniz had noted a few months earlier in *Studies on the Universal Characteristic* (late 1671), "Existence [*Existentia*] is the distinct sensibility [*sensibilitas*] of something. That is, an existing thing [*Existens*] is what can be sensed or perceived [*sentiri sive percipi*] distinctly ... in much the same way that a *Being* [*ens*] is able to be conceived distinctly" (A VI ii, 487). Nothing can exist without existing *as that particular thing*, and it is its particular act of existing that makes it an "it" in the first place.

The significant point to note here is that for Leibniz, as for Berkeley, a thing is not defined first by having an essence to which existence happens to be added, for the essence or complete concept of a thing is unintelligible apart from its actual (i.e. harmonious) relations to an entire universe that God chooses either to create or not to create. Rather, in keeping with the teachings of Francisco Suárez, both Leibniz and Berkeley hold that it is the actual existence of a thing – its act of being (*ens* as a participle) – that identifies it as that thing (*ens* as a noun).[20] To say of any determinate thing that it exists means that it is identified (i.e. "perceived" or "sensed") as that thing: that is, it has a sense or meaning for some mind and can thus be said to be perceived. Accordingly, Leibniz can claim that "everything that exists is sensed [*sentiri*]. ... Whatever is sensed exists [*existit*]. ... Whatever exists is sensed clearly and distinctly" (*On Endeavour and Motion, Sensing and Thinking* [1671]: A VI ii, 282) and "to exist [*existere*] is nothing other than to be sensed [*sentiri*]" (*Certain Physical Propositions*: A VI iii, 56). So too for Berkeley, a thing's being (its *esse*) seems to consist in its being perceived (*percipi*) (PHK §3).

However, this is where things get tricky and where we need to be careful about how we translate *sentiri* and how we understand the additional Suárezian distinction between *esse* and *existere*.[21] As the quote above indicates, Leibniz permits *sentiri* to be interchanged with *percipi*, but only so long as "to be perceived" is understood as the experience of a thing in harmonious relations with other things. For God, of course, things are perceived for all eternity in just this way, so the *sense* of a thing always exhibits its relations to (and distinction from) other things. But for creatures, the sense of a thing's identity (that is, its *existentia*) depends on our thinking of it in terms of its being an expression of harmony. Indeed, as Leibniz writes in his draft of *On Endeavour and Motion*, thinking itself "is nothing other than the sense [*sensus*] of harmony," or as the final version puts it, "the sense of relation [*comparitionis*], or more briefly, the perception of many things at the same time or the one in the many" (A VI ii, 282). More than forty years later in a letter to Christian Wolff, Leibniz makes the point again, this time equating the perfection of a thing to the extent to which its essence is thinkable and perceived as related to all else:

Perfection is the harmony of things or the observability of things as universally connected [observabilitas universalium], that is, their agreement [consensus] or identity in variety or, you might say, their degree of thinkability [considerabilitas]. After all, order, regularity, and harmony amount to the same thing. You can also say that perfection is a thing's degree of essence, if essence is calculated from the harmonious properties which give it, so to speak, its weight and momentum. Hence it surely follows that God (the supreme mind) is endowed with perception, indeed to the greatest degree; otherwise he would not care about harmonies. (18 May 1715: GW 172)

To think at all (for both God and creatures) is to perceive objects of thought as related (that is, in harmony); for if we did not identify objects in terms, for example, of their differential weight and momentum, we could not distinguish what it is that we are thinking. Accordingly, the essence of a thing is thinkable and perfected in virtue of its being perceived as existing in harmony with all other things.

To put this differently, the very conceivability or essence of things includes their being perceived as existing in greater or lesser degrees of harmony with other things. In any possible universe, the *sense* or meaning of things consists in their *con-sensus* or *consentientia*.[22] So, to the degree that things are not perceived as being in agreement or "consenting" to another, their existence is at most (to use Berkeley's term) "relative" to finite minds. However, in the best of possible worlds, everything in the universe is in essential agreement or harmony with all else. That such harmony might not be recognized by finite minds in no way detracts from the fact that, in such a universe everything – including objects that are considered possible by finite minds but that are not in complete harmony with all else – is perceived by God and has (in Berkeley's phrase) "eternal existence" (TDHP: LJ II, 252).

Both Leibniz and Berkeley are thus more than willing to describe something that really is sensible, determinate, and related to other things as a body in the order of nature. As Leibniz remarks, "[h]aving already posited that to exist [existere] is to be perceived [sentiri], it follows that to be a body is to exist" (*Certain Physical Propositions*: A VI iii, 56).[23] For to be a body in nature means to exist or be sensed as a determinate object of thought, and that requires that it be related to other things in the order of nature. The mere perception of a body does not determine its existence, for then we would have no means to determine whether it was real or imaginary. That is why we rely on the perception or sense of a body's harmonious place in nature to characterize its existence.

In saying that the being [esse] of sensible things consists in their being perceived [percipi] (PHK §3; TDHP: LJ II, 230), Berkeley makes the same point. The real bodies that exist in nature are not reducible to *our* perceptions of the world (PHK §§34, 48), for the "eternal existence" of things in the mind of God is not reducible to the "relative existence" of things with respect to created minds (TDHP: LJ II, 252). Nonetheless, for a thing to be (*esse*) requires that it be perceived (even if only by God) in relation to other things; otherwise, "it" has no discernible identity. That act of perceiving is itself not perceived and cannot be said to be or have a discernible identity, for it is the means by which discernment or identification comes into being. In short, it "exists" (*existit*) or, more formally, "subsists" as the principle of being. In claiming that "*existere* is *percipi* or *percipere*" (NB §429), Berkeley thus reinforces the point that an existing thing can be either an object of perception *or* the perceiving activity whereby that object is identified, and that neither of the two can be thought apart from one another.

This distinction between *existere* and *esse* is important for appreciating the ontological implications of the *percipi* – *percipere* distinction. Typically, the latter distinction is explained simply by saying that, for Berkeley, ideas or bodies are things that are perceived and minds are the things that do the perceiving. But such accounts ignore Berkeley's warnings against treating minds as things in the first place.[24] It becomes harder to gloss over these warnings when they are understood in the context of Leibniz's use of *esse* and *existere*. For in that context a mind's existence – including that of a windowless monad – is understood in terms of how its specific activity in perceiving bodies is *related* to the actual activity of other minds.

According to Leibniz, the divinely pre-established harmony of perceivers not only constitutes their identities relative to one another but also guarantees the order of the things they perceive. For Berkeley, the co-ordination of bodies described by laws of nature reveals the same kind of harmony as Leibniz's postulation of an infinity of monads. But with Berkeley the divine regulation of experience is less obvious unless we also recognize the constitutive role mind plays in determining the identities of the objects of acts of perceiving and willing. By thinking that laws of nature describe merely the interaction of things whose identities are independent of the minds that identify them, we fail to appreciate how created minds are essential to the delineation and order of bodies in the world. Therefore, to ask Berkeley (as Samuel Johnson does twice) "what is the *esse* of spirits?" (Cf. Johnson to Berkeley, 10 September 1729: MA 343; 5 February 1730: MA 351–2) is to fail to see how minds have no *esse* at all, because minds, souls, or spirits are instead the "very existence" (*existere*) of ideas (Berkeley, NB §577). It is no wonder that Berkeley does not respond to Johnson's question.

In sum, both Leibniz and Berkeley provide a phenomenalist account of bodies that not only spells out what it means for something to exist but also highlights the need for a doctrine that explains how the perceptions of individual perceivers are co-ordinated. This latter feature reveals the realist character of their thought in that it characterizes real bodies as those that are independent of the particular perceivers in terms of whose perceptions they are intelligible.

This realism explains why when Leibniz says that "to exist [*existere*] is nothing other than to be peceived [*sentiri*]" (*Certain Physical Propositions*: A VI iii, 56) and that "to be [*esse*] is simply nothing other than being able to be perceived [*percipi*]" (*On Matter, Motion, Minima, and the Continuum*: A VI iii, 466/ P 11), he appeals to two complementary frameworks for understanding existence.

The first is concerned with mechanics, the second with metaphysics. If one objects, as Berkeley has Hylas do in *Three Dialogues* (LJ II, 234), that there is a difference between being perceived and being perceivable, Berkeley replies that *the thing* that is perceivable is by that very fact perceived as *that thing*. This, as Parkinson notes (P 127), is Leibniz's point as well, since "to exist" does not mean simply the abstract concept to be perceived, but rather being able to be perceived *as a such and such* even if only in one's mind (as in the case of a chimera).

With this explanation, Berkeley would have no quarrel. He would object only to the claim that one can think of existence itself, that is, existence abstracted from any particular thing's existence. For if we ask what is meant by existence itself (or in Berkeley's preferred expression, "absolute existence"), we discover that "it" has no identity. That is why Berkeley concludes that "the question between the materialists and me is not, whether things have a real existence out of the mind of this or that person, but whether they have an absolute existence, distinct from being perceived by God, and exterior to all minds" (TDHP: LJ II, 235). In this respect, Berkeley and Leibniz are on the same page: what we perceive are real things whose intelligibility depends on their being perceived (i.e. known) either eternally by God or within the "well-founded" patterns of experience summarized in laws of nature. Efforts by commentators to characterize their philosophies as an exclusive choice between phenomenalism and realism are thus beside the point.[25]

As Leibniz repeatedly remarks, though, this is not to say that everything *we* sense (e.g. illusions, chimeras) really exists. Nor does it mean that everything that exists is actually perceived:

Sensation does not constitute the existence of things, because obviously there are things that exist that are not sensed. Furthermore, the coherence of sensations must itself spring from some cause. Existence, therefore, is the quality of a subject that accounts for our having coherent sensations. From this it can be understood that there also exist things that are not sensed, since that quality can exist even if (because of our own deficiency) the thing is not sensed. (*On Mind, the Universe, and God*: A VI iii, 464/ P 9)

If we did not limit the notion of existence to well-ordered (law-governed) phenomena that are coherent with other sensations, we would be unable to distinguish dreams or imaginary phenomena from reality.[26] Accordingly, a phenomenon is real "if it is vivid, complex, and internally coherent [*congruum*]" (*On the Method of Distinguishing Real from Imaginary Phenomena*: GP VII, 319/ L 363). Furthermore, "God alone produces the connection or communication between substances: it is through him that the phenomena of one coincide or agree with those of another, and as a result that there is reality in our perceptions" (*Discourse on Metaphysics* §32: WFPT 84). The things we perceive are thus said to be real in virtue of the fact that our perceptions of them are coherent with one another.

This is precisely the point Berkeley makes as well, although instead of referring to individual and idiosyncratic perceptions as sensations, Berkeley refers to them as images (PC §823) or ideas of imagination (PHK §§3, 33; TDHP: LJ II, 215).

To drive home his point, he simply observes that the things we call real are nothing other than the things we ordinarily (but coherently) sense:

> The ideas of sense are more strong, lively, and distinct than those of the imagination; they have likewise a steadiness, order, and coherence, and are not excited at random, as those which are the effects of human wills often are, but in a regular train or series, the admirable connexion whereof sufficiently testifies the wisdom and benevolence of its Author. Now the set rules or established methods, wherein the mind we depend on excites in us the ideas of sense, are called the *Laws of Nature*; and these we learn by experience, which teaches us that such and such ideas are attended with such and such other ideas, in the ordinary course of things. (PHK §30)[27]

To Hylas' question "[w]hat difference is there between real things and chimeras framed by the imagination or the visions of a dream, since they are all equally in the mind?" Philonous replies that ideas perceived by sense ("real things") are distinguished by being connected in the sequences or orders of experience ("laws of nature") ordained by God (TDHP: LJ II, 234):

> The ideas formed by the imagination are faint and indistinct; they have, besides, an entire dependence on the will. But the ideas perceived by sense, that is, real things, are more vivid and clear; and, being imprinted on the mind by a spirit distinct from us, have not a like dependence on our will. There is therefore no danger of confounding these with the foregoing: and there is as little of confounding them with the visions of a dream, which are dim, irregular, and confused. And, though they should happen to be never so lively and natural, yet, by their not being connected, and of a piece with the preceding and subsequent transactions of our lives, they might easily be distinguished from realities. (TDHP: LJ II, 235)

Consistent with Leibniz's marginal note on the *Principles*, Berkeley insists that ideas should not be equated with images and that our experience of perceptions should be understood as divinely coordinated. Such coordination is exhibited in the laws of nature whose function it is to identify the regular patterns of perceptions we have or would have under certain circumstances, as, for instance, if I were in my study.

Here again, Leibniz anticipates Berkeley: "[s]ince what we can judge about the existence of material things is no more than the consistency of our senses, we have sufficient reason to conclude that we can ascribe nothing to matter apart from being sensed in accordance with certain laws"(*On Truths, the Mind*: A VI iii, 508).[28] The real identity, unity, or "substance" of a material body thus consists in its being a well-founded and regulated phenomenon (*On the Method of Distinguishing Real from Imaginary Phenomena*: GP VII, 321/ L 365). However, a body's identity is determined by its motion and since no material body contains within itself its own principle of motion, no body can be said to be a substance as such, even if "[w]e rightly regard bodies as things, for phenomena too are real" (To Des Bosses, 15 March 1715: GP II, 492/ L 609). Thus, bodies are not substances, because the unity or identity of a true substance is internal and is not merely the product of its regularization according to laws of nature.

3. THE METAPHYSICAL CHARACTER OF INFINITE DIVISIBILITY

According to Leibniz, the differentiations of matter (i.e. bodies) constituted by mind can be correlated with the practical regularities of law-governed, well-founded phenomena by showing how a mechanical account of nature is intelligible ultimately only if it is supplemented by metaphysics. As he tells Arnold Eckhard in 1676, "*Everything in nature happens mechanically, but metaphysics is the principle of mechanism* that constitutes not only the absolute necessity of the motions and laws of nature but also the will behind sensible causes (though not based on my choice but on the mutual convenience of things)" (To Eckhard, November 1676?: GP VII, 258). And to Arnauld he writes, "[w]e can explain the particularities of nature mechanically, I agree, but only after having accepted or taken for granted the principles of mechanism itself, which can only ever be established a priori by metaphysical reasoning" (30 April 1687: GP II, 98 /WFPT 124–5). As the rationale for the differentiation of bodies and their ordered network of relations, metaphysics is the presupposition of mechanics, but it is not part of natural science. In fact, in *Specimen Dynamicum* Leibniz recommends that in mechanics we avoid invoking talk of souls, entelechies, and even God except to praise his wisdom in ordering things (GM VI, 242–3/ WFPT 163).

This is the same point that Berkeley makes in his *De Motu* when, in commenting on *Specimen Dynamicum* in particular, he claims that Leibniz improperly introduces metaphysical abstractions, such as force, gravity, impetus, and attraction, into mechanics (§§16–20). For Berkeley, mechanical explanations should be limited to experiments and observations. However, he acknowledges that natural philosophy presupposes God as the ultimate cause (§34) and mind as the principle of motion (§42). He points out that to imagine the motion of physical objects requires that we consider the cause or principle of such motion, because the concept of a cause of motion is already implicit in stipulating the limits of the proper domain of physics. But when we admit that the domain of physics has a limit, we also affirm the need to respect the fact that its principles are not included in the domain. As Berkeley puts it,

metaphysical principles and real efficient causes of the motion and existence of bodies or corporeal attributes in no way belong to mechanics or experiment, nor throw light on them, except in so far as by being known beforehand they may serve to define the limits of physics, and in that way to remove imported difficulties and problems. (§41: LJ IV, 42)

As in the case of other disciplines, the limits of physics are not part of physics even though they indicate which kinds of problems are appropriate for it. By knowing these limits we know that the proper concerns of physics are the motion and existence of bodies. At the same time we acknowledge that the principles and causes of motion and existence are intrinsically related to bodies *as their principles and causes*. This means that physics cannot be fully explained without invoking concepts (e.g. mind) that go beyond what is properly the domain of physics. However, because this invocation risks the possibility of misapplying categories proper to one domain onto another – for example, as in saying of minds that they are things, or of bodies that they are substances – Berkeley recommends avoiding such expansions if possible:

> If anyone were to extend natural philosophy beyond the limits of experiments and mechanics so as to cover a knowledge of incorporeal and unextended things, that broader interpretation of the term permits a discussion of soul, mind, or vital principle. But it would be more convenient to follow the usage which is fairly well accepted, and so to distinguish between the sciences so as to confine each to its own bounds. (§42: LJ IV, 42)

Here Berkeley admits that the motions or existence of bodies can be explained physically by using notions such as force or attraction. But to think of souls, minds, or vital principles as the determinate *causes* of bodily motion is to risk ignoring how mind serves as the limit concept of our understanding of physical objects. Mind is not an object of physical enquiry and cannot be associated with bodies other than as the metaphysical principle by which bodies are identified as scientific objects. To extend natural philosophy beyond experience to include mind or God – or even forces – is to apply the notion of physical cause illegitimately. This can result, for example, in treating minds as if they were things in the world that cannot be described as physical causes. Instead, mind must be understood as a principle for explaining the order of nature (*De Motu* §§42, 69; TDHP: LJ II, 257) that leads to human well-being.[29] We can still give a metaphysical account of the motion and existence of bodies, but in such an account the cause of motion is nothing more than the indicator of how physics cannot account for the ultimate intelligibility of the regularity of motion.

In Leibniz's philosophy, this concern to distinguish the domains of natural philosophy and metaphysics is particularly evident regarding the question of the infinite. But whereas Berkeley invokes laws of nature to describe the infinite sequence of divinely constituted orderings of perceptions that would occur *if* there were an infinity of perceivers, including angels, human beings, mites, and who knows what all else (NTV §§80–1; TDHP: LJ II, 188–9), Leibniz describes an actual infinity of minds that are related to one another and their objects in virtue of their perceptions of all parts of the universe. That is to say, Leibnizian objects of experience are composed of infinite parts, each of which in turn depends for its identity on an endlessly differentiating principle of activity that provides its unity and distinctness.

By contrast, in Berkeley's account, the activity by which an object is differentiated cannot be endless because it would otherwise remain indeterminate. Besides, talk of endless determination, like that of insensible points and infinitely divisible angles or lines, smacks of abstraction run amok. "We Irish men," he says, "cannot attain to these truths" (NB §392), for a theory of abstraction that permits infinite divisibility ignores the fact that thinking in terms of numbers always originally presumes some sensible, determinate experience.

This is a theme to which Berkeley appeals often. It is found in his early *Arithmetic Demonstrated without Algebra or Euclid* (1704, published 1707) where he notes that "nature itself teaches us the way of working arithmetical questions on the fingers" (LJ IV, 171/ SW I, 8).[30] He insists that by subordinating arithmetic to algebra and geometry, Euclid and other mathematicians make it impossible to provide *true* mathematical demonstrations (applicable to real things), because such demonstrations would be based ultimately on axioms that are not grounded in particular ideas.[31] In place of the abstract method of mathematical reasoning found in Euclid, Berkeley suggests that we think of arithmetic "demonstrations" as statements of algorithms that relate signs of particular ideas to one another. His point is that unless we think of mathematical objects as signs of discrete ideas instead of as abstractions from sensible objects, we will always be in doubt about the legitimacy of applied mathematics.

He acknowledges, though, that few mathematicians would endorse such a critique of abstraction. But this is not to say that he was alone in his beliefs, for in *Letters to Serena* (1704) his Irish countryman John Toland publishes criticisms of Leibniz in which he argues that errors in mathematics often occur "when abstracted notions are taken for real beings, and then laid down as principles whereon to build hypotheses":

Thus mathematical lines, surfaces, and points have been maintained to exist in reality, and many conclusions thence deduced, though very unhappily; as that extension was compounded of points, which is to say, that length, breadth, and thickness are formed of what is neither long, nor broad, nor thick, or measure of no quantity. So the word *infinite* has been wonderfully perplexed; which has given occasion to a thousand equivocations and errors. ...Whatever is really infinite, does actually exist as such; whereas what only may be infinite, is very positively not so. (GG 179–80)[32]

According to Toland, whatever is truly infinite cannot be considered as yet one more thing over and against others. Nor can it be objectified as a mathematical abstraction or extension in general, for the former fails to provide the determinate characteristics necessary to explain the existence of real, sensible objects; and the latter supports a form of Spinozistic pantheism by portraying God in terms of extensional (i.e. material) properties. Instead, drawing on ideas from Joseph Raphson and Henry More, Toland proposes that the infinite must be understood as the immaterial activity or (in More's term) "substance" of all that exists (GG 181–2, 212–20).[33] This entails thinking about infinity no longer as the Newtonian "space" in which already determinate objects are located, but as the subject by which finite, created things are posited as differentiated and associated with one another.

Berkeley is understandably reluctant to endorse this explicitly "pantheistic" view. Instead, in his paper *Of Infinites* delivered to the Dublin Philosophical Society in November 1707, he adopts Locke's claim (Essay II, xvii, 3) that our *idea* of infinity is simply the endless ("infinite") repetition of finite ideas. There he concludes that, when we speak of infinity, we do not mean to communicate any positive idea at all (LJ IV, 235–8).[34] Peter Browne (Trinity College Dublin Provost) and William King (Archbishop of Dublin) quickly warn Berkeley (who had only recently been appointed a Trinity College fellow) that such a view empties claims about God of any cognitive content.[35] Their objections fail to recognize, however, how Berkeley shifts the discussion away from treating the infinite as either an idea or the space in which determinate ideas/things are associated to thinking of the infinite (as Toland suggests) as the substantive principle of the actual differentiation of bodies. That is, if the infinite (God) is not an idea at all, it cannot be confused with any material thing or even (as in pantheism) with the totality of material things.

This point is central for understanding how Berkeley's position is much closer to Leibniz's than Berkeley realizes. For in *Of Infinites* Berkeley criticizes Leibniz for collapsing metaphysics into mathematics by failing to appreciate the difficulties of "applying the idea of infinity to particles of extension exceedingly small, but real and still divisible" (LJ IV, 237). This is to interpret Leibniz in Lockean terms by assuming that he thinks of particles of extension as initially finite and only derivatively infinite. But Locke's attempt to define the infinite in terms of the finite ignores how Leibniz links the infinity of differentiations and associations of things in the universe to how they are perceived. To the extent that Berkeley thinks of Leibniz in such terms, he misinterprets him – just as Leibniz misinterprets Berkeley in his *Principles* marginal note when he claims that Berkeley refuses to countenance the infinite division of extension. What Berkeley objects to is not the belief that there might be an infinite number of ways of perceiving the world: indeed, my way of carving up experience is certainly different from that of the mite. What Berkeley objects to is the actual infinite divisibility of sensible objects when they are considered the *same* for me and the mite, that is, when they are considered apart from the specific integrating, associative activities of mind by which they are identified. But this is the same point that Leibniz makes when he doubts actual infinitesimal quantities; for understood in mathematical terms, sensible objects would be quantities that are unintelligible apart from their being related (by mind) to an infinity of other quantities. In this sense, both thinkers agree that no sensible object can be perceived apart from the *act* of perceiving or willing by which it is differentiated and associated to other objects.

As I have indicated above, Berkeley is willing to accept the concepts of material substance and matter as long as they are understood in terms of perceptions. And just as individual perceptions are made intelligible and real by being understood in terms of patterns or laws of nature, so too, those patterns or laws are seen as congruent and even beautiful when they are placed in a metaphysical context. But if such patterns occurred only in *my* mind or even in all human minds, then experience would be indistinguishable from dreaming and ultimately pointless. What makes the perceptions of bodies real, though, is not merely that they are experienced, but that they are experienced as a harmony, a "regular train or series, the admirable connexion whereof sufficiently testifies the wisdom and benevolence of its Author" (PHK §30). The point Berkeley emphasizes is that the experience of that harmony – for example, in the experience of perceptions as constituting a language that informs us about how to act (*Alciphron* IV,12: LJ III, 157) – is not part of sensible experience itself. That is why we have to appeal to metaphysics to explain the things we experience. And that opens up the possibility that, just as metaphysics serves to define the limits of science, so the notion of infinity might serve to define the possibility of mathematical reasoning.

This is not a problem for Leibniz because he believes that, unlike the determinate, non-divisible primary forces that constitute real bodies (i.e. corporeal substances), the derivative forces described by mathematical accounts of nature are abstractions. Thus "not all truths about corporeal things can be derived from logical or geometrical axioms alone" (*Specimen Dynamicum*: WFPT 162). For Berkeley the idea of an infinitely divisible force – even one that is only derivative – threatens to destabilize the distinction between the known laws of nature, from which follow "very elegant theories and mechanical devices of practical utility" and the "most excellent considerations" implicit in the metaphysical, theological, and moral knowledge of the Author of nature (*De Motu* §42: LJ IV, 42).

So, Leibniz and Berkeley agree that metaphysics must be understood to include, but not be reducible to, a phenomenalistic account. This is also how – despite oft-repeated claims by commentators to the contrary – their doctrines about *minima sensibilia* can be understood as complementary rather than contradictory. According to Berkeley, either *minima sensibilia* are properly scientific objects (in which case they are not further analysable) or they are limit concepts for scientific discourse (in which case they are further analyzable in terms of mind and relations to other ideas). But since we cannot *perceive* minds or relations, we cannot incorporate them into a science of physics or mechanics other than as the metaphysical principles of our experience of order or harmony in the world (PHK §§89, 142). In Leibniz's opinion, questions about monads are always properly metaphysical and questions about the infinite divisibility of matter are always only about phenomena. As long as such notions (e.g. force) are understood as merely phenomenal, then Berkeley is comfortable in treating them in instrumentalist rather than ontological terms (*Alciphron* VII, 6: LJ III, 294–5). That is, as long as we limit our claims about *minima sensibilia* to either actual bodies or heuristic, instrumentalist accounts of bodies, we need not imagine any conflict between him and Leibniz. It is only when the boundaries between their views of mechanics and metaphysics are not respected that the issue of their seeming difference arises.

The attempt, therefore, to distinguish Berkeley and Leibniz by saying that Berkeley allows only a finite number of perceivers and Leibniz postulates an infinite number, overlooks both how Leibniz limits science to the finite or phenomenal and how Berkeley allows for the infinity of possible perceptions encompassed by the laws of nature (PHK §§72, 147, 151; TDHP: LJ II, 212, 215, 257–8) and perhaps even an infinity of minds (but that would be a purely metaphysical issue). For Berkeley, the existence of the physical world does not depend on the actual perceptions of particular perceivers. Rather, it depends upon the perceivability of things as determined by the network of minds God creates. As part of their understanding of the Mosaic account of creation, some of those minds will think of things *as if* those things existed before there were finite minds (TDHP: LJ II, 251–2). But of course, that is simply to say that the harmony of experience requires that we fill in the gaps of what is perceivable (e.g. the desk when we are out of the room) when we are not actually perceiving. So just as there are no gaps in Leibniz's world, there are none in Berkeley's either.

In short, for both Leibniz and Berkeley, all of creation is orderly, and all things are in "exact harmony" and in correspondence with everything else (PHK §146).

The identities of all things depend on the differentiating and associating activities of mind. Minds cannot properly be thought of as entities existing apart from either their relations to one another or the things that they identify through perceiving and willing. This way of speaking of minds (or monads) might sound familiar in respect to Leibniz, but by reading Berkeley in the context of Leibniz we can better understand Berkeley in this way as well. In turn, Berkeley's cautions regarding the proper limits of natural philosophy and metaphysics reveal how he agrees with Leibniz on the very points that are often cited as dividing them.

By focusing on how certain features of Leibniz's and Berkeley's doctrines complement one another, I have argued that their purported differences are much less profound than is often thought. Specifically, I have suggested that Leibniz and Berkeley do not in fact differ on three important issues: (1) bodies (or perhaps more specifically, *aggregate* bodies as opposed to corporeal substances) are phenomena whose existence consists in being perceived by substances; (2) perceptions of real, scientifically knowable things cannot be understood fully apart from their appearance in a sequence of ordered experiences; and (3) recognition of the congruence of such experiences requires understanding the relation of metaphysics and natural philosophy in a way that overcomes what is often thought to be the topic that most separates Leibniz and Berkeley, namely, how Leibniz's doctrine of infinite divisibility relates to Berkeley's doctrine of *minima sensibilia*. By recognizing these similarities, we are in a much better position to detect and explain aspects of their philosophies individually.

NOTES

[1]   See, for example, MacIntosh 1970–71: 147, 157; McRae 1976: 139–40; Adams 1983: 222; Brown, S. 1984: 42, 91, 147–8; Adams 1994: 169, 224–27, 237n; Berlioz 1999: 437–41; Brykman 1999: 103–4, 111–2.

[2]   The first association of Leibniz with Berkeley appears in 1716 in the *Histoire Critique* 11: 117–8n, written either by Pierre Desmaizeaux or the journal's editor, Samuel Masson. See Lamarra 1990: 93.

[3]   See Furth 1967: 186; Ross 1984: 179, 183; Jolley 1986: 44, 51; Adams 1994: 219–21, 239; Look (forthcoming).

[4]   See MacIntosh 1970–71: 156; Berlioz: 1999: 138, 148.

[5]   See Parkinson 1965: 166–7; Robinet 1983: 220; Brown, S. 1984: 141–8, 153; Ross 1984: 180–3.

[6]   See Jolley 1986: 43–4; Wilson, M. D. 1987: 9–13.

[7]   See McRae 1976: 140; Brown, S. 1984: 141–8, 153; Adams 1994: 221, 238–9.

[8]   See Berlioz 1999: 138, 148; Brykman 1999: 113–4; Peterschmitt 2003: 125.

[9]   *Notebooks* (NB) §333; *An Essay towards a New Theory of Vision* (NTV) §54; *Of Infinites*: LJ IV, 236–7; *De Motu*, §§8, 16–20, 43; *Alciphron* VII, 6: LJ III, 295; *The Analyst* §18: LJ IV, 75. Unless otherwise noted, all NB, NTV, and *De Motu* citations are from MA.

[10]   *Theory of Vision Vindicated and Explained*, §6: MA 233.

[11]   The class of men to which Leibniz refers no doubt includes Berkeley's Irish countryman, John Toland, whose behaviour, Leibniz says (quoting from Luke 2:34), serves as a sign to be contradicted (To Spanheim, 24 June 1702: K VIII, 353). See also Daniel 1984: 149.

[12]   Also see Charles 2007.

[13]   Cf. *Of Infinites*: LJ IV, 236–7; *Alciphron* VII, 6: LJ III, 295.

[14]   Cf. Peterschmitt 2003: 116–25.

[15]   All PHK citations are from Part I (the only part Berkeley published) as found in MA.

[16] Cf. NB §§517, 700.

[17] See also Essay II, xxiii, 5.

[18] See also McCracken 1992: 197; Daniel 2000: 631–6; 2001a: 244–5.

[19] The passage is also discussed by Mercer 2001: 398. Cf. Berkeley: "I wonder not at my sagacity in discovering the obvious tho' amazing truth, I rather wonder at my stupid inadvertancy in not finding it out before" (NB §279). See also NB §491.

[20] See Daniel 2000: 622–5.

[21] See Daniel, 2000: 627.

[22] See *On Truths, the Mind, God, and the Universe*, 15 April 1676: A VI iii, 511/ P 63. On the concept of consent, see Daniel 1994: 72–3, 175–87; and Daniel 2007a: 164–5, 173–7.

[23] "Posito jam existere esse sentiri, necesse est, corpus existere, esse."

[24] See Daniel 2000: 629–36; Daniel 2001a: 245; Daniel 2001c: 58, 61–7.

[25] On the phenomenalism versus realism issue in Leibniz, see Parkinson 1965: 166–7; Furth 1967: 186; Ross 1984: 179, 183–4; Jolley 1986: 51; Wilson, M. D. 1987: 4; Adams, 1994: 219–21; Rutherford 1995: 144–7; Look (forthcoming). On the issue in Berkeley, see Yolton 1984: 142; Grayling 1986: 99–111; Pappas 2000: 198–204; McCracken 2007.

[26] See *On Truths, the Mind*: A VI iii, 511/ P 63; *On the Method of Distinguishing Real from Imaginary Phenomena*: GP VII, 319–20/ L 363–4.

[27] See also PHK §33.

[28] Cf. P 59. See also *On Truths, the Mind* (A VI iii, 511/ P 63) and Castañeda 1978: 106–7.

[29] See also *De Motu* §§39, 71.

[30] See Jesseph 1993: 94.

[31] See Hooykaas 1958: 58; Jesseph 1993: 16n.

[32] See Brown, S. 1999: 60.

[33] See More 1662: 165; Daniel 1997; Daniel 2001b.

[34] See also Berman 1985: 129.

[35] See Berman 1994: 14–6.

12. SYNECHISM AND MONADOLOGY

*Charles Sanders Peirce's reading of Leibniz**

1. INTRODUCTION

The consideration of modern philosophers played a substantial role in the development of Peirce's philosophy. But while his views on other modern philosophers such as Kant and the British empiricists have been studied extensively,[1] his references to Leibniz have been generally ignored.[2] Yet the American thinker gave a prominent position to Leibniz, not only because Peirce regarded his reasoning as even "far more accurate than that of Kant" (CN II, 186) but mainly because he believed that his thought furnished key ideas "universally esteemed as highly fruitful" (CN II, 186), particularly his law of continuity. However, this appraisal contrasts with what he considered a "blind spot" on Leibniz's logical retina since, according to Peirce, some of his metaphysical doctrines are in contradiction with certain of his most emblematic principles.[3] My purpose in this paper is to focus on those inconsistencies Peirce thought he found in Leibniz's reasoning.

In 1899, and after distinguishing his own conception of continuity from Cantor's view, the publication of Robert Latta's edition of the *Monadology* (Latta ed. 1898) gave Peirce the occasion to set forth his argument. Firstly, the American philosopher remarked that

He is a declared nominalist, and his theory of monads breathes nominalistic individualism. But he strangely fails to see how contrary to all this is his law of continuity; and it is more curious that he found himself, at last forced to revive the substantial forms of the mediaeval realists. (CN II, 187)

But the law of continuity (hereafter LC) also conflicts with the hypothesis of preestablished harmony (hereafter HPA). He writes:

This principle will do away with the isolated monads, and render the extravagant and unverifiable hypothesis of preestablished harmony superfluous by directly solving the riddle of the transitivity of causation, while it would form the basis of a philosophy in deepest unison with the ideas of the last half of the nineteenth century. (CN II, 209)

Peirce also opposes Leibniz's principle of the identity of indiscernibles, which states that "[...] things other than one another must differ in some quality [...]" (CN II, 207), on the basis that existence is not a predicate. He writes:

* Special thanks to the conference organizers, S. Brown and P. Phemister and to Sara Barrena from the Spanish Peircian Group (GEP), R. Arthur, P. Beeley and particularly Greg Brown, who in different ways made this paper possible.

P. Phemister and S. Brown (eds.), Leibniz and the English-Speaking World, 181–193.
© 2007 *Springer.*

In his fourth letter to Clarke, he offers, as an argument in favour of his logical "principle of the identity of indiscernibles," the fact that a nobleman of his acquaintance, on hearing it enunciated, long searched in vain to find two leaves of trees exactly alike[4] [...] Here lies one of the capital errors upon which the Leibnizian metaphysics comes to wreck, namely that he does not see that existence is no general predicate or intellectual conception, but an affair of brute fact. (CN II, 187)

At the same time he acknowledges Leibniz's remark that the existence of a thing cannot be demonstrated but then, Peirce concludes, the principle of sufficient reason must be false; Leibniz's doctrine of the creation of the best possible world is not acceptable, he argues, and cannot be used in defence of the principle, also no reasons can be given to account for the correspondence between our perceptions and their causes. He writes:

This falsifies, too, the other principle which Leibniz in the same letter lays down as fundamental, the law of sufficient reason. There is no proving existence, as he himself once remarked; for though a thing be in itself possible, it may not, in his phrase, be "compossible" with other things which have forestalled it in the struggle for existence. Leibniz fancies he answers this objection by saying that God has created the best of all possible worlds; but that this proves itself upon discussion to be a quite meaningless proposition has long been apparent. Nor this is the only such objection to the law of sufficient reason, for nobody has answered the old question what reason there can be why red and blue light should not excite each the sensation that the other does excite. (CN II, 187)

However, Peirce agrees with Leibniz that there are reasons or final causes acting in the universe but he claims that this view is in contradiction with denying the reality of general concepts:

But though the doctrine that everything has a sufficient reason is thus untenable, yet it still may be true that reasons ("raisons"), that is final causes, should be operative in the universe. Only this cannot consistently be maintained by a philosopher who insists upon denying the reality of all generals; unless indeed he resorts to the device of supposing a deity in whose mind those reasons and purposes should reside – his nominalism probably passing to the conceptualistic variety. But what, after all, is such a theological nominalism but the attribution to the system of generals, not only of reality, but also of life? (CN II, 187)

Again, it is to Leibniz's nominalistic commitment that Peirce objects. So, it seems that Peirce's objections are these, that the monadology and the HPA are in conflict with the LC, and that final causes, i.e., reasons, are inconsistent with nominalism. I will attempt to show how all of Peirce's criticisms have the same ground, namely, that these inconsistencies arise from the acceptance of the LC. At the same time it will give content to the view that existence cannot be a predicate.

In the same context Peirce offers a brief version of his mature conception of continuity: "Continuity is nothing but that modification of generality which is proper to the logic of relatives" (CN II, 209). Although the meaning of this definition is not evident, we may consider whether he attributes a similar view to Leibniz himself. Firstly, he had criticised other conceptions of continuity such as Kant's, Cantor's, and even Aristotle's conception of continuity, but he does not say that Leibniz's conception is wrong. Rather, he regards the acceptance of LC as inconsistent with what he considers false metaphysical theses. Also, he acknowledges two key features of his own notion of continuity in Leibniz. In

Leibniz Rewritten, for example, he assumes that for Leibniz infinite multitudes are consistent notions, a thesis which, according to Peirce, has been established by contemporary number theory.[5] Furthermore, he believes that Leibnizian continuity involves "an evolution of all things" (CN II, 186).

In what follows I will briefly explain Peirce's conception of continuity and analyse why he argued that it was inconsistent with the theory of monads and the HPA as well as its relation to final causes. I will then compare this notion with some aspects of Leibniz's own conception of continuity and propose an account of the differences.

2. PEIRCE'S CONCEPTION OF CONTINUITY

Multitudes, Possibilities and Generals

As we have seen in the introduction, Peirce defines continuity as the kind of "generality which is proper to the logic of relatives." He had introduced this definition in a series of lectures he gave in Cambridge in 1898. In the last session, devoted to the logic of continuity, he says:

Now continuity is shown by the logic of relatives to be nothing but a higher type of that which we know as generality. It is relational generality. (CL 258)

In order to support this thesis, Peirce claims, we must consider what the logic of relatives shows about generality and continuity. He compares the *classes* used in traditional logic to the *systems* of his logic of relatives.[6] His argument assumes that the nominalist accepts that classes are composed of possibilities.[7] While a class consists of *individual* objects brought together by their relation of similarity, a system consists of objects brought together by any kind of relation.[8] Now systems differ from each other in terms of multitude (CL 157) and the relations determining them will have different properties. A multitude can be finite or infinite. In finite multitudes, "[...] if there be a relation in which every individual in such a system stands to some other but in which no third stands to that other, then to every individual of the system some other individual stands in that relation" (CL 157). The multitude of all possible different finite multitudes is called the *denumeral* multitude, that is the multitude of the whole numbers. In a system of denumeral multitude the individuals have generative relations, that is

These are dyadic relations of relate to correlate such that, taking any of them, whatever character belongs to the correlate of that relation wherever it belongs to the relate, and which also belongs to a certain individual of the system , which may be called the *origin* of the relation, belongs to every individual of the system. (CL 157)

A multitude that is greater than that of all the finite whole numbers is called an abnumerable multitude.[9] It is important to notice that each abnumeral multitude is the multitude of possible collections formed from the members of the collections of the preceding multitude (so they can be compared to Cantor's alephs as Peirce himself remarked). Peirce thinks he can prove that there is no multitude greater than every abnumerable multitude since abnumerable collections cannot have a multitude as great as that of the collection of possible collections of its individual members (CL 158–9). A collection of every abnumerable multitude would be a collection of a multitude as great as that of all possible collections of its members. This cannot be true, Peirce claims, of any collection whose individuals are distinct from each other: consider for example, two collections, A and B, of distinct objects so that the collection B is greater in multitude than the collection A. For every object in A there will be a distinct object in B assigned to it exclusively but there will not be an object in A assigned exclusively to every object in B. Now suppose that A and B are abnumerable collections so that all possible collections of different objects in A form the collection B of the next higher abnumerable multitude. It will be impossible to assign to every collection of objects in B a distinct object in A. But the impossibility of a greater multitude than every abnumerable multitude, Peirce claims, holds for collections of different individuals:

> When I say that the series of abnumerable multitudes has no limit, I mean that it has no limit among multitudes of distinct individuals. It will have a limit if there is properly speaking any meaning in saying that something that is *not* a multitude of distinct individuals is *more* than every multitude of distinct individuals. (CL 247)

It may be the case that something that is not a multitude of different individuals can be more than every multitude of distinct individuals. In fact, this is the case of continua:

> We, therefore, find that we have now reached a multitude so vast that the individuals of such a collection melt into one another and lose their distinct identities. Such a collection is *continuous.* (CL 159)[10]

Peirce can conclude that a true continuum is composed of possibilities, as a line is composed of possible points, and therefore it is general; in other words, the continuum is the true universal:[11]

> If there is room on a line for any multitude of points, however great, a genuine continuity implies, then, that the aggregate of points on a line is too great to form a collection: the points lose their identity; or rather, they never had any numerical identity, for the reason that they are only possibilities, and therefore are essentially general. They only become individual when they are separately marked on a line; and however many be separately marked, there is room to mark more in any multitude. (EP II, 100)

But what is this true universal, according to Peirce? He claims that continuity is possibility since the greatest multitude does not contain individuals but the highest grade of possibilities. He distinguishes this possibility from the abstract possibility of nominalists, so he writes:

> That which is possible is in so far *general*, and as general, it ceases to be individual. Hence remembering that the word "potential" means *indeterminate yet capable of determination in any special case*, there may be a *potential* aggregate of all the possibilities that are consistent with certain conditions; and this may be such that given any collection of distinct individuals whatsoever, out of that potential aggregate there may be actualized a more multitudinous collection than the given collection. Thus the potential aggregate is with the strictest exactitude greater in multitude than any possible multitude of individuals. But being a potential aggregate only, it does not contain any individuals at all. It only contains general conditions which permit the determination of individuals. (CL 247)

Peirce's argument from the logic of relatives proceeded from what he took to be the nominalist assumption that what is general is possible. In the last Cambridge Lecture he identifies the general with the possible; the potential aggregate of all the possibilities, for example, the possible points of a line, is greater than any possible multitude of individuals because an individual represents a discontinuity, the potential aggregate contains the general conditions to determine them. But what are those general conditions? He writes:

A potential collection more multitudinous than any collection of distinct individuals can be [,] cannot be entirely vague. For the potentiality supposes that the individuals are determinable as distinct. But there cannot be a distinctive quality for each individual; for these qualities would form a collection too multitudinous for them to remain distinct. It must therefore be by means of relations that the individuals are distinguishable from one another. (CL 248)

These relations, Peirce argues, cannot be dyadic but triadic, since no perfect continuity can be defined by dyadic relations (CL 250). He illustrates this with the example of the point on a circle. In sum, the study of multitudes has shown, according to Peirce, that the maximum possibility does not contain individuals but has become continuous. As he writes in his article on synechism for the Baldwin Dictionary:

A true continuum is something whose possibilities of determination no multitude of individuals can exhaust. (CP VI, 170)

The Reality of the Continuum

Continuity as law Once he had established that continuity is the true universal, Peirce claims, the question of nominalism and realism depends on showing that the continuum is real (CL 160). Some Peirceian scholars think that since continuity is the highest grade of possibility, the reality of continuity depends on the reality of the possible.[12] Peirce explicitly says that he had shown that continuity is not a contradictory fiction by proving that the greatest possibility becomes continuous (CL 162). But showing that it is not contradictory is not the same as showing that it is real, unless we assume that possibilities are real.

Another line of argumentation assumes that our processes of reasoning correspond to the processes of the real. He claims that

Every attempt to understand anything – every research – supposes, or at least *hopes*, that the very objects of study themselves are subject to a logic more or less identical with that which we employ. [...] Looking upon the course of logic as a whole we see that it proceeds from the question to the answer, – from the vague to the definite. And so likewise all the evolution we know proceeds from the vague to the definite. (CL 258)

Now as logic proceeds from the vague to the determinate, so does evolution proceed from indeterminate potentiality to habit or law.[13] For our present purpose it suffices to say that in Peirce's cosmology evolution is a process of generalization which consists in "spilling out" continuous systems (CL 163).[14] The crucial point is that the evolution from the indeterminate to the determinate is a process from chance[15] to law. The existing universe emerges from a world of possibilities:

From this point of view we must suppose that the existing universe with all its arbitrary secondness is an offshot from, or an arbitrary determination of, a world of ideas, a Platonic world [...] The evolutionary process is, therefore, not a mere evolution of the existing universe, but rather a process by which the very Platonic forms themselves have become or are becoming developed. (CL 261)

And if we regard the universe as a system of relations, connecting things together, these relations may obey some laws which must be operative in the universe. But Peirce also thinks that "Continuity is nothing but perfect generality of a law of relationship" (CP VI, 172). In order to understand in what sense Peirce regards law as relational generality or continuity I must introduce another point of view on continuity.

Continuity as final cause   For generality can be understood in two senses, as resemblance but also as purpose, and the generality involved in law must be understood as purpose. He writes:

The green shade over my lamp, the foliage I see through the window, the emerald on my companion's finger, have a resemblance. It consists in an impression I get on comparing those and other things, and exists by virtue of their being as they are. But if a man's whole life is animated by a desire to become rich, there is a general character in all his actions, which is not caused by, but it is informative of, his behavior. [...] it is the law that shapes the event, not a chance resemblance between the events that constitutes the law. (EP II, 72n)

He also claims that a law as a general rule induces one fact to cause another.[16] As Aristotle had recognized, he argues, a final cause acts from the future.[17] In order to act from the future as a final cause a law must be real:

The objector may, however, take somewhat stronger ground by confessing himself to be a scholastic realist, holding that generals may be real. A law of nature, then will be regarded by him as having a sort of *esse in futuro*. That is to say they will have a present reality which consists in the fact that events *will* happen according to the formulation of those laws. (EP II, 153)

Even if we accept with Peirce that a law is a final cause and final causes are real, it is not evident how they relate to continuity as relational generality. He has to argue for the importance for metaphysics of the abstract notion of continuity. According to Peirce, continuity represents an order of possibilities exceeding all multitudes. But then if the regularities expressed in a law could exceed all multitude, a law would have the same kind of generality he ascribed to continuity. On the other hand, we have seen that the generality of a law is that of final causes as ingredients of reality acting from the future. The effectiveness of law is attested by the fact that predictions based on it will be realized by actual events[18] in the future.[19] So he can say that law influences matter in the same way words produce physical effects, that is, as a symbol or representation since a law is a general formula.[20] Although evolution determines that the universe tends in a teleological manner to increase the reasonableness (CP VII, 520), the creation of representations has no limits. Moreover, without relational generality, signs would not be possible.[21] Thus, the inherent potentiality of real generality in nature is the condition of possibility for representation. By proving the reality of continuity he proves the reality of generals because he assumes the efficacy of determinable potentialities, a view which he associates with scholastic realism.

Peirce's Continuity and Leibniz's Metaphysics

Now we can examine this conception of continuity in connection with those Leibnizian theses which Peirce considered in contradiction with it:

(i) The application of the LC is in contradiction with the acceptance of monads: the monadological doctrine, Peirce claims, states that "the universe is composed of unities, indivisible and endowed with consciousness (CN II, 207)." These unities are the real beings from which compound things result. But the conception of continuity as relational generality involves that determinable possibility is a condition for determining individuals.

(ii) Final causes and the denial of the reality of generals: as we could see final causes in the Peirceian sense are future events which are relationally general but real inasmuch as they are the potentialities included in laws.

(iii) Continuity makes superfluous the HPA: For Peirce the HPA is an improved form of occasionalism and as such a form of dualism. But if we assume with Peirce that purposes are operative in the universe in the form of representation, then symbols can influence facts. Peirce illustrates the way he conceives that mind differs from matter by using the diagram of a continuous series of curves approaching and departing from a circle.[22] Briefly, we can conceive the hypothesis that matter is effete mind or regard mind as an extremely complex chemical genus (CP V, 4). So if there is continuity between mind and matter it is not necessary to suppose their ideal agreement.

For Peirce the study of infinite multitudes showed that continuity consists of possible relations by which their elements are determined as discontinuities but at the same time the relational generality of continuity is real. However, it is the thesis that asserts the reality of the possibles as the potentialities included in the general laws of nature that gives content to his denial of the nominalistic conceptions of universals and so, of Leibniz's monadology. For the same reason Leibniz's rehabilitation of substantial forms cannot resolve the inconsistencies.

3. LEIBNIZ'S CONCEPTION OF CONTINUITY

I will have to be excessively brief for the intrincated developments of Leibniz's conception, and focus on the status he conferred on *continua* since the acceptance of the conception I presented gives content to the other aspects by which Peirce opposes Leibniz.

For Leibniz, the problem of continuity is the so-called problem of the labyrinth of the composition of continuity,[23] that is, as he writes to Sophie, how can geometry show that matter is divisible to infinity and composed of individuals (K IX, 145–5). According to Leibniz mathematical considerations on the infinite can shed light on the problem since it is based on the nature of infinity (L 264). A whole is infinitely divisible if its parts are similar to the whole, as in time or space.[24] Two things are similar if they have the same qualities.[25]

Although extended matter can be infinitely divisible, from this he concludes that matter is only mere appearance or a phenomenon.[26] Bodies are aggregates and their reality supposes true unities but these true unities, he claims, are not the extended parts in which matter can be divided. In the third paragraph of the *New System* he writes:

> At first, when I had freed myself from the yoke of Aristotle, I was in favour of atoms and the void, because this view best satisfies the imagination. But thinking again about this, after much meditation I saw that it is impossible to find *the principles of a real unity* in matter alone, or in what is only passive, since this is nothing but a collection or aggregation of parts *ad infinitum*. Now a multiplicity can derive its reality only from *true unities* which come from elsewhere, and which are quite different from points*, from which it is obvious that something continuous cannot be composed. So, in order to get to these *real unities* I had to have recourse to a formal atom, since a material thing cannot simultaneously be material and perfectly indivisible, or possessed of a genuine unity. (WF 11–2/ GP IV, 478)

In commenting this passage Simon Foucher complains that Leibniz did not follow all the consequences of this view or he would have concluded that the foundations of extension cannot exist.[27] In his reply to this objection Leibniz argues that extension and number do not have constitutive principles in the sense of ultimate elements because they are only relations and then they cannot be conceived as resulting from these elements.[28] Moreover, the fractions of a number or the points of a line are indefinite, and so they are mere possibilities.[29] In existing things, on the other hand, the whole is a result of a multiplicity of real unities. For this reason the labyrinth of the composition of continuity has its origin in the confusion of the ideal and the actual.[30] He writes:

> But in actual substantial things, the whole is a result, or assembly, of simple substances, or indeed of a multiplicity of real unities. It is this confusion of the ideal and the actual which has quite obscured, and made a labyrinth of, "the composition of the continuum". Those for whom lines are made up out of points have quite mistakenly looked for primary element in ideal things, or in relations; and those who realized that relations like number, or space (which comprises the system or relations of possible coexistent things), could never be formed by the putting together of points, have for the most part then gone wrong by saying that substantial realities have no basic elements, as if they have no primary unities, and there are no simple substances. (WF 45–6/ GP IV, 491)

In other words, from a Leibnizian point of view Peirce entangles himself in the labyrinth and confuses the ideal and the actual.

4. SYNECHISM AND MONADOLOGY

It might seem that Peirce's appraisal and criticism are based on ascribing to Leibniz a conception of continuity that is foreign to him. However, both philosophers point out similar aspects of the abstract notion of continuity. For example, both emphasise that the elements of continua are indeterminate and consist of possible relations from which those elements are determined; in addition, they accept that an infinite multitude can be greater than its infinite part and there is no number of all number[31] or greatest multitude.

Nevertheless Leibniz and Peirce have different views regarding the consequences of the mathematical conception of continuity. For the American philosopher, mathematical reasoning has consequences for the actual world to the extent that the truth of synechism implies that actual things are phenomenal.[32]

For Leibniz, existing things are in accordance with ideal reasons since they are actualized possibilities:

> Meanwhile the knowledge of the continuous, that is of possibilities, contains eternal truths which are never violated by actual phenomena, since the difference is always less than any given assignable amount. And we do not have, nor ought we hope for, any other mark of reality in phenomena than they correspond with each other and with eternal truths as well [...]. (L 539/ GP II, 283)

Note that the difference between the ideal conception and actual phenomena is smaller than any value that can be assigned to them, just like a circle can be regarded as a polygon with infinite sides in respect to its properties. But the fact that bodies do not have shapes which exactly correspond to geometrical figures and extended matter attest to their being mere appearances[33] in need of a genuine principle of unity.

From a "pragmaticist" point of view it is not possible to admit the ontological priority of substances; on the contrary, individual objects are constituted by the categories of firstness, secondness and thirdness. If we agree with the nominalists that the real is totally independent of the conceptual, we introduce a gap between real things, being external to the mind, and the properties we conceive they have; in other words, we render the real an incognizable thing-in-itself. In order to account for the possibility of objective knowledge we must supersede the gap the nominalist introduced between the way things are and the way we conceive them by appealing to the reality of thirdness or relational generality. For this reason Peirce could claim that Leibniz admitted contradictory theses, since he had the right premises (LC, substantial forms and final causes) but failed to draw the right conclusion, that is, the rejection of monads, to which Peirce ascribed a mind-independent reality.

5. CONCLUSION

In sum, for Leibniz and Peirce the reflection on the abstract notion of continuity was central in the development of their thought. Yet, they regard specific instances of rational knowledge of phenomena as playing different roles in terms of their connections with their metaphysical ground. For Peirce, what underlies a phenomenon is to a certain extent, phenomenal; reality is the regulative ideal that investigation will attain in the indeterminate future, then the acceptance of ultimate elements in reality would block the road of inquiry. His approach to Leibniz's thought emphasises the difficulties of jointly admitting the actual infinite of simple substances and the heuristical value of the application of LC in nature, situating a key problem of Leibniz's metaphysics in his own horizon, the mathematical logic developments of the end of the nineteenth century and the emergence of pragmatism.

NOTES

[1]   See, for example, Apel 1975 and Goudge 1950.

[2]   A remarkable exception is Max Fisch's programmatic paper (Fisch 1986b). See also L 57.

[3]   "... while the reasoning of Leibniz was nearly, if not quite, of the highest order, being far more accurate than that of Kant or almost any metaphysician that can be named, and abounding in luminous, simplifying methods, yet he seems to have had a sort of blind spot on his logical retina that rendered him capable accepting tremendous inconsistencies and absurdities" (CN II, 186).

[4]   See GP VII, 372.

[5]   "An important departure from Leibniz is the rejection of all actual infinite multitude (and hence of all continuity) as self–contradictory" (CN II, 207). "Modern logic enables us to show that it is absurd to say there is contradiction in supposing an infinite multitude of substances. There is certainly an infinite multitude of finite whole numbers. True, these are only possibilities, not substances" (CN II, 209).

[6]   See CP III, 423–4 for the origin of this notion of system.

[7]   "these general classes are composed not of real objects, but of possibilities, and hence it is that the nominalist for whom [...] a mere possibility which is not realized is nothing but what they call an 'abstraction,' and little better, if at all, than fiction" (CL 156-7).

[8]   "Consequently, in place of a *class*, which is composed of a number of individual objects or facts brought together in ordinary logic by means their relation of similarity, the logic of relatives considers the *system*, which is composed of objects brought together by any kind of relations whatsoever" (CL 156).

[9]   "An *abnumerable* multitude is one of a denumeral succession of multitudes greater than the denumeral multitude. I have proved that there is no multitude greater than every abnumerable multitude; [...] It will, therefore, suffice to define an abnumerable multitude as a multitude greater than that of all the finite whole numbers" (EP II, 100).

[10] Properly speaking, true continua are not collections but aggregates: "By a *collection*, I mean an individual object whose actual presence in any part of experience consists in the actual presence of certain other individual objects called its *members*, so that if one of them were absent, the same collection would not be present, and these members are such that any part of them might logically be present or absent irrespectively of the presence or absence of any others; and the truth [...] Having thus defined a collection, I call attention in passing to the circumstance that a time, as ordinarily conceived, is not a collection of instants, nor a line of points, but any instant when present is a part of time and instants with their relations may be conceived as constituting time, and therefore I will use the word *aggregate* in such a sense that time may be said to be an aggregate of instants and any collection to be an aggregate also" (EP II, 98).

[11] "Namely a continuum is a collection of so vast a multitude that in the whole universe of possibility there is no room for them to retain their distinct identities; but they become welded into one another. Thus the continuum is all that is possible, in whatever dimension it be continuous. But the general or universal of ordinary logic also comprises whatever of a certain description is possible. And thus the *continuum* is that which the Logic of Relatives shows the *true* universal to be" (CL 160).

[12] See, for example, (Fisch 1986a) and Noble 1989. For a different view see Murphey 1993: 395–6.

[13] "And so likewise all the evolution we know of proceeds from the vague to the definite. The indeterminate future becomes the irrevocable past" (CL 261).

[14] "This habit is a generalizing tendency, and as such a generalization, and as such a general, and as such a continuum or continuity. It must have its origin in the original continuity which is inherent in potentiality. Continuity, as generality, is inherent in potentiality, which is essentially general" (CL 262).

[15] "The very first and most fundamental element that we have to assume is Freedom, or Chance, or Spontaneity, by virtue of which the general vague nothing-in-particular-ness that preceded the chaos took a thousand definite qualities. The *second* element we have to assume is that there could be accidental reactions between those qualities. The qualities themselves are mere eternal possibilities. But these reactions we must think of as *events*" (CL 260).

[16] "Every law, or general rule, expresses a thirdness; because it induces one fact to cause another" (CL 148).

17 "Aristotle himself, as I need not remind you, recognizes four distinct kinds of cause, which go to determining a fact, the *matter* to which it owes its existence, the *form* to which it owes its nature, the *efficient cause* which acts upon it from past time, and the *final cause* which acts upon it from future time. [...] They seem to me to mark different types of retroductively inferred acts, – facts which it was supposed furnished the universal process of Nature [,] the occasions from which different features of the [facts] were brought about. The conception is that Nature syllogizes from one grand major premise; and the causes are the different minor premises of nature's syllogistic development" (CL 197).

18 "The idea of Futurity, meaning what affirmatively *will* be, is a conception of Thirdness, for it involves the idea of *certainty*, and certainty is *knowledge*, and knowledge is *representation*. But the idea of what *may* in the future be, is a singular mixture in which possibility seems to predominate. If we discriminate Futurity from certainty and uncertainty the result seems to have no logical interest. That such ideas of Law, of Purpose, of Thought, have Thirdness as their dominant element is too evident to be dwelt upon. It is better worth while to remark upon the conception of Life, that Thirdness essentially involves the production of effects in the world of existence;-not by furnishing energy, but by the gradual development of Laws" (EP II, 271).

19 "In a still fuller sense, Thirdness consists in the formation of a habit. In any succession of events that have occurred there must be some kind of regularity. Nay, there must be regularities exceeding all multitude. But as soon as time adds another event to the series, a great part of those regularities will be broken, and soon indefinitely. If, however, there be a regularity that never will be and never will be broken, that has a mode of being consisting in this destiny or determination of the nature of things that the endless future shall conform to it, that is what we call law. Whenever any such a law be discoverable or not, it is certain we have the idea of such a thing, and should there be such a *law*, it would evidently have a *reality, consisting in* the fact that predictions based on it would be borne out by actual events" (EP II, 269).

20 " [...] now it is proper to say that a general principle that is operative in the real world is of the essential nature of a representation and of a symbol because its *modus operandi* is the same as that by which *words* produce physical effects. Nobody can deny that words do produce such effects. [...] But how do they produce their effect? [...] They certainly do not, in their character as symbols, directly react upon matter. Such action as they have is merely logical. [...] All this is equally true of the manner in which the laws of nature influence matter. A law is in itself nothing but a general formula or symbol" (*ibid.*).

21 " [...] continuity is an indispensable ingredient of reality, and that continuity is simply what generality becomes in the logic of relatives, and thus, like generality, and more than generality, is an affair of thought, and is the essence of thought. [...] a proposition the pragmaticist holds and must hold, [...] that the third category, – the category of thought, representation, triadic relation, mediation, genuine thirdness, Thirdness as such,- is an essential ingredient of reality [...]" (EP II, 345).

22 " [...] This shows that the supposition that thought acts directly only on thought and matter directly only on matter does not in the least interfere with the mutual action of matter and thought. Only it is requisite to suppose that in speaking of matter acting on matter and mind on mind we have adopted a mode of analysis of the phenomenon which requires us to suppose an infinite series, just as Achilles and the Tortoise. [...] That no doubt is a wild hypothesis enough. But perhaps it may help to show that there is no contradiction in the idea of *symbols* influencing the *blind* reactions and the reverse" (EP II, 186).

23 See for example Bayle's article on Zeno.

24 "*Time can be continued to infinity.* For since a whole of time is similar to a part, it will be related to another whole of time as its part is to it. Thus it must always be understood as capable of being continued into another greater time [...] The same argument can be used to show that space, as well as a straight line and time, or in general, any continuum, can be subdivided to infinity. For in a straight line as in time, a part is similar to the whole and can therefore itself be cut in the same ratio as the whole" (L 669/ GM VII, 22).

25 "*Quality, on the other hand, is* what *can be known in things when they are observed singly, without requiring any comprescence.* Such are the attributes which can be explained by a definition or through the various modes which they involve" (L 667/ GM VII, 19).

[26] "I do not understand how matter can be conceived as *extended* and yet without either actual or ideal (*mentales*) parts; if it can, I do not know what it is for something to be extended. In fact, I hold that *matter* is essentially *an aggregate*, and consequently that it always has actual parts. Thus it is by reason, and not only by the senses, that we see that it is divided, or rather that it is ultimately nothing but a multiplicity. I hold it true that matter (and indeed every part of matter) is divided into a greater number of parts than it is possible to imagine. This is why I often say that each body, however small, is a world of infinitely many creatures. Thus I do not believe there are atoms, that is to say parts of matter which are perfectly hard or of unbreakable solidity; nor, on the other hand, do I believe that there is perfectly fluid matter: my opinion is that each body is *fluid* as compared with more solid bodies, and *solid* (*ferme*) as compared with more fluid ones" (*Journal des Savants* 1696 (38): 455/ WF 66–7).

[27] "Je demeure d'accord avec vous, qu'on a raison de demander des unites qui fassent la composition et la réalité de l'étenduë. Car sans cela, comme vous remarquez fort bien; une étenduë toujours divisible n'est qu'un compose chimérique, don't les principes n'existent point, puisque sans unites il n'y a point de multitude véritablement. Cependant je m'étonne que l'on s'emdorme sur cette question; car les principes essentials de l' étenduë ne sçauroient exister réellement. En effet, des points sans parties ne peuvent être dans l'Univers, et daux points joints ensemble ne forment aucune extension. It est impossible qu'aucune longueur subsiste sans largeur, ni aucune superficie sans profondeur. Et il ne sert de rien d'aporter des points physiques, puisque ces points sont étendus et renferment toutes les difficultés que l'on voudroit éviter" (GP IV, 424/ cf. WF 41–2).

[28] "Il semble que l'auteur de l'objection n'a pas bien pris mon sentiment. L'entendue ou l'espace, et les surfaces, lignes et points qu'on y peut concevoir, ne sont que des rapports d'ordre, ou des orders de coexistence, tant pour l'existent effectif que pour le possible qu'on pourroit y mettre à la place de ce qui est. Ainsi ils n'ont point de principes composans, non plus que le Nombre. Et comme le Nombre rompu, par exemple 1/2, put ester rompu d'avantage en deux quatriemes ou 4 huitiemes etc. et cela à l'infini, sans qu'on puisse venir aux plus petites fractions ou concevoir le nombre comme un Tout formé par l'assemblage des desrniers elemens, il en est de meme d'une ligne qu'on peut diviser, tout comme ce nombre. Aussi à proprement parler, le nombre 1/2 en abstrait est un rapport tout simple, nullement formé par la composition d'autres fractions, quoyque dans les choses denombrées il se trouvee de l'egalité entre deux quatriemes et un demi. Et on peut dire autant de la ligne abstraite, la composition n'estant que dans les concrets, ou masses don't ces lignes abstraites marquent les rapports. Et c'est aussi de cette sorte que les points mathematiques on lieu, qui ne sont encore des modalités, c'est à dires des extremités" (GP IV, 491/ cf. WF 45).

[29] "Et comme tout est indefini dans la ligne abstraite, on y a égard à tout ce qui est possible, comme dans les fractions d'un nombre , sans de mettre en peine des divisions faites actuellement, qui designent ces points de differente maniere" (GP IV, 491/ cf. WF 45).

[30] "From the things I have said it is also obvious that in actual bodies there is only a discrete quantity, that is, a multitude of monads or of simple substances, though in any sensible aggregate or one corresponding to phenomena, this may be grater than any given number. But a continuous quantity is something ideal which pertains to possibles and to actualities only insofar as they are possible. A continuum, that is, involves indeterminate parts, while on the other hand, there is nothing indefinite in actual things, in which every division is made that can be made. Actual things are compounded as is a number out of unities, ideal things as is a number out of fractions; the parts are actually in the real whole but not in the ideal whole. But we confuse ideal with real substances when we seek for actual parts in the order of possibilities, and indeterminate parts in the aggregate of actual things, and so entangle ourselves in the labyrinth of the continuum and in contradictions that cannot be explained" (L 539/ GP II, 282).

[31] See GM III, 535/ GP I, 338.

[32] "I carry the doctrine so far as to maintain that continuity governs the whole domain of experience in every element of it" (EP II, 1).

"Synechism certainly has no concern with any incognizable; but it will not admit a sharp sundering of phenomena from substrates. That which underlies a phenomenon and determines it, thereby is, in a measure, a phenomenon" (EP II, 2).

[33] "Et quoyque dans la nature il ne se trouve jamais des changements parfaitement uniformes, tels que demande l'idée que les Mathematiques nous donnent du movement, non plus que des figures actuelles à la rigueur de la nature de celles que la Geometrie nous enseigne, parce que le monde actuel n'est point demeuré dans l'indifference des possibilities, estant venu à des divisions ou multitudes effectives, dans les resultants sont les phenomenes qui se presentment et qui sont varies dans les moindres parties: meantmoins les phenomenes actuels de la nature sont menagés et doivent l'estre de telle sorte, qu'il ne se rencontre jamais rien, où la loy de la continuité (que j'ay introduite […]) ou toutes les autres règles les plus exactes des Mathematiques soient violées. Et bien loin de cela, les choses ne sauroient ester rendues intelligibles que par ces règles, seules capables, avec celles de l'Harmonie, ou de la perfection, que la veritable Metaphysique fournit, de nous faire entrer dans les raisons et veues de l'Auteur des choses […] qu'on est plus capable de ménager la consideration de l'infini, comme nos dernieres methods l'ont fait voir. Ainsi quoyque les méditations Mathematiques soient idéales, cela ne dimunue rien de leur utilité, parce que les choses actuelles ne sauroient s'écarter de leurs règles; et on peut dire en effect, que c'est en cela que consiste la réalité des phénomènes, qui les distinguee des songes" (GP IV, 568–9/ cf. WF 123).

NORMA B. GOETHE

13. HOW DID BERTRAND RUSSELL MAKE LEIBNIZ INTO A "FELLOW SPIRIT"?*

1. INTRODUCTION

Bertrand Russell's book *A Critical Exposition of the Philosophy of Leibniz* (1900) opened the century by expressing a "new" paradigm of the role of a *philosophical* commentator on a great philosopher of the past. Russell devoted himself to the study of Leibniz at a turning point in his intellectual development. He was asked to lecture on the philosophy of Leibniz in Cambridge (1898/1899) when he was still struggling to overcome the idealist views he had adopted as a student there under the guidance of Ellis McTaggart.[1] As he recalls in *My Philosophical Development*, between 1894 and 1898 he had been a "full-fledged Hegelian" who aimed at constructing a complete dialectic of the sciences:

> I accepted the Hegelian view that none of the sciences is quite true, since all depend upon some abstraction, and every abstraction leads, sooner or later, to contradiction. *Whenever Kant and Hegel were in conflict, I sided with Hegel.* (1959: 42)[2]

But siding with Hegel meant, sooner or later, siding with the "*historical* spirit" and this was going to drastically change as of 1899 when Russell takes upon himself to examine the leibnizian views from "a *different* spirit".

2. A "*PURELY* PHILOSOPHICAL ATTITUDE" AGAINST THE SO-CALLED "HISTORICAL SPIRIT"

In his book on the philosophy of G.W. Leibniz, Russell claims to favour a "purely philosophical attitude" as opposed to a tendency greatly increased by the so-called "historical spirit," to pay much attention to questions concerning the influence of the time or of other philosophers, concerning such issues as, for instance, "the growth of a philosopher's system as a whole." The attitude that Russell espouses is one in which, without regard to dates or influences, we seek to *discover* what are the "great types" of possible philosophies. We guide ourselves in the search by investigating the systems advocated by the great philosophers of the past. In this inquiry, what may be the most important of the *historical* questions – the problem as to the actual views of the philosopher – is yet not to be neglected but examined in "a *different* spirit." The latter will reveal what is *timeless* about such views.

* For helpful comments on an earlier version of this paper I would like to thank Philip Beeley, Ivor Grattan-Guinness, Emily Grosholz and Markus Stepanians.

P. Phemister and S. Brown (eds.), Leibniz and the English-Speaking World, 195–205.

How is this "purely philosophical" attitude to be characterized? The suggestion here seems to be that learning from the philosophical past is like learning mathematics – which brings to light *Russell's appreciation of the great influence of the geometrical method upon seventeenth century philosophy.* In the case of his only full-scale study of an important historical figure, Russell's idea is that by learning to understand the views advocated by Leibniz, "we shall ourselves *acquire* knowledge of important *philosophic* truths." Yet it is essential to such inquiries that the philosopher is no longer explained psychologically, Russell insists, but examined as "the advocate of what he holds to be a body of philosophic truth" (Russell 1900: xii). By what *process* of development the philosopher came to the opinion may be an interesting and important question in itself, but it is not *logically* relevant to the inquiry how far the opinion itself is *correct.* At this stage of his intellectual development Russell upholds the Kantian view that consistency is the first principle of truth.[3] It should thus not come as a surprise to find him putting great emphasis on detecting any form of inconsistencies in Leibniz's philosophy. Having no interest in "dialectical" resolutions of antinomies, Russell conceives a basic two-step strategy in the design of his book: in the first place, among the opinions of Leibniz, the philosopher, it becomes desirable *to prune away* the views, which seem inconsistent with his main doctrines, before those doctrines themselves are subjected to *critical scrutiny.* The reason Russell offers for this strategy is no other than his reason for rejecting the "historical method" of inquiry *tout court.* Such method is inspired by the so-called "historical spirit" he is now so eager to call into question: "Philosophic truth and falsehood, in short, rather than *historical* fact, are what primarily demand our attention in this inquiry" (Russell 1900: xii). Accordingly, questions pertaining to the growth of knowledge – as all alteration, the evolution of human knowledge included, takes place in time – are to be sharply distinguished from questions pertaining to the grounds for truth.

3. WHY FOCUS ON LEIBNIZ'S PHILOSOPHY AS AN OBJECT OF INQUIRY?

Russell is convinced that a careful examination of Leibniz's work shows a coherent system, which would have lent itself – far better than Spinoza's philosophy – to *geometrical deduction* from definitions and axioms. But, in contrast with Spinoza, Leibniz in his philosophical writings did not even attempt to make use of the "synthetic mode" of presentation characteristic of seventeenth century textbooks of geometry. Russell has a psychological explanation for the fact that Leibniz never presented his work as a systematic whole: "It is in the character and circumstances of the man, not of his theories, that the explanation of his way of writing is to be found" (Russell 1900: 2). So, for everything Leibniz wrote he seems to have required an immediate motivation, while for the sole purposes of exposition he seemed to have cared very little. Also, few of Leibniz's works are free of reference to some particular person. From such circumstances Russell draws a rather extraordinary conclusion: that his desire for persuasiveness, ambition and versatility all combined to prevent Leibniz from doing himself justice in a coherent exposition of his system.[4]

We thus come to Russell's explicit purpose in composing his book: because of what he sees as "Leibniz's neglect", the work of the commentator becomes more important than in the case of most other philosophers, given that what is required is nothing less than "to attempt a *reconstruction* of the system, which Leibniz *should* have written" (Russell 1900: 2). In such a demanding enterprise, exposition and criticism ought not be separated. We recall here Russell's design to throw light on the correctness of Leibniz's views, and "since *philosophic* error chiefly appears in the shape of inconsistency", he tells us, we can hardly avoid considering how far these views are consistent – how far the views held can possibly be true.

Russell claims to have found inconsistencies of two kinds in Leibniz's philosophy. The first kind arises through the fear of admitting consequences shocking to the prevailing opinions of the time – such as, for instance, the inconsistencies that follow from the maintenance of the ontological argument for God's existence (Russell 1900: vii).[5] For such cases Russell has a quick and painless cure: since "we do not depend upon the smile of princes, we may simply admit the consequences, which Leibniz shunned" (Russell 1900: 2–3). By performing this task we shall finally uncover Leibniz's true system of thought, which according to Russell follows almost entirely from a small number of premises. (Russell then goes on to argue that in the course of this deduction we become aware of a second kind of inconsistency, but I shall not go into this here.)

4. RUSSELL'S WAY OF DOING JUSTICE TO THE PHILOSOPHY OF LEIBNIZ

In his exposition of "the system that Leibniz should have written" Russell endeavours to discover what is "the beginning, and what the end, of his chains of reasoning, to exhibit the interconnections of his opinions and to fill in from his other writings the bare outlines of works such as the *Monadology* and the *Discours de Métaphysique*" (Russell 1900: v). In 1899, Russell was lecturing on Leibniz's philosophy at Trinity College, Cambridge. The written lectures led to the book, which in a way "came about by accident"[6] and was to be first published a year later. The principal thesis of Russell's book holds that Leibniz's philosophy "was almost entirely derived from his logic". By logic, Russell meant traditional Aristotelian logic.[7]

As Russell writes in the (new) Preface to the second edition of the book in 1937, his thesis received independent confirmation from the publication of a collection of MSS prepared by L. Couturat, which had been overlooked by previous editors: "No candid reader of the *Opuscules et Fragments inédits de Leibniz* (1903) can doubt that Leibniz' metaphysics was derived from the subject-predicate logic" (Russell 1900: 8). But Couturat's own book *La Logique de Leibniz* (1901) also made Russell aware of a second important aspect concerning Leibniz's work which he had not properly taken into account: "Mathematics, and specially the infinitesimal calculus, greatly influenced Leibniz's philosophy".[8] Moreover and perhaps more importantly, Russell concedes in 1937 that around the time he composed his book on Leibniz (1899) he knew little of the new mathematical logic. In the meantime, he had met Peano en Paris (in August 1900) and had studied Frege's work and also published together with Whitehead the monumental *Principia Mathematica*. The newly available materials from the *Nachlass* and such remarkable intellectual development gave Russell a first hand perspective for a re-evaluation of Leibniz's philosophy. Yet, given his way of telling the story of the "*philosophical* history" of philosophy as utterly detached from the history of science, the said development seems to have had little or no impact upon his understanding of the philosophy of Leibniz. (I shall say more on this issue in the concluding section of the paper.)

5. THE ASSUMPTIONS UNDERLYING RUSSELL'S READING OF LEIBNIZ

In his reading of Leibniz Russell takes up two fundamental points of view, which are not open to debate. The first and most fundamental assumption underlying Russell's book is to be found in the opening lines of Chapter II entitled "Necessary propositions and the law of contradiction". He opens the second chapter thus: "That all sound philosophy should begin with an analysis of propositions is a truth too evident, perhaps, to demand a proof." Russell believes that Leibniz also made such an assumption concerning the starting point of all philosophy and the priority of (the analysis of) propositions. The latter may be less evident, but according to Russell it seems to be no less true (Russell 1900: 8).

As we stated earlier, the aim of Russell's exposition was to fill in what he saw as the outlines of such works as the *Monadology* and the *Discours*. Wishing to exhibit a coherent whole, which contains a *logical* beginning Russell confines his reading to Leibniz's mature views thus far published:

> By the beginning of 1686 he had framed his notion of an individual substance and [sent] Arnauld what is perhaps the best account he ever wrote of it – the *Discours de Métaphysique*. With this and the letters to Arnauld his mature philosophy begins, not only the temporal beginning, also the *logical beginning* is, in my opinion, to be sought there. (Russell 1900: 7, my emphasis)

About 1686 Leibniz conceives of an argument which, as he writes to Arnauld, is "drawn from the general nature of propositions", and gives the definition of substance. Russell reads this argument as a *purely logical* argument from which the notion of substance is derived.[9] He concedes that the reasoning does not explicitly occur in any other passages, but he thinks that it alone explains why Leibniz held the view that substances do not interact.[10] Perhaps more importantly, the argument in question relates to Leibniz's notion of necessity, for it yields the "eternal truths" – these are propositions which are true in all *possible* worlds. Again, to Russell, this logical beginning makes sense, given that the notion of substance is *logically* prior to the discussion of perception and knowledge of facts – which is relevant to the *actual* world and the notion of contingency. In Russell's terminology, this means that truth (and necessity) is logically prior to (and independent of) knowledge. We thus come to the second of Russell's fundamental assumptions underlying his reading of Leibniz, that truth is independent of knowledge. As it will turn out, both assumptions are indeed closely related.

But in order to understand what motivates Russell's interpretation, let us first focus on the first assumption, that all sound philosophy should begin with an analysis of propositions and, in particular, what he calls "the logical argument" in Chapter II of his book. According to Russell, the argument by which Leibniz obtains his definition of individual substance assumes that *every proposition is reducible to one which attributes a predicate to a subject* (Russell 1900: 9).

Now, are all propositions reducible to the subject-predicate form? Is this form universal? This is Russell's way of asking whether Leibniz was correct in making such assumption. The above question, Russell tells us, is of great importance to any philosophy which uses the notion of substance. But this would seem to be the case only provided that we understand the notion of substance as derivative from logical notions, which is just another way of saying that fundamental metaphysical notions must ultimately begin with a logical analysis.[11] This brings us back to Russell's first assumption. Moreover, and perhaps more importantly, concerning the *logical* basis of metaphysics, there is the more basic assumption being made by Russell that there are propositions – state of affairs, he just disagrees with the traditional analysis of the "general nature of the proposition" in subject-predicate form. Also, can we think of propositions not being true, Russell would ask? Not really, this is why we may call them "eternal truths".[12]

The question whether the traditional form of logical analysis is universal, deserves close attention, Russell insists here. He discusses the traditional view, which as we all know goes back to Aristotle. But there is no explicit reference to Aristotle in this context. So, just how important was this issue towards the end of the nineteenth century, on the eve of a radical transformation, which was just getting started around 1879 with the publication of Frege's *Begriffsschrift*?[13]

6. THE "PURELY LOGICAL" – SIDING WITH KANT (REVISITED)?

According to the Kantian view of seventeenth century philosophy, traditional *ontology* was an encumbrance to epistemology. Now, Russell thinks that something went wrong with subsequent developments consisting in shedding this burden, if we look at the *Hegelian transition from substance to subject*. The reason for this misfit lies in the fact that the (traditional) logical doctrine at the basis of traditional ontology was not called into question. Among those still attached to the traditional logical doctrine, interestingly enough, Russell discusses Bradley. He suspects that Bradley's attachment to the traditional view was ultimately responsible for his deep entanglement with idealism.[14]

Russell himself, as he recognizes in the 1937 Preface, knew little of the new logic at the time, when he composed his book on Leibniz. This, together with the fact that about 1899 – still unaware of important MSS – he mistook some of the most fruitful methodological ideas of Leibniz for old currency, blinded him from recognizing how rich Leibniz's notion of analysis was.[15] At this stage of his career, Russell did not defend an alternative form of logical analysis, yet in the context of his study of Leibniz he had thought carefully about the limitations of the traditional scheme. Indeed, it will prove illuminating to take a look at Russell's grounds for rejecting the traditional doctrine. This will bring us back to Leibniz's views and Russell's motivation.

According to Russell, the clearest examples of propositions not reducible to the traditional subject-predicate form are mathematical propositions – assertions of numbers and relational properties – e.g. relations of position, of greater or less, of whole and part. Leibniz himself discusses this very issue, and Russell decides to illustrate the problem by quoting a passage directly from him:

> The ratio or proportion between two lines L and M may be conceived three several ways, as a ratio of the greater L to the lesser M, as a ratio of the lesser M to the greater L, and lastly, as something abstracted from both, that is, as the ratio between L and M, without considering which is the antecedent, or which the consequent, which the subject, and which the object... In the first way of considering them, L the greater is the subject, in the second M the lesser is the subject of that accident which philosophers call *relation* or *ratio*. But which of them will be the subject, in the third way of considering them? It cannot be said that both of them, L and M together, are the subject of such an accident, for if so, we should have an accident in two subjects, with one leg in one, and the other in the other, which is contrary to the notion of accidents. Therefore we must say that this relation, in this third way of considering it, is indeed *out of* the subjects, but being neither a substance, nor an accident, *it must be a mere ideal thing, the consideration of which is nevertheless useful.* (GP VII, 401, my emphasis)

For an understanding of Russell's interpretation of Leibniz this passage is of great importance. Leibniz's closing remarks here seem clear enough: for "being neither a substance, nor an accident, it (a relation) *must be a mere ideal thing.*" For Russell this is tantamount to saying that relations are "the work of the mind", and the only ground for denying the "independent reality" of relations is that propositions must have a subject and a predicate (Russell 1900: 14–5). Russell thus draws the conclusion that Leibniz, in order to maintain the traditional doctrine, was forced to the theory that relations – as e.g. those of space, time, and number – are the work of the mind, "a mere ideal thing." And this is a view Russell feels strongly against. In this context, he is quick to point out that the view implicit in this Leibnizian point of view had great impact upon Kant's idea of a "Copernican revolution" concerning our philosophical understanding of human knowledge. Russell's unorthodox way of stating the Kantian view is that "propositions may acquire truth by being believed" or more concisely that "truth is dependent on knowledge". This is a view that Russell strongly rejects as it goes against his second assumption that *truth is independent of knowledge.*[16] I shall return to this issue in the next section.

But first, let me briefly refer to what Russell sees as his "most destructive task" concerning Leibniz's *notion of analysis and its connection with necessity,* a connection Russell is eager to call into question. These are perhaps some of the most polemical lines of the book: Russell believes that Leibniz, "like all who have held analytic propositions to be fundamental, was guilty of much confusion" (Russell 1900: 18). In this context, again, Russell establishes a revealing link with

Kant's notions. According to Russell, Leibniz and Kant both held that there is a fundamental distinction between *necessary* and *contingent* propositions. Keeping the Leibnizian terminology is somewhat confusing if you want to focus on Kant's views,[17] but this strategy allows Russell to claim (in general terms) that the propositions of mathematics are necessary, while those asserting particular existence are contingent.[18] Now, whatever view we adopt, as regards the necessity of existential propositions, Russell writes, "it must be admitted that *arithmetical* propositions are both *necessary and synthetic*" and this, he continues, "is enough to destroy *the supposed connection of the necessary and the analytic*" (Russell 1900: 24).[19] Russell will be able to correct such remarks, elaborating on them after having been exposed to Frege's work. I shall say a little more on this in the concluding section of the paper.

7. THE VIEWS ON TRUTH AND KNOWLEDGE SUGGESTED BY LEIBNIZ

After having shown the "fallacies" involved in Leibniz's deduction of God from the eternal truths, Russell tries to reinforce his arguments by offering some general remarks on truth and knowledge. He thinks that the views suggested by Leibniz's proof are problematic, and the proof itself he describes as "scandalous" (Russell 1900: 174ff.). What Russell finds most shocking is that in the case of the eternal truths, in general, and relations, in particular, the view defended by Leibniz seems to boil down to *esse* is *percipi*. For instance, God's understanding appears "described as the region of the eternal truths" (GP VI, 115; VII, 311). But this, on Russell's reading, is just another way of saying that all eternal truths and relations, in particular, derive their reality from the supreme reason, i.e. from the fact that they exist in the divine mind. Here, again Russell is quick to point out that, as a matter of fact, such a view is indeed widespread among philosophers and has been explicitly encouraged from Kant to Hegel. For this reason he would like to make it clear that everything that he urges against Leibniz applies equally against all who make *truth dependent upon knowledge:*

> It is a view commonly held that, as Leibniz puts it, the eternal truths would not subsist if there were no understanding, not even God's. (GP VI, 226. Cf. Spinoza, *Ethics*, II, 7, Schol.) *This view has been encouraged by Kant's notion that a priori truths are in some way the work of the mind, and it has been exalted by Hegelianism into a first principle...*Since, on this view, *nothing can be true without being known*, it has become necessary to postulate either a personal God, or a kind of pantheistic universal Mind from whose nature truths perpetually flow or emanate. *What I wish to point out is, that Leibniz's proof of God is merely a theological form of this argument.* (Russell 1900: 181)

What are the problems with this view? Russell argues that making truth dependent upon knowledge faces a number of difficulties. The main difficulty that seems relevant to this paper is the first one he discusses, that knowledge is a complex notion, compounded of truth and belief. (Here I am keeping Russell's terminology.) Belief, from *a psychological point of view* is just the same when the proposition believed is true, as when it is false. So, the first difficulty encountered by this view is, according to Russell, to distinguish between true knowledge and human error.

It is worth noting that in a way, Russell is rehearsing here Kant's objection against Locke's emphasis on the source of knowledge and his interest in psychological origination. Let's have a closer look at Russell's objection against "Kant's notion that a priori truths are in some way the work of the mind" (Russell 1900: 181). While rejecting what he sees as Kant's psychological view of the a priori, Russell claims that, in opposition to Kant, by "a priori" he means something "purely logical." According to Russell (1900) the Kantian distinction between the empirical and the a priori depends upon confounding the sources of knowledge with the grounds of truth.[20]

Let's get back to Leibniz himself and Russell's objection. The most solid reply to the difficulty Russell is addressing can be found in Leibniz's proposal to *firmly connect truth with the grounds for truth* by the notion of an a priori proof, a view Russell was not willing to accept or perhaps not even able to fully grasp, because in the context of Leibniz's conception of an a priori proof Russell was reading "a priori" in the Kantian sense (which for Russell was psychological), thus missing Leibniz's most interesting point.

8. SOME CONCLUDING REMARKS

I would like to close here with some concluding remarks on some of the principal issues brought up in my paper.

(a) Russell's proposal of a *rational* reconstruction of Leibniz's philosophy guided by a *purely philosophic* attitude is based on specific assumptions that have their own history.

Firstly, his strategy to transform Leibniz into a "fellow spirit" goes back to Kant who was a distinct "presentist" – he conducted his discussions with past philosophers as if with contemporaries, urging that we should deal with the history of philosophy not as historical and empirical but as rational, i.e. possible a priori – a "philosophical archaeology" of reason.[21]

Secondly, Russell upholds the Kantian view that became canonical for a "reconstruction" of seventeenth century philosophy, that is, that the relevant *philosophical* question was not how to acquire knowledge (i.e. the growth of knowledge) – a merely historico-psychological question – but the issue of grounding truth by offering reasons. According to this view, seventeenth century philosophers failed to keep both issues apart. Leibniz was no exception, and on Russell's reading of Kant, the latter did not manage to completely get out of the ambiguity either.[22] Russell's remedy to this problem is to sharply separate truth and knowledge of the truth.

(b) There are different ways of considering *the relationship between mathematics and philosophy* in the seventeenth century.

Firstly, Russell chooses to focus on the idea of the great impact of the geometrical method upon Leibniz's philosophical writings. The paradigm of classical textbooks presentation was the axiomatic method – also called the "synthetic mode" of presentation. Given the importance of Leibniz's contributions to the field of mathematics this may not be the most fruitful way of approaching the study of his philosophy, which was indeed greatly marked by mathematics.

Secondly, this remark relates to our previous remarks (a) concerning the assumptions underlying the idea of a "rational" reconstruction. Russell's strategy of interpretation has a narrowing effect upon the important Leibnizian notions of "analysis" and "synthesis".[23] Just how restrictive Russell's understanding of Leibniz's notion of analysis turns out to be for us today, and how little justice it does to the philosophy of Leibniz, may not have been clear at the time when Russell worked on his book. However, it is perhaps unfair to argue along these lines, since Russell's book depended on the materials available at the moment, and in this sense the book is but product of his time.[24] Last but not least, the book tells us more about Russell's intellectual development than about Leibniz himself. This brings me to my final remark.

(c) As I pointed out, in the Preface to the second edition of his book Russell addresses two issues of particular interest that give us some hints as to some of the shortcomings of his reading.

Firstly, only a few years after the publication of Russell's book, Couturat's work made him aware that "Mathematics, and specially the infinitesimal calculus, greatly influenced Leibniz's philosophy" (Russell 1937: vii). The latter is an aspect Russell almost completely ignored in this research on Leibniz's philosophy.

Secondly, at the time Russell composed his book, as he recognizes some decades later, he "knew little of mathematical logic, or of Cantor's theory of infinite numbers" (1937: vii). He thus corrects himself in the 1937 Preface:

I should not now say [...] that the propositions of mathematics are "synthetic". The *important distinction is between propositions deducible from logic and propositions not so deducible.* The former may be defined as "analytic", the latter as "synthetic" [...] *modern logicians, for the most part, regard pure mathematics as analytic.* (1937: viii)

In the meantime, not only his own work on logic and the foundations of mathematics, but also the study of Frege's work conducted Russell to this insight.[25]

Both considerations should bear upon Russell's attempt at doing justice to Leibniz's philosophy. Conceding that his importance as a philosopher has become more evident owing to the growth of mathematical logic and the discovery of his MSS, Russell thus writes in 1937:

His philosophy of the empirical world is now only a historical curiosity, but in the realm of logic and the principles of mathematics many of his dreams have been realized, and have been shown at last to be more than the fantastic imaginings that they seemed to all his successors until the present time. (Russell 1937: xii–xiii)

Yet, in spite of such a clear recognition, Russell proceeds to close his New Preface with the words: "my views as to the philosophy of Leibniz are still those which I held in 1900" (Russell 1937: xii).

NOTES

[1] Russell spent the academic year 1898–1899 as a fellow of Trinity College with no teaching duties. But he was asked to deliver the Leibniz lectures because the regular lecturer, Ellis McTaggart was on leave of absence. For a short account of how it came about that Russell was asked to lecture on Leibniz, see Slater 1992: iii–iv.

[2] My emphasis. For a discussion of Russell's idealist period, see Hylton 1990: Chapter 3.

[3] According to Kant, while there cannot be a general "positive" criterion of truth, consistency (as it follows from the logical principle of non-contradiction) is the first "negative" general criterion of truth. This relates to the Kantian view that the logical principles are a *canon* of truth only concerning the formal correctness of our judgments and reasoning. But they can never take the place of an *organon* of truth and thus never contribute to the advancement of learning as heuristic principles may do. It is this fact that disengages general logic from the evolution of human knowledge and the temporality of history. See AA IX; Abbott ed. & trans. 1885: 3.

[4] Russell 1900:2. Russell here regrets that Leibniz's desire to please princes and princesses contributed to the dissipation of his immense energies! However, in his review of the most recent work on Leibniz by L. Couturat he offers a slightly different evaluation. See Russell 1903: 365. On this issue, see also Russell 1945: Chapter XI.

[5] Leibniz's *desire to distance himself from pantheism* would be another instance of this fear. See, for instance, Russell's remarks concerning his attempt to take distance from Spinozism in his published works: "Leibniz fell into Spinozism whenever he allowed himself to be logical, *in his published works, accordingly, he took care to be illogical*" (Russell 1900: vii, my emphasis).

[6] See Slater 1992: iii and note (1) above.

[7] On this issue, see Russell 1900: Sections 101–103.

[8] When Russell (1903) discusses Couturat's work on Leibniz he is paying closer attention to some of the methodological issues in Leibniz. This is not the case in his Leibniz book, and although he claims that Couturat's work offers overwhelming confirmation for own work on Leibniz, there are many important disagreements between them. Russell partly acknowledges this in Russell 1903. For a historical consideration of the development of some of Leibniz's methodological ideas leading to his innovations in mathematics during the stay in Paris, see Lamarra 1978.

[9] It is worth noting that the expression "purely logical" is closely related to Russell's notion of a "purely philosophical" attitude.

[10] Russell 1900: 7. Russell claims that Leibniz often suggests the argument from the "general nature of the proposition", and to support this view he refers to (GP IV, 496/ L 326).

[11] For the view that fundamental logical notions must ultimately begin with a metaphysical analysis, see Vuillemin 1984.

[12] Russell 1900, see on this issue Section. 113. "Eternal truths" are propositions which are true in all possible worlds. Russell regards Leibniz's conception of the eternal truths as sound philosophy – once we prune away the argument that makes them dependent upon God's understanding! All that is required is to get clear about the distinction between truth and knowledge and draw the consequences. I say more on this issue in the next section.

[13] Frege introduced his new form of functional analysis in *Begriffsschrift* (1879).

[14] As I indicated in the Introduction, Russell had been struggling to distance himself from the idealist views he inherited from his teachers at Trinity. He held such views from early in 1894 until late in 1898. In the Preface to *An Essay on the Foundations of Geometry*, for instance, Russell writes "In Logic I have learnt most from Mr. Bradley, and next to him, from Sigwart and Bosanquet." This teaching was but a recasting of general logic in terms of the results of Kant's transcendental philosophy, as Kemp Smith writes: "Modern Logic, as developed by Lotze, Sigwart, Bradley and Bosanquet, is, in large part, the recasting of general logic in terms of the results reached by Kant's transcendental enquiry" (1923: xxxviii).

[15] See, for instance, Russell's evaluation of the Leibnizian idea of "mathesis universalis", Chapter IV. For a historical consideration of the different conceptions of analysis to be found in Leibniz see Pasini 1997.

[16] Russell 1900, Section 113.

[17] This is so especially in the context of Kant's First Critique where the notion of "contingent propositions" *tout court* does not play central role.

[18] For a remark about the fact that Russell changed his mind a few years later as to how Leibniz understands the dichotomy of the necessary and the contingent, see Russell 1903: 377, 8n.

[19] According to Russell, by radically moving away from Leibniz, Kant prepared the way for the view that all propositions are both necessary and synthetic. But "it must be confessed that, if *all* propositions are necessary, the notion of necessity is shorn of most of its importance" (Russell 1900: 24).

[20] See, for instance, Russell 1900: 74. However, it should be noted that a psychologistic reading of Kant is not the outcome of Russell's rejection of his earlier idealistic views. See Hylton 1990: Chapter 3.

[21] Kant, AA XX, 341 (*Lose Blätter: Zu den Fortschritten der Metaphysik*, F 3). The section is entitled "*Von einer philosophierenden Geschichte der Philosophie*"; see pp. 340–1).

[22] Interestingly enough, already former critics such as Hegel made this objection against Kant. See Hylton 1990: 78.

[23] For a discussion of Kant's reading of Leibniz's use of the notions of "analysis" and "synthesis", see Grosholz and Yakira 1998.

[24] We recall that at the time when Russell wrote his Leibniz book (1899), he was neither well acquainted with the unpublished Leibniz *Nachlass* nor with Couturat's project of publishing an important part of it as *Opuscules et Fragments Inédits* (1903).

[25] For the view that Frege represents an important conceptual link with Leibniz's views see my "Frege on Understanding Mathematical Truth and the Science of Logic", *Foundations of the Formal Sciences IV, The History of the Concept of the Formal Sciences* (2006).

14. LEIBNIZ AND RUSSELL

The number of all numbers and the set of all sets *

1. INTRODUCTION

In *My Philosophical Development* Bertrand Russell wrote:

There is one major division in my philosophical work: in the years 1899–1900 I adapted the philosophy of logical atomism and the technique of Peano in mathematical logic. This was so great a revolution as to make my previous work, except such as was purely mathematical, irrelevant to anything that I did later. The change in these years was a revolution; subsequent changes have been of a nature of evolution. (Russell 1959: 11)

It is well known that, precisely during these years, Russell was intensively occupied in lecturing and writing a book on Leibniz. It is less well known to what extent and in what ways Leibniz's work influenced Russell. It is fairly clear, nonetheless, that his engagement with Leibniz's philosophy significantly influenced Russell – both in positive and negative ways. For example, Russell noted that it was through his study of Leibniz that he realized the importance of relations. The logic of relations is one of Russell's most significant contributions to logic and philosophy in general, and, it goes without saying, to that of the English-speaking world in particular. Incidentally, "The Logic of Relations" was Russell's early title for what was later titled *Principia Mathematica* (1903).

It is also largely due to Russell's pioneering role that philosophy in the English-speaking world has become mathematical or, as we have come call it, analytical.[1] Although Leibniz might have been a source of inspiration for the establishment of a mathematically oriented philosophy,[2] Leibniz was the "other" with respect to Russell's logic of relations. With regard to Russell's (and Frege's) fundamental innovative logic, namely that all predicates are types of relations, some being monadic and some being polyadic, Leibniz was the adversary.[3] At the time that Russell was producing his book on Leibniz he set himself two major objectives: (1) to reduce mathematics to logic and (2) to replace the traditional subject-predicate logic with his own logic of relations (that is, to analyze predication by using propositional functions). There is little doubt that it was in light of these objectives that Russell wrote:

I found what so many books on Leibniz failed to make clear – that his metaphysic was explicitly based upon the doctrine that every proposition attributes a predicate to a subject and (what

* I would like to thank Martha Bolton, Meir Buzaglo, Emmanuel Farjoun, Haim Gaifman, and Zohar Yakhiny for very helpful discussions and comments on early versions of this paper. I would also like to thank the editors, Pauline Phemister and Stuart Brown, for organizing the conference and providing the stimulus for writing this paper.

P. Phemister and S. Brown (eds.), Leibniz and the English-Speaking World, 207–218.
© 2007 *Springer.*

seemed to him almost the same thing) that every fact consists of a substance having a property.
I found that this same doctrine underlies the systems of Spinoza, Hegel, and Bradley [...].
(Russell 1959: 61)

A substantial portion of Leibniz's scholarship in the twentieth century was devoted
to grappling with this claim – showing that, however insightful and interesting it
may be, it is strongly overstated, if not entirely misguided. What led Russell to this
view of Leibniz's system wasn't just his attempt to reduce all notions to logical
ones (his logicism) but also the role Leibniz played in his philosophical agenda
of refuting the traditional subject-predicate logic. Russell argued that Leibniz's
commitment to the subject-predicate logic, on the one hand, and his use of relations,
on the other, rendered his system incoherent.[4] In this way, Leibniz's work provided
Russell with a formulation of the doctrine he was trying to refute and to produce
an alternative for. Although Russell's agenda led him to serious misinterpretations
of Leibniz (which are familiar by now), Russell and Frege's logic of relations has
known a great success, so much so that it has become the common language of
contemporary philosophers and logicians.[5]

As far as the logic of relations is concerned, Leibniz played the role of the
"other" – an illustration why an altogether different approach to relations is needed.
In this respect, Russell's agenda was a very successful one. Curiously enough, it
seems that Leibniz played quite a different role in the development of Russell's
agenda and, consequently, in the development of logic, mathematics and philosophy
in the English-speaking world.

2. THE NUMBER OF ALL NUMBERS AND THE CLASS OF ALL CLASSES

It is well known that Russell's logicist programme (presented in *Principles of
Mathematics*, 1903) to reduce all mathematical notions to logical ones was unsettled
by a paradox. Frege showed how to define numbers by means of classes. Russell
noticed that this gives rise to the notion of the class of all classes. He then asked
whether this class is a member in the class of all classes (or in it self). As it
turns out, both options, viz., that it is a member of itself or not, are impossible.
Hence, the definition of numbers in terms of classes seems to generate a paradox.
Russell himself did not at first see the devastating effect of the paradox he had
discovered. This was conveyed to him in a letter from Frege who wrote: "not only
the foundations of my arithmetic, but the sole possible foundations of arithmetic,
seem to vanish."[6] As Lavine remarks, this is how Russell's "conundrums" became
Russell's Paradox and changed the course of his agenda.

Whether the paradox constitutes a problem for Cantor's set theory or for set
theory in general is a controversial matter (see especially Lavine 1994). What
is clear beyond any controversy is that the paradox had enormous influence on
Russell's philosophy, on the development of set theory, on logic and on the
project of providing a foundation for mathematics and for knowledge through logic.

I will therefore assume that the impact of Russell's paradox on Anglo American philosophy requires no further argument.

Let us first take note of some reference points in the chronology of Russell's discovery of the paradox:[7]

- In 1895 Cantor discovered that the assumption that the system of all numbers is a set leads to contradictions. He called such a set an inconsistent absolutely infinite multiplicity.[8]
- In 1896, Russell learned about Cantor's work.[9]
- During 1899–1900 Russell was writing his book on Leibniz and translating passages from the Latin into English for the appendix to his book.[10]
- By early March 1900, Russell completed his *Critical Exposition of the Philosophy of Leibniz* (RCP, vol.2, liii).
- In May 1901, Russell discovered a paradox but, as Lavine remarks, "he did not discuss at the time the class of all classes that are not members of themselves, but only the class of all predicates that cannot be predicated of themselves. The class version ('There is no class of all classes that do not belong to themselves as members') appears only a year later in his letter to Frege" (Lavine 1994: 60–1 note 21).
- In June 1902, Russell wrote to Frege and Peano about the paradox.
- While Frege was devastated by Russell's Paradox, Russell set out to develop his theory of Types in an attempt to avoid the paradox.

Long before he first formulated "Russell's paradox" in May 1901, in 1899 and 1900, Russell was preoccupied with what he variously called "the contradiction of infinity" or "the antinomy of the greatest number." For example, in a draft of the *Principles of Mathematics* (of 1899–1900) he wrote:

Mathematical ideas are almost all infected with one great contradiction. This is the contradiction of infinity. All antinomies, I believe, so far as they are valid at all, will be found reducible to the antinomy of infinite number. (RCP vol.3, Paper #1, 70 and 11)

As G. H. Moore notes in his introduction to *The Collected Papers of Bertrand Russell*, "In 1899, in 'Fundamental Ideas', he [Russell] had been very concerned with the antinomy of infinite number. He wrote that the totality for 'classes seems necessary; but if we make it so, infinite number with its contradictions becomes inevitable, being the number of concepts or of numbers'" (RCP vol.2, p.266).[11] In the same chapter Russell spells out the antinomy as follows: "there are many numbers, therefore there is a number of numbers. If this be N, N + 1 is also a number, therefore there is no number of numbers" (Russell 1899b 265 and xxi).[12] This reasoning gives rise to Russell's summary of the Antinomy of Infinite Number (in Fundamental Ideas, Chapter VII), as follows: "This [the Antinomy] arises most simply from applying the idea of a totality to numbers. There is, and is not, a number of numbers" (RCP, vol2: 267/RCP xx).

The formulations in terms of the number of all numbers will ring familiar to Leibniz's readers (and especially to readers of his early texts). Leibniz explicitly and quite frequently stated that "The number of all numbers is a contradiction"

(e.g. A VI iii, 463/P 7). We already noted that Russell was studying and translating Leibniz's texts intensively at the time. In his book on Leibniz, Russell
cites him as saying that the number of all numbers implies a contradiction[13] and
adds: "Leibniz denied infinite *number*, and supported his denial with very sound
arguments."[14]

As Russell notes, Leibniz not only stated that the number of all numbers is a
contradiction but also explained it in some detail. Although his arguments are not
perspicuous, they are worth quoting. For example, in his Paris notes, he wrote:

> The number of finite numbers cannot be infinite; from which it follows that there cannot be an infinity
> of square numbers, taken in order starting from one. From which it seems to follow that an infinite
> number is impossible. It seems that one only has to prove that the number of finite numbers cannot
> be infinite. If the numbers are assumed to exceed each other continuously by one, the number of such
> finite numbers cannot be infinite, for in that case the number of numbers is equal to the greatest number,
> which is assumed to be finite. It has to be replied that there is no greatest number. But even if they
> were to increase in some way other than by ones, yet if they always increase by finite differences, it is
> necessary that the number of all numbers always has a finite ratio to the last number; further, the last
> number will always be greater than the number of all numbers. From which it follows that the number
> of all numbers is not infinite; neither, therefore, is the number of units. Therefore there is no infinite
> number, or, such a number is not possible. (A VI iii, 477/ P 31–3)[15]

In alluding to Galileo's paradox (that there are as many natural numbers as square
numbers), Leibniz is explicitly arguing here that the number of all finite numbers
cannot be a number since it cannot be either finite or infinite. Therefore, he
concludes that such a notion is contradictory or impossible.

Given the obvious similarity between the number of all numbers and the class of
all classes, it is interesting to consider the relation between Leibniz's formulations
of the impossibility of the number of all numbers and Russell's paradox. It is
significant in this regard that Russell has three different formulations of the paradox.
As we have seen, he first formulated the paradox (or antinomy) in terms of numbers.
He then formulated it in terms of predicates, namely, "the predicate of a predicate
being impredicable of itself" (in RCP xxxvii); and finally in the now familiar terms
of classes (the class of all classes that do not belong to themselves). The first
formulation in terms of numbers sounds very Leibnizian. The second, in terms of
predicates, also has interesting relations to Leibniz.

If one recalls Leibniz's use of the *in-esse* principle, that is, the inclusion of a
predicate in a subject, a principle which Russell placed at the center of Leibniz's
philosophy, and if one interprets the notion of a number of all numbers in these
terms, i.e., a number, seen as a subject term including all numbers as its proper
predicates, it becomes clear that such a number has to include itself as a predicate.
If this number be N, then it is clear that it does not include $N + 1$ as a predicate.
But, if so, it is not the number of all numbers for there is a number that it does not
include.

The third formulation in terms of classes, with the precise definitions of classes
and of the membership-relation is altogether foreign to the seventeenth century
context. These notions were spelled out rigorously by Cantor. The concepts introduced in Cantor's set theory clearly stand between Leibniz notion of the greatest

number and Russell's Paradox. Furthermore, this formulation utilizes classes in an extensional sense (which was foreign to Leibniz). It seems reasonable to suppose that Russell's paraphrase of the paradox in extensional terms (i.e., in terms of classes) is related to his attempt to engage Frege in the problem (as testified by his letter to him). Russell's initial formulation in terms of predicates does not make sense in the context of Frege's system. In order to engage Frege, he had to formulate the problem in extensional terms.[16]

Yet it seems that the intuition, as well as the basic logical structure of the paradox, can be read into Leibniz's formulations, that is, *if* they are interpreted with Cantorian concepts in mind. It is therefore arguable that Russell's paradox could be generated by applying Cantor's set theory to Leibniz's notion of the number of all numbers. This is the exercise I propose to engage in.

Let me be very clear on this point. I do not suggest that Russell's paradox was invented by Leibniz. Such a claim is not only false but is a significant distortion in the sense that it ignores the subtle historical context in which both Leibniz and Russell's formulations arise. Yet the syntactical similarity between the number of all numbers and the class of all classes is striking and suggestive. It is an interesting exercise, therefore, to bring out points of similarity as well as points of difference between Leibniz's claim that the number of all numbers is a contradiction and Russell's paradox.

A particularly interesting question in this regard is whether the self-reflexivity of Russell's formulation, (viz. the class of all classes which is not a member of itself) is already implicit in Leibniz's formulations. From a current perspective, it seems that Leibniz's observation that the notion of the number of all numbers is inconsistent anticipates some of the dramatic consequences and discoveries about number, infinity, and some well-known paradoxes. For example, Leibniz's argument that "there is no infinite number" or that "the number of all numbers is not a number" anticipates Cantor's treatment of infinite cardinality as powers rather than as numbers in the traditional sense. More generally, Leibniz's argument points to the insight that infinite magnitudes cannot be quantified by numbers or cannot be expressed by numbers. One can see Cantor's development of infinite cardinality as closely related to Leibniz's arguments that the number of all numbers is not a number.

One can also see in Leibniz's argument an anticipation of Wittgenstein's remark that Russell's paradox (as well as other confusions regarding the infinite) stem from a problematic extension of the notion of number from the context of finite numbers to that of infinite numbers.[17]

Leibniz's argument against the number of all numbers does seem to employ, though not explicitly, the self-referential aspect of this notion. As is well known, self-reference is endemic to some well-known paradoxes. We have seen that, in Russell's formulation, "the class of all classes which is not a member of itself", self-reference is essential to the paradox. Self-reference is most explicit in the liar paradox in its various formulations (e.g. "this sentence is false" or "what I am now saying is false"). It is also worth observing that Gödel incompleteness proof also employs self-referential claims. In fact, it is arguable that Gödel's proof is a very sophisticated mathematical recast of the liar paradox. In any event, it is clear that self-reference plays an important role not only in Russell's paradox but also in other important paradoxes and theorems.

Intuitively, it seems that the notion of "the number of all numbers" is self-referential. The syntactical form of the phrase strongly supports this intuition. Further, the semantics also speaks in favor of this intuition. After all, the subject of the phrase is a number, which numbers (or quantifies over) all numbers. Let us call this number N. Since (by hypothesis) N is a number, the phrase "the number of all numbers" must also apply to itself. In this sense, the phrase "the number of all numbers" is clearly self-referential. Likewise the phrase "the class of all classes" refers to itself in the sense that it includes itself. Thus Russell's formulation seems to make explicit what was implicit in Leibniz's formulation.

As I have already noted, Russell's antinomy of infinite number became a paradox in the context of the Frege-Russell programme. The goal of Russell's logicist programme was to define all concepts in logical terms. The definition of numbers was as difficult as it was crucial to the success of this programme. To define number in logical terms, Russell used classes as the logical objects and membership as the logical relation (Russell 1903: 166–7). As Lavine put it, "for Russell, a number was a class of all systems equinumerous to any member of the class. For example, on Russell's account, the number 2 is the class of all pairs" (Lavine 1994: 66).[18] When numbers were recast as classes, Russell's "antinomy of infinite number" became a severe problem for this programme. We have already noted that Russell articulated the problem in the form of the following contradiction: "there is and is not a greatest number". Once numbers are defined in terms of classes and the membership relation in a class, so that one can think of the number 2 as including the class of all pairs and the class of all units, it becomes natural to recast the notion of the number of all numbers as the class of all classes. Since the number of all numbers is to "number" all numbers, and, since it is itself a number, it also has to number or include itself or, in short, it has to refer to itself. In terms of classes, this notion is naturally rendered as a class of all classes that includes itself as a member. In this way, it is fairly easy to see how the self-reflexive character implicit in 'the number of all numbers' becomes explicit in Russell and Frege's attempt to define all numbers in terms of classes and membership in a class. By rendering Russell's formulation "there is and is not a number of all numbers" in terms of classes we would get the more straightforward paradoxical formulation: "there is and there is no class of all classes that do not belong to themselves."

Thus it seems that the definition of numbers in logical terms can naturally lead from Leibniz's argument to Russell's paradox. This also explains why it was such a devastating effect on the logicist programme of Russell and Frege. As we know, Frege was indeed entirely devastated – both personally and professionally. By contrast, Russell didn't give up the programme; rather, he set out to solve the paradox and save the programme. The result was his theory of types. Whether the theory of types saved the reductive programme is doubtful. In any event, the theory of types pays a heavy price for elegance and simplicity. In the end, it seems fair to conclude with Lavine that, "Russell's logicist programme failed as a result of the paradox" (Lavine 1994: 73).

3. THE GREATEST NUMBER AND THE GREATEST BEING

Thus far I have stressed the striking similarity between Leibniz and Russell's formulations. I would now like to show that they arose in very different contexts and play very different roles in each thinker's agenda. Let us turn to Leibniz's agenda. Leibniz's point that the number of all numbers is a contradiction makes its appearance in the context of an altogether different programme. In 1675–76, the period during which Leibniz develops his views about infinity (see Levey 1998), Leibniz is also engaged, among many other projects, in distinguishing possible and impossible notions. More precisely, in the texts from this period, Leibniz is attempting to demonstrate that some notions are possible while others are impossible. Leibniz presupposes a fairly crystallized theory of possibility. In brief, he identifies the possible with the thinkable or the conceivable in God's mind and he explicates the thinkable (or the intelligible) in terms of self-consistency among the terms of complex notions. Leibniz also presupposes a universally applicable method to distinguish possible notions from impossible ones. Leibniz's method can be stated roughly as follows: if the terms which compose a given notion are consistent *inter se*, then the notion indicates a possible thing; if the terms are inconsistent so that they imply a contradiction, the notion indicates an impossible thing. The method involves the analysis of complex notions into their constituents and in this way the determination of whether they involve internal contradictions.

It is very clear that Leibniz is using the notion of the number of all numbers in this context as an illustration of an impossible notion, i.e., one whose internal constituents imply a contradiction. For example, he states that the number of all numbers is a contradiction and goes on to discuss the twofold origin of impossibility. He writes: "The number of all numbers is a contradiction, i.e., there is no idea of it; for otherwise it would follow that the whole is equal to the part, or that there are as many numbers as there are square numbers" (A VI iii 463/ P 7). Immediately after that he writes that, "Impossible is a two-fold concept: that which does not have essence and that which does not have existence..." (A VI iii 463/ P 7). 'The number of all numbers' is an example of the first type of impossibility.[19]

At the same time, he is also using the notion of the number of all numbers in a more specific context, namely *in contrast* to a notion whose possibility he is very keen to prove, namely, the notion of the greatest or the most perfect being (*Ens Pefectissimum*) (A VI iii, 572/ P 91).[20] His objective in this context is to support Anselm's argument, revived by Descartes, according to which God exists since existence is included in his notion as one of his perfections. For Anselm's argument to be valid, one has to show that the definition of the greatest being is possible. As he writes, "God is a being from whose possibility (or, from whose essence) his existence follows. If a God defined in this way is possible, it follows that he exists"

(A VI iii, 582/ P 105). Descartes, as well as the rest of the tradition, simply assumed that the definition of the most perfect being is non-problematic. Leibniz points out that this supposition requires proof. In *A Specimen of Discoveries* (c.1686), Leibniz writes:

A real definition is one according to which it is established that the defined thing is possible, and does not imply a contradiction. For if this is not established for a given thing, then no reasoning can be safely taken about it, since if it involves a contradiction, the opposite can perhaps be concluded about the same thing with equal right. And this was the defect in Anselm's demonstration, revived by Descartes, that the most perfect or the greatest being must exist, since it involves existence. For it is assumed without proof that a most perfect being does not imply a contradiction; and this gave me occasion to recognize what the nature of real definition was. (RA 305–7)

While Leibniz's preoccupation with the notion of the greatest being is familiar, it has not been recognized that Leibniz traded on the connection between the possibility of the greatest being and the impossibility of the greatest number. I will try to show that this connection is evident – both textually and conceptually – and that it has very interesting implications. Leibniz defines the notion of the most perfect being as "the subject of all perfections" (A VI iii, 580/ P 103) – "one which contains all essence, or which has all qualities, or all affirmative attributes" and attempts to demonstrate that this notion "is possible or (*seu*) does not imply a contradiction" (A VI iii, 572/ P 91). It appears in these formulations that the notion of God as the greatest being is closely related to the notion of a totality taken in a quantitative sense; for it is defined as that which contains all essence, all perfections, all qualities or all affirmative attributes. In short, the notion of God is defined in quantitative terms and as the subject of *all* perfections or attributes.

Now we might wonder why Leibniz is anxious to show that such a notion is possible. Why does he see it as something requiring a proof? Why should the possibility of the greatest being – a traditionally accepted and apparently innocuous notion – be in question at all? After all, Leibniz fully accepts the traditional view of God as entailing all knowledge, as entailing all power, all wisdom and all Being.

A general answer to this question derives from what I have already mentioned, namely that Leibniz was deeply committed to the project of distinguishing between possible and impossible notions by analyzing complex concepts into their constituents and examining their internal consistency. This general reply, however, does not explain Leibniz's particular interest in proving the possibility of the notion of the greatest being, which otherwise would seem non-problematic. This is why a more specific reply is needed. I suggest the following: Leibniz is concerned about the possibility of the notion of a totality and, in particular, about God as the maximal totality because he clearly sees that similar notions, namely, the notion of the greatest number (and that of the most rapid motion and the greatest shape) are problematic. The syntactical similarity between the notion of the greatest number, seen as the totality of all numbers, and that of the greatest being, seen as the totality of all perfections, is clear. Hence it is likely to have evoked Leibniz's intellectual concerns about the traditional notion of God.[21] It hardly needs mentioning that, if it turned out the notion of the *Ens Perfectissimum* would be inconsistent, disastrous consequences would follow: not only for rational theology in general but also for the very foundations of Leibniz's own metaphysics.[22]

That the relations between the notions of the greatest being and the greatest number concern Leibniz is evident. He juxtaposes and contrasts these definitions in the very same papers and notes from the Paris writings (e.g. A VI iii, 520/ P 79). In this very paper Leibniz explicitly draws an analogy between the essence of God and the essence of the number 6 as being composed of six units (A VI iii, 518/ P 77). He is clearly toying with the analogy between God as the subject of all perfections and number as subject of units. Direct evidence for Leibniz connecting the notions of the greatest being and the greatest number appears in a later text. He wrote explicitly that Descartes agrees to the analogy between these notions:

Mons. Des Cartes in his reply to the second objections, article two, agrees to the analogy between the most perfect Being and the greatest number, denying that this number implies a contradiction.[23] It is, however, easy to prove it. For the greatest number is the same as the number of all units. But the number of all units is the same as the number of all numbers (for any unit added to the previous ones always makes a new number). But the number of all numbers implies a contradiction, which I show thus: To any number, there is a corresponding number equal to its double. Therefore, the number of all numbers is not greater than the number of all evens, i.e., the whole is not greater than its part. (GP I, 338; cited from Russell's appendix, 244)

It seems reasonable to suppose that Leibniz's clarity about the impossibility of the greatest number (as well the most rapid motion and the greatest shape) plays a role in his concerns about the possibility of the greatest being – which is partly why its possibility required a proof in the first place.

In any event, it is clear that Leibniz is investigating these notions by comparing and contrasting them. In Leibniz's eyes, these examples provide paradigmatic cases of possible versus impossible notions. It is also clear that each of these notions is of great consequence to Leibniz's philosophy. For this reason, the relations between them are all the more interesting. Yet it is very curios that, while these concepts have a striking structural similarity and both seem to imply infinite quantity the concept of the greatest being serves Leibniz as a paradigm of a *possible* notion and the notion of the greatest number serves as a paradigm of an *impossible* notion.

Since these notions seem analogous, Leibniz's position is very intriguing. What makes the notion of the greatest being a paradigm of possibility and that of the greatest number a paradigm of impossibility? As we shall see, the distinction between these notions points to a deep insight in Leibniz's metaphysics. To see this, let us try to advance the analogy a bit further. As we noted, Leibniz analyzed the notion of the greatest being in quantitative terms, i.e. as "the subject of all perfections" (A VI iii, 580/ P 103), "one which contains all essence, or which has all qualities, or all affirmative attributes." In the same texts he also draws an explicit analogy between God's essence and whole numbers.[24] In this analogy, numbers consist of units as God's essence consists of simple forms or perfections. Since Leibniz defines whole number as consisting of units, the greatest number is seen as including all units. Since he defines God as consisting of all essence or all perfections, the greatest being is seen as the subject of all perfections. Just as there are infinitely many units in the notion of infinite number, so there are infinitely many perfections in the notion of God. In this sense, these notions seem perfectly analogous. Therefore, it seems that they should be considered to be equally problematic. Yet we have seen that Leibniz considers the one as a paradigm of possibility, the other as a paradigm of impossibility. What then is the dissimilarity Leibniz sees between these notions? What makes him consider the one notion to be possible and the other to be impossible?

Let me make a conjecture. In spite of the close similarity between these notions, there is in fact substantial difference between them. The dissimilarity stems from the difference between beings and numbers – a distinction that cuts deep in Leibniz's metaphysics. We know that Leibniz does not consider numbers to be true beings. As he writes, "Numbers, modes, and relations are not entities" (A VI iii, 463/ P 7). A major difference between these notions might hinge on the distinction between the concept of the greatest being and that of a greatest non-being. While numbers are universal, non-active, and not true units, beings for Leibniz, are individual, active units. In short, beings, for Leibniz, are agents.

Furthermore, the notion of God or the greatest being serves as the paradigm of Being. It is the first being and the source of all created beings. In fact, it also serves as the model for Leibniz's notion of created beings – individuals that have power and internal source of activity. Even so, the question why the notion of the greatest being, seen as consisting of infinitely many perfections, is possible stands. Let us not forget that Leibniz's strategy to prove that the greatest being is possible is to show that all positive perfections or attributes are compatible *inter se* and therefore may be included in one subject. So, how is such a notion possible if the notion of infinite number is not?

In fact, this is precisely what becomes clear when we compare the notion of God to that of infinite number. Unlike the notion of a number, the notion of God (and, if fact, of any true being) is not additive; it is not *composed* of infinite units or of perfections. It is not a sum of all perfections; rather, it is initially a *subject* which includes all perfections. In this context, the notion of a subject seems to indicate individuality, unity and activity.[25] Unlike numbers, ideas and other incomplete notions, subjects act. Subjects, for Leibniz, are agents. God, of course, is the primary agent. This indicates that, unlike the notion of number, the notion of God is not purely quantitative. The source of being, according to Leibniz, is intrinsic activity. God's intrinsic activity is also the source of its unity and perfection. In fact, the notion of the *Ens Perfectissimum* is more accurately rendered as the highest being or the most perfect being, which points that the highest or most perfect being need not pertain primarily to a quantitative aspect but rather to a qualitative one.

This also clarifies the grounds for Leibniz distinction between true entities and aggregates. Beings or true unities are not composed. He writes, for example, that, "...no entity that is truly one [*ens vere unum*] is composed of parts. Every substance is indivisible and whatever has parts is not an entity but only a phenomenon".[26] This distinction becomes all the more significant when we consider the context of infinity. The context of infinity clarifies that the greatest number is impossible while and greatest being is possible. Unlike a number, a being is not defined quantitatively or compositionally; rather, it is defined through its basic ability to act.[27] Similarly, Leibniz defines created beings (as well as their infinite concepts) by their unique method of production or law of formation, not as a sum of their predicates.[28] This is why Leibniz can accept infinite beings while rejecting infinite numbers. In this light, it becomes rather clear why Leibniz states the following: "It is not surprising that the number of all numbers (*numerum omnium numerorum*), all possibilities, all relations or reflections, are not distinctly understood; for they are imaginary and have nothing that corresponds to them in reality" (A 399/ P 115).

NOTES

[1] Consider his book *Introduction to Mathematical Philosophy* (1919) and his explicit desire to establish a school of Mathematical Philosophy as evidence.

[2] Leibniz wrote: "Ma Metaphysique est toute mathematique, pour dire anisi, ou la pourroit devenir" (Letter to de l'Hospital, GM II, 258, cited from Couturat 1901: 281–2.

[3] I thank Meir Buzaglo for an illuminating discussion of this point.

[4] In his *A Critical Exposition of the Philosophy of Leibniz*, Russell described Leibniz as attempting to reduce all relations and polyadic predicates to monadic ones. Since such a reduction has shown to be formally impossible, Russell argued that Leibniz's system fails.

[5] From a perspective of the history of philosophy in the English-speaking world (which has of course enormous influence on the philosophical world at large) this point is evidenced by two simple observations: (1) Logic – that is, mathematical Logic – has become an obligatory course in almost any academic philosophical training (so that formal logic became an essential part of a philosopher's knowledge and one of his or her basic working tools). (2) The logic taught in the basic philosophy courses is the logic of relations introduced by Russell and Frege.

[6] Letter to Russell, cited from Lavine 1994: 55. See p. 293 for a translation of the whole letter.

[7] This chronology is mainly based on two sources: G. H. Moore's introduction to RCP and Lavine 1994.

[8] Lavine 1994: 56–7.

[9] In his *Autobiography* (Russell 1967–69: 200) he later wrote: "At the time I falsely supposed all his arguments to be fallacious, but I nevertheless went through them in the minutest detail. This stood me in a good stead when later on I discovered that all the fallacies were mine." (See Lavine 1994: 57).

[10] Incidentally, the majority of his correspondence with Moore at the time deals with questions of these translations. Russell also corresponds with Louis Couturat who invites him to participate in the Paris conference, where his first encounter with Peano (mentioned above) takes place.

[11] Moore goes on to remark: "Here again, he [Russell] stood at the brink of the Paradox of the Largest Cardinal" (RCP xxiii).

[12] Here is another one of Russell's formulations of this point: "...there is a number after any given number and therefore no number N that may be specified is the number of all numbers" (RCP III, 32).

[13] See Moore and Garciadiego 1981.

[14] For which he cites GP VI, 629; GP I, 338; GP II, 304–5; GP V, 144; Langley ed. 1896: 161 (Russell, 1937: 111).

[15] See also the following argument from 1672: "Or perhaps we should say, distinguishing among infinites, that the most infinite, or all the numbers, is something that implies a contradiction, for it were a whole it could be understood as made up of all the numbers continuing to infinity, and would be much greater than all other numbers that is, greater than the greatest number" (A VI iii, 168/ RA 116).

[16] This point is due to Haim Gaifman.

[17] See Shanker 1987: 187. Wittgenstein wrote: "It seems to me that we can't use generality – all, etc. – in mathematics at all. There's no such thing as 'all numbers', simply because there are infinitely many". Wittgenstein 1974: §126.

[18]   Russell and Frege adopt the extensional interpretation of numbers because they attempt to reduce all concepts (particularly, number concepts) to logical concepts. But in response to the question "What is numbered?" they cannot refer to any non-logical objects. For this reason they use equi-numerousity between classes as their basic notion. On this see Lavine 1994: 65–6. Lavine writes: Russell was a logicist. He wished to show that mathematics and logic are one by showing how to develop all of mathematics within a framework free of any special conditions or empirical and psychological assumptions. That is a programme substantially similar to Frege's for arithmetic and analysis. Frege and Russell faced a common problem: mathematics is apparently about objects (numbers and so forth), and yet the assumption that objects exist apparently goes beyond logic [...] Russell used classes as the logical objects and membership as the logical relation (Russell 1903: 166–7)".

[19]   I do not discuss in this paper the other (very interesting) type of impossibility.

[20]   In a letter to Conring (1677) Leibniz writes: "*At qui subtiliores sunt adversarii ajunt Ens perfectissumum tam implicare contraditionem quam numerum maximum*" (A II i, 325).

[21]   "There cannot be a most rapid motion or a greatest number. For number is something discrete, where the whole is not prior to its parts, but conversely. There cannot be a most rapid motion, because motion is a modification, and is the transference of a certain thing in a certain time. (Just as there cannot be a greatest shape.) There cannot be one motion of the whole, *but there can be a kind of thinking of all things*. Whenever the whole is prior to its parts, then it is a maximum, as in space and in a continuum. If matter is like a shape, namely that which makes a modification, then it seems that there is no totality of matter" (A VI iii, 520/ P 79, my italics).

[22]   In 1678, Leibniz writes to Elizabeth: "Mais à présent, il me suffit de remarquer, que ce qui est le fondement de ma caractéristique l'est aussi de la demonstration de l'existence de Dieu" (A II i, 437).

[23]   In his second objection to Descartes's *Meditations* Caterus argued that humans may invent or think out the concept of the greatest being from their own resources, just as they may think the concept of the greatest number though it is impossible.

[24]   "It seems to me that the origin of things from God is of the same kind as the origin of properties from an essence; just as $6 = 1 + 1 + 1 + 1 + 1 + 1$, therefore $6 = 3 + 3, = 3 \times 2, = 4 + 2$, etc. [...] So just as these properties differ from each other and from essence, so do things differ from each other and from God" (A VI iii, 518–9/ P 77. See also A VI iii, 523/ P 83; A VI iii, 512/ P 67 for similar analogies and A VI iii, 521/ P 81).

[25]   See Fichant 1997.

[26]   Cited from Brown, G. 2000: 41.

[27]   This point might have interesting bearing on the debate between Richard Arthur and Gregory Brown (in *Leibniz Review* 1998, 1999, 2001) regarding Leibniz's denial of infinite number and infinite whole. The question I discuss above, what justifies Leibniz to regard the notion of an infinite being as possible and that of an infinite number impossible is at the background of the debate between Arthur and Brown.

[28]   A very interesting corollary to this view is Leibniz's definition of infinite series. He does not define infinite series as a sum of numbers but as a product of its formation rule. In this connection see the interesting discussion in Couturat 1973: 476. Couturat cites this passage from the letter to des Bosses (of 11 March 1706): "*Neque enim negari potest, omnium numerorum possibilium naturas revera dari, saltem in divina mente, adeoque numerorum multidudinem esse infinitiam*" (cited from Couturat, 1973: 476).

15. LEIBNIZ AND THE PERSONALISM
OF L. E. LOEMKER

L. E. Loemker (1900–1985) was one of the twentieth century's foremost students of the philosophy of Gottfried Wilhelm Leibniz, the great seventeenth century German philosopher and polymath. Loemker's translations of Leibniz's papers, originally published in two volumes by the University of Chicago Press, and later by Reidel in a single volume edition, his many essays devotedly collected and edited by Ivor Leclerc, and his monograph on the seventeenth century intellectual background of Leibniz's thought, published by Harvard under the title *Struggle for Synthesis*, are central monuments in recent Leibniz study.[1] As Robert Sleigh noted in his memorial announcement of Loemker's death, this work brought Leibniz scholarship in America to its maturity (*Studia Leibnitiana* 1987, XIX: 1). What is less well-known is that Loemker had long hoped to write a reexamination of American personalism, the philosophical position in which he was schooled at Boston University. As he put it in an unpublished statement of "research plans," dating from 1969, "A third project, which I may never carry out, involves a fresh appraisal and interpretation of the personalistic tradition, in terms of its relations to other philosophical and theological trends".[2] Loemker did finish four relatively complete papers on personalism. These papers, along with a number of notes from a variety of sources, indicate what direction his reappraisal would have taken. What I propose to do in this paper is to look at the intersection of the two central foci of Loemker's career, and to show some of the ways in which Loemker's reading of Leibniz influenced his critical interpretation of personalism. At the same time this paper might be called "L. E. Loemker and the Personalism of Leibniz," since a complementary goal is an examination of Leibniz's candidacy for membership in the personalist tradition. Does Loemker's work suggest Leibniz belongs there? What follows then is a brief summary of some basic personalist positions, an account of Loemker's critique, his appropriation of Leibniz in the project of a reconstructed personalism, and some concluding remarks on the viability and promise of a renewed personalistic philosophy.

But let me set the scene with a bit of classical enthusiasm and a few lines of great verse:

By Hercules! I'd say, cleverly and wittily does Gavius Bassus explain the derivation of the word *persona*, suggesting that it is formed from *personare*, for, as he says, the head and the face are shut in on all sides by the covering of the *persona*, or mask, and only one passage is left for the issue of the voice; and since this opening is neither free nor broad, but sends forth the voice after it has been concentrated and forced into one single means of egress, it makes the sound clearer and more melodious. Since then that covering of the face gives clarity and resonance to the voice, it is for that reason called *persona*...[3]

P. Phemister and S. Brown (eds.), Leibniz and the English-Speaking World, 219–230.

So the great second century Roman truffle-hunter, Aulus Gellius, in his splendid collection of essays, *Attic Nights*, offers his etymology of the term "person." The ancient masks of players were actually megaphones of a kind, allowing the player to be heard from a distance, in theatres mostly in the open air. However likely this derivation may be, and it has been challenged by scholars from Scaliger to Trendelenburg,[4] Gellius draws our imagination to the deeper dimensions of personality, its announcement of individuality, of one's presence on stage so to speak, a character in the great theatre of the world, unique and of surpassing importance. That someone at sometime should make personhood the centerpiece of a philosophical reconstruction should not surprise us. Persons announce their individuality, their this-ness, their calling, as Gerard Manley Hopkins, the great poet of Scotistic individuality, wrote so well:

> Each mortal thing does one thing and the same:
> Deals out that being indoors each one dwells;
> Selves – goes itself; *myself* it speaks and spells,
> Crying *What I do is me: for that I came.*[5]

Let us explore a bit more in depth the position hinted at by the Roman orator and the Victorian poet, now from the vantage point of philosophy. Personalism is in some eclipse these days, save perhaps in the few cells of Boston influence. Flower and Murphey's history of American philosophy hardly alludes to the personalist school, and even identifies Borden Parker Bowne with Cornell rather than with Boston University (1976: xx). Barbara MacKinnon's "historical" anthology of American philosophy has no selection from a prominent personalist, and subsumes brief remarks on Howison and Bowne under her chapter on Royce, entitled "The Idealism and Absolute Pragmatism of Josiah Royce."[6] Professional philosophical societies and journals pay scant attention to personalism, even though the personalist discussion group is one of the oldest group societies affiliated with the American Philosophical Association. We must return half a century to find personalism adequately represented, in works like W. H. Werkmeister's.[7] So some account of the history of personalism may not be out of order.[8]

We start with a working definition of the term "personalism." Personalism is a form of idealism, containing a powerful and haunting central intuition, namely that the ultimate unit of philosophical experience and discourse, is the free, self-conscious and creative person. The term "personalism" like all "isms" does not much antedate the nineteenth century. Its first appearance apparently is found in Schleiermacher writing in 1799 during the so-called Pantheism Controversy.[9] The transcendentalist, Bronson Alcott, seems to have been the first American to use the term, in his radical educational theories.[10] The term became popularized among philosophically inclined educators such as William Torrey Harris. Walt Whitman used the term politically and culturally in his essay *Democratic Vistas*, in his usual exuberant style: "In addition to established sciences, we suggest a science as it were of healthier average personalism [...] the object of which should be to raise up and supply through the States a copious race of superb American men and women, cheerful, religious, ahead of any yet known" (1912: 330). As a more technical and generalized philosophical position, American personalism is associated with two intellectual centers, on opposite sides of the continent. One lies in Boston, the other in California. Both had their respective guiding founders, George Holmes Howison (1834–1916)[11] at the University of California; and Borden Parker Bowne (1847–1910)[12] at Boston University. It is probably the case that Howison should be credited with introducing the position into the mainstream of American philosophical life. But the stronger case can be made for individuality and creative impact on Bowne's part. Indeed, no less a figure than William Ernest Hocking claimed in 1922 that "there is no more powerful and convincing chapter in American metaphysical writing than that of Bowne on 'the failure of impersonalism'."[13] Although we concentrate on American personalism, we should note the international appeal it enjoyed, in Europe and South America especially. Particular mention should be made of Emanuel Mounier in France, whose personalism enjoyed great vogue before his untimely death in 1950.[14]

In the hands of its ablest adherents personalism developed into a full philosophical position. While stressing moral and religious issues, philosophers like Bowne and his student and successor at Boston University, Edgar Sheffield Brightman (1884–1953), explored the full range of philosophical topics, to undergird their central concerns. I shall examine some of these positions at this point, focusing on Bowne, because of his thoroughness and influence, and the fact that as leader of the Boston school, he established the matrix in which L. E. Loemker was nurtured. Loemker has Bowne and Brightman in mind in his own critical assessment of personalism, and when I use the term "personalist," I shall have these two chiefly in mind, but especially Bowne.

The central philosophical intuition of personalism, again, is the absolute irreducibility of persons, defined, as we noted above, as self-aware, spontaneous and creative beings. The position is comprehensive, ontologically and epistemologically. Being is personal, and knowledge is personal. Philosophical questions are to be answered only in terms of what we, as persons, must think about them. Modern personalism stands in sharp opposition to nineteenth century impersonalistic alternatives, such as forms of naturalism holding the radical independence of a physical world, and forms of idealism holding the absoluteness of some supreme principle transcending the world of nature and persons, including God. Personalism is theistic and pluralistic. As primarily a moral philosophy, its philosophy of religion is suffused with moral themes and a social anthropology. Moral law is objective and discovered, however creative human responses to the moral order may be. So there is a realistic core to the personalistic project, holding a theory of knowledge committed to a world outside and beyond the experiencing subject, a world of moral agents and order. On the side of nature, however, this world is phenomenal in much of its structure and has no radically independent existence beyond the mind, finite or infinite. Bowne sometimes called his position "Kantianized Berkeleyanism." This term helps us orient ourselves to Bowne's chief philosophical sources for his theory of knowledge and metaphysics. In epistemology he is a kind of Kantian;

in metaphysics a kind of Berkeleyan. In brief what this amounts to is a modified empiricism, the position that the knowing self contributes to knowledge the basic structure and organization of objects of knowledge, and is not simply affected by sensory input. And, in matters of reality, the only absolutely real things in the universe are immaterial selves. Personalists are fond of quoting a passage from Berkeley's *Commonplace Book*: "Nothing properly but persons, i.e. conscious things, do exist. All other things are not so much existences as manners of ye existence of persons."[15] The world is other than the knowing mind, as ideas are other than knowers, but its organization, structure and reality are dependent upon the inner, causal resources of mind, either finite or infinite. The world of nature, as experienced, is thus a set of phenomena, reducible causally and cognitively to creative and experiencing persons.

The place of a Supreme Person in this scheme of things is increasingly obvious, although not via the traditional arguments for God's existence, even the teleological argument. God is known to exist through analogy with the inner life and choices of experiencing persons, and the world is God's creature because of God's life as a person, willing and knowing the world as it really is. Such argumentation rests upon the total experience of the person, a kind of holism in natural theology reminiscent of the so-called "moral" argument for God's existence. Finally, for most personalists the system is pluralistic, and the existence of an indefinite number of personal centers beyond the individual knower and God is fundamental, at least to Boston personalism. A communitarian ethics, then, depending upon a very Kantian respect for persons, and an experiential and interactive epistemology and metaphysics, flow from some of the central personalistic foundational principles. Personalism's chief bequest to recent thought has been a philosophy of religion and ethics founded in a fundamentally moral view of basic reality, one where "life is deeper than logic," as Bowne was fond of saying. Martin Luther King, Jr. claimed that personalism was the major philosophical influence on his ethics and social activism (1958: 100).

We turn now to Loemker's critical remarks on personalism, as found in his published papers.[16] Because there is some overlap, I shall not consider them one by one, but rather adopt a more synoptic approach, pointing to some common themes. After this account of Loemker's critique, I shall address his suggested reconstruction of personalism, with particular attention to the relevance Leibniz has to this reconstruction.

Loemker was primarily a historian of philosophy, and we should not be surprised to find some historical estimate of personalism even in these few papers. In the first of his surviving personalist papers, "American Personalism as a Philosophy of Religion," dating from 1958, Loemker claims that, along with empiricism, activism and pragmatism, personalism constitutes one of the four characteristic tendencies of American thought. These four characterize both Santayana's "aggressive enterprise" and "genteel tradition," both the idealistic and naturalistic, the pluralist and monist, the tender-minded and tough-minded traditions of American thought, from Edwards down to Royce and James. In particular, personalism is characteristically American "in its sensitivity to the claims of the whole person as opposed to psychological abstractions" (Loemker 1993: 9). At its heart then, personalism forms one of the integrative characteristics of the American tradition, a striking generalization that ought to attract the attention of students of American thought and culture.

Loemker's criticism of personalism takes the form of some enthusiastic endorsement, including this historical claim, and some sharp and pointed reservations. On the positive side, Loemker finds himself in full sympathy with the core intuition that personhood is the ultimate touchstone of philosophical reconstruction, its "central core of concern," offering its synthesis in terms of "a plural order of persons, including a personal God" (Loemker 1993: 19). Its "opposition to all abstract theories of human nature," (Loemker 1993: 15) to which we have already alluded, suggests a concreteness in methodology and basic themes that Loemker returns to, time and again, leading him to stress the experiential and non-rationalistic quality of its anthropology and epistemology. And it leads him of course to stress the moral character of personality, over against metaphysical and psychological readings of the meaning of the term: "It is the concrete unity of the moral situation which requires a *person* as the focal center of perspectives of knowledge and action" (Loemker 1993: 37). This moral quality of personalism, indebted as it is to the Kantian tradition, extends to its theological side: "Involved in all religion, regardless of differences in tradition and cultural pattern, is a moral change in which the will of the individual is involved" (Loemker 1993: 38). These free acts of the person lead in turn to the claim that all individuals share a creative power, at least "in a measure" (Loemker 1993: 38), thereby constituting their own unique character or form. "Personality is woven out of components – experienced qualities, structures, and uniformities provided by memory, and arising from bodily processes and from the natural and social environment" (Loemker 1993: 38). All these strengths serve to champion personalism's superiority over alternative theories of religion, whether they be linguistic, existentialist, naturalist or organic. (Loemker 1993: 43ff.) At the center of these competing theories is some variant of the impersonal that Loemker, in continuity with Bowne, never tired of criticizing. Loemker united ethics with a philosophy of religion, very much in the tradition of American liberal Protestantism. This is perhaps personalism's most enduring thematic strand, and one where Loemker professes his most unflagging commitment.

In spite of all this, Loemker's negative criticisms are more prominent in all but one of his personalist papers. He clearly regards the position as in need of some radical overhaul, one recovering a pre-modern, or at least pre-Enlightenment, methodology and mood, if it is to continue as a viable philosophical option.

These criticisms dominate "Personalism as a Philosophy of Religion," a paper he wrote in 1955 for the Southern Society for the Philosophy of Religion. Basically, Loemker finds in classical personalism an incoherence, or at least incompatibility, of basic philosophical themes. Its fundamental empiricism, borrowed especially from the Berkeleyan tradition, although admirably resistant to reified abstractions, tends to conflict with the transcendentalism, both of Kant's ethics, and of his organizing unified ego. And both run counter to the central personalist voluntarism derived from Kant's primacy of practical reason. The "transcendental empiricism"

Bowne espouses involves for Loemker a double and mutually inconsistent tendency, one to a realistic epistemology, the other to a private and inner empiricism. "Observed data are experience, and the person [...] is the experienced ground of all meaning" (Loemker 1993: 23). But a pluralistic metaphysics, at least one containing God and the self, requires a realism in conflict with this empiricist subjectivism. The result is "a double language of exposition, the realistic and the subjective" (Loemker 1993: 23). The problem is exacerbated by the unclear status of phenomena in Bowne's writings. Bowne seems committed to an independent world of real things, but the relation of this order to the inner perceived order of phenomena, is never clarified. Personalists need a theory of well-foundedness to establish a proper relation between the phenomenal and the real, where universal struc-tures and logical principles themselves are gradually discerned in the phenomenal order, through a process more of discovery than invention. Science deserves more of a place in personalism, provided of course it is to be seen as "a human enterprise affected by the complete order of human interests and activities" (Loemker 1993: 61).

These methodological difficulties lead to serious problems in a philosophy of religion, since a realistic epistemology renders knowledge of God more, not less difficult. It renders an argument from analogy with human purposiveness insuf-ficient, and marks an approach to God that is always approximative, subject to the "infinite analysis" of phenomenal and real orders that is always beyond us. The "moral argument" for God's existence demands a more realistic account of the world, an "objective order of existence [...] given in *personal* action" (Loemker 1993: 29), and can escape some of the problems outlined above, but only if the concept of personality itself is empirically enriched. Person-alists perhaps should sacrifice their analogical arguments for God's existence in favor of "deepened analysis of human beings as persons" (Loemker 1993: 30). Such analysis can produce a more profound awareness of the divine, and an enriched argument from analogy. As things stand, the inwardness of the individual person is more absolute even than Leibniz's monadism, since the latter is at least reflective of the entire universe, from its own point of view, whereas person-alists focus and refocus on the inner "scaffolding of their own hypotheses" (Loemker 1993: 31). In this very telling and promising passage, Loemker argues that Leibniz is more an appropriate source for "political, social and Christian order" (Loemker 1993: 31) than personalism has so far been able to achieve. The tension remains between the external, activist conception of personality and the inner, subjective and solitary notion of the person, and religion must satisfy both, but even this inwardness requires mutual programmatic openness to moral and social problems and order. We shall recall this passage more completely as we now move to a more direct consideration of Loemker's consideration of Leibniz.

L. E. Loemker was not the first personalist to recognize a link with Leibniz. And, in fact, many of the first scholars and philosophers writing in English to have recognized Leibniz's stature were Americans.[17] The first important translations of

Leibniz, including the *Monadology*, the *Discourse on Metaphysics*, and the *New Essays*, were made by Americans. The first anthology of his writings in English, and some of the first important scholarly articles, all came from this country, including a fine piece in the very first volume of the *Atlantic*, written by a "minor transcendentalist," Frederic Henry Hedge, a close friend of Emerson's and one of the founders of the Transcendental Club. John Dewey's examination of the *New Essays* preceded Russell's book on Leibniz by more than a decade. So we should not be surprised to find personalists as well intrigued by Leibniz's thought. Howison thought Leibniz at the forefront of the movement historically, and Bowne's studies in Germany with Lotze and Erdmann brought him in close contact with much of Leibniz's basic writings.[18] On the whole, however, this recognition is curiously grudging. So Brightman, Loemker's major professor at Boston University, thought Leibniz "too rationalistic," (Loemker 1993: 55) to be of much use to personalists. Interestingly, Loemker replied to this criticism in a 1942 letter to Brightman (Loemker 1993: 55–56), and by 1950 Brightman could write: "The founder of modern personalism is Gottfried Wilhelm Leibniz" (1950: 340–52). Brightman had changed his mind, and it is likely that Loemker made him do so. Loemker's appropriation of Leibniz takes place against a rich background of American research, and should reward some close consideration.

First of all, Leibniz offers a theory of knowledge more adequate to the investigation of the phenomenal world. The empiricism espoused by Bowne and succeeding personalists is compatible with James's "radical empiricism," but not with some of the more metaphysical and theological concerns at the heart of personalist intuitions. In order for these issues to be more adequately dealt with, a return to what Loemker calls "a pre-Kantian (perhaps a pre-Ockhamist) theory of knowledge" (Loemker 1993: 17), is demanded, one where a greater confidence in the power of intellection, is found. Thus the well-foundedness of phenomena stands a greater chance of being understood in terms of objective and independent reality (Loemker 1993: 17). On the side of metaphysics too, Loemker repeatedly criticizes the personalist account of phenomena, particularly Bowne's treatment, and calls for a more adequate theory of "well-foundedness" in an independent order of reality. Berkeleyan empiricism reduces the phenomenal order to a series of mind-dependent ideal entities, enjoying no existence beyond this objective status. Although the point is a controverted one in Leibniz exegesis, I think Loemker is correct that Leibniz would have rejected this extreme. The most coherent account we can give of Leibniz's position is that phenomena are confused perceptions of ultimately real things, ordered in hierarchies of substantial entities, from the lowest "naked" monads to the highest, "spirits," or we could say, persons. The order, one of super- and sub-ordination, and employing the political metaphor of domination, is discoverable through analytic procedures, and, to be sure, involves an analysis *ad infinitum*, one never finally achieved by a finite intellect. But the relegation of these entities to a simple subjective form of idealism trivializes the methodology and makes science a distinctly second-order activity. For Loemker the well-foundedness of the phenomenal order is inadequately developed by the personalist tradition.

Leibniz's phenomenalism is very different in character from Bowne's and offers a useful corrective of his subjectivism.

Leibniz's theology is in part useful, in part not. Loemker shares personalism's traditional hesitations over the ontological argument, and prefers the moral argument espoused by Kant. All substantialist and causal approaches to God depend upon an analogy from finite personal centres of action to some independent ground of all phenomena and personal agents. But this analogy is rendered impossible of completion, given the objective infinity of phenomena and their analyzed elements. Loemker calls upon Leibniz's analysis *ad infinitum* at this point to bolster his critique of personalist theology (Loemker 1993: 28), although there is an irony here in that Leibniz certainly thought traditional arguments for God's existence were possible and not vitiated by the infinite complexity of the phenomenal world. But perhaps Leibniz here is less consistent than he ought to be, and points more toward a Kantian moral argument than he himself thought he did. For Loemker the primacy of the practical reason suggests an analogy from the order of moral objectivity, uncovering "an objective order of existence...given in *personal action*." (Loemker 1993: 29) Therefore, arguments even like the ontological, depend upon some immediate intuition of the nature of a perfect being, and this is not possible except where the knower has a rich appreciation of the demands of an objective moral order.

And so we are led to the ethics. It always comes as a surprise to those immersed in Leibniz as a metaphysician and mathematician, that he considered himself more a moralist than a speculative or theoretical thinker. "You (Locke) had more to do with the speculative philosophers, while I was more inclined towards moral questions" (A VI vi, 71). But a glance at Leibniz's biography should have alerted us to the truth of this claim. Leibniz was trained in law, spent his entire life in the practical service of rulers, counseled countless persons of influence in matters of public benefit, and engaged himself in political, ecumenical and diplomatic activities. He merits being counted among the last great public philosophers. Indeed, given his learning, Leibniz may be considered a late survivor of the Renaissance tradition of civic humanism.[19] Although in many issues his ethics is not so original as his metaphysics, there are some noteworthy themes. Among these is his fundamental position that love, tempered by wisdom, constitutes justice, the central moral value in his scheme. As early as his first years in Hanover,[20] Leibniz began to define justice as "*charitas sapientis*," "the charity of the wise person." (I hasten to add that my translation of this term uses "person" to avoid sex-specific language, not to reinforce Leibniz's personalism.) Leibniz uses this definition throughout his life, in juridical, moral and theological settings. This definition is a key, I think, to Leibniz's arguments for God's justice in the *Theodicy*, but we cannot explore this issue right now.

Loemker had a deep appreciation of the moral dimension of Leibniz's thought. It forms a central motif of his reconstructed personalism. In conversation he once said he thought the *Monadology* was a groundwork for an aristocratic ethics. There is a striking passage in one of Loemker's papers, excerpted above, that I should now quote in full:

It is well to emphasize, these days, the self-determining nature of human beings and the essential privacy, the self-experience and self-value in which their worth resides. But here too it seems that personalism has gone too far. The inward approach to human beings, prematurely hardened into an ontology, has caused the social conditions and power of their nature to be neglected. (The social nature of religion has therefore not received adequate treatment.) Indeed, the windows of the individual are darkened even more completely than were those of Leibniz's monads, for these perceived the entire world, each from its point of view, while in personalism persons seem to construct only the scaffolding of their own hypotheses about the living conscious core of their experience, the qualitative richness of this experience being the subjective effects of causes internal or external. Leibniz was able to outline a basis for political, social, and Christian order based upon the harmony constituted by the interlaced patterns of perceptions; personalism has not done this. (Loemker 1993: 31; Loemker 2002: 182–3)

As this text shows, Loemker clearly thinks a modified monadism can be a useful addition to the personalist arsenal, but only because of the validity of Leibniz's self-description as primarily a moral philosopher rather than a speculative or theoretical one. The famous "windowlessness" of Leibniz's monads may seem to support a metaphysics of isolated individualism, but his theory of universal representation modifies this insularity, and justifies a fairly radical involvement in public activity. As Loemker puts it: "... monads see one another, even though they depend only upon God." (2002: 183) This supports Loemker's characterization of concrete personhood as having "... two distinct sides, an external side available to other persons, and an internal side available only to themselves and to God, who sees and orders all" (Loemker 1993: 39). Without this position, amounting to Leibniz's repeated statement that the nature of the monad is to represent or mirror the world, his own extensive public activity seems radically at odds with a central feature of his monadic theory, an intolerable gap between life and logic for any personalist.

Thus Leibniz's windows are opened, at least enough for a theory of moral action, and for a response in love to perceived monadic states. It will appear strange that monads can love anything, since their perceptions are the only immediate objects of their conscious life, volitionally or cognitively. Furthermore, in a tradition reaching back to Augustine, Leibniz claims a community of causal action only between God and the individual, not between the individual and any other created or finite substance. Yet Leibniz speaks of love as the coordinated basic element of justice. Loemker thought much about this, and we find throughout his papers a number of remarks on Leibniz and love. So it would be useful to cite a passage in which Loemker addresses this issue in the context of Leibniz's usefulness to a reconstructed personalism:

Both political and religious thought have, it is true, often undertaken an explanation of human social order on the basis of a sharp assertion of the separateness of persons. Persons are after all the locus of values and the sources of creativity, not communities and institutions. Hence solitariness is sometimes seen as the essence not merely of religion, but of all cultural and spiritual life; even Christian love is commonly defined as my joy (or assent) in the joy or well-being or perfection of another. But unless this individualism involves immediacy of responsiveness, the "knowing of others" not merely by a set of propositions but directly and through a sharing of the issues and outcomes of life, political and religious unity is weak and thinly conceptual indeed. (Loemker 2002: 184 – a less ambiguous version of Loemker 1993: 32–3)

Now, however "commonly defined" love may be in the Christian tradition as joy in the happiness of another, it is explicitly the definition given by Leibniz, in his many tables of moral definitions. So, again in an important paper of 1693 we find the following definitions: "*Charity* is universal benevolence, and *benevolence* is the habit of loving or of cherishing. But to love or to cherish is to find pleasure in the happiness of another, or what amounts to the same thing, to accept the happiness of another as one's own."[21] This definition pleased Leibniz enormously and he thought it the way to reconcile Bossuet and Fénelon in their famous dispute over pure love. And at least verbally it seems to satisfy many of the moral aims espoused both by Leibniz and recent personalism. But for Loemker it highlights the great ambiguities in Leibniz's usefulness for a satisfactory theory of community, political or religious. Leibniz's monads reflect the universe in a way far more comprehensive than any personalist has been able to devise, but they continue to be closed to any real action except God's and the most one can hope for in the relations of charity, benevolence and intimacy is a variant of enlightened self-interest, where individuals find their own fulfillment in the happiness of others. Some central demands of vital charity seem lost here.[22] Leibniz seems not to have seen them, and Loemker cannot really reconcile the conflict. Leibniz may have been touched by Augustine, but he seems not to have been moved by Augustine.

So, in summary, Loemker's critique, enthusiastically positive regarding personalism's core intuitions and applicability to ethics and the philosophy of religion, is strongly at odds with some of its theory of knowledge and metaphysics. In his reconstruction he appropriates some of Leibniz's realism and his objectivism. But there is a deep ambivalence in Leibniz's ethics that may make these heroic efforts only partially successful. Leibniz's representationalism seems to require that persons enter each other's world only ideally and not in reality. So Leibniz's monads may have less darkened windowlessness even than traditional personalism. But in some critical ways the windows remain closed, and Loemker's Leibnizianism has somewhat diminished force in his critique.

Writing in 1951, W. H. Werkmeister said, "… contemporary personalism is still largely a project and a program; and it is good that such is the case" (1951: 349). He could have said much the same of Loemker's personalism, that it is an incomplete project. While we may wish that it had been otherwise, and that Loemker had finished his "re-appraisal," perhaps here too, we might echo Werkmeister: "it is good that such is the case." The incompleteness of personalism is oddly analogous to the incompleteness in personal knowledge itself, and coming to understand personalism is like coming to know a person. This incompleteness, occasionally fragmentary and tantalizing, can lead contemporary and future personalists to continue the project, and use Loemker's analysis as one of many keys to its further development.

Of course, one might wonder why bother? Personalism has a curious mustiness to it. Sixty years ago, Herbert Schneider thought Bowne "antiquated."[23] Are we not simply stirring dead bones? Possibly, of course. But are there impersonalisms in the new millennium that should excite a personalistic revival? It certainly seems that we haven't far to look for them. The age of depersonalization might be a good title for a contemporary critique of individual life and culture. The triumph of technique is a common enough theme these days. Ray Kurzweil's intelligent machines are maturing into spiritual ones, and Kurzweil (1999) says some of his machines have "personalities," but chooses not to define the term. Leibniz too thought it was possible for machines to have moral identity, but, as such a thing was contrary to nature, only God could produce such a machine, through a miraculous act.[24] Perhaps the age of miracles has not yet passed, and the future doesn't need us at all, as Bill Joy and other doomsday forecasters warn us. Jonathan Margolis's brief history of the future (Margolis 2000) may be altogether too brief, as our social and individual lives become increasingly mechanized. Will future history be neither history nor "herstory," but "itstory"? The term "personal computer" becomes ever more an ominous oxymoron. Fragmented responses to all this, found in innumerable anti-modernist manifestoes, give little solace. But there are signs throughout recent literature of a kind of recovery, of modernism itself in J. W. Burrow's work, and more narrowly of the concept of personhood, in Warren Breckman's recent study of Marx.[25] Some personalists, even Bowne at one point, suggested that Descartes was a source of modern personalism. (Loemker 1993: 11) Maybe, but how then can personalism be enriched by pre-modern moves? I think we can say that, well before Rousseau and Romanticism, Leibniz himself was championing an infinitely richer conception of individuality than the *res cogitans*. Finally, idealism in some form or other may survive to bury its undertakers. The perennial philosophy, perhaps philosophy itself, is stubbornly idealistic. Recovery of the spirit of idealism, perhaps in its personalist form, may be the needed response to technique in all its forms, including technical philosophy. It is probably time to look at work like Bowne's as part of a classic American tradition, to be rediscovered and mined anew. In this task of recovery, L. E. Loemker will be a fine critical guide, and G. W. Leibniz his inspiration.

NOTES

[1] Loemker 1969 and 1972, Leclerc ed. 1973.
[2] Loemker's papers are maintained in the Special Collections department of the Woodruff Library at Emory University.
[3] Aulus Gellius, *Attic Nights* V, 7, trans. John C. Rolfe (Cambridge, MA: Harvard University Press, 1946–1952).
[4] See Trendelenburg 1910: 336–63.
[5] Gerard Manley Hopkins, "As kingfishers catch fire, dragonflies draw flame." (Gardner ed. 1953: 51)
[6] MacKinnon ed. 1985: chapter 9, especially p. 287.
[7] Werkmeister 1949: chapter 7 "The Personalism of Bowne," and chapter 8 "The Pluralistic Personalism of Howison."
[8] An excellent brief account of personalism, its history and major themes, can be found in Buford 2000, Flewelling 1950–51. A classic account remains Knudson 1927.
[9] See "Personalismus," in Joachim Ritter hrsg. *Historisches Wörterbuch der Philosophie* Band 7, Columns 338–42.
[10] On many of these details regarding personalism in the nineteenth century, see Flewelling 1950–51: esp. 233–43.

[11] Howison published only one major work (Howison 1901) but a number of his essays appear in Buckham and Stratton eds. 1934.

[12] Unlike Howison, Bowne was prolific. See his bibliography in McConnell 1929. Bowne's most important books are Bowne 1898 and Bowne 1908.

[13] Hocking 1922: 374. The reference is to chapter 5 of Bowne's *Personalism.*

[14] See Mounier 1950.

[15] F I, 59.

[16] The sources for these papers are Loemker 1993 and 2002.

[17] For the following details see Mulvaney 1996.

[18] See Mulvaney 2001.

[19] See Mulvaney 1980.

[20] See Mulvaney 1968.

[21] "Preface" to *Codex Juris Gentium Diplomaticus,* GP III, 387/ L 421.

[22] See Guitton 1951: 103–4.

[23] Schneider 1946: 467. Thirty years later, however, Schneider was able to revise his opinion and to make a favourable comparison between Bowne and William James. See Schneider 1981: xi–xv.

[24] Cf. New Essays II, xxvii, 9/ A VI vi, 235–7.

[25] See Burrow 2000 and Breckman 1999.

REFERENCES

Abbott, T. K. ed. & trans. 1885. *Kant's Introduction to Logic and his Essay on the Mistaken Subtlety of the Four Figures.* London: Longmans, Green & Co.

Adams, R. M. 1983. "Phenomenalism and Corporeal Substance in Leibniz." *Midwest Studies in Philosophy* 8: 217–257.

Adams, R. M. 1994. *Leibniz: Determinist, Theist, Idealist.* New York: Oxford University Press.

Aiton, E. J. 1985. *Leibniz – A Biography.* Bristol: Hilger.

Antognazza, M. R. 2002. "Leibniz and Religious Toleration: The Correspondence with Paul Pellisson Fontanier." *American Catholic Philosophical Quarterly* 76: 601–622.

Apel, K. -O. 1975. *Der Denkweg von Charles S. Peirce.* Frankfurt: Suhrkamp.

Ariew, R. ed. & trans. 2000. *G. W. Leibniz and Samuel Clarke: Correspondence.* Indianapolis, CA: Hackett.

Arthur, R. 1998. "Infinite Aggregates and Phenomenal Wholes: Leibniz's Theory of Substance as a Solution to the Continuum Problem." *Leibniz Review* 8: 25–45.

Arthur, R. 1999. "Infinite Number and the World Soul: In defence of Carlin and Leibniz." *Leibniz Review* 9: 105–116.

Arthur, R. 2001. "Leibniz on Infinite Number, Infinite Wholes, and the Whole World: A Reply to Gregory Brown." *Leibniz Review* 11: 103–116.

Ashworth, E. J. ed. 1985. *Robert Sanderson: Logicae artis compendium* (Oxoniae, 1618). Reprint. Bologna: Editrice CLUEB.

Ashworth, E. J. 1986. "Renaissance Man as Logician: Josse Clichtove (1472–1543)." *History and Philosophy of Logic* 7: 15–29.

Ayers, M. 1991. *Locke: Epistemology and Ontology.* London: Routledge.

Baines, B. J. and Williams, G. W. eds. 1994. *Renaissance Papers* 1993. Southeastern Renaissance Conference.

Barbour, R. 1994. "Between Atoms and the Spirit: Lucy Hutchinson's Translation of Lucretius," in B. J. Baines and G. W. Williams, eds. 1994: 1–16.

Barbour, R. 1997. "Lucy Hutchinson, Atomism, and the Atheist Dog," in L. Hunter and S. Hutton, eds. 1997: 122–137.

Battigelli, A. 1998. *Margaret Cavendish.* Lexington: University Press of Kentucky.

Beeley, P. 2004. "A Philosophical Apprenticeship: Leibniz's correspondence with the Secretary of the Royal Society, Henry Oldenburg," in P. Lodge, ed. 2004: 47–73.

Berlioz, D. 1999. "On Leibniz's Final Note to Berkeley's *Treatise*," in D. Berlioz and F. Nef, eds. 1999: 437–457.

Berlioz, D. and Nef, F. eds. 1999. *L'Actualité de Leibniz: les deux labyrinthes.* Stuttgart: Franz Steiner Verlag.

Berlioz, D. 2002. "Jurisprudence, résolution des controverses et philosophie," in H. Poser, ed. 2002: 150–157.

Berman, D. 1985. "The Irish Counter-Enlightenment," in R. Kearney, ed. 1985: 119–140.

Berman, D. 1994. *George Berkeley: Idealism and the Man.* Oxford: Clarendon Press.

Bernstein, H. 1980. "*Conatus*, Hobbes, and the Young Leibniz." *Studies in History and Philosophy of Science* 11: 25–37.

Birch, T. 1756–57. *History of the Royal Society.* 4 vols. London: A. Millar.

Boucher, W. I. ed. 1999. *Spinoza: Eighteenth and Nineteenth Century Discussions.* 6 vols. Bristol: Thoemmes Press.

Bouveresse, R. ed. 1999. *Perspectives sur Leibniz.* Paris: J. Vrin.

Bowerbank, S. 1984. "The Spider's Delight: Margaret Cavendish and the 'Female' Imagination." *English Literary Renaissance* 4: 392–408.

Bowne, B. P. 1898. *Metaphysics*. New York: Harper.

Bowne, B. P. 1908. *Personalism*. Boston: Houghton Mifflin.

Boyle, R. 1996. *A Free Enquiry into the Vulgarly Received Notion of Nature*. Ed. by E. B. Davis and M. Hunter. Cambridge: Cambridge University Press.

Breckman, W. 1999. *Marx, the Young Hegelians and the Origins of Radical Social Theory: Dethroning the Self*. Cambridge: Cambridge University Press.

Brightman, E. S. 1950. "Personalism," in V. Ferm, ed. 1950: 340–352.

Brown, G. 1992. "Is there a Pre-Established Harmony of Aggregates in the Leibnizian Dynamics, or do Non-Substantial Bodies Interact?" *Journal of the History of Philosophy* 30: 53–75.

Brown, G. 1995. "Miracles in the Best of all Possible Worlds: Leibniz's Dilemma and Leibniz's Razor." *History of Philosophy Quarterly* 12: 19–39.

Brown, G. 1998. "Who's' Afraid of Infinite Numbers? Leibniz and the World Soul." *Leibniz Review* 8: 113–125.

Brown, G. 2000. "Leibniz on Wholes, Unities and Infinite Number." *Leibniz Review* 10: 21–51.

Brown, G. 2004. "'[...] et je serai tousjours la même pour vous': Personal, Political, and Philosophical Dimensions of the Leibniz-Caroline Correspondence," in P. Lodge, ed. 2004: 262–292.

Brown, S. 1984. *Leibniz*. Brighton, Sussex: The Harvester Press and Minneapolis: University of Minnesota Press.

Brown, S. 1990. "Leibniz and More's Cabbalistic Circle," in S. Hutton, ed. 1990: 77–95.

Brown, S. 1996. "Leibniz's *New System* Strategy," in R. S. Woolhouse, ed. 1996: 37–61.

Brown, S. 1997. "F. M. Van Helmont: His Philosophical Connections and the Reception of his Later Cabbalistic Philosophy," in M. A. Stewart, ed. 1997: 97–116.

Brown, S. 1999. "Two Papers by John Toland: His 'Remarques Critiques sur le Systême de M. Leibnitz ...' and the last of his *Letters to Serena*." *I castelli di Yale* 4: 55–79.

Brunschwig, J. ed. 1966. *Gottfried Wilhelm Leibniz: Nouveaux essais sur l'entendement humain*. Paris: Garnier-Flammarion.

Brykman, G. 1999. "Leibniz et les 'paradoxes' de Berkeley," in R. Bouveresse, ed. 1999: 97–114.

Buckham, J. W. and Stratton, G. M. eds. 1934. *George Holmes Howison, Philosopher and Teacher*. Berkeley: University of California Press.

Buford, T. O. 2000. "American Idealism and Personalism," in J. J. Stuhr, ed. 2000: 646–652.

Buford, T. O. and Oliver, H. H. eds. 2002. *Personalism Revisited: Its Proponents and Critics*. Amsterdam and New York: Rodopi.

Burrow, J. W. 2000. *The Crisis of Reason: European Thought 1848–1914*. New Haven: Yale University Press.

Burtt, E. A. 1932. *Metaphysical Foundations of Modern Science*. London: Routledge & Kegan Paul.

Čapek, M. 1973. "Leibniz on Matter and Memory," in I. Leclerc, ed. 1973: 78–113.

Carr, H. W. 1922. *A Theory of Monads. Outlines of the philosophy of the principle of relativity*. London: Macmillan.

Carr, H. W. 1930. *Cogitans Cogitata*. London: Favil Press.

Carr, H. W. ed. 1930. *The Monadology of Leibniz: With an Introduction, Commentary & Supplementary Essays*. London: Favil Press.

Castañeda, H. 1978. "Leibniz's Meditation on April 15, 1676 about Existence, Dreams, and Space." *Studia Leibnitiana Suppl.* 17: 91–129.

Cavendish, M. 1653. *Philosophicall Fancies*. London: J. Martin & J. Allestrye.

Cavendish, M. 1655. *The World's Olio*. London: J. Martin & J. Allestrye.

Cavendish, M. 1664. *Philosophical Letters: Or, Modest Reflections upon some Opinions in Natural Philosophy*. London: A. Maxwell.

Cavendish, M. 1666. *Observations upon Experimental Philosophy*. London: A. Maxwell.

Cavendish, M. 1668. *Grounds of Natural Philosophy*. London: A. Maxwell.

Charles, S. 2007. "Berkeley and the *Lumières*: Misconception and Reconstruction," in S. H. Daniel, ed. 2007b.

Charleton, W. 1652. *The Darknes of Atheism dispelled by the Light of Nature*. London: J. F. for W. Lee.

Charleton, W. 1654. *Physiologia Epicuro-Gassendo-Charletoniana: Or a Fabric of Science Natural upon the Hypothesis of Atoms*. London: Tho. Newcomb for Thomas Heath..

Charleton, W. ed. & trans. 1656. *Epicurus's Morals: collected partly out of his owne Greek text, in Diogenes Laertius, and partly out of the rhapsodies of Marcus Antonius, Plutarch, Cicero & Seneca; and faithfully Englished*. London: W. Wilson for Henry Herringman.

Clucas, S. 2003. "Variation, Irregularity and Probabilism," in S. Clucas, ed. 2003: 199–209.

Clucas, S. ed. 2003. *A Princely Brave Woman: Essays on Margaret Cavendish, Duchess of Newcastle*. Aldershot: Ashgate.

Cole, P. and Morgan, J. eds. 1975. *Syntax and Semantics. Vol.3: Speech Acts*. New York: Academic Press.

Coleridge, S. T. 1829. *Aids to Reflection, in the Formation of a Manly Character* …Together with a preliminary essay and additional notes, by James Marsh. First American Edition. Burlington: Chauncey Goodrich. Further edition London: G. Bell, 1913.

Conway, A. 1996. *Principles of the Most Ancient and Modern Philosophy*. Ed. by A. P. Coudert and T. Corse. Cambridge: Cambridge University Press.

Coudert, A. P. 1995. *Leibniz and the Kabbalah*. Dordrecht: Kluwer Academic Publishers.

Couturat, L. 1901. *La logique de Leibniz d'après des documents inédits*. Paris: Félix Alcan. Reprinted Hildesheim: Olms, 1961, 1966, 1969, 1985.

Couturat L. 1973. *De l'infini mathématique*. Paris: A. Blanchard.

Cowie, F. 1999. *What's Within: Nativism Reconsidered*. Oxford: Oxford University Press.

Cudworth, R. 1678. *The True Intellectual System of the Universe: The First Part; Wherein, all the Reason and Philosophy of Atheism is Confuted; and its Impossibility Demonstrated*. London: R. Royston.

Cummins, P. D. and Zoeller, G. ed. 1992. *Minds, Ideas, and Objects: Essays on the Theory of Representation in Modern Philosophy*. Atascadero, CA: Ridgeview Publishing Co.

Dalgarno, G. 1661. *Ars Signorum. Vulgo character universalis et lingua philosophica*. London: J. Hayes. Repr. and trans. by David Cram and Jaap Maat, *George Dalgarno on universal language: the art of signs (1661), the deaf and dumb man's tutor (1680), and the unpublished papers*. Oxford and New York: Oxford University Press, 2001.

Daniel, S. H. 1984. *John Toland: His Methods, Manners, and Mind*. Toronto: McGill-Queen's University Press.

Daniel, S. H. 1994. *The Philosophy of Jonathan Edwards*. Bloomington: Indiana University Press.

Daniel, S. H. 1997. "Toland's Semantic Pantheism," in P. McGuiness, A. Harrison and R. Kearney, eds. 1997: 303–312.

Daniel, S. H. 2000. "Berkeley, Suárez, and the *Esse-Existere* Distinction." *American Catholic Philosophical Quarterly* 74: 621–636.

Daniel, S. H. 2001a. "Berkeley's Christian Neoplatonism, Archetypes, and Divine Ideas." *Journal of the History of Philosophy* 39: 239–258.

Daniel, S. H. 2001b. "Berkeley's Pantheistic Discourse." *International Journal for Philosophy of Religion* 49: 179–194.

Daniel, S. H. 2001c. "Edwards, Berkeley, and Ramist Logic." *Idealistic Studies* 31: 55–72.

Daniel, S. H. 2007a. "Edwards as Philosopher," in S. J. Stein, ed. 2007: 162–180.

Daniel, S. H. ed. 2007b. *New Interpretations of Berkeley's Thought*. Amherst, NY: Humanity Books.

Dascal, M. 2001. "Nihil sine ratione → Blandior ratio," in Poser et al. eds. 2001: 276–280.

Dascal, M., Racionero, Q. and Cardoso, A. eds. & trans. (forthcoming). *G. W. Leibniz: The Art of Controversies and Other Writings in Dialectics and Logic*. Dordrecht: Springer.

De Quehen, H. ed. 1996. *Lucy Hutchinson's Translation of Lucretius De Rerum Natura*. London: Duckworth.

Des Maizeaux, P. ed. 1720. *Recueil de diverses pièces, sur la philosophie, la religion naturelle, l'histoire, les mathématiques, & c.* 2 vols. Amsterdam.

Dewey, J. 1888. *Leibniz's New Essays concerning the Human Understanding: A critical exposition*. Chicago: S.C. Griggs.

Digby, K. 1644. *Two Treatises, in One of Which, the Nature of Bodies: In the Other, the Nature of Mans Soule, is Looked into: In the Way of Discovery, of the Immortality of Reasonable Soules.* Paris: Gilles Blaizot.

Dobbs, B. J. T. 1991. *The Janus Faces of Genius: The Role of Alchemy in Newton's Thought.* New York: Cambridge University Press.

Dooren, W. van 1975. "Der Dialog als Diskussionform." *Studia Leibnitiana, supplementa* 15: 195–205.

Duchesneau, F. 1993. *Leibniz et la Méthode de la Science.* Paris: Presse Universitaire de France.

Duchesneau, F. 1994. *La dynamique de Leibniz.* Paris: J. Vrin.

Duchesneau, F. 1998. *Les modèles du vivant de Descartes à Leibniz.* Paris: J. Vrin.

Duchesneau, F. and Griard, J. eds. 2006. *Leibniz selon 'les Nouveaux essais sur l'entendement humain'.* Montreal: Bellarmin & Paris: J. Vrin.

Duhem, P. 1954. *The Aim and Structure of Physical Theory.* Trans. by P. P. Wiener. Princeton: Princeton University Press.

Duncan, G. M. ed. 1890. *The Philosophical Works of Leibniz.* New Haven: Tuttle, Morehouse & Taylor.

Evelyn, J. 1656. *An essay of the first book of T. Lucretius Carus 'De rerum natura.'* Interpreted and made Engl. verse by J. Evelyn. London: G. Bedle & T. Collins.

Feller, J. F. ed. 1718. *Otium hanoveranum sive Miscellanea, ex ore et schedis illustris viri, piae memoriae, Godofr. Guilielmi Leibnitii ...* Lipsiae: Johann Christiani Martini.

Ferm, V. ed. 1950. *A History of Philosophical Systems.* New York: Philosophical Library.

Fichant, M. 1978. "Les concepts fondamentaux de la mécanique selon Leibniz en 1676." *Studia Leibnitiana, Supplementa* 17: 219–232.

Fichant, M. 1994. *Gottfried Wilhelm Leibniz. La Réforme de la dynamique: De corporum concursu (1678) et autre textes inédits.* Paris: J. Vrin.

Fichant, M. 1997. "*Actiones sunt suppositorum*: l'ontologie leibnizienne de l'action." *Philosophie* 53: 135–148.

Fichant, M. 2003. "Leibniz et les machines de la nature." *Studia Leibnitiana* 35: 1–28.

Firth, C. ed. 1885. *The Memoirs of Colonel Hutchinson.* London: Nimmo.

Fisch, M. H. 1986a. "Peirce's Progress from Nominalism Toward Realism," in K. L. Ketner and C. J. W. Kloesel, eds. 1986: 184–200.

Fisch, M. H. 1986b. "Peirce and Leibniz," in K. L. Ketner and C. J. W. Kloesel, eds. 1986: 249–260.

Flewelling, R. T. 1950–51. "Studies in American Personalism." *The Personalist* XXXI: 229–244; 341–351 and XXXII: 5–10.

Flower, E. and Murphey, M. G. 1976. *A History of Philosophy in America.* New York: Putnam.

Frankfurt, H. G. ed. 1972. *Leibniz, A Collection of Critical Essays.* New York: Doubleday.

Fraser, A. C. 1856. *Essays in Philosophy.* Edinburgh: W. P. Kennedy.

Fraser, A. C. 1904. *Biographia Philosophica: A Retrospect.* Edinburgh: Blackwood.

Frege, G. 1879. *Begriffsschrift: eine der arithmetischen nachgebildete formelsprache des reinen denkens.* Halle: L. Nebert.

Furth, M. 1967. "Monadology." *Philosophical Review* 76: 169–200.

Garber, D. 1985. "Leibniz and the Foundations of Physics: The Middle Years," in K. Okruhlik and J. R. Brown, eds. 1985: 27–130.

Garber, D. 1995. "Leibniz: Physics and Philosophy," in N. Jolley, ed. 1995: 270–352.

Gardner, W. H. ed. 1953. *Poems and Prose of Gerald Manley Hopkins.* Hardmondsworth: Penguin.

Gassendi, P. 1647. *De vita et moribus Epicuri, libri octo* Lugduni [i.e. Lyon]: Guillelmum Barbier. Facsimile reprint Amsterdam: Rodopi, 1968.

Gaukroger, S. ed. 1991. *The Uses of Antiquity: The Scientific Revolution and the Classical Tradition.* Dordrecht: Kluwer.

Gibson, J. 1917. *Locke's Theory of Knowledge and Its Historical Relations.* Cambridge: Cambridge University Press.

Goethe, N. 2006. "Frege on Understanding Mathematical Truth and the Science of Logic." *Foundations of the Formal Sciences IV: History of the Concept of the Formal Sciences,* vol.3, Logic Studies, Lowe, B., Peckhavs, V.T.Rash eds. London: College Publications.

Good, J. A. ed. 2002. *The Journal of Speculative Philosophy, 1867–1893.* Bristol: Thoemmes Continuum.

Goudge, T. A. 1950. *The Thought of C. S. Peirce*. Toronto: University of Toronto Press.

Grandy, R. E. and Warner, R. eds. 1986. *Philosophical Grounds of Rationality*. Oxford: Clarendon Press.

Grant, D. 1957. *Margaret the First*. London: Rupert Hart-Davies.

Grayling, A. C. 1986. *Berkeley: The Central Arguments*. La Salle, IL: Open Court.

Grice, H. P. 1975. "Logic and Conversation," in P. Cole and J. Morgan, eds. 1975: 41–85.

Grosholz, E. and Yakira, E. 1998. *Leibniz's Science of the Rational. Studia Leibnitiana, Sonderheft*: 26.

Guitton, J. 1951. *Pascal et Leibniz: Etude sur Deux Types de Penseurs*. Paris: Aubier.

Hacking, I. 1988. "Locke, Leibniz and Hans Aarsleff." *Synthese* 75: 135–153.

Hamilton, W. 1859–60. *Lectures on Metaphysics and Logic*. Ed. by H. L. Mansel and J. Veitch. 4 vols. Edinburgh and London: W. Blackwood & sons.

Hartley, H. ed. 1960. *The Royal Society. Its Origins and Founders*. London: The Royal Society.

Haynes, M. 1988. "Hume's Tu Quoque: Newtonianism and the Rationality of the Causal Principle," *Man and Nature* 7: 131–139.

Henry, J. 1990. "Henry More versus Robert Boyle: The Spirit of Nature and the Nature of Providence," in S. Hutton, ed. 1990: 55–76.

Henry, J. 1994. "Boyle and Cosmical Qualities," in M. Hunter, ed. 1994: 119–138.

Hill, C. 1965. *Intellectual Origins of the English Revolution*. Oxford: Clarendon Press.

Hintikka, J. 1986. "Logic of Conversation as a Logic of Dialogue," in R. E. Grandy and R. Warner, eds. 1986: 259–276.

Hobbes, T. 1655. *De corpore. Elementorum philosophiae sectio prima*. Ed. by K. Schumann and M. Pécharman. Paris: Vrin, 1999.

Hobbes, T. 1668. *Malmesburiensis opera philosophica, quae Latine scripsit, omnia*. Amsterdam: Ioannes Blaeu.

Hocking, W. E. 1922. "The Metaphysics of Borden P. Bowne." *Methodist Review* 105: 371–374.

Hofmann, J. E. 1973. "Leibniz und Wallis." *Studia Leibnitiana* 5: 245–281.

Hooke, R. 1665. *Micrographia* [...] London: J. Martyn & J. Allestry.

Hooykaas, R. 1958. *Humanisme, Science, et Réforme: Pierre de la Ramée (1515–1572)*. Leyden: E. J. Brill.

Howison, G. H. 1901. *The Limits of Evolution and Other Essays*. New York: Macmillan.

Hunter, L. and Hutton, S. eds. 1997. *Women in Science and Medicine 1500–1700*. Gloucestershire: Sutton.

Hunter, M. ed. 1994. *Robert Boyle reconsidered*. Cambridge: Cambridge University Press.

Hutchinson, L. 1885. "Dedication to the Earl of Anglesea," in C. Firth, ed. Reprinted in H. de Quehen, ed. 1996: 25.

Hutton, S. ed. 1990. *Henry More (1614–1687): Tercentenary Studies*. Dordrecht and Boston: Kluwer Academic Publishers.

Hutton, S. 1997. "In Dialogue with Thomas Hobbes: Margaret Cavendish's Natural Philosophy." *Women's Writing* 4: 421–432.

Hutton, S. 2003. "Margaret Cavendish and Henry More," in S. Clucas, ed. 2003: 185–194.

Hylton, P. 1990. *Russell, Idealism and the Emergence of Analytic Philosophy*. Oxford: Clarendon Press.

Jacob, A. 1991. "The Neoplatonic Conception of Nature in More, Cudworth, and Berkeley," in S. Gaukroger, ed. 1991: 101–121.

James, S. 1999. "The Innovations of Margaret Cavendish." *British Journal for the History of Philosophy* 7: 219–244.

Jesseph, D. M. 1993. *Berkeley's Philosophy of Mathematics*. Chicago: University of Chicago Press.

Jesseph, D. M. 1999. *Squaring the Circle. The War between Hobbes and Wallis*. Chicago and London: University of Chicago Press.

Jolley, N. 1984. *Leibniz and Locke: A study of the 'New Essays on Human Understanding'*. Oxford: Clarendon Press.

Jolley, N. 1986. "Leibniz and Phenomenalism." *Studia Leibnitiana* 18: 38–51.

Jolley, N. 1990. *The Light of the Soul*. Oxford: Clarendon Press.

Jolley, N. ed. 1995. *The Cambridge Companion to Leibniz.* Cambridge and New York: Cambridge University Press.

Kalinowski, G. 1977. "La Logique Juridique de Leibniz." *Studia Leibnitiana* 9: 168–189.

Kearney, R. ed. 1985. *The Irish Mind: Exploring Intellectual Traditions.* Dublin: Wolfhound Press.

Kemp Smith, N. 1923. *A Commentary to Kant's "Critique of Pure Reason".* 2nd ed. London: Macmillan.

Ketner, K. L. and Kloesel, C. J. W. eds. 1986. *Peirce, Semeiotic and Pragmatism: Essays by Max H. Fisch.* Bloomington: Indiana University Press.

King, M. L. Jr. 1958. *Stride Toward Freedom.* New York: Harper & Brothers.

King, W. 1702. *De origine mali.* London: B. Tooke.

Klaaren, E. 1977. *Religious Origins of Modern Science: Belief in Creation in Seventeenth Century Thought.* Grand Rapids and Michigan: William B. Eerdmans.

Knobloch, E. 1973. *Die mathematischen Studien von G. W. Leibniz zur Kombinatorik; auf Grund fast ausschliesslich handschriftlicher Aufzeichnungen dargelegt und kommentiert. Studia Leibnitiana, Supplementa* 11.

Knobloch, E. ed. 1976. [Leibniz] *Ein Dialog zur Einführung in die Arithmetik und Algebra.* Stuttgart-Bad Cannstatt: Frommann-Holzboog.

Knobloch, E. ed. 1993. *De quadratura arithmetica circuli ellipseso et hyperbolae cujus corollarium est trigonometria sine tabulis.* Göttingen: Vandenhoeck & Ruprecht.

Knudson, A. C. 1927. *The Philosophy of Personalism: A Study in the Metaphysics of Religion.* New York: Abingdon.

Kortholt, C. ed. 1734–42. *Viri illustris G. G. Leibniz: Epistolae ad diversos, theologici, iuridice, medici, philosophici, mathematici, historici et philologici argumenti.* 4 vols. Lipsiae: Bern. Christoph. Breitkopfii.

Koyré, A. 1965. *Newtonian Studies.* Cambridge: MIT Press.

Koyré, A. and Cohen, I. B. 1962. "Newton and the Leibniz-Clarke Correspondence." *Archives Internationales d'Histoire des Sciences* 15: 63–126.

Kurzweil, R. 1999. *The Age of Spiritual Machines: When Computers Exceed Human Intelligence.* New York: Viking.

Lamarra, A. 1978. "The Development of the Theme of the '*logica inventiva*' During the Stay of Leibniz in Paris." *Studia Leibnitiana, Supplementa* 18: 55–71.

Lamarra, A. 1990. "An Anonymous Criticism from Berlin to Leibniz's Philosophy: John Toland Against Mathematical Abstraction." *Studia Leibnitiana, Sonderheft* 16: 89–102.

Langley, A. G. ed. & trans. 1896. *New Essays Concerning Human Understanding by Gottfried Wilhelm Leibniz, Together with an Appendix Consisting of some of his Shorterpieces.* New York and London: Macmillan.

Latta, R. ed. & trans. 1898. *Leibniz: The Monadology and other Philosophical Writings.* Oxford: Oxford University Press.

Lavine, S. 1994. *Understanding the Infinite.* Cambridge, MA: Harvard University Press.

Leclerc, I. ed. 1973. *The Philosophy of Leibniz and the Modern World.* Nashville: Vanderbilt University Press.

Leibniz, G.W. 1686. Review of J. Wallis, *A Treatise of Algebra both Historical and Practical. Acta eruditorum* VI: 283–289.

Leibniz, G.W. 1696. Review of J. Wallis, *Opera mathematica*, vols. I and II. *Acta eruditorum* VI: 249–259.

Levey, S. 1998. "Leibniz on Mathematics and the Actually Infinite Division of Matter." *Philosophical Review* 107: 49–96.

Lodge, P. ed. 2004. *Leibniz and his Correspondents.* Cambridge: Cambridge University Press.

Loemker, L. E. 1955. "Boyle and Leibniz." *Journal of the History of Ideas* 16: 22–43.

Loemker, L. E. ed. & trans. 1969. *G. W. Leibniz: Philosophical Papers and Letters: A Selection Translated and Edited, with an Introduction.* 2nd ed. Dordrecht: Reidel. 1st ed. Chicago: University of Chicago Press, 1956.

Loemker, L. E. 1972. *Struggle for Synthesis; the Seventeenth Century Background of Leibniz's Synthesis of Order and Freedom.* Cambridge, MA: Harvard University Press.

Loemker, L. E. 1993. "The Personalism of L. E. Loemker." Ed. by R. J. Mulvaney. *The Personalist Forum* 9: 1–61.

Loemker, L. E. 2002. "Some Problems in Personalism," in T. O. Buford and H. H. Oliver, eds. 2002: 169–185.

Look, B. (forthcoming). "Idealism and the Ideals of Mechanism: The Case of Leibniz and Berkeley."

Maat, J. 2004. *Philosophical Languages in the Seventeenth Century: Dalgarno, Wilkins, Leibniz.* Dordrecht: Kluwer.

MacCarthy, B. G. 1946. *Women Writers: Their Contribution to the English Novel 1621–1744.* Cork: University Press and Oxford: B.H. Blackwell.

MacIntosh, J. J. 1970–71. "Leibniz and Berkeley." *Proceedings of the Aristotelian Society* 71: 147–163.

MacKinnon, B. ed. 1985. *American Philosophy: A Historical Anthology.* Albany: State University of New York Press.

Mander, W. J. and Sell, A. P. eds. 2002. *Dictionary of Nineteenth-Century British Philosophers.* Bristol: Thoemmes Press.

Margolis, J. 2000. *A Brief History of Tomorrow: The Future, Past and Present.* New York: Bloomsbury.

Marsh, D. 1989–2001. "Dialogue and Discussion in the Renaissance," in *The Cambridge History of Literary Criticism,* 9 vols. (Cambridge: Cambridge University Press, 1989–2001), vol. 3: 265–270.

Marsh, J. 1913. "Preliminary Essay," in S. T. Coleridge 1829.

Masham, D. 1696. *A Discourse Concerning the Love of God.* London: A. & J. Churchill.

Masham, D. 1705. *Occasional Thoughts in Reference to a Vertuous or Christian Life*: London: A. & J. Churchill.

McConnell, F. J. 1929. *Borden Parker Bowne: His Life and His Philosophy.* New York: Abingdon.

McCracken, C. J. 1992. "Berkeley on the Relation of Ideas to the Mind," in P. D. Cummins and G. Zoeller, eds. 1992: 187–200.

McCracken, C. J. 2007. "Berkeley's Realism," in S. H. Daniel, ed. 2007b.

McGuinness, P., Harrison, A. and Kearney, R. eds. 1997. *John Toland's "Christianity Not Mysterious": Text, Associated Writings and Critical Essays.* Dublin: Lilliput Press.

McGuire, J. E. 1972. "Boyle's Conception of Nature." *Journal of the History of Ideas* 33: 523–542.

McRae, R. 1976. *Leibniz: Perception, Apperception, and Thought.* Toronto: University of Toronto Press.

Meli, D. B. 1993. *Equivalence and Priority: Newton versus Leibniz.* Oxford: Clarendon Press.

Meli, D. B. 1999. "Caroline, Leibniz, and Clarke." *Journal of the History of Ideas* 60: 469–486.

Mercer, C. 2001. *Leibniz's Metaphysics: Its Origins and Development.* Cambridge and New York: Cambridge University Press.

Merchant, C. 1979. "The Vitalism of Anne Conway: The Impact on Leibniz's Concept of the Monad." *Journal of the History of Philosophy* 17: 255–269.

Merz, J. T. 1884. *Leibniz.* Philosophical Classics Series. Edinburgh and London: Blackwood.

Meyer, G. D. 1955. *The Scientific Lady in England, 1650–1760.* Berkeley: University of California Press.

Mill, J. S. 1865. *An examination of Sir William Hamilton's Philosophy.* 2nd ed. London: Longmans, Green. Ed. by J. M. Robson. *Collected Works of J. S. Mill.* 9 vols. Toronto: University of Toronto Press, 1979.

Molesworth, W. ed. 1839–45. *Thomae Hobbes Malmesburiensis Opera philosophica quae Latine scripsit omnia.* 5 vols. London: J. Bohn.

Moll, K. 1968–96. *Der junge Leibniz.* 3 vols. Stuttgart: Frommann-Holzboog.

Moore, G. H. and Garciadiego, A. 1981. "Burali-Forti's Paradox: A Reappraisal of its Origins." *Historia Mathematica* 8: 319–350.

More, H. 1662. An Appendix to the Foregoing Antidote against Atheism, in *A Collection of Several Philosophical Writings of Dr Henry More.* 2nd ed. London: William Morden.

More, H. 1671. *Enchiridion metaphysicum: sive, de rebus incorporeis succincta & luculenta dissertatio. Part one.* London: E. Flesher.

Mounier, E. 1950. *Le Personnalisme.* Paris: Presses Universitaires de France. Trans. by P. Mairet as *Personalism.* London: Routledge & Paul, 1952.

Mulvaney, R. J. 1968. "The Early Development of Leibniz's Concept of Justice." *Journal of the History of Ideas* 29: 53–72.

Mulvaney, R. J. 1980. "Leibniz and the Survival of Renaissance Humanism." *Akten des III. Internationalen Leibniz-Kongresses* 1: 218–224.

Mulvaney, R. J. 1996. "Frederic Henry Hedge, H. A. P. Torrey, and the Early Reception of Leibniz in America." *Studia Leibnitiana* 28: 163–182.

Mulvaney, R. J. 2001. "Leibniz and American Personalism," in H. Poser et al. eds. 2001: 854–860.

Murphey, M. G. 1993. *The Development of Peirce's Philosophy*. 2nd ed. Indianapolis: Hackett.

Newton, I. 1952. *Opticks, or a Treatise of the Reflections, Refractions, Inflections and Colours of Light*. New edition, based on 4th ed. London 1730. New York: Dover.

Noble, B. N. 1989. "Peirce's Definitions of Continuity and the Concept of Possibility." *Transactions of the Charles S. Peirce Society* 25: 149–174.

Okruhlik, K. and Brown, J. R. eds. 1985. *The Natural Philosophy of Leibniz*. Boston: D. Reidel.

Olaso, E. de. 1975. "Leibniz et l'art de disputer." *Studia Leibnitiana, supplementa* 15: 207–228.

Otte, M. and Panza, M. eds. 1997. *Analysis and Synthesis in Mathematics, History and Philosophy*. Dordrecht: Kluwer.

Pacheco, A. ed. 1998. *Early Women Writers*. London and New York: Longman.

Pappas, G. 2000. *Berkeley's Thought*. Ithaca, NY: Cornell University Press.

Parkinson, G. H. R. 1965. *Logic and Reality in Leibniz's Metaphysics*. New York: Oxford University Press.

Parmentier, M. ed. 1995. *Estime des apparences: 21 manuscrits de Leibniz*. Paris: J. Vrin.

Parmentier, M. 2006. "Leibniz lecteur de Locke," in F. Duchesneau and J. Griard, eds. 2006: 11–18.

Pasini, E. 1997. "*Arcanum artis inveniendi*: Leibniz and Analysis", in M. Otte and M. Panza, eds. 1997: 35–46.

Peterschmitt, L. 2003. "La critique du réalisme leibnizien dans le *De Motu* de Berkeley." *Astérion: Revue de philosophie, histoire des idées, pensée politique* 1: 112–126.

Phemister, P. 2005. *Leibniz and the Natural World: Activity, Passivity and Corporeal Substances in Leibniz's Philosophy*. Dordrecht: Springer.

Piro, F. 1990. *Varietas identitate compensata. Studio sulla formazione della metafisica di Leibniz*. Naples: Bibliopolis.

Poser, H. et al. eds. 2001. *Nihil Sine Ratione. Mensch, Natur und Technik im Werken von G. W. Leibniz*. Proceedings of the VII Internationaler Leibniz Kongress. 3 vols. Hanover: Gottfried-Wilhelm-Leibniz-Gesellschaft.

Poser, H. ed. 2002. *Nihil sine Ratione*, Proceedings of the VII. Internationaler Leibniz-Kongress, suppl. Hannover: Gottfried-Wilhelm-Leibniz-Gesellschaft.

Prag, A. 1931. "John Wallis (1616–1703). Zur Ideengeschichte der Mathematik im 17. Jahrhundert." *Quellen und Studien zur Geschichte der Mathematik, Astronomie und Physik B* 1: 381–412.

Probst, S. 1997. *Die mathematische Kontroverse zwischen Thomas Hobbes und John Wallis*. Diss. Univ. Regensburg: Hanover.

Raspe, R. E. ed. 1765. *Oeuvres philosophiques latines et françoises de feu M. de Leibnitz*. 7 vols. Amsterdam and Leipzig: Jean Schreuder.

Rauzy, J. -B. 2001. *La doctrine leibnizienne de la vérité. Aspects logiques et ontologiques*. Paris: J. Vrin.

Riley, P. 1996. *Leibniz' Universal Jurisprudence: Justice as the Charity of the Wise*. Cambridge, Mass: Harvard University Press.

Robinet, A. 1983. "Leibniz: Lecture du *Treatise* de Berkeley." *Les Études philosophiques* n.v.: 217–223.

Robinet, A. 1997. "Les Différentes Lectures du *System* de Cudworth par G. W. Leibniz," in G. A. J. Rogers, J. M. Vienne, and Y. C. Zarka, eds. 1997: 187–195.

Rogers, G. A. J., Vienne, J. M. and Zarka, Y. C. eds. 1997. *The Cambridge Platonists in Philosophical Context: Politics, Metaphysics and Religion*. Dordrecht: Kluwer.

Rogers, G. A. J. 1998. "Locke and the Latitude Men: Ignorance as a Ground of Toleration," in G. A. J. Rogers, ed. 1998: 113–132.

Rogers, G. A. J. ed. 1998. *Locke's Enlightenment: Aspects of the Origin, Nature, and Impact of his Philosophy*. Hildesheim: Olms.

Ross, G. MacD. 1984. "Leibniz's Phenomenalism and the Construction of Matter." *Studia Leibnitiana Sonderheft* 13: 26–36. Reprinted in R. S. Woolhouse 1994: 173–186.

Russell, B. 1900. *A Critical Exposition of the Philosophy of Leibniz*. London: Allen & Unwin.

Russell, B. 1903. "Recent Work on the Philosophy of Leibniz." *Mind* 12: 177–208. Reprinted in H. G. Frankfurt, ed. 1972: 365–400.

Russell, B. 1910–1913. *Principia Mathematica*. With A. N. Whitehead. 3 vols. Cambridge: Cambridge University Press.

Russell, B. 1937. *A Critical Exposition of the Philosophy of Leibniz*. 2nd ed. London: Allen & Unwin, PB. ed. London: Routledge, 1992.

Russell, B. 1945. *A History of Western Philosophy*. London: Allen & Unwin 2nd ed., London: Allen & Unwin. 1961.

Russell, B. 1959. *My Philosophical Development*. London: Allen & Unwin.

Russell, B. 1967–69. *The Autobiography of Bertrand Russell*. 3 vols. London: Unwin Books.

Rutherford, D. 1995. "Metaphysics: The Late Period," in N. Jolley, ed. 1995: 124–175.

Rutherford, D. 1996. "Demonstration and Reconciliation: The Eclipse of the Geometrical Method in Leibniz's Philosophy," in R. S. Woolhouse, ed. 1996: 181–201.

Schaffer, J. D. 1988. "Dialogue," in J. -C. Seigneruet, ed. 1988: 387–395.

Scheidt, C. L. ed. 1749. *Summi polyhistoris Godefridi Guilielmi Leibnitii protogaea, sive, De prima facie telluris et antuquissimae historiae vertigiis in ipsis naturae monumentis dissertation*. Göttingen: J. G. Schmidii.

Schnath, G. 1938–82. *Geschichte Hannovers im Zeitalter der neunten Kur und der englischen Sukzession 1674–1714*. 4 vols. Hildesheim: August Lax.

Schneider, H. W. 1946. *A History of American Philosophy*. New York: Columbia University Press.

Schneider, H. W. 1981. "Bowne's Radical Empiricism," in W. E. Steinkraus, ed. 1981: xi–xv.

Scott, D. 1987. "Platonic Anamnesis Revisited."*Classical Quarterly* 37: 346–366.

Scott, D. 1988. "Innateness and the Stoa." *Proceedings of the Cambridge Philological Society* 214: 123–153.

Scott, J. F. 1938. *The Mathematical Work of John Wallis, D.D., F.R.S. (1616–1703)*. London: Taylor & Francis. Reprint New York: Chelsea Publishing, 1981.

Scott, J. F. 1960. "The Reverend John Wallis, F.R.S.," in H. Hartley, ed. 1960: 57–67.

Scriba, C. J. 1966. *Studien zur Mathematik des John Wallis (1616–1703)*. Wiesbaden: F. Steiner.

Seigneruet, J. -C. ed. 1988. *Dictionary of Literary Themes and Motifs*. New York: Greenwood Press.

Shaftesbury, Anthony Ashley Cooper, third Earl of. 1711. *Characteristicks of Men, Manners, Opinions, Times*. 3 vols. London: John Darby.

Shanker, S. G. 1987. *Wittgenstein and the Turning-Point in the Philosophy of Mathematics*. London and Sydney: Croom Helm.

Slater, J. 1992. "Introduction," to B. Russell 1937. Pb ed. London: Routledge.

Smith, D. E. 1917. "John Wallis as Cryptographer." *Bulletin of the American Mathematical Society* 24: 82–96.

Smith, J. E. H. 2006. "The Leibnizian Organism between Cudworth's Plastic Natures and Locke's Thinking Matter," in F. Duchesneau and J. Griard, eds. 2006: 129–140.

Smith, S. 1998. "Margaret Cavendish and the Politics of the Female Subject," in A. Pacheco, ed. 1998: 111–132.

Sorley, W. R. 1920. *A History of English Philosophy*. Cambridge: Cambridge University Press.

Sosa, E. ed. 1987. *Essays on the Philosophy of George Berkeley*. Dordrecht: D. Reidel.

Stahl, D. 1655. *Compendium Metaphysicae In XXIV. Tabellas redactum, Nuncque post Auctoris obitum emendatiùs et auctiùs editum* ...Jena: Georg Sengenwald.

Stahl, D. 1657. *Regulae philosophicae*. 2 vols. Jena: Georg Segenwald.

Stanley, T. 1655–60. *The History of Philosophy* [...] London: H. Moseley & T. Dring.

Stein, L. 1890. *Leibniz und Spinoza*. Berlin: Reimer.

Stein, S. J. ed. 2007. *The Cambridge Companion to Jonathan Edwards*. Cambridge: Cambridge University Press.

Steinkraus, W. E. ed. 1981. *Representative Essays of Borden Parker Bowne*. Utica, NY: Meridian Publishing Co.

Stewart, D. 1829. *Works*. 7 vols. Cambridge: Hilliard & Brown.

Stewart, M. A. ed. 1997. *Studies in Seventeenth Century European Philosophy*. Oxford: Clarendon Press.

Strasser, G. F. 1988. *Lingua Universalis: Kryptologie und Theorie der Universalsprachen im 16. und 17. Jahrhundert*. Wiesbaden: Harrassowitz Wolfenbütteler Forschungen 38.

Stuhr, J. J. ed. 2000. *Pragmatism and Classical American Philosophy: Essential Readings and Interpretive Essays*. New York: Oxford University Press.

Stump, E. 1982. *Dialectic and its Place in the Development of Medieval Logic*. Ithaca: Cornell University Press.

Thomasius, J. 1676. *Dilucidationes Stahlianae in partem priorem regularum philosophicarum Danielis Stahlii*. Leipzig: Fromann (reprint Hildesheim: Olms 2005).

Toland, J. 1696. *Christianity not Mysterious, or, a Treatise Shewing, that there is Nothing in the Gospel Contrary to Reason, Nor Above it*. London.

Tönnies, F. 1887. "Leibniz und Hobbes." *Philosophische Monatshefte* 23: 557–573.

Trendelenburg, A. 1910. "A Contribution to the History of the Word Person." *The Monist* 20: 336–363.

Vailati, E. 1997. *Leibniz and Clarke: A study of their correspondence*. Oxford and New York: Oxford University Press.

Vasilyev, V. 1993. "Hume: Between Leibniz and Kant (the role of pre-established harmony in Hume's philosophy)." *Hume Studies* 19: 19–30.

Vuillemin, J. 1984. *Nécéssité et Contingence*. Paris: Minuit.

Wallis, J. 1693–99. *Opera mathematica*. 3 vols. Oxford: at the Sheldonian Theatre.

Watkins, J. N. W. 1973. *Hobbes's System of Ideas*. 2nd ed. London: Hutchinson.

Webster, C. 1975. *The Great Instauration. Science, Medicine and Reform 1626–1660*. London: Duckworth.

Werkmeister, W. H. 1949. *A History of Philosophical Ideas in America*. New York: Ronald Press.

Werkmeister, W. H. 1951. "Some Aspects of Contemporary Personalism." *The Personalist* 32: 349–357.

Whiteside, D. T. 1960–62. "Patterns of Mathematical Thought in the Later Seventeenth Century." *Archive for History of Exact Sciences* 1: 179–388.

Whitman, W. 1912. *Leaves of Grass (I) & Democratic Vistas*. London: Dent.

Wilkins, J. 1668. An *Essay Towards a Real Character: And a Philosophical Language*. London: S. Gellibrand & J. Martyn.

Wilson, C. 1989. *Leibniz's Metaphysics. A Historical and Comparative Study*. Manchester: Manchester University Press & Princeton, NJ: Princeton University Press.

Wilson, C. 1990. "Nostalgia and Counterrevolution: The Case of Cudworth and Leibniz." *Studia Leibnitiana, Supplementa* 27: 138–146.

Wilson, C. 1995. "The Reception of Leibniz in the Eighteenth Eentury," in N. Jolley, ed. 1995: 442–474.

Wilson, C. 1997. "Motion, Sensation, and the Infinite: The Lasting Impression of Hobbes on Leibniz." *British Journal for the History of Philosophy* 5: 339–351.

Wilson, M. D. 1987. "The Phenomenalisms of Leibniz and Berkeley," in E. Sosa, ed. 1987: 3–22.

Wittgenstein, L. 1974. *Philosophical Grammar*. Ed. by R. Rees. Tr. by A. Kenny. Oxford: Basil Blackwell.

Wojcik, J. W. 1997. *Robert Boyle and the Limits of Reason*. Cambridge: Cambridge University Press.

Woolhouse, R. S. ed. 1994. *Gottfried Wilhelm Leibniz: Critical Assessments*. Volume IV. New York: Routledge.

Woolhouse, R. S. ed. 1996. *Leibniz's 'New System' (1695)*. Florence: Olschki.

Yolton, J. 1984. *Perceptual Acquaintance from Descartes to Reid*. Minneapolis: University of Minnesota Press.

Yrojonsuuri, M. 2000. "Disputations, Obligations and Logical Coherence." *Theoria* 66: 205–223.

INDEX

Abstraction, 11, 54, 57, 163–64, 167, 174–76, 190 (note 7), 198
action at a distance, 10, 12, 147, 153
America, reception of Leibniz in, 15–16, 224–25
analysis, 53, 57, 67, 85, 198–99, 200, 203, 204
Aiton, Eric J., 16 (note 7)
Antognazza, Maria Rosa, 133, 138, 139, 142
Archeus, 96, 100, 105
Aristotle, 2, 3, 19, 46, 47, 98, 182, 186, 188, 191 (note 17)
Arnauld, Antoine, 198
atheism/atheist, 31, 36, 37, 95, 96, 108–09, 164
attitude, 'purely philosophical', 195–96, 202
attraction, 32, 145–49, 153–57, 174

Bacon, Francis, 1, 2, 19, 47, 83, 85, 152
Bayle, Pierre, 12, 95, 119, 155
Beeley, Philip, 5, chapter 5 (author)
being, most perfect, 213–14
belief, involuntariness of, 138–39
Berkeley, George, chapter 11, *passim*
best of all possible worlds, 143, 170, 182
Blank, Andreas, 5, chapter 6 (author)
Bolton, Martha, 9, chapter 8 (author)
Boston 'school', 221
Bowne, Borden Parker, 225, 226, 229
Boyle, Robert, 2, 3, 4, 5, 37, 44, 45, 50, chapter 6 *passim*
Brightman, Edgar, 221, 225
Britain, reception of Leibniz in, 12–15

Brown, Gregory, 10, chapter 10 (author), 218
Brown, Stuart, 5, chapters 1 & 6 (author)
Burnett, Thomas (of Kemnay), 4, 7, 8, 9, 129

Calculating machine, 5
calculus, 10, 29, 43, 44, 69, 72, 114, 152, 198, 203
Cambridge Platonists 6, chapter 7 *passim*
Caroline, Princess of Wales, 9–10, 11
Carr, H. Wildon, 16, 18 (note 37)
Cartesianism, 26, 35, 39, 42, 102, 104, 108, 120, 150, 155, 160
Cantor, Georg, 203, 208, 209, 211
causes, final, 21, 98, 102, 103, 182, 186, 187
Cavalieri, Bonaventura, 65–66
Cavendish, Margaret, chapter 3 *passim*
characteristic, universal, 6, 21, 22, 23–24, 51, 53, 54, 56, 57, 59
Charleton, Walter, 35, 37
Clarke, Samuel, 1, 5, 9–11, 143, 146, 147, 148, 154, 156, 157
Clucas, Stephen, 44, 50 (note 30)
co-ercion, 135–38
Collins, John, 4, 5
combinations, art of, 21, 27, 53, 66
computation, 21–22
conatus, 24–27, 30, 100
concepts, metaphysical, chapter 4 (*passim*), 107, 164
consubstantiation, 134, 141
Conti, Abbé Antonio-Schinella, 153

The New Synthese Historical Library
Texts and Studies in the History of Philosophy

Series Editor: Simo Knuuttila (*University of Helsinki*)

The New Synthese Historical Library

21. J.V. Buroker: *Space and Incongruence*. The Origin of Kant's Idealism. 1981
ISBN 90-277-1203-4
22. Marsilius of Inghen: *Treatises on the Properties of Terms*. A First Critical Edition of the *Suppositiones, Ampliationes, Appellationes, Restrictiones* and *Alienationes* with Introduction, Translation, Notes and Appendices by E.P. Bos. 1983
ISBN 90-277-1343-X
23. W.R. de Jong: *The Semantics of John Stuart Mill*. 1982   ISBN 90-277-1408-8
24. René Descartes: *Principles of Philosophy*. Translation with Explanatory Notes by V.R. Miller and R.P. Miller. 1983   ISBN 90-277-1451-7
25. T. Rudavsky (ed.): *Divine Omniscience and Omnipotence in Medieval Philosophy*. Islamic, Jewish and Christian Perspectives. 1985   ISBN 90-277-1750-8
26. William Heytesbury: *On Maxima and Minima*. Chapter V of *Rules for Solving Sophismata*, with an Anonymous 14th-century Discussion. Translation from Latin with an Introduction and Study by J. Longeway. 1984   ISBN 90-277-1868-7
27. Jean Buridan's *Logic. The Treatise on Supposition*. The Treatise on Consequences. Translation from Latin with a Philosophical Introduction by P. King. 1985
ISBN 90-277-1918-7
28. S. Knuuttila and J. Hintikka (eds.): *The Logic of Being*. Historical Studies. 1986
ISBN 90-277-2019-3
29. E. Sosa (ed.): *Essays on the Philosophy of George Berkeley*. 1987
ISBN 90-277-2405-9
30. B. Brundell: *Pierre Gassendi: From Aristotelianism to a New Natural Philosophy*. 1987   ISBN 90-277-2428-8
31. Adam de Wodeham: *Tractatus de indivisibilibus*. A Critical Edition with Introduction, Translation, and Textual Notes by R. Wood. 1988   ISBN 90-277-2424-5
32. N. Kretzmann (ed.): *Meaning and Inference in Medieval Philosophy*. Studies in Memory of J. Pinborg (1937–1982). 1988   ISBN 90-277-2577-2
33. S. Knuuttila (ed.): *Modern Modalities*. Studies of the History of Modal Theories from Medieval Nominalism to Logical Positivism. 1988   ISBN 90-277-2678-7
34. G.F. Scarre: *Logic and Reality in the Philosophy of John Stuart Mill*. 1988
ISBN 90-277-2739-2
35. J. van Rijen: *Aspects of Aristotle's Logic of Modalities*. 1989   ISBN 0-7923-0048-3
36. L. Baudry: *The Quarrel over Future Contingents (Louvain 1465–1475)*. Unpublished Latin Texts collected and translated in French by L. Baudry. Translated from French by R. Guerlac. 1989   ISBN 0-7923-0454-3
37. S. Payne: *John of the Cross and the Cognitive Value of Mysticism*. An Analysis of Sanjuanist Teaching and its Philosophical Implications for Contemporary Discussions of Mystical Experience. 1990   ISBN 0-7923-0707-0
38. D.D. Merrill: *Augustus De Morgan and the Logic of Relations*. 1990
ISBN 0-7923-0758-5
39. H.T. Goldstein (ed.): *Averroes' Questions in Physics*. 1991   ISBN 0-7923-0997-9
40. C.H. Manekin: *The Logic of Gersonides*. A Translation of *Sefer ha-Heqqesh ha-Yashar* (The *Book of the Correct Syllogism*) of Rabbi Levi ben Gershom with Introduction, Commentary, and Analytical Glossary. 1992   ISBN 0-7923-1513-8

The New Synthese Historical Library
Texts and Studies in the History of Philosophy

41. George Berkeley: *De Motu* and *The Analyst*. A Modern Edition with Introductions and Commentary, edited en translated by Douglas M. Jesseph. 1992   ISBN 0-7923-1520-0
42. John Duns Scotus: *Contingency and Freedom*. Lectura I 39. Introduction, Translation and Commentary by A. Vos Jaczn., H. Veldhuis, A.H. Looman-Graaskamp, E. Dekker and N.W. den Bok. 1994   ISBN 0-7923-2707-1
43. Paul Thom: *The Logic of Essentialism*. An Interpretation of Aristotle's Modal Syllogistic. 1996   ISBN 0-7923-3987-8
44. P.M. Matthews: *The Significance of Beauty*. Kant on Feeling and the System of the Mind. 1997   ISBN 0-7923-4764-1
45. N. Strobach: *The Moment of Change*. A Systematic History in the Philosophy of Space and Time. 1998   ISBN 0-7923-5120-7
46. J. Sihvola and T. Engberg-Pedersen (eds.): *The Emotions in Hellenistic Philosophy*. 1998   ISBN 0-7923-5318-8
47. P.J. Bagley: *Piety, Peace, and the Freedom to Philosophize*. 1999
        ISBN 0-7923-5984-4
48. M. Kusch (ed.): *The Sociology of Philosophical Knowledge*. 2000
        ISBN 0-7923-6150-4
49. M. Yrjönsuuri (ed.): *Medieval Formal Logic*. Obligations, Insolubles and Consequences. 2001   ISBN 0-7923-6674-3
50. J.C. Doig: *Aquinas's Philosophical Commentary on the Ethics*. A Historical Perspective. 2001   ISBN 0-7923-6954-8
51. R. Pinzani: *The Logical Grammar of Abelard*. 2003   ISBN 1-4020-1246-2
52. J. Yu: *The Structure of Being in Aristotle's Metaphysics*. 2003   ISBN 1-4020-1537-2
53. R.L. Friedman and L.O. Nielsen (eds.): *The Medieval Heritage in Early Modern Metaphysics and Modal Theory, 1400-1700*. 2003   ISBN 1-4020-1631-X
54. J. Maat: *Philosophical Languages in the Seventeenth Century: Dalgarno, Wilkins, Leibniz*. 2004   ISBN 1-4020-1758-8
55. L. Alanen and C. Witt (eds.): *Feminist Reflections on the History of Philosophy*. 2004
        ISBN 1-4020-2488-6
56. O. Harari: *Knowledge and Demonstration*. Aristotle's Posterior Analytics. 2004
        ISBN 1-4020-2787-7
57. J. Kraye and R. Saarinen (eds.): *Moral Philosophy on the Threshold of Modernity*. 2005
        ISBN 1-4020-3000-2
58. P. Phemister: *Leibniz and the Natural World*. Activity, Passivity and Corporeal Substances in Leibniz's Philosophy. 2005   ISBN 1-4020-3400-8
59. V. Mäkinen and P. Korkman (eds.): *Transformations in Medieval and Early-Modern Rights Discourse*. 2006   ISBN 1-4020-4211-6
60. M. Dascal: *G.W. Leibnitz: The Art of Controversies*. 2006   ISBN 1-4020-5227-8
61. O. Nachtomy: *Possibility, Agency and Individuality in Leibniz's Metaphysics*. 2006
        ISBN 1-4020-5244-8
62. P. Phemister and S. Brown (eds.): *Leibniz and the English-Speaking World*. 2007
        ISBN 978-1-4020-5242-2

springer.com

Printed in the United States
78673LV00001B/118-165